A New American TQM

A New American TQM

Four Practical Revolutions in Management

Shoji Shiba
Alan Graham
David Walden

Foreword by Ray Stata and Thomas H. Lee
Publisher's Message by Norman Bodek

Productivity Press
Portland, Oregon

The Center for
Quality
Management

Center for Quality Management
Cambridge, Massachusetts

135676

Productivity Press
P.O. Box 13390
Portland, OR 97213-0390
(503) 235-0600 (telephone)
(503) 235-0909 (fax)

Designed by Gary Ragaglia
Printed and bound by Maple-Vail Book Manufacturing Group
Printed and bound in the United States of America

Library of Congress Cataloging-in-Publication Data

Shiba, Shoji, 1933-
    A new American TQM: four practical revolutions in management/ Shoji Shiba, Alan Graham, David Walden; foreword by Ray Stata and Thomas H. Lee; publisher's message by Norman Bodek.
      p.   cm.
    "Center for Quality Management."
    Includes bibliographical references and index.
    ISBN 1-56327-032-3
    1. Total quality management.   I. Graham, Alan, 1949-
II. Walden, David, 1942- . III. Lee, Thomas H., 1923-
IV. Stata, Ray. V. Center for Quality Management (Boston, Mass.)
VI. Title.
HD62.15.S55   1993   93-906
658.5′62 — dc20   CIP

97 96 95 94 10 9 8 7 6 5

Contents

Publisher's Message   xi
Foreword   xv
Preface   xix

Introduction: THE EVOLUTION OF QUALITY   1

1. The Evolution of the Quality Concept   3
    Quality Concept 1: Fitness to Standard   4
    Quality Concept 2: Fitness to Use   5
    Quality Concept 3: Fitness of Cost   8
    Quality Concept 4: Fitness to Latent Requirement   11
    Cost versus Price   12

2. Evolution of Quality Methods   15
    Development of the Four Fitnesses   16
    Evolution of Methodology   18
    Evolution of Company Integration   20
    Quality of Conformance versus Quality of Design   23
    From Deviations to Weaknesses to Opportunities   24
    TQM Companies Must Be Aware of All
        Four Fitnesses   25
    Future Fitnesses   26
    Four Revolutions in Management Thinking   27
    Four Levels of Practice   29

The First Revolution: FOCUS ON CUSTOMERS   33

3. Change in the Work Concept   35
    Market-in   35
    Customers   40

135676

The Second Revolution: CONTINUOUS IMPROVEMENT 43

4. Improvement as a Problem-solving Process 45
   Management by Process 45
   WV Model of Continuous Improvement 47
   Process Control 59
   Process Control and Process Improvement 64
   Process versus Creativity 65

5. Reactive Improvement 73
   Identifying the Problem 75
   Standard Steps and Tools 85
   The 7 Steps: A Case Study 87
   The 7 QC Tools 101

6. Management Diagnosis of the 7 Steps of Reactive
       Improvement 107
   General Guidelines for Managers Diagnosing a
       QI Story 108
   Diagnosing Step 1: Select Theme 112
   Diagnosing Step 2: Collect and Analyze Data 116
   Diagnosing Step 3: Analyze Causes 118
   Diagnosing Step 4: Plan and Implement Solution 121
   Diagnosing Step 5: Evaluate Effects 123
   Diagnosing Step 6: Standardize Solution 125
   Diagnosing Step 7: Reflect on Process
       (and Next Problem) 126
   Case Study for Diagnosis of the 7 Steps 127
   Run PDCA and Develop Skill 139

7. Proactive Improvement 141
   Introduction to Proactive Improvement 141
   Toward Standard Steps for Proactive Improvement 150
   Semantics 161
   An Example of Proactive Improvement:
       Customer Visitation 170

8. Applying Proactive Improvement to Develop
      New Products   189
   [Stage 1] Step 1: Plan for Exploration   192
   [Stage 1] Step 2: Collect the Voice and Context
      of the Customer   196
   [Stage 1] Step 3: Develop an Image of the Customer's
      Environment   205
   [Stage 2] Step 4: Transform the Voice of the Customer
      into Customer Requirements   207
   [Stage 2] Step 5: Select the Most Significant Customer
      Requirements   216
   [Stage 2] Step 6: Develop Insight into the Relations
      between Requirements   217
   [Stage 3] Step 7: Investigate Characteristics of
      Customer Requirements   221
   [Stage 3] Step 8: Generate Metrics for Customer
      Requirements   231
   [Stage 3] Step 9: Integrate Understanding about
      Customer Requirements   232
   Summary of Stage 3: Operationally Defining
      Customer Requirements   237
   From the Operationally Defined Customer
      Requirements to a Product   240

The Third Revolution: TOTAL PARTICIPATION   247

9. Teamwork Skill   249
   The Dual Function of Work   249
   Teams and Teamwork   255
   Principles for Activating Teamwork   289
   Creativity in Team Processes   301

10. Initiation Strategies   307
   CEO Involvement   307
   Example Strategies for TQM Introduction   321

11. Infrastructure for Mobilization   337
     Goal Setting (Vision/Mission)   339
     Organization Setting   344
     Training and Education   347
     Promotional Activities   359
     Diffusion of Success Stories   360
     Awards and Incentives   365
     Monitoring and Diagnosis   368

12. Phase-In   377
     Orientation Phase   380
     Empowerment Phase   381
     Alignment Phase   383
     Evolution of the Parallel Organization   384

13. U.S. Strategies for Phase-In   391
     Benchmarking   393
     Six Sigma and Cycle Time Reduction   401

14. Hoshin Management   411
     What Is Hoshin Management?   411
     Phase 1 — Strategic Planning (Proactive)   417
     Phase 2 — Hoshin Deployment   426
     Phase 3 — Controlling with Metrics (Control)   437
     Phase 4 — Check and Act (Reactive)   440
     President's Diagnosis   443
     Hoshin Management versus Management by
         Objectives   445
     Hoshin Management and Conventional Business
         Planning   451
     An Alternative Hoshin Deployment System   454
     Hoshin Management as "Systems Engineering"
         for Alignment   457

15. Managerial Development   461
     Case Study of NIMS   461

Company Strategies 470
Individual Practice of CAPD by Managers 491

The Fourth Revolution: SOCIETAL NETWORKING 505

16. Networking and Societal Diffusion: Regional and
Nationwide Networking 507
Infrastructure for Networking 510
Openness with Real Cases 521
Change Agents 522
CQM Case Study 522
Dynamics of a Societal Learning System 528

17. TQM as a Learning System 533
Keeping Pace with the Need for Skill 534
A TQM Model for Skill Development 537
Summary of Skill Development 554

Afterword 559
About the Authors 563
Index 565

Publisher's Message

Productivity Press has been dedicated for more than a decade to educating manufacturers about eliminating process waste on the floor — just-in-time approaches to inventory control and supplier relations, quick changeover, one-piece flow and small lot production, plant floor redesign (such as u-shaped cells), and defect control in process flow (such as poka-yoke devices). Mostly recently, our focus has been on eliminating waste in product design. With this book, we turn our attention squarely to the role of top management in the quality control movement.

As with most Productivity Press books, implementation is at the heart of Shiba's, Graham's and Walden's textbooks on the evolution and practices of the quality movement. A strong mix of historical survey, theory, case studies (some Japanese, many American), and tools focused on bottom-line results. *A New American TQM: Four Practical Revolutions in Management* gives managers the lessons needed to successfully implement company-wide quality practices. *A New American TQM* was created for and drawn from the first-hand experiences at seven major high-tech firms in Massachusetts in conjunction with MIT professor Thomas Lee and visiting professor Shoji Shiba from Tsukuba University. The book captures the shared learning of senior executives from Digital, Teradyne, Polaroid, Bolt Beranek and

Newman, Analog Devices, General Electric, and Bose, the founding corporate members of the Center for Quality Management.

To see the shared learning process at the heart of TQM as the active operating strategy among these industry competitors should encourage leaders in all industries to embark on the quality path. The scope offered here demonstrates the axiom "think globally — act locally." Starting with analysis and measurement of discrete processes through iterative improvement cycles, the authors show the evolving impact on a company, its industry, and the social network within which the company functions. This simple yet thorough course of study can lead your company to global leadership.

This book provides the best information we have seen on management's role in the implementation of quality practices and on application of those practices to strategic planning. Because it was prepared for and by top managers, based on their own learning, the material included here can be directly and successfully applied by other managers. Senior executives as well as middle managers will discover the means to achieve competitive practices in their companies at every level. In one place, under a unifying model and seven-step process, managers will find QFD, benchmarking, translating customer voice, hoshin management, teamwork methods, QC story and diagnosis, seven quality control tools, seven new management and planning tools, and where process control fits into all of these.

We are very pleased to offer this book to our readers and grateful for the opportunity to work with each of the authors as well as the members and staff of the Center for Quality Management, in particular Toby Woll and Emily DiMaggio. We also extend our thanks to our own staff who produced the book: Karen Jones for her patience and meticulous attention to detail; Julie

Zinkus for proofreading; David Lennon, Gayle Joyce, and Karla Tolbert for their skills in book design, graphics arts, and typesetting; and Gary Ragaglia for the cover design.

Norman Bodek, President
Diane Asay, Series Editor

Foreword

In the last quarter of 1989, seven companies in the greater Boston area decided to organize the Center for Quality Management (CQM) in order to accelerate the implementation of total quality management systems in their companies by sharing their learning experiences. A design team was organized to study TQM and plan the operation of the center. The team consisted of 10 senior executives from the founding companies and 3 members from the Massachusetts Institute of Technology. The team's planning effort was led by Professor Shoji Shiba from the University of Tsukuba, Japan, a renowned authority on TQM. We asked Professor Shiba to lead this effort because many executives of the founding companies were impressed by his explanation of how world-class TQM works. His systems orientation, with real life cases of what works in companies, was extremely effective in empowering executives for TQM implementation. In addition, his emphasis on creating learning networks among corporations, as is done so effectively in Japan, was seen as a vital missing link in the United States.

The design team spent five weeks working full time together, often from sunup to sundown. The research phase included a one-week visit to Japan and three company visits in the United States. The group studied TQM firsthand and applied

TQM methodologies to planning the CQM. Two primary conclusions emerged from the planning effort.

1. The dedicated involvement of topmost executives is key to the success of TQM implementation.
2. Because TQM is a thought revolution, the competence to lead the revolution must be developed within the organization.

Acting on these conclusions, efforts in 1990 concentrated on the training of senior executives. A six-day course was organized and taught by Professor Shiba to 48 senior executives. During the course, many people assisted Professor Shiba to organize cases and facilitate. Alan Graham and David Walden (the coauthors of this book) spent an enormous amount of time organizing the lectures into written documents, with the intention that their efforts would help the member companies to take over the training responsibility from Professor Shiba. This book is the result of those efforts.

Even though the fundamental principles of TQM described in this book were all taught by Professor Shiba and therefore are Japanese principles and practices, nevertheless we have decided to name this book "A New American TQM" for several reasons:

- We firmly believe that imitation is the first step in innovation. A number of our companies have applied Professor Shiba's teaching in their TQM implementation. In that process, they have adapted the teaching to American culture and industrial practices. This is evidenced by the cases described in the book.
- Many CEOs and senior executives of the CQM member companies have become teachers for the six-day course, teaching CEOs and senior executives from other member companies. This is the first occurence of this type of mutual learning effort in the United States.
- We have a close relationship with 10 universities. They are our University Affiliates. We cooperate in both the

teaching and research of TQM. Some of the work described in the chapter on proactive problem solving originated from that cooperation.

In 1992, the CQM gave the six-day course eight times, taught by CEOs, president, vice presidents, and other senior managers. 360 senior managers had taken the six-day course as of the end of 1992. We now have a cadre of capable instructors who are real practitioners of TQM at the senior executive level. We celebrate the completion of this book because it represents the first strategic success of CQM and we salute the numerous people who contributed to this effort in addition to the authors.

Ray Stata
Chairman, Analog Devices, Inc.

Thomas H. Lee
President, Center for Quality Management
Professor Emeritus and Senior Lecturer
Massachusetts Institute of Technology

Preface

Total quality management (TQM) is an evolving system of practices, tools, and training methods for managing companies to provide customer satisfaction in a rapidly changing world. Total quality management improves the performance of companies in several areas: eliminating product defects, enhancing attractiveness of product design, speeding service delivery, and reducing cost, among others.

ABOUT THE TITLE

We have titled the book *A New American TQM* to indicate the continuing renewal and evolution of TQM in the United States. The phrase "revolutions in management" in the subtitle comes from Kaoru Ishikawa, in many ways a father of Japanese TQM, whose motivation for working at TQM was to "accomplish a revitalization of industry and effect a thought revolution in management."[1] This book talks about and is organized around no less than four "revolutions." The approach stems from looking at TQM as a system, or more precisely, an ensemble of management technologies. Technological breakthroughs often occur when several previously existing technologies are brought together; the most interesting variety occurs when the component technologies all have existed for some time, but only have a revolutionary effect when joined together.[2]

We believe that companies cannot succeed in the long run without systems and practices that support customer focus, continuous improvement, total participation, and societal networking. All four revolutions are necessary; absence of any one is an obvious major strategic weakness. We formulated the four revolutions based on Professor Shiba's experiences in Japan, validated them through observation of Baldrige- (and Deming-) winning American companies, and validated them through experiment (successfully, so far) through member companies of the Center for Quality Management implementing TQM based on this viewpoint. Indeed, the materials of this book are the basis for those implementations.

HOW AND WHY THIS BOOK CAME TO BE WRITTEN

This book is the brainchild of Shoji Shiba, a professor at Tsukuba University and currently adjunct professor at MIT. One source of the book is a course Shiba taught at MIT twice a year from 1990 to 1993 to students in the Sloan School of Management and in the Leaders for Manufacturing program. The MIT program offers courses and work-study experience leading to two master of science degrees: one in management, granted by the MIT Sloan School, and one in engineering, granted by the MIT School of Engineering. The purpose of the program is to train students to be future leaders in manufacturing.

A second source for the book was a course offered by Shoji Shiba and the Center for Quality Management (CQM), an organization of companies formed with the purpose of sharing TQM implementation experiences and resources. This six-day course, started in the fall of 1990, gave senior managers from CQM member companies an overview of TQM and strategies for its implementation. This book came together during the second course, for which participants from the CQM companies prepared relevant case studies and helped Shoji Shiba organize and give the course.

Throughout this book, examples from Japan are cited, especially from winners of the Deming Prize and from JUSE (Union of Japanese Scientists and Engineers). Other examples are winners of the American Baldrige Award and members of the CQM. The authors have used examples from these sources because those were the examples they had available to them. In addition, Shoji Shiba drew on his wide experience of bringing TQM practice to Western countries, and many anecdotes of his are cited in the book. In its description of TQM, the book does not take the viewpoint of any particular institution or individual; rather, it synthesizes successful practices used around the world.

We have focused on issues of general management within organizations using TQM, rather than on specialized skills such as those of a quality assurance director, a design assurance director, or a reliability engineer. It is an axiom of TQM that total quality improvement starts from the top and must have the commitment of senior management. Therefore, we direct our attention to general management concerns first, and treat well-known quality control and assurance aspects only very lightly.

Many books have been written about the concepts of TQM, but few exist that describe the practice of it in detail. Here, we have focused on the practice of TQM methods, with anecdotes and examples from actual experiences of people using these methods. The book's purpose is to provide commentary and explanation of TQM concepts. It also can be used as the basis for a course on TQM for senior managers and as reading material for those studying the topic.

In many cases we focused on what was "a half-step ahead" — not merely on the present, but always on concepts and practices directly tied to the present. In selecting topics, thinking a half step ahead meant emphasizing practices that have been adopted in state-of-the-art companies but are not yet in common practice worldwide. Chapter 1 discusses this evolutionary dynamic further. For example, one tool, the KJ method of analyzing qualitative data, is widely used in Japan but seldom taught and little understood in the United States.

Related to "half a step ahead," readers will find that the chapters on U.S. phase-in strategy (Chapter 13) and on societal networking (Chapter 16) have less of the "how-to" focus of the other chapters. The U.S. experience in these areas is still formative, but nonetheless important to include here.

A SETTING FOR LEARNING

Our model of learning and skill acquisition has the following three parts:[3]

1. Information + commentary ⟶ knowledge

When people talk about something they have read, the words they use tend to come right out of the information source; this is knowledge. If the subject contains pure facts, this way of learning can be quite useful.

2. Knowledge + feedback ⟶ understanding

You deepen knowledge into understanding by speaking about the subject with someone who already understands it, attempting to use the knowledge in different ways. In turn, the person who already knows the subject can correct any misunderstandings the learners might have and thereby enable them to deepen their mastery of the subject.

3. Understanding + drive to use and schedule ⟶ skill

Ideas have to be used and practiced before they become skills. It is a rare discipline in which a person can jump immediately from talking about something to doing it at a fully professional skill level, in a real setting for real stakes. In practice, developing a skill useful in actual situations takes both motivation — a powerful reason to use new skills instead of playing it safe — and a commitment to use the skills, which often takes the form of a schedule. Once a skill is developed, benefit can be given to the customer and money can be made.

Corporate users of this book have a straightforward charter: Get the information, work to understand it in the training context, and then use it on the job for real problems, following actual schedules, and with actual management oversight. An effective method for carrying out this charter has been the "cascade" method. First managers learn the skills, then they teach them to their direct reports, who then use the skills and teach them to their direct reports, and so on. Xerox Corporation calls this process LUTI: learn, use, teach, inspect.

In the corporate setting, and for that matter in a university classroom, reading the book is only the first step. Results come from skill. Gaining skill requires commitment to three things: serious application, mutual learning, and openness to learning.

Commitment to Serious Application

Proficiency in TQM skills cannot be achieved through study of the methods and examples in this book alone. Study must be accompanied by a well-organized sequence of applications to actual processes. For example, let's say that a manager senses a problem and has some idea of what to do about it. Unless there is a common language for discussing improvement among the people who work for him, and unless the members of the group have some common experience of following the improvement process, it will be difficult for him to solve the problem or even to communicate its importance to his colleagues. Therefore, this book deals not only with concepts but with the applications for these concepts.

Aggressive Learning

Much of the material in this book concerns the development of skills. One skill often neglected in the training process is capturing and structuring information. TQM cannot be practiced effectively with knowledge only. Understanding and skill are necessary, and these start with aggressive learning and listening. One example of aggressive listening is drawn from the section on management diagnoses of improvement activity: When improvement activities are being presented to management, at any point during the presentation, an aggressively listening manager will have a question or insightful observation. Simply listening passively to a presentation is not aggressive learning.

Another example is note taking. Course materials in well-designed courses are closely linked to lectures and exercises. But reality doesn't come so neatly packaged, and neither does much new information. The material in this book may not always match that heard in a lecture course based on it, both because the written word is different from the spoken word and because the lectures are constantly being revised and improved.

Therefore, we ask participants in courses to develop the skill of copious, verbatim note taking, in which they write down everything they hear. This activity will sharpen their focus on the information, preserve knowledge, and demonstrate interest and concern for the presenters. In addition, by disciplining themselves to take effective notes, the participants will acquire a useful skill.

Moving Forward

After we reviewed this list of commitments with the students in MIT's Leaders for Manufacturing program, we showed them a small ceremony, the "yo-one." The mechanics of the ceremony are simple: Once a task has been completed, everyone stands in a circle, so that they can all see each other. The leader starts by saying "yo-oh" (in two syllables). Other people join in, and then the group says the word "one" in a louder voice, and everyone claps their hands together once, simultaneously. The rhythm of this chant is approximately "one, two, THREE." A group needs only a couple of rehearsals to learn how to perform this ceremony.

The yo-one ceremony signifies completion and agreement. It is typically used when a phase of team activity is finished. *Yo* has no meaning, and *one* simply means one. The chanting of those words provides closure to an activity. The time just before the yo-one ceremony, when people are asking "are we ready to yo-one?" is explicitly designed to give people an opportunity to voice final doubts. If no one speaks up and the group goes ahead with the yo-one ceremony, everyone observes everyone else clearly and forcefully saying "yo-one" and clapping. Thus there is no doubt that each person is unambiguously committed to making their work or their decision final. If someone attempts to reverse or rework a position, the group can remind that person firmly that he or she has "yo-oned" and is therefore violating a publicly made commitment. As an added value, a cheer at the end of hard work is invigorating and acknowledges a task successfully done. It makes people feel good.

The particular words used in the chant may differ according to corporate or national culture. One group of Chinese students used "Don't go BACK!" which worked equally well. What matters is that the ceremony is always used and is mutually understood by the group. Learning to perform the yo-one ceremony is the class's first work as a group; it is a micro-demonstration of commitment to move forward to real application.

Commitment to Mutual Learning

The traditional classroom learning environment, in which an instructor talks and students listen and then do homework, differs greatly from most learning environments on the job. In classrooms, students learn primarily from the instructor and from the teaching materials provided. Even much corporate training takes place in this manner. But the most common learning situation in work settings, and the one that TQM practices support, is learning in groups, in which no one is much more knowledgeable than the others. Therefore, this book emphasizes work in groups, whether on the job or in the classroom. In the TQM method we describe, reading is the only activity that each person undertakes alone from beginning to end.

Commitment to Openness to Learning

At least three attitudes block openness to learning, and we ask students to commit themselves to giving these up. They are the following:

I Already Know It (IAKI)

Knowing something is quite different both from having exposure to information and from possessing actual skill. IAKI must not become an excuse to tune out information and abandon the acquisition of skills.

Not Invented Here (NIH)

It is easy to reject ideas and practices simply because they are new or foreign. Some TQM practices are foreign to us in the sense that they are widely practiced in Japan and seldom practiced in the United States. Some practices seem foreign to people because they differ from their habitual styles of analysis and problem solving. Some practices may seem foreign because the examples given are from industries, functions, or situations other than the ones they work in. Many people proclaim their company's situation to be unique, but this assertion is seldom true. Students of TQM must make a commitment either to avoid NIH or to abandon this attitude if they now hold it.

Prove It to Me (PITM)

In junior high school, students don't have a vote on whether to include essay writing and spelling in the English curriculum, although some students do question the teacher about the usefulness of these activities. No one can guarantee that all the skills we learn will be essential to us in the future, and indeed, some things we learn may never be used. But much of what we learn in the English curriculum turns out to be valuable and applicable later.

The same is true of TQM practices. Before they become skills, it is difficult to see how they will be applicable. Therefore students of TQM must forswear the use of PITM as an obstacle to full participation in or full comprehension of the subject being taught. In American education, we are often taught to "listen critically." But this may have been poor advice. A better approach is to listen *empathetically* and later to *think* critically. If you listen critically from the start, you may be so busy finding flaws that full comprehension eludes you. To understand a lesson, you must assume temporarily that what is being said is correct. Only then are you in a position to form alternative opinions about the subject being taught.

Following the Process

One school of academic thought encourages instructors to give minimal guidance to students so that the students can practice the skill of discovering things on their own. This idea has become somewhat embedded in American culture, so that people are commonly expected to experiment with variations and try out shortcuts to learning on their own. This approach can speed the conversion of knowledge into understanding. At the stage where understanding is turned into skills, however, it is less useful. Encouraging individual variation at the beginning of the learning process slows down progress considerably, and may engender bad habits that have to be unlearned.

A general maxim in quality control for engineering or marketing is *Standardize routine tasks and avoid routine defects, so that you can focus on being creative.* For TQM practices, this means following the procedures closely at first and introducing variations only after the practices have become familiar to you. Trying to take shortcuts too early can undermine the learning process and interfere with getting useful results.

CONTRIBUTORS AND ACKNOWLEDGMENTS

First of all, we are deeply grateful to Japan and especially the administration and colleagues at the University of Tsukuba who have made it possible for Shoji Shiba to contribute so substantially to the quality effort in the United States through MIT and the CQM. Also, without the help of Robert Mosbacher (former U.S. Secretary of Commerce), the Japanese Ministry of Education, the Japanese Ministry of Foreign Affairs, and many others too numerous to mention individually, this process would not have been possible.

We are indebted to the Japanese and American companies that hosted our initial visits in 1990 and 1991. In alphabetical order they are: Florida Power & Light Co.; Fuji Xerox Co. Ltd.; Hitachi Ltd., Mito Works; Motorola; NEC Corporation; NEC IC Microcomputer Systems, Ltd.; NEC Shizuoka, Ltd.; Toto Ltd.; Xerox Corporation; and Yaesu Book Center. Senior executives and managers Akira Kuroiwa and Morio Katsuta from NEC Kansai, Ltd. and Mitsuru Nitta from Tokyo Electric Power Company were also extremely generous in visiting MIT and the CQM. JUSE, the Union of Japanese Scientists and Engineers, has been invaluable in sharing its experience in societal networking. We also appreciate the great efforts of the Deming Prize Committee that has been selecting Deming Prize winners since 1951. We have had a great opportunity to learn at MIT from some recent winners.

We are likewise indebted to the *sensei*s and practitioners who have directly given us the benefit of their experience. In alphabetical order they are: Mr. Jim Bakken (vice president, Ford Motor Company [retired]), Dr. George Fisher (chairman of Motorola), Mr. Robert Galvin, (former chairman of Motorola), Professor Emeritus Masao Kogure (who was also kind enough to comment on drafts of Chapter 14 on hoshin management), Dr. Yokio Mizuno (senior executive vice president, NEC Corporation), and Mr. Junji Noguchi (executive director of JUSE).

Our special acknowledgment to Professor Emeritus Jiro Kawakita, whose ingenious concepts and methods have catalyzed our progress continually.

Finally, we must acknowledge the remarkable ability of the MIT community to bring people and knowledge together. Although this preface recounts the chronology of this book and the Center for Quality Management elsewhere, an acknowledgment can point to common themes: Tom Lee, an MIT professor, was able to meet Shoji Shiba because he was not at MIT, but in Vienna, being director of IIASA, an international research institute. Shiba was able to begin teaching a new subject at MIT because the Leaders for Manufacturing program systematically seeks out new viewpoints to teach. This same openness later allowed

Shiba to become an adjunct professor. Lee was able to extend the TQM message into corporations through the MIT community, via the management of many of the founding companies of the Center for Quality Management, particularly through Ray Stata, chairman of Analog Devices, Inc., and also a member of the MIT Corporation. Stata and Lee continue their cross-organizational roles as chairman and president, respectively, of the CQM. There are other synergies with MIT too numerous to mention.

We have benefited from the ideas and teaching of so many that we fear we have forgotten to list some of them. We greatly appreciate the long experience of individuals in many countries. We also know that in some cases we may have misunderstood or misinterpreted what we were taught. We trust that our many teachers will forgive our missteps and continue to guide us.

The Center for Quality Management was founded by seven companies: Analog Devices, Inc.; Bolt Beranek and Newman, Inc.; Bose Corporation; Digital Equipment Corporation; General Electric's division in Lynn, Massachusetts; Polaroid Corporation; and Teradyne, Inc. In March and April 1990, the following individuals from these companies and MIT participated in a full-time 5-week project to study TQM and design how the CQM would function and the services it would provide: Ron Butler, Dave Darsney, Ralph Goldwasser, Steve Graves, Joe Junguzza, Tom Lee, John Petrolini, Ken Potashner, Art Schneiderman, Goodloe Suttler, and the three authors of this book. The initial outline of the course on which this book is based and many of the case studies were developed by many of these same individuals.

Many people helped directly or indirectly with the preparation of this book. Gary Burchill, Rich Lynch, Ira Moskowitz, Ron Santella, Diane Shen, and John Sheridan contributed to various instruction manuals to be used with this book and the CQM course based on this book. Ron Butler, Charlie Fine, Phil Gulley, Joe Junguzza, Mike LaVigna, Rich

Lynch, Ira Moskowitz, Yogesh Parikh, John Petrolini, Owen Robbins, Art Schneiderman, and Del Thorndike presented case studies during the first two CQM courses. Gary Burchill provided a major case study for the book. Gary Burchill and Tom Heller were teaching assistants for the MIT courses, and they assisted in the CQM course as well. Donna McGurk provided administrative support for the CQM course. Stella Tarnay transcribed the bulk of the notes we took on these first courses. Trish McKinnon typed redrafts of the material. Deborah Melone provided editorial assistance. The staff of the CQM office dealt with the final logistics of submitting the manuscript for publication. Diane Asay and Karen Jones of Productivity Press edited the book and patiently accepted endless revisions. Gayle Joyce and Karla Tolbert of Productivity Press deserve special mention for their heroic typesetting and graphics contribution.

While many people from the CQM and many CQM companies have been supportive of this book and the course on which it was based, we would like to specially acknowledge the support and encouragement of Alex d'Arbeloff, Sherwin Greenblatt, Tom Lee, Steve Levy, and Ray Stata.

Shoji Shiba
Alan Graham
David Walden

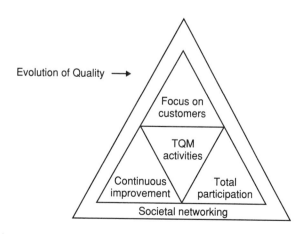

NOTES

1. *What Is Total Quality Control? The Japanese Way* (Englewood Cliffs, NJ: Prentice-Hall, 1985), Chapter 6.
2. This general pattern was articulated by Graham, with examples in software development and airplane design ("Software Design: Breaking the Bottleneck," *IEEE Spectrum* (March 1982): 43-50).
3. We have derived this model of learning from Matthew J. Culligan, C. Suzanne Deakins, and Arthur H. Young, *Back to Basics Management* (New York: Facts on File, Inc., 1983).

Introduction:
THE EVOLUTION
OF QUALITY

1

The Evolution of
the Quality Concept

What is quality? This is a multifaceted question, difficult to address in the abstract. It is easier to understand quality by considering its evolution in leading companies. In the United States and Europe, quality control of one sort or another has been part of manufacturing for more than a hundred years, and the use of various quality concepts has come and gone and come again.[1] By contrast, in Japan quality control was not significant until after World War II. In Japan as in the United States, however, the spectrum of quality practices ranges from none at all to the leading edge, where progress has been rapid and uniform.

At the beginning of this evolutionary process, quality of any kind is not noticed or measured. Goods are produced and shipped. If customers want to send something back, they do so — end of story. This situation characterized Japanese companies in the early 1950s, when "made in Japan" meant shoddy, unreliable goods. The story of Japan's transformation of that term into one signifying products of excellent quality is the story of their adoption of TQM. The different stages in the evolution of quality can be seen clearly in leading Japanese companies.

In this chapter we trace the evolution of TQM by explaining some of its basic concepts, beginning with the four *fitnesses* or levels of quality, and their weaknesses. These concepts characterize four eras in the history of Japanese TQM.

The four fitnesses are

- fitness to standard
- fitness to use
- fitness of cost
- fitness to latent requirement

QUALITY CONCEPT 1: FITNESS TO STANDARD

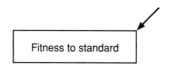

Fitness to standard evaluates whether a product built as described in the manual passes the standard. In other words, fitness to standard defines quality as the product that does what the designers intend it to do. Determining whether a product meets fitness to standard is mainly a question of inspection: does the product pass or not? To achieve fitness to standard, managers and engineers define each manufacturing task, record those tasks as standard practices in manuals, and define inspection procedures to enforce the standard practices. To evaluate fitness to standard, companies sometimes use the concept of statistical quality control (SQC), an approach the American quality expert W. E. Deming brought to Japan in the early 1950s.

When considered from a modern-day rather than a historical perspective, fitness to standard used alone as a definition of quality has two weaknesses.

The first is the notion that quality can be achieved through inspection. According to fitness to standard, you assure quality by inspecting the output of a manufacturing process and culling out and discarding the defective or low-quality items. In reality, however, this process often leads to an adversarial relationship between those who make a product and those who inspect it. Professor Shiba tells of a case in which the factory manager proudly described to him his factory's excellent inspection system, emphasizing that the inspection function was completely separate from the rest of the plant; indeed, the inspectors were government employees, not plant employees. When Professor Shiba talked to the workers, however, he learned that they considered the inspectors to be the enemy.

The second weakness of fitness to standard is its neglect of market needs. Creation of production standards and inspection geared to these standards orients people to the product and whether it does what it was designed to do, rather than to the needs of customers and whether the product fills those needs. Acting to correct this weakness brought leading Japanese companies to the next level of quality in the early 1960s.

QUALITY CONCEPT 2: FITNESS TO USE

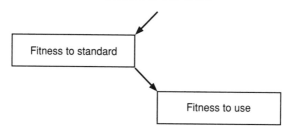

Fitness to use is the means to assure satisfaction of market needs. Can the product be used as the customers want to use it? For instance, a tool company makes screwdrivers to turn a certain size screw. For how many of us is the real need to have the tool turn whatever size screw we have, and for how many is it to open a can of paint? (The Sears Craftsman Tools no-questions-asked guarantee may have been an attempt to promise fitness to use.) It is not easy to forecast the diverse usage of the market, as the following amusing example from Japan illustrates.

A major appliance company made a new washing machine. However, there were many complaints about it from the customers living in rural areas. The company sent its engineers to the field to observe. They found that farmers were using the machines to wash the dirt off potatoes. Although such use wasn't prohibited by the manual, the machines weren't designed for such dense loads, and they would often break. When the manufacturer realized the use to which customers were actually putting the machines, the machine was redesigned to tolerate potato washing, and the machines returned to normal reliability. Fitness to use addresses the real needs or desires of the customer, not just the standards set by the producer.

As was the case with fitness to standard, fitness to use is achieved by inspection. Thus a certain amount of conflict between inspectors and workers arises. Further, if the company wants products that can be absolutely counted on to perform as expected, that is, to have high "fitness to use," then inspectors must rigorously reject products that deviate from the standard.

Any production process has variability from one unit to the next. Not all cars that come off an assembly line have exactly the same horsepower. Some bottles of soda will have caps too small, so that they don't quite stay on. Other bottles will have caps that leak because they are too large. Extremes on one or both sides of the standard must be rejected and reworked or thrown away.

Figure 1-1 illustrates this principle. The upper curve shows the statistical variation in some product characteristic such as horsepower, size of bottle cap, or amount of ice cream in the cone at an ice cream parlor. The products with characteristics beyond the acceptable tolerances must be rejected; this is a costly approach. As shown in the lower curve, if higher quality is desired, the inspection limits must be narrowed so that even more items are rejected; this approach is even more costly.

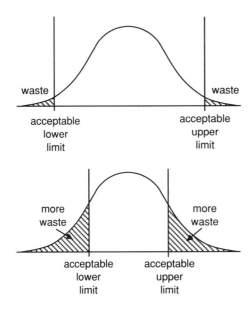

Figure 1-1. Statistical Variation in Product Characteristics

Another weakness of focusing on fitness to use is that use-based competitive advantage is tenuous. If a company has clearly understood fitness to use (meeting the needs of users), it may gain a monopoly position, so that it can charge prices high enough to compensate for the higher cost of higher quality through inspection. Competitors offering equally good products for cheaper prices quickly spring up, eliminating the monopoly position and the ability to offset costs incurred during the inspection process. For instance, from 1960 to 1970, a major Japanese camera company monopolized its market and charged high prices. But then the competition for cameras in Japan became fierce; sales of this camera company went down, and those of other brands went up. The camera company lost much of its market share in Japan.

Moving away from the high costs of "inspecting quality in" and toward "building quality in" brought leading Japanese companies during the early 1970s to the next level of quality.

QUALITY CONCEPT 3: FITNESS OF COST

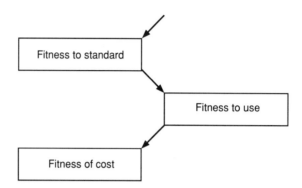

Fitness of cost means high quality *and* low cost. These are the two most universal requirements for virtually all customers, products, and services. To achieve cost reduction while maintaining high quality (with no products outside the bounds), you must reduce the variability of the production process, so that all units produced are already within the inspection limits and none have to be discarded (see Figure 1-2).

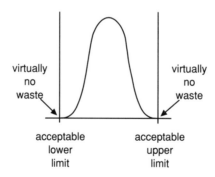

Figure 1-2. Reduced Variability Reduces Waste

We seek 100 percent quality without culling. This requires feedback and correction at each step rather than just at the end of the production process. To achieve this level of quality, you must completely change the production system. Worker focus must shift from controlling the output through inspection to controlling the process (see Figure 1-3).

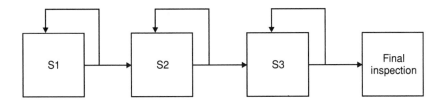

Figure 1-3. Feedback at Each Production Step

The modern methods to accomplish this shift are

- using statistical quality control (SQC)
- monitoring the process in addition to the output
- providing for feedback at each step, whereby every line worker notices the work of his or her predecessor, and can ensure that mistakes are corrected immediately
- instituting line worker participation in the design and improvement of the production process, to make it continuously more reliable

Workers are empowered to create this kind of continuous change through standardized, mass-taught tools and practices, such as the seven steps for quality control (7 QC steps, or 7 steps) and the seven tools for quality control (7 QC tools), which are described later.

The fitness of cost requirement has made the concept of quality multidimensional. Its original meaning (circa 1950) was product defects per hundred units. Today, even on the manufacturing floor, quality never means just identifying product defects. At Toto Limited in Japan, we saw five dimensions of quality improvement listed on a factory-floor bulletin board:

- Q Quality
- C Cost

- D Delivery
- S Safety
- M Morale

At Motorola, two driving forces are considered to create customer satisfaction:

1. Cycle time (for example, time from beginning to end of product development, time to ship a product, or time to make a product)
2. Normalized process defect rate (errors per million opportunities to make errors — for example, in insurance claims handling, customer order taking, semiconductor fabrication, or "beeper" manufacturing)

For several organizations (Motorola, Xerox USMG, Yaesu Book Center, Florida Power & Light), the most important aspect of quality is customer satisfaction, measured directly by survey. Some organizations, such as 3M, make product innovation a quality to be improved or maintained, with explicit corporate goals.

However, a weakness remains. Companies that have achieved the quality level of fitness of cost are producing highly reliable, functional products at low cost. But competitors can create similarly reliable and inexpensive products. Newly industrialized countries can copy their skills of fitness to standard and fitness to use but have much cheaper labor, yielding low cost. This happened to Japan in the 1980s. Korea, Hong Kong, and Taiwan adopted Japanese technology, but had labor costs that were only one-half or two-thirds the Japanese cost.

For this weakness, the cure that leading Japanese companies began pursuing in a standardized way in the early 1980s, is creating innovative products that will outsell competitors' products. This raises product quality to the next level.

QUALITY CONCEPT 4:
FITNESS TO LATENT REQUIREMENT

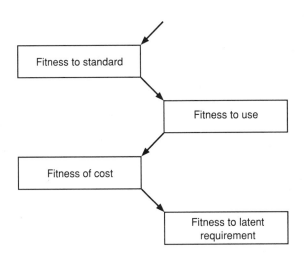

Fitness to latent requirement means meeting customer needs before customers are aware of those needs. If a company can find the latent requirement of the market, it may achieve a monopoly for a little while. The company can ask a higher price, which can be very profitable.

One of the most famous examples of a latent requirement occurred with the Polaroid Land camera. In 1944, while on vacation in Santa Fe, New Mexico, Edwin Land took a picture of his young daughter. She asked him why she had to wait to see the picture. On a solitary walk around Santa Fe, Land solved the puzzle implicit in her question, visualizing most of the requirements for a camera, film, and physical chemistry that permit what is now called instant photography.

A more recent example of a latent requirement is the Sony Walkman. This is a product we didn't know we needed, but as soon as it was available we found that our children couldn't walk or ride in the car without one, and the Walkman definitely improved the time we spent jogging and standing in grocery store lines.

Watches provide an example of all four levels of the quality concept:

- If a watch is put together with parts missing, it doesn't fit the standard. It must be thrown away or reworked.
- Watches must keep time to be fit for use. High-quality (accurate) chronometers of the 18th and 19th centuries were made of expensive components and were rigorously tested. Their cost was high, but they met the second quality standard. The classic mechanical Swiss watch of the 20th century continues this tradition.
- Watches with electronics are both cheap and accurate, meeting the standard of fitness of cost. Many companies in many countries make such watches. Now watches can be had for under $10 that are more accurate than the finest mechanical watches of the pre-electronic era, but competition is brutal.
- Fashion and individuality were introduced into the low-end watch market by Swatch, a Swiss company. Meeting these latent requirements allowed the company to charge more and make a higher profit than for commodity watches.

Weaknesses can remain even in companies that systematically meet their customers' latent requirements. These weaknesses arise not from the companies' current processes for product and production process design, but from the variable speed and appropriateness of improvement and change. Many companies are going out of business simply because they are not able to improve as quickly as their competitors. The tools and practices to address this weakness are discussed later in this book.

COST VERSUS PRICE

The preceding sections describe the evolution of quality in Japan. One of the most profound results of the differing ways quality developed in Japan and the United States is the difference in attitude about quality and the price of products.

The following account, related to us by Alex d'Arbeloff, CEO of Teradyne, illustrates how the Japanese think about price and clarifies fitness to use versus fitness of cost.

Japanese Companies Worry about Cost, Not Price

Despite new features and middlemen, Japanese companies want 10 percent cost reduction per year. They tell their suppliers to reduce costs 10 percent per year and tell them to tell their suppliers. They use the slogan CD10, or cost down 10 percent. All levels of the company work on this goal. Many quality circles' themes are aimed at reaching a 10 percent cost reduction. The engineers' and managers' cross-functional teams cooperate to reduce costs. The senior managers work with suppliers of materials and parts, and they audit and invest in suppliers to get cost reductions.

This way of running a plant is different from the methods used in the United States.

The Japanese assume that the market sets the price, and that you have to include the next features within that price. This is a great revolution in thinking. In the United States, we think we can get a higher price if we add features. In Japan, companies assume that you must both add new features and decrease the cost. Monopolistic power lets you raise prices. However, within six months any company can produce a better product than yours at a lower cost. Latent requirements only last a year or less. The price is set by the market, by your competitors, or by the demands of the customer. If you don't control your price, the only thing you can control is your costs.

Some American engineers regard the Japanese method as incorrect. They adhere to the fitness to use concept. Japanese engineers assume that the market sets the price, and they constantly work to reduce costs.

Fitness of Cost May Work Better in Japan than in the United States

Cultural differences between Japan and the United States may account for different approaches. In the United States people are used to paying more for added features. In Japan this is not the case. In addition, in Japan people at the same level in a company hierarchy tend to have the same ability to approve purchase prices across all departments and subsidiaries, regardless of the size of the company; in the United States, purchasing limits tend to be proportional to the size of the company.

NOTE

1. David A. Garvin gives a thorough history of quality in the United States in Chapter 1 of *Managing Quality* (New York: Free Press, 1988).

2

The Evolution
of Quality Methods

As the world changes, societal and economic forces drive the evolution of quality concepts and the tools and practices used to achieve them. Throughout the world people have intuitively understood and attempted to address the four fitnesses. Edwin Land's instant Polaroid photography, for example, addressed a latent requirement. His insight comprised both the concept and the means of its implementation. In Japan there has been an attempt to systemize and diffuse the quality improvement process.

The dominant quality concept of leading Japanese companies has changed roughly every 10 years. In the 1950s, fitness to standard best met the needs of mass production. The 1960s, 1970s, and 1980s were dominated, respectively, by fitness to use, fitness of cost, and fitness to latent requirement (see Figure 2-1).

Standardized tools and practices were developed, deployed, and validated for each of the fitnesses and stages of the quality concept. These tools and practices were modified as corporations and their customers responded to the changes in the larger economy. We can expect to see further changes as compe-

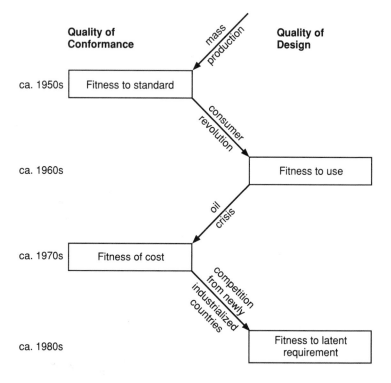

Figure 2-1. Changes in Dominant Quality Concepts in Leading Japanese Companies

tition develops along new dimensions and societal needs find new expression.

Let us now look more closely at how and why the four fitnesses evolved in Japan, and consider the methods developed to deal with each.

DEVELOPMENT OF THE FOUR FITNESSES

Following the devastation of World War II, the primary aim of Japanese industry was to increase production in order to rebuild both the individual standard of living and the country's commercial infrastructure. In the 1950s, concern for quality was considered to be an obstacle to mass production. Some avant-garde Japanese companies applied the Deming tools of statistical quality control (SQC) to output.

By the early 1960s, Japan no longer had an urgent need to replace essential goods. Manufacturers started competing not on how many usable units they could make but on the variety of goods they made. Between 1960 and 1965, previously hard-to-get nonconsumables such as televisions, washing machines, cameras, and vacuum cleaners became standard features in Japanese homes. This so-called consumer revolution gave rise to the concept of market, which differed from the concept of simple production.

The oil crises triggered by OPEC oil embargoes and price hikes during the 1970s shook Japanese society. Japan has no real domestic sources of oil; nearly 100 percent of domestic oil for consumption is imported. The OPEC actions raised the possibility of a Japan crippled by inability to earn foreign exchange to pay for oil imports. During a 1990 visit to TQM companies in Japan, the authors asked the executives why their company took up TQM. The answer was always the same: the oil crises. The need to export created a need to compete with foreign products in their home markets, a near impossibility without products that met actual customer requirements better than foreign competition. Fitness to all customer requirements became the dominant quality concept of the leading Japanese firms.

However, in the 1980s, Japanese successes of the 1970s had begun to create resistance on two fronts. First, because of consistent trade surpluses with the rest of the world, the value of the yen increased relative to most other currencies. This meant that Japanese-produced goods became more expensive on world markets solely because of exchange rate shifts; thus, the competitiveness of Japanese goods was reduced. Second, Japanese production technologies and management methods had spread elsewhere in Asia: to Korea, Taiwan, Singapore, and Hong Kong, the "four tigers" of Asia. With comparable production technologies and cheaper labor, Asian competitors became a serious threat.

As the concept of quality evolved, there were three "great leaps," or revolutionary changes in how people thought about quality.

- From fitness to standard to fitness to use — shift to the concept of market
- From fitness to use to fitness of cost — shift to the concept that the price is set in the market
- From fitness of cost to fitness to latent requirement — shift to the concepts of continuous change in market need and thus the continuous shortening of product development cycles

EVOLUTION OF METHODOLOGY

As the concept of quality evolved, the practices and tools of quality also evolved. We call this the evolution of methodology (see Figure 2-2).

Fitness to Standard → Fitness to Use

Standardization, statistical process control, and inspection were the main tools used to achieve fitness to standard. With the consumer revolution and fitness to use came a new tool: market research to find out what the customer wanted and cross-functional involvement to deliver it.

Fitness to Use → Fitness of Cost

At the next quality level, fitness of cost, the emphasis was on reducing costs while increasing quality (and hence on the need for low-variance production). This made it necessary to control and improve each production process, actively involve production workers, and develop the tools and practices suitable for a mass movement. Quality control circles are described in Chapter 9. The 7 QC tools and the 7-step improvement process that uses them are listed in Table 2-1 and described in Chapter 5.[1]

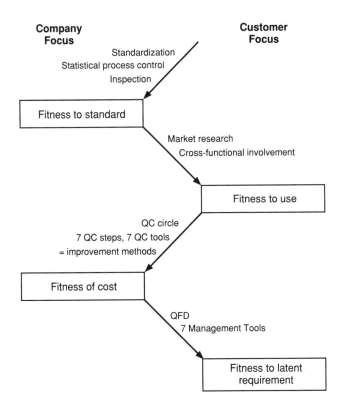

Figure 2-2. The Evolution of Methodology

Table 2-1. The Tools and Steps of Quality Control

The 7 QC Tools	The 7 QC Steps
1. Check sheet*	1. Select theme
2. Pareto diagram	2. Collect and analyze data
3. Cause-and-effect diagram	3. Analyze causes
4. Graphs/Stratification	4. Plan and implement solution
5. Control charts	5. Evaluate effects
6. Histogram	6. Standardize solution
7. Scatter diagram	7. Reflect on process (and next problem)

*Some companies include stratification or
process flowcharts as one of the 7 QC
tools instead of check sheet.

Fitness of Cost → Fitness to Latent Requirement

The next level in quality methods added design value, with products developed to satisfy latent needs. The standardized means for accomplishing this new kind of quality are quality function deployment (QFD) and the 7 management and planning tools, which are listed in Table 2-2 and described in Chapter 7. These tools help companies identify latent needs and translate those needs into plans for products and production processes. The term *management tools* is somewhat misleading, because the tools are for engineers and staff people as well. Indeed, perhaps the most prominent and standardized application of these tools is QFD, which is designed specifically to forge a common understanding among marketing people, engineers, and managers.

Table 2-2. The Seven Management and Planning Tools

1. Affinity diagram (KJ method)
2. Relations diagram
3. Matrix diagram
4. Tree diagram
5. Arrow diagram
6. PDPC
7. Matrix data analysis

EVOLUTION OF COMPANY INTEGRATION

As industrialization increased during the first half of this century, companies evolved from craft shops, with the entire staff in one room, into highly compartmentalized organizations. Such companies were capable of producing a few standard products with great efficiency. In the second half of this century, however, compartmentalization left companies unable to address the changing definition of quality; thus, a reintegration process began.

In Japan, the integration of various parts of companies and their environments occurred as a result of successive innovations in TQM. As Figure 2-3 suggests, the pattern of integration has alternated between vertical integration (lower parts better connected with upper parts) and horizontal integration (better connection of different functions, such as marketing, customers, or development).

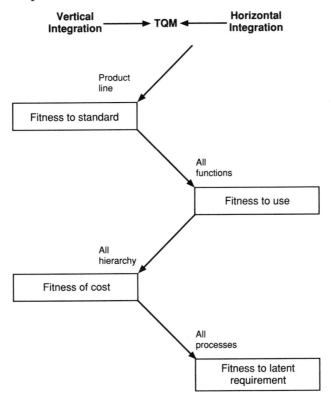

Figure 2-3. Horizontal and Vertical Integration Due to Successive TQM Innovations

Fitness to standard and fitness of cost have to do with where quality improvement takes place in the vertical hierarchy of the company.

With fitness to standard came the hierarchical *integration* of engineering, in which specifications were provided for the production line and the QA department assured that the production line met those specifications. However, improvement (by management and engineering) and daily work (by workers on the production line) remained strictly separated.

With fitness of cost came the imperative to focus on cost goals and to move information for improvement activities up and down the hierarchy. Quality circles not only improved the way line workers did their daily work, but they revealed ways for managers and engineers to reduce cost through process changes and product design. Thus production and improvement work were integrated at all levels of the organization.

Fitness to use and fitness to latent requirement have to do with how quality improvement takes place across an organization, that is, with horizontal integration.

Fitness to use required integration of all functions so that the company could provide quality in the customer's terms. Functions became interdependent: Market research data had to be taken, the design and planning people had to design a product based on those data, production had to work from the design to make a product, sales and support had to sell and deliver the product to the customer, and the cycle would be repeated. In fact, the *total* in *total quality management* originally meant integration of all company departments (see Figure 2-4). Companies sought to "totalize" all divisions in order to unify efforts to satisfy customers.

Fitness to latent requirement requires that processes be integrated. Integration of process has two meanings. First, it refers to integrating processes beyond the functional departments of the company (for example, customer processes used to identify anticipated needs) into the internal processes of the company. Second, it refers to extrapolating what is learned about processes in one area of the company to processes in other parts of the company so that the entire company may better anticipate customer needs.

Achieving fitness to latent requirement "totalizes" or systematically integrates quality practices across the customer's en-

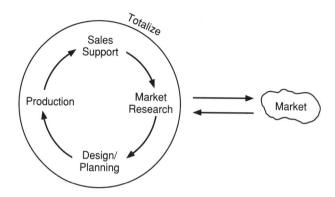

Figure 2-4. Total Integration of Company Functions

vironment. Information about customer lifestyles and ways to improve them reach throughout the entire corporation.

QUALITY OF CONFORMANCE VERSUS QUALITY OF DESIGN

Several other aspects of the evolution of quality should be noted. First, the fitnesses, or quality concept levels (standards, use, cost, and latent requirement), have alternated between quality of conformance and quality of design (see Figure 2-5).

Quality of conformance indicates the degree to which a product or service conforms to a standard, whether it be an internal, product-oriented standard, like those of the 1950s, or a standard set by customer requirements, like those of the 1970s. Standardization and some of the statistical process control tools support basic fitness to standard, and the 7 QC steps and 7 QC tools support conformance to evolving customer requirements (such as higher quality and lower cost).

Quality of design assumes expansion of the scope of standards, use of market research to support fitness to use, and use of QFD and the 7 tools for proactive improvement, which allow redesign of products or services and the processes that create them to support fitness to latent requirement.

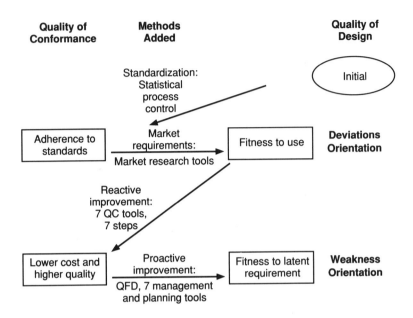

Figure 2-5. Quality of Conformance and Quality of Design, with Supporting Methods

FROM DEVIATIONS TO WEAKNESSES TO OPPORTUNITIES

As Figure 2-5 shows, there has been another evolution, from a deviations orientation with fitness to standard and fitness to use, to a weakness orientation with fitness of cost, to an opportunities orientation for fitness to latent requirement. A deviations orientation is static: it provides the mechanism to assure that a company meets the existing standards and usage needs. Companies using only this orientation were neither able to address customer demands for continually low cost nor to meet latent requirements.

A weakness orientation creates dynamic quality levels. It provides the mechanisms necessary to address weaknesses on a continuing basis — as improvements are made, elimination of the next weakness is always sought. The 7 Steps for reactive improvement seek to find and eliminate the next most important weakness.

An opportunities orientation proactively seeks new definitions of quality based on newly discovered customer needs. A major difference between the reactive approach and the proactive approach to quality is a shift from a weakness orientation (as when one is reducing the cost of an existing product) to an opportunities orientation (as when one is developing a new product).

Table 2-3 summarizes the key features and weaknesses of the four fitnesses.

Table 2-3. Evolution and Features of the Four Fitnesses

	1950s	1960s	1970s	1980s
Quality concept	Fitness to standard	Fitness to use	Fitness of cost	Fitness to latent requirement
"Totalization" among	Products from same line	Functions	Hierarchy	Customer's environment
Weakness	Unresponsive to market needs	Costly "inspecting in" quality	Imitable	Can create artificial unnecessary demand

TQM COMPANIES MUST BE AWARE OF ALL FOUR FITNESSES

In this and the preceding chapter we described the evolution of the concept of quality, in response to societal pressure, through the four fitnesses. However, companies today can't evolve through the four fitnesses in the historical order — it would take so many years that the company would lose competitively to pressures of companies already skilled in all four fitnesses.

Companies may not have to implement all four fitnesses for every product, and some companies may decide to focus on just some of the fitnesses. In general, however, companies today have to be aware of and probably implement the four fitnesses in parallel.

Companies must also avoid the mistake of thinking that the later fitnesses are higher or better than the earlier fitnesses and thus worthy of greater attention. For instance, some product development people become fixated on fitness to latent requirement. In product development, companies must always address fitness to standard and probably need to address fitness of use and fitness of cost. They need address only a few latent requirements.

FUTURE FITNESSES

Since the world is still rapidly changing, it is very likely that the concept of quality will continue to evolve and expand. Some hints about the direction of the quality movement follow.

Fitness to Corporate Culture and
Fitness to Societal and Global Environment

Increasingly, companies are making decisions about products and promoting themselves on the basis of their corporate culture. For instance, NEC views itself as a company of computers and communications. We might call this *fitness to corporate culture*. As seen in Figure 2-6, fitness to corporate culture fills out the stream of production from its starting point with the individual worker, through team efforts to address quality and cost simultaneously, to the product's place within the corporate strategy.

There is also increasing pressure for companies to improve the fitness of their work environment for employees and the fitness of their products and manufacturing processes for the surrounding environment — what might be called *fitness for*

135676

societal and global environment. This is a market-focused issue extending from fitness to latent requirement to include meeting the needs of the environment in which the customer lives.

FOUR REVOLUTIONS IN MANAGEMENT THINKING

We define total quality management as an evolving system, *developed through success in industry,* for continuously improving products and services to increase customer satisfaction in a rapidly changing world.

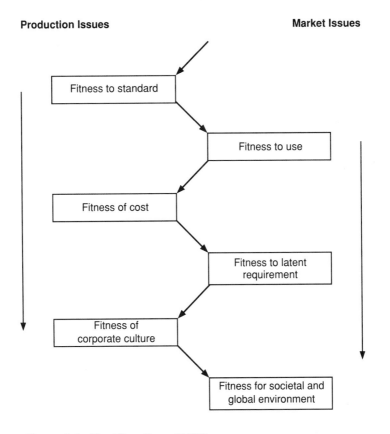

Figure 2-6. The Direction of TQM

TQM concepts and practices have been developed over many years by companies seeking to improve the quality of their products and services. TQM is not an abstract philosophy. Neither is there a single correct way to implement TQM; it must be customized to each company's culture and history.

Although each company must find its own way to implement TQM, four areas of concepts and practices are common to most successful implementations, and these differ from practices in many non-TQM companies. They represent four revolutions in management thinking (see Figure 2-7).

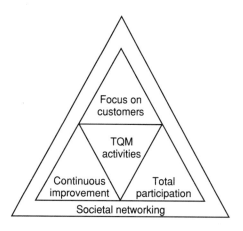

Figure 2-7. Four Revolutions of Management Thinking

1. TQM companies *focus on customers* and on satisfying their needs. Therefore, they must be able to react fast to changing customer needs and to focus their limited resources on activities that satisfy customers.
2. TQM companies *seek continuous improvement* of the processes that lead to higher quality products and services. Continuous improvement involves using a scientific approach to make improvements (analyze facts, base actions on facts, test results empirically), doing step-by-step improvements to get to market fast and acquire real

experience, and doing iterative improvement to reach ever-higher levels of quality.

3. TQM companies *seek total participation* of their staffs. All capabilities of all company members must be used if companies are to make continuous improvement and to seek customer satisfaction.

4. TQM companies must *participate in societal learning* (that is, shared learning with other companies) to avoid reinvention of methods, to implement quality practices more quickly, and to create a quality culture in which to do business.

FOUR LEVELS OF PRACTICE

Implicit in the four revolutions of management thinking is the need to practice TQM at four levels: individual, work group, organization, and regional or industry levels (see Figure 2-8). To some extent, these four levels of practice parallel the four revolutions in thinking.

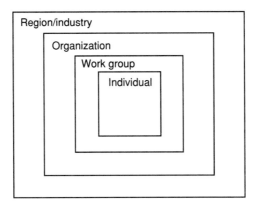

Figure 2-8. The Four Levels of TQM Practice

The individual level of TQM practice is necessary to shift the purpose of each employee's work from just doing the work assigned to satisfying the customer, and to give the individual employee the tools necessary to accomplish this task. It brings the idea of customer/supplier relationships to everyone in the company. If employees are to meet and satisfy the customer or next process, their skills must shift from just doing daily work to doing both daily work and improvement work. Making such shifts effectively requires a system.

At the work group level, you also want to unite daily work and improvement work (which requires a focus on process). You do this by encouraging mutual learning and teamwork, by providing a system that makes clear that daily work and improvement are both part of the job, and by taking the time for improvement.

At the organizational level, you want to integrate innovative improvements with the corporate goals, and mobilize the entire company in systematic pursuit of the corporate goals.

The industrywide, regional, or national level of TQM practice is directed toward a broader quality culture that supports an individual company's TQM efforts. This support can be through informal "networking," collaboration for mutual gain, and transfer of successful practices among companies and others interested in quality. The Center for Quality Management (CQM) was established to provide such sharing of experiences and resources. It also motivates us to keep going when we are flagging. In Japan, successful practices are integrated into the JUSE and JSA training materials, which many companies use; the journals and seminars of national quality societies also serve this purpose. National quality awards, such as the Baldrige Award in the United States, encourage nationwide awareness of quality; Japan's Deming Prize is part of an extensive system of national quality awareness.

Chapters 3 through 17 describe the systems TQM puts in place to implement the four revolutions and the four levels of practice.

NOTE

1. The 7 QC steps are described in Hitoshi Kume's book *Statistical Methods for Quality Improvement* (Tokyo: AOTS Press, 1985).

The First Revolution:
FOCUS ON CUSTOMERS

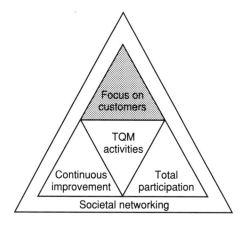

3

Change in
the Work Concept

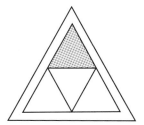

MARKET-IN

TQM teaches that understanding and fulfilling the expectations of customers is the best and only lasting means to business success.

To this end, TQM emphasizes a concept called *market-in*, which focuses on customer satisfaction as the purpose of work, in contrast to the older concept of *product-out*, which focuses on the product as the purpose of work.

The traditional concept of work says that a job is done and done well if a product is produced according to the manual for making it and the product works up to its specification or standard. This is called the product-out concept, because the focus is on the company's effort to output what it considers to be a good product (see Figure 3-1).

The product-out concept is often practiced in a fashion that suggests that the customers are stupid — that they don't understand their real needs. Often companies with a product-out orientation reject a customer's complaint about a product with the statement, "you are using it incorrectly," or "it's not meant

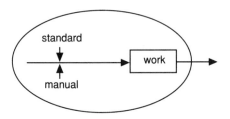

Figure 3-1. The Product-out Concept

to do that." Also, workers frequently believe that their job is just to do what is specified in their description, product standard, or production manual, and nothing more; managers may have this same attitude of "not my job."

But why do we work? Work is the means to the purpose of satisfying customers. The market-in concept focuses on input from the market and says that the job is not done well until the customer is satisfied (see Figure 3-2). The market-in concept says, "the customer is king" (or queen — the Japanese translate their version of this saying as "the customer is god").

The market-in concept says that every employee has customers. The company has outside customers, of course, and

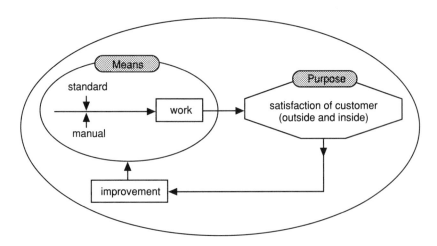

Figure 3-2. The Market-in Concept

they must be satisfied; however, each person in the company, no matter how far from the external customers, also has customers. The now famous TQM slogan, "The next process is your customer," means that each product or service step must satisfy or serve all subsequent processes. Therefore, internal customers (the next processes) have the same importance as external customers. Whoever uses the product of your work is your customer. In fact, each person may have many customers (and be a customer of many others). The market-in concept keeps your focus on customer satisfaction: the person you are talking to now is your customer, and you must try to satisfy that person.

The TQM ideal is for the market-in concept to penetrate the entire company and reach all employees at all levels. Of course, customer requirements change, so you need feedback from the customer and processes to improve the product over time — its specifications, the way it works, and the way you produce it. The Japanese call this improvement process *kaizen*. The market-in concept includes the idea of an improvement process for adjusting the work and the product produced as dictated by changing customer needs.

Why is market-in necessary? The product-out concept adheres to Taylor's theory of division of labor: some people follow standard processes, and others work on improvement.[1] Market-in tries to eliminate this concept of separation of labor. Instead, the market-in concept includes the dual function of work; that is, everyone works on both standard processes (daily work) and on improvement. The difficulty with Taylor's theory of division of labor is that it does not allow for reaction fast enough to satisfy customers in today's fast-paced, rapidly changing world. The key phrase here is "rapid change" — of customer requirements, technology, staff requirements, the communities around you, the monetary system, and the international geopolitical situation — and such change is frequently unforeseeable. As shown in Figure 3-3, TQM can be thought of as management in the face of rapid change.

Corning provides the following analogy to this increased pace and change in society and the need for business to keep

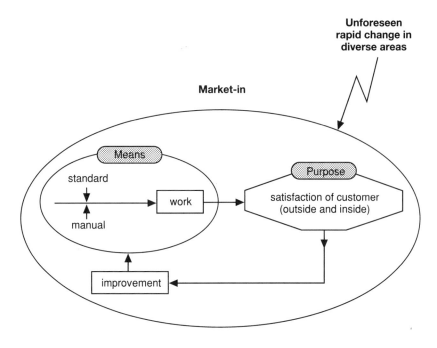

Figure 3-3. TQM Is Management in the Face of Rapid Change

up: For centuries, running a four-minute mile was believed to be impossible. In the 1950s, Roger Bannister ran a mile in under four minutes for the first time. Today, running a four-minute mile is a basic requirement for any competitive miler. The business situation is similar. Companies that pioneered in achieving total quality have raised the standard for competitive performance. Today, unless a company is achieving total quality, it is, or soon will be, uncompetitive.

Bill Smith of Motorola offers a related viewpoint summarized below:

> You must be best in class in terms of people, product, marketing, manufacturing, technology, and service. Otherwise, you will not be competitive. Best in class means you do as well as L.L. Bean in order entry, as well as the Federal Reserve Bank in transaction processing, and so forth. Fur-

thermore, once product quality is high, the customer will take it for granted and other factors (e.g., billing, order entry) will become more important to the customer.

These viewpoints suggest why many companies are adopting TQM. In a fast-paced world they are under many pressures that threaten their survival — the threat of insolvency, poor staff morale, increased costs, and diminished market share or sales (the latter two are forms of market pressure).

The practitioner of market-in knows the customer is not concerned with a company's internal functional organization. The customer is interested in product quality, cost, and delivery (QCD, in TQM terminology). These require cross-functional effort — no one department or function can provide quality, cost, and delivery by itself. This means you must have two overlaid organizational structures — a hierarchy for doing daily work and a cross-functional organization to ensure customer satisfaction. The cross-functional organization is needed to align the efforts of all parts of the company — divisions, departments, and individual employees — in a continuous effort to understand root issues (customer and internal) and improve and adapt to changing circumstances.

Traditional management structures are typically not well suited to working on total customer satisfaction. U.S. companies have functional management but not cross-functional management. They focus on results, not root causes: that is, they focus on the dependent variable, not the independent variable. They focus on trying to develop perfect standards and policies rather than viewing them as part of a continuous improvement process. They manage their workers rather than involving them in the improvement process.

TQM is a mass movement. It is not a movement of the elite within a company. The leverage in TQM comes from getting everyone in the company to play their appropriate role skillfully — from focusing everyone on doing what they can do to satisfy the customer. It is the job of the manager to practice and teach market-in.

As you look at companies that are practicing TQM, you may sometimes wonder what it is that makes the focus on quality so effective. There are, in fact, two major alignments behind the success of TQM.

First, the best way to satisfy customers is to deliver a high-quality product at a low price when the customer wants it. To reach these goals you must figure out what product the customer really wants, design and manufacture it so it works really well (removing all defects), and design and build it quickly (without any unnecessary cycle time). In addition to satisfying customers, all of these things save the company money by reducing wasted resources. *The focus on customer-defined quality does double duty — it satisfies customers, and it lets the company run as efficiently as possible.*

Second, customers want many different things. Some focus exclusively on low cost, some are motivated by personal ambition, some want to avoid a controversial buying decision, and some enjoy dominating the supplier. However, the majority of customers are concerned with something else: some 70 to 80 percent of them want a quality product at a low price. Company staff members also want many different things. Some want profits above all else, some want to perform social good, some want to work with the highest technology, and some only seek personal promotion. Most, however, are striving primarily for excellence in their work. *Quality is perhaps the only area where there is such great alignment between the goals of the customer and the goals of the staff. Achieving this alignment is the second way in which a focus on quality does double duty.*

CUSTOMERS

Many companies in the United States provide examples of a market-in approach to quality. Corning's quality goal is "Meeting the requirements of the customer completely, on time, 100 percent of the time." Corning goes on to explain that in its view every valid business activity has a customer and a supplier; that the requirements of the customer must be defined, understood, communicated, and agreed to by the supplier; and that agreed-to requirements will be met completely.

Xerox Corporation also adheres to the market-in concept. Xerox says, "Quality is the basic principle of Xerox. Quality means providing our external and internal customers with innovative products and services that fully satisfy their requirements." It goes on to say, "The customer will ultimately decide whether we have a job or not. The attitude of the customer will be the critical factor in determining our success. Everyone must decide that our first duty is to our customer." Motorola's approach is simply, "Total customer satisfaction."

Under the concept of market-in, for each piece of work you do, you must seek customer satisfaction. To achieve customer satisfaction, first determine who your customer is.

A customer is the person or group who receives the work you do. That work may be a product, or it may be a service. The customer who receives your output may be either external or internal. An external customer is someone who does not work for the company but receives the company's products or services. Notice, these are not only the immediate customers of your company; they may also be anyone in the customer stream to which your products flow. An internal customer is someone who works for the company and depends on the work of other company employees to get work done. Everyone has customers for every valid business function: a secretary types a letter for a customer, an accountant produces a financial report for a customer, an engineer does a detailed design for a customer, an employee submitting a trip report has a customer for that trip report. *A business function without a customer should not be performed.*

The market-in concept includes the idea of a process for improvement aimed at continuing customer satisfaction. TQM companies often have an explicit process or set of guidelines for dealing with customers (either external or internal). For instance, in its *Total Quality Control Pocket Guide*, Hewlett-Packard uses the following steps:

1. Who are my customers?
2. What are their needs?
3. What is my product or service?
4. What are my customers' measures or expectations?
5. What is my process for meeting their needs?
6. Does my product or service meet their needs and expectations?
7. What actions are needed to improve my process?

Motorola uses approximately the following steps:

1. Identify the work you do (i.e., the product).
2. Identify whom you do it for (i.e., the customer).
3. What do you need to do your work and from whom (i.e., the suppliers) do you need it?
4. Map the process.
5. Mistake-proof the process and eliminate delays (including non-value-added time).
6. Establish quality and cycle time measurement and improvement goals.

These are standard steps for executing and describing improvement. People are taught that the first step in identifying a problem is to see what customers want and aren't getting. Managers of improvement efforts therefore require this analysis. Market-in is not just a slogan, but is built into the way things are done. Senior executives plan the sequence in which market-in is institutionalized.

NOTE

1. J.M. Juran, "The Taylor System and Quality," *Quality Progress* 6 (May 1972): 42.

The Second Revolution:
CONTINUOUS
IMPROVEMENT

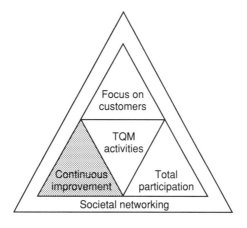

4

Improvement as a
Problem-Solving Process

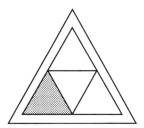

Chapter 3 introduced the concepts of market-in, continuous quality improvement, and customer satisfaction through an improvement process. According to TQM, because every product or service is the outcome of a process, the effective way to improve quality is to improve the process used to build the product. The corollary of focusing on process is that the focus is not on the results — results are the dependent variable. The results come from whatever process is followed — process drives results.

This practice differs significantly from the methods used in most U.S. non-TQM companies, where the emphasis is on objectives. TQM teaches that objectives alone cannot produce sustainable results. The value of objectives is to help decide what process needs to be put in place to produce the desired results. That process (and the way you follow it) then determines the results.

MANAGEMENT BY PROCESS

TQM calls this focus on process *management by process*. It consists of realizing that results come from process, building a process to produce the desired results, implementing the process so one can later figure out why it produced the results it did, and then feeding this insight back to improve the process next time it is used (see Figure 4-1).

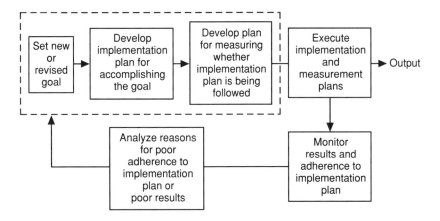

Figure 4-1. Management by Process

Management by process works as follows. First, set a goal and then develop an implementation plan for accomplishing the goal, including assignment of the people necessary to accomplish the effort. Develop a system for measuring whether you are adhering to the plan and accomplishing the desired results. Then undertake the task, monitoring adherence to plan and results. With this information, analyze why you were unable to adhere to the implementation plan or why the plan didn't work, and use this analysis to revise the goal, implementation plan, and measurement plan. The emphasis is on changing the process and changing the inputs to accomplish the desired results. The outputs are important for the light they shed on how the process is working.

Implicit in the concept of focus on process is the idea that any activity can be improved if you systematically plan the improvement, understand the current practice, plan solutions and implement them, analyze the result and its causes, and cycle around again. TQM applies this scientific approach both to improving a company's process for anticipating its customers' needs and also to improving the capabilities of individual staff members or groups of staff members. Throughout the rest of this book we will show examples of process as the means of making learning and improvement more efficient, simplifying communication, reducing variability of diverse results, building intuition and creativity, and improving ability to predict the future. TQM itself can be thought of as a process for helping a company to learn and improve — to change noncontrollable items into controlled or controllable items.

The theme of management by process, and more generally the process focus, recurs throughout TQM. Managers need such a viewpoint to understand and improve their own daily work. And, as this chapter suggests, managers must be able to see the improvement process as a process in order to provide guidance and support to subordinates engaging in improvement activity. The manager's job is to treat improvement as a problem-solving process, as described in the rest of this chapter.

WV MODEL OF CONTINUOUS IMPROVEMENT

TQM uses the phrase *continuous improvement* to stand for the idea of improvement as a problem-solving process. Continuous improvement is based on two major ideas — systematic (or scientifically based) improvement and iterative improvement.

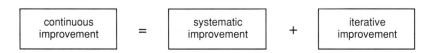

The WV model is used in this section to illustrate the key issues of continuous improvement.

Systematic Improvement

Improvements are derived from use of a scientific approach and tools and a structure for team or individual effort. A scientific approach considers a variety of possible solutions until the best — not just the most obvious — is identified factually. Structuring a team's efforts facilitates the participation of all members, eliciting information from even the more reticent of them.

Having made a first step at improvement using these methods, repeat the methods to get continuous improvements. Shoji Shiba modified Kawakita's W model for application to TQM.[1] Shiba calls this the *WV* model; we will use it to explain the concepts relating to improvement as a problem-solving process. The WV model is not a prescription for making specific improvements — it is too abstract for that. Rather, it is an aid to understanding and remembering three generally used stages of quality improvement and quality maintenance. It also conveys the idea of moving systematically back and forth between abstract thought and empirical data during the process of solving a problem. Like all models, it is an abstraction and idealization, useful for figuring out where you are and where you need to go next.

The WV model depicts the overall form of problem solving as alternation between thought (rumination, planning, analyzing) and experience (getting information from the real world, e.g., through interviews, experiments, or numerical measurements). The path between these two levels over time forms the shape of a *W*, then a *V*; hence the name WV.

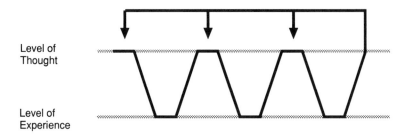

Level of
Thought

Level of
Experience

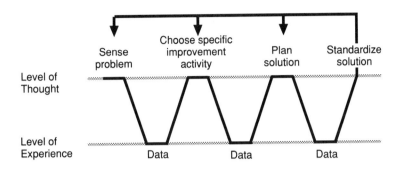

Figure 4-2. Using the WV Model for Problem Solving

For instance, as shown in Figure 4-2, you sense a problem and then collect data on where it might be; choose a specific improvement activity and then collect data on exactly what is wrong; plan a solution and then collect data to be sure it works; and then standardize on the new solution.

The WV model reminds you not to skip directly from "sense problem" to "standardize solution" — for example, from "sales are down" to "reorganize the company."

Three Types of Improvement

In addition to illustrating the interplay between thought and experience, the WV model illustrates three types of problem solving, as shown in Figure 4-3.

The three types of improvement — process control, reactive improvement, and proactive improvement — are described below. Quality management started with process control in the United States in the 1930s and in Japan in the 1950s. Reactive improvement was added in the 1960s and 1970s, followed by proactive improvement in the 1980s.

Process control. Assume that you have an effective standard process to perform some business or manufacturing function. You must monitor the process to make sure it is working

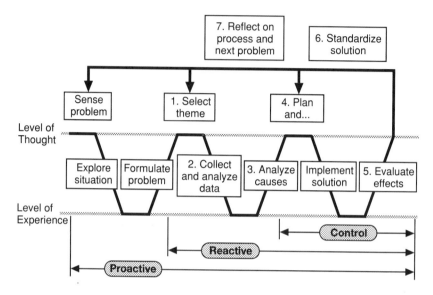

Figure 4-3. Three Types of Problem Solving

as intended and bring it back into proper operation if it gets out of alignment. Suppose a worker is charting her process with a control chart, such as the one shown below. In the figure, results of a process are plotted from left to right over time; the resulting chart highlights those results that exceed certain limits of acceptability.

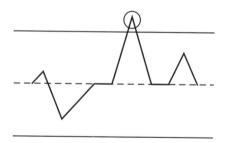

If the process produces results that are out of its control limits, the worker takes corrective action as predetermined and described in the maintenance manual to correct the defect in the process. This cycle, known in TQM terms as the SDCA (standard, do, check, act) cycle, is shown in the rough shape of a V in Figure 4-4. For example, you have a standard bill-paying process (S); you use, or do, it (D) to decide which bills are valid to pay and when to pay them; you take data and evaluate or check (C) the results to make sure you are maximizing your cash position without paying so late that you incur payment penalties; and you act (A) to return to the standard process if it has gotten out of kilter and you are paying incorrectly, too soon, or too late.

Thus the method is to have a standard process, to use it to

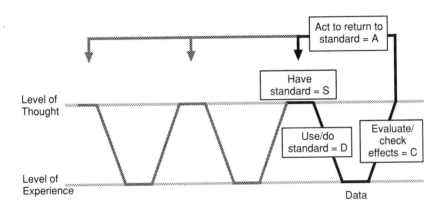

Figure 4-4. The SDCA Cycle

check whether the product meets the specification, and then to act to bring the process back to the standard. The concept is depicted as a cycle because one continues to apply the standard as long as the production procedure continues. This cycle to control or maintain the operation of a good process is known as process control. The monitoring system of process control includes use of inspection and some of the 7 QC tools. Process control itself is described more fully later in this chapter.

Reactive improvement. The next stage of the WV model addresses the improvement of a weak process. Suppose you have a specific process that simply isn't good enough — there are many points outside the control limits. Suppose, even if the worker corrects the process according to the process manual, it repeatedly produces results that are out of its control limits. There is obviously something wrong with the process.

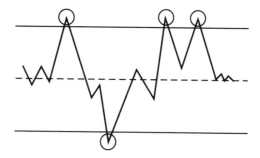

In this case, the worker must take data, analyze it, find the root causes of the problem, and implement appropriate counter-measures. In other words, the worker reacts to a specific problem by using a problem-solving process to make the improvement — hence the title of this section. For this case, TQM has a specific standard methodology to follow.

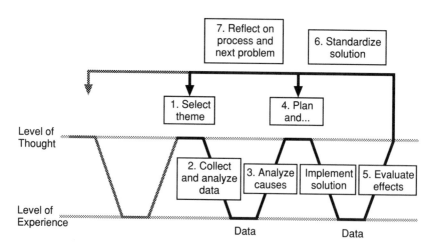

Figure 4-6. The Seven Improvement Steps

As shown in Figure 4-5, the steps of the methodology are as follows:

1. Select a theme (a specific improvement, such as "decrease after-shipment bugs reported in product X").
2. Collect and analyze data (to discover what types of bugs occur most often).
3. Analyze causes (to discover the root cause of the most frequent type of bug).
4. Plan and implement solution (to prevent the root cause from recurring).
5. Evaluate effects (to check the new data to make sure the solution worked).
6. Standardize solution (to permanently replace the old process with the improved process).
7. Reflect on process and the next problem (to consider how the problem-solving process could have been better executed and to decide which problem to work on next, such as the next most frequent type of bug from step 2).

These steps, known as the 7 QC steps or 7 steps, are TQM's standard methodology for improving weak processes. This approach is known as *reactive improvement,* because it reacts to already existing weaknesses. Note that for a successful improvement, the last few steps become the SDCA cycle for maintaining the improvement. The 7 QC tools, and more sophisticated statistical tools such as multivariate analysis and experimental design, are also frequently used in reactive problem solving. Chapter 5 describes reactive problem solving in more detail.

Proactive improvement. In many situations you do not start with a clear idea of a specific needed improvement. Rather, you have to choose a direction for the company before starting an improvement activity. For instance, you may need to decide what the customer wants, which product to develop, or which process needs improvement most. This situation is addressed by the final portion of the WV model, known as proactive improvement, as shown in Figure 4-6.

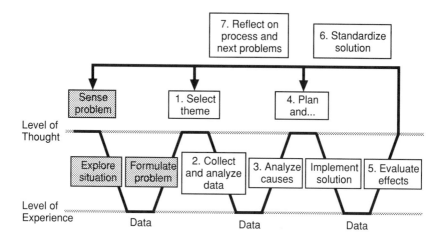

Figure 4-6. Proactive Improvement Steps

At first you are only generally aware that there is a problem — you sense a problem. Then you explore the situation broadly to understand what is going on (what customers appear to want, what you are able to build, what processes need fixing). Having explored the situation broadly, you are in a position to formulate a problem, and then in many cases you can move into the 7 QC steps. The 7 management and planning tools and QFD (described in Chapter 7) are useful for proactive improvement, especially in the initial steps.

Action Based on Facts

At each stage in the WV model, as you move between formulating problems or solutions and taking data, you move between the upper and lower lines on the WV model, or the level of thought and the level of experience. In the proactive stage you have a feeling or image of a problem — you are at the level of thought. Next, take some data (for example, look at how the process or machine is actually operating) — you are at the level of experience. Continue to move back and forth: formulating a theme (thought), taking data upon which to base root cause analysis (experience), planning a solution (thought), taking data to confirm that the solution works (experience), and standardizing successful solutions (thought). This alternation between thought and experience illustrates the important TQM principle of basing actions on facts. *At no time do you use speculation or opinion as the basis of decision making.*

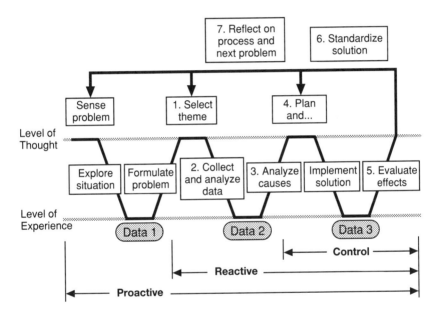

Figure 4-7. Three Kinds of Data for Problem Solving

As shown in Figure 4-7, each of the three stages of the WV model uses a different kind of data. Data 1, the data of proactive improvement, is most often qualitative — in language, not numbers; its purpose may be unclear, the data is fuzzy and comes in many different forms, and you don't know in advance what kind of data you'll get. Jiro Kawakita's advice on how to collect Data 1 is discussed in Chapter 6. Data 2, the data of reactive improvement, comes in both numbers and language, but you try to eliminate the language by defining a purpose (theme), which can be handled numerically. You must then define the data to solve the problem. Data 3, the data of process control, is typically accounting data and QC data in specific formats, mainly numbers, and is defined to be used for a special purpose.

Focus on the Vital Few

The WV model points toward another important aspect of systematic improvement: focusing on the "vital few" issues that will most affect your business if you improve them. At each state in the WV model and in each iteration, you will have many problems and improvements to choose from. Focus on the few vital things to improve, maximizing the impact of actions taken. There are many opportunities for making improvements, but the resources for doing so are limited. Furthermore, experience has shown that only a few of the actions taken have significant effect. Therefore, work only on those improvements that are both critical to a company's future (for example, those that improve customer satisfaction) and produce the biggest payback.

TQM uses current and future customer satisfaction as guidelines to making key decisions about company products, practices, and systems — highlighting the few activities that will have the greatest impact on business success.

Iterative Improvement

Implicit in the WV model is the idea of iterative improvement — the cycling back to work on the next problem or to continued improvement of an already improved process. This is the famous PDCA (plan, do, check, act) cycle of TQM (see Figure 4-8). PDCA was contributed to Japanese quality control by W.E. Deming, who learned it from W.A. Shewhart.[2]

    Plan: Determine analytically and quantitatively what the key problems are with an existing process or existing activities and how they might be corrected.

    Do: Implement the plan.

Check: Confirm quantitatively and analytically that the plan works and results in improved performance.

Act: Modify the previous process appropriately, document the revised process, and use it.

PDCA symbolizes the principle of iteration in problem solving — making improvements in a step-by-step fashion and repeating the improvement cycle many times.

If you are sailing a boat with the intent to intercept another boat, you periodically recalculate the course to the target. Each time you make the best calculation you can.

What you don't do is follow the initial course calculation without correction until the calculation indicates that you have reached the target. You realize that despite your best initial efforts to calculate the course to the target, the target may be moving in unforeseen ways, and the currents and winds in which you are sailing may carry you off course. You follow the principle of seeking frequent feedback about your position and the target's position in relation to your course.

In business, however, people tend to think that they should be able to develop the correct plan or procedure for meeting business needs without trial and feedback.

The PDCA principle of iteration gives you a system for making improvements in a step-by-step way, doing the best job you can within relatively short improvement cycles. In that way

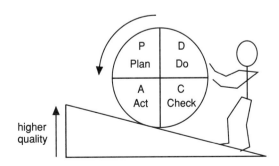

Figure 4-8. The PDCA Cycle

you can try an improvement and get real feedback regarding the direction and distance to targets or goals. It is important to get improved products or services rapidly to market or in the hands of the next process, in order to get this user feedback. In addition, PDCA is a system for making continuous improvements to achieve the target or ever-higher performance levels.

The PDCA cycle is always shown as a circle to indicate the continuous nature of improvement. All types of improvement and improvement maintenance require iteration.

PDCA is a method for dealing with all sizes of problems, including some that may be beyond the scope of the 7 steps. As will be discussed in more detail in Chapter 15, TQM explicitly addresses the differing methods needed for incremental improvements and breakthrough improvements. We call these $PDCA_1$ and $PDCA_2$ (see Figure 4-9).

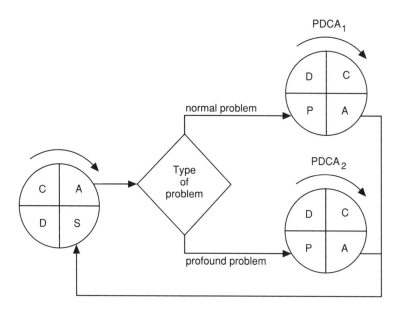

Figure 4-9. PDCA for Incremental and Breakthrough Improvements

PROCESS CONTROL

This section contains a brief sketch of some of the principles of process control. There is nothing original in this section; all of the ideas here have been expressed by Shewhart, Deming, Ishikawa, and the other practitioners of statistical process control. An enormous literature exists on the subject.[3]

However, few senior managers — especially if they did not rise through the manufacturing side of the organization — are familiar with the basic concepts of process control. If they know process control exists, they don't imagine that it could apply outside the manufacturing area. In fact, process control does not apply just to manufacturing processes. It can also apply to the processes for order entry, training course delivery, billing, recruiting, daily cash forecasting, the monthly financial close, servicing service requests, forecasting telecommunications capacity needs, developing product documentation, or corporate budgeting. In fact, process control can be applied to any process that repeats and that can be measured; in other words, process control can be applied to a large number of diverse tasks. No matter what length the process cycle or how complex the task, process control can be applied to it.

A basic understanding of the principles of process control will improve anyone's understanding of PDCA, and of the TQM principles that systemization and iterative improvement are valuable in every aspect of business. In addition, such a basic understanding will help managers understand that creativity is based on disciplined application of methods that are known to work.

We do not have space in this book to develop the basic principles of process control and provide an intuitive basis for them. Therefore, we will state the principles as clearly as we can in a short space.[4]

Here are several basic principles that every manager should understand:

- Customer needs determine the desired output.
- The process used determines the actual output.
- The actual output inevitably has variance.
- Inspection is a poor primary control method.
- To meet the desired output specification, reduce the variance of the actual output by finding and removing the sources of variation in the process.

These principles are described in more detail below.

Customer needs determine the desired output. The goal of business processes should be to satisfy a customer, whether external or internal. Therefore, customer needs must determine the desired outputs of the processes of companies — you need to know what customers care about, and you need valid quantitative measures to track what they care about. In Chapters 7 and 8 we consider at length how to hear, interpret, and quantitatively

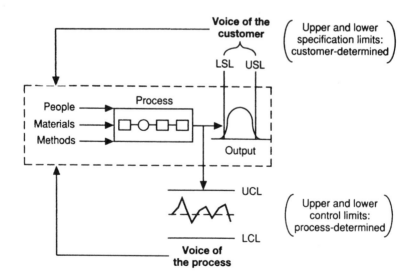

Figure 4-10. A Model for Process Control

specify the "voice of the customer." In Figure 4-10, this voice of the customer determines the upper and lower specification limits (USL and LSL) for the results produced; results outside of these limits are defects that must be discarded or reworked.[5] Notice in the figure that the voice of the customer is outside the process and, in fact, is independent of it.

The process used determines the actual output. As Figure 4-10 shows, the actual results produced, indicated by the output distribution, come from the process and its inputs and not from the voice of the customer or specification limits. If you have a process that produces outputs within a certain range, the outputs will be within that range regardless of the outputs customers desire. Suppose, for instance, you have a cash management department only good enough to maintain cash balances within a range of no better than plus or minus $3 million as a weekly target. If the system cannot perform any more accurately than this, simply wishing it would improve will not make it do so.

The actual output inevitably has variance. Any process has some variability in its results. This variability of response has two characteristics that can be learned from the statistics on the output: a central tendency (average response), and natural variability (distribution of responses over the range of responses). For instance, in the cash management system example, the actual cash balance at the end of each week will vary plus or minus from the target for the week. Some of these variations will be acceptable (fall within specification), and some results will vary so widely that they fall outside of specifications.

Historically, people have tried two methods for producing results within specification — inspection and reduction of variance.[6]

Inspection is a poor primary control method. With some processes you can avoid shipping defective products by inspecting the outputs and discarding those outside specification or sending them back for rework. Likewise, if the numbers in a departmental budget are not justified satisfactorily, the budget can be redone. Of course, this produces waste or extra expense, and perhaps delay. With other processes, such as the cash management example mentioned in the last paragraph, inspection will show that you are producing results outside of specification but that doesn't stop them from happening. The point is that inspection is an ineffective method of trying to control a process.

Shewhart, Deming, and those who followed them teach that by focusing on meeting specification, one is unlikely to meet specification reliably. As long as inspection is used as the method of meeting specification, there will continue to be waste and extra expense, some bad products will slip through inspection, results that were acceptably good will become unacceptably bad without warning, and in general continued good performance is tenuous.

To meet the desired output specification, reduce the variance of the actual output by finding and removing the sources of variation in the process. The second method of producing results within specification is reducing the variance in the process until the average and virtually all the output measurements are within specification; the results are inspected and the process or the way it is followed is modified to reduce the variance in the results. Poor results may still have to be discarded until the variance is so small that the products outside of specification are no longer produced.

Shewhart, Deming, and others teach that focusing on reducing variation is the best approach to meeting specification reliably. Low variation indicates expertise; just meeting specification may be luck. With sufficiently small variation, there are no bad products to slip through inspection, and the system is stable and will provide warning of impending failure. However, as Shewhart said, reduced variation can only be achieved through careful study of the sources of variation in the process and through action to reduce or eliminate sources of extraneous or excessive variation.

A process may have two types of variation: variation that has a stable and consistent pattern over time (controlled variation, due to what Deming calls common causes) and variation that has a changing pattern over time (uncontrolled variation, due to what Deming calls special causes). Controlled variation is the variation inherent in the process — natural variation imposed by the physical limits of the process. Controlled variation is statistically the same each time, as the process is run from one day to the next. Uncontrolled variation typically results from not following the process reliably. That is, each time the process is run, it is run differently. This can happen because of poor operator training, poor process documentation, unreliable supplier performance, or many other factors that can change over time. Uncontrolled variation usually has a large effect compared with controlled variation.

Since controlled variation is inherent in the process, it cannot be reduced except through a change in the process. Demanding that workers do a better job will not reduce the controlled variation inherent in the process; demanding that specifications be met will have no effect on the natural variation of a process. Many managers don't realize this. They think that by setting objectives they can affect the results of a process. Whether the results of a process are within specification depends on the natural variation of the process, not the specification. This is not to say that setting objectives is not useful; setting an objective is useful because without it one will not know what process to try to develop to produce the desired result. However, the process then produces the result it is capable of producing — not the result demanded by the objective.

On the other hand, you can remove uncontrolled variation by controlling the inputs and following the process accurately. The larger uncontrolled variation usually masks the smaller controlled variation, so that it is not possible to find and eliminate the sources of controlled variation until the sources of uncontrolled variation have been eliminated. Deming argues that until the sources of variation have been understood, changes to a process are likely to make it perform worse than before; he

calls this "tampering." Reorganizing in response to poor performance without understanding the causes of poor performance
is a form of management tampering that is frequently practiced.
Therefore, the scenario to follow in reducing process variation
is, first, to control the process by removing uncontrolled variation and, second, to find the sources of controlled variation and
change the process to remove them, thus decreasing the variation until virtually all results are within specification.

The control chart and other tools of statistical process control enable results of a process to be plotted over time and clearly
show whether the process is out of control (has uncontrolled
variation) or in control (has no uncontrolled variation). For instance, a control chart plotting the difference between forecast
and actual revenues will show whether one has an effective (in-
control) process for achieving and forecasting revenues. These
tools also show whether a process that is in control is capable of
achieving the desired results. Ford Motor Company likes to say
that statistical process control provides the "voice of the process"
— it enables you to learn what the process wants to say to you
(see Figure 4-10). Once you can hear the voice of the process, you
should be able to change the process so it can meet customer
specifications, revealed through the "voice of the customer."

PROCESS CONTROL AND PROCESS IMPROVEMENT

The basic cycle of process control is often called the SDCA
cycle. In the SDCA cycle, there is a standard (S), and it is used to
do the process (D). Then the results of the process are checked
(C), and appropriate action is taken (A). If the results are within
specification, the appropriate action is to continue to use the
standard and repeat the cycle. If the results are beginning to
drift or are actually out of specification (i.e., not meeting customer needs), take standard corrective actions.

However, from time to time you may decide that the specifications are not stringent enough and that you must improve

the process (reduce the variance) so that tighter specifications can be met. When this happens, use a form of PDCA, the method of reactive improvement (described in Chapter 5), to find the source of the greatest natural variation and to improve the process by eliminating it. This interaction between the SDCA cycle of process control and the reactive improvement cycle was sketched earlier in the chapter and is shown more precisely in Figure 4-11.

A scenario of interaction between the two cycles might run something like this:

SDCA   Run an existing process for a while.
       Compute the natural variation, thus highlighting uncontrolled variation.
PDCA   Find and eliminate the sources of uncontrolled variation.
SDCA   Continue running the new or now accurately followed process.
       Eliminate the source of any out-of-control condition that begins to occur.
PDCA   Use the 7 steps to find and reduce the largest source of controlled variation.
SDCA   Continue running the new process.
       Eliminate the source of any out-of-control condition that begins to occur.

This alternation of SDCA and PDCA cycles also can be shown graphically as in Figure 4-12.

PROCESS VERSUS CREATIVITY

When people introduce TQM and its focus on management by process to their companies, the typical reactions are, "Won't this focus on process stifle innovation and creativity?" or, "Innovation is our competitive advantage, and process will stifle innovation." The fact is, the focus on process increases efficiency, as we will show through many examples in this

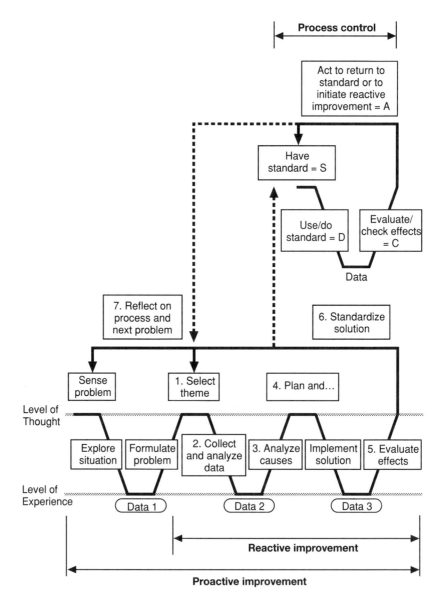

Figure 4-11. Interaction between the SDCA Cycle and the Reactive Improvement Cycle

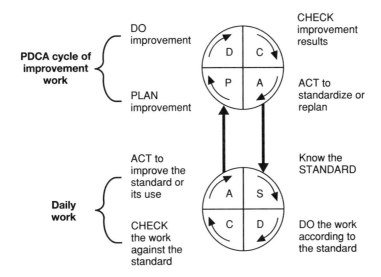

Figure 4-12. Alternation of SDCA and PDCA Cycles

book. Figure 4-13 indicates how effectiveness may change as a function of focus on process.

Without any process, effectiveness is limited. People don't work smoothly together, they don't learn from each other, they don't learn from past experience, and, in general, a company gains no leverage beyond individual capabilities. A certain amount of debilitating conflict will probably also be present. As companies begin to manage by process, efficiency goes up. However, there is surely some point beyond which process ceases to be a tool to achieve improved results and becomes an end in itself. When process becomes an end in itself, the organization ossifies. Somewhere on the horizontal axis lies the balance point between too much and too little process. This is the point where companies will get substantial financial payoff from process — for example, learning how to get products to market faster. The

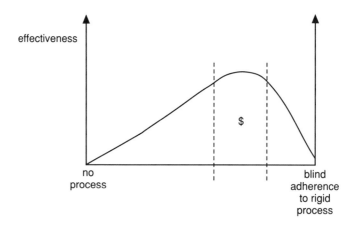

**Figure 4-13. Optimum Balance Between Too Little and
Too Much Process**

job of managers is to use process sensibly and to teach its sensible use to gain maximum effectiveness. For most companies it is safe to err in the direction of more process for a few years more. Figure 4-14 from Ishikawa shows a Japanese view of the relationship between process and innovation.[7]

In the United States, companies typically have a history of occasional innovation-based breakthroughs with periods of status quo in between. In Japan, companies also have occasional breakthroughs, but in between they make continuous improvements. As shown in the figure, if the two approaches start at the same level on the left side of the figure, over time the Japanese approach results in a significant advantage. Since both approaches include breakthrough, the source of the Japanese advantage is continuous improvement.[8] The U.S. approach is losing because it doesn't include continuous improvement. Recently Japanese companies have been using the extra profits gained through continuous improvement to invest in developing systematic methods of innovation and breakthrough.[9] Companies that do not correct the imbalance between innovation and continuous improvement will fall further and further behind.

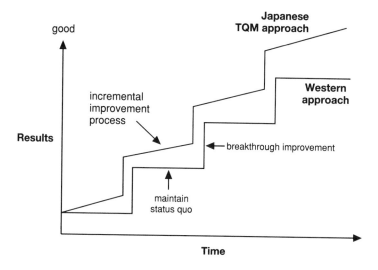

Figure 4-14. The Improvement Process and Innovation

NOTES

1. Jiro Kawakita, *The Original KJ Method* (Tokyo: Kawakita Research Institute, 1991), 422.

2. W.A. Shewhart was a member of the Quality Assurance Department of Bell Telephone Laboratories. In 1931, he put the quality movement on scientific footing when he published *Economic Control of Quality of Manufactured Product* (New York: Van Nostrand Reinhold, 1931; republished Milwaukee: ASQC, 1980). Kozo Koura described the history of the development of the PDCA cycle very nicely in "From Deming Cycle to Management Cycle," *Quality, JSQC* 20, no. 1 (1990).

3. Following is a list of standard texts on process control. The books marked with asterisks are essentially textbooks; the rest are guidebooks.

   David Amsden, Howard Butler, and Robert Amsden, *SPC Simplified for Services* (White Plains, NY: Quality Resources, 1991).

AT&T, *Achieving Customer Satisfaction*, AT&T doc. no. 500-443 (Indianapolis: AT&T Customer Information Center, 1990).

Idem., *Statistical Quality Control Handbook*, 2d ed., AT&T doc. no. 700-744 (Indianapolis: AT&T Customer Information Center, 1958).

Augustus Donnell and Margaret Dellinger, *Analyzing Business Process Data: The Looking Glass*, AT&T doc. no. 500-445. (Indianapolis: AT&T Customer Information Center, 1990).

E.L. Grant and R.S. Leavenworth, *Statistical Quality Control*, 5th ed., (New York: McGraw-Hill, 1980).

*Kaoru Ishikawa, *Introduction to Quality Control* (Tokyo: 3A Corporation, 1990).

*Douglas C. Montgomery, *Introduction to Statistical Quality Control* (New York: John Wiley & Sons, 1985).

*H.M. Wadsworth, K.S. Stephens, and A.B. Godfrey, *Modern Methods for Quality Control and Improvement* (New York: John Wiley & Sons, 1986).

Donald J. Wheeler and David S. Chambers, *Understanding Statistical Process Control* (Knoxville, TN: Statistical Process Controls, Inc., 1986).

4. Managers who doubt the validity of these principles should immediately sign up for one of the numerous three-day seminars on statistical process control, view the tapes in the Deming Library (particularly 7, 8, and 9), arrange to participate in a simulation of just-in-time manufacturing (Coopers & Lybrand has something called "the JIT wheel game," and other institutions offer similar simulations), have a long discussion with the company's quality control staff, or read a book on process control. Books particularly recommended for their ease of understanding are AT&T, *Achieving Customer Satisfaction;* Donnell and Dellinger, *Analyzing Business Process Data;* and Wheeler and Chambers, *Understanding Statistical Process Control.*

5. The "voice of the process" concept and elements of Figure 4-10 were presented by James Bakken (formerly of Ford Motor Co.) at the Annual Conference, Center for Quality Management, Cambridge, MA, April 1992; AT&T's *Achieving Customer Satisfaction* also provides an excellent discussion of how to find out what customers care about and how to decide on the appropriate measures.

6. We draw here on Wheeler's and Chambers' excellent discussion of this topic in their book *Understanding Statistical Process Control.*

7. Ishikawa, *Introduction to Quality Control,* 70.

8. We don't read any significance into the fact that the breakthroughs in the Japanese approach occur slightly to the left of the western breakthroughs, which we assume was for visual separation of the vertical lines.

9. Sheridan M. Tatsuno, *Created in Japan* (New York: Harper Business, 1990); James Womack, et al., *The Machine that Changed the World* (New York: Harper Collins, 1991).

5

Reactive
Improvement

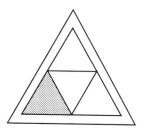

Recall that in Chapter 3 we discussed two major components of developing individual skill: the market-in concept and
improvement skill. In Chapter 4 we said that improvement skill
also has two components — reactive skill and proactive skill.
Proactive skill is what we need to design new products, choose
new directions for our companies, and design new systems.
Chapter 7 contains a detailed discussion of this approach. Reactive improvement (the subject of this chapter) deals with correcting or improving existing processes — reacting to flaws such as
defects, delays, and waste. The WV model (introduced in Chapter 4) shows the connections among proactive and reactive improvement and process control (see Figure 5-1).

Process control is shown at the right side of Figure 5-1,
which illustrates the realm of statistical process control. Assume
that there is a standard process, for example, in a factory or an
administrative activity. Decide on the standard process or solution for the task at hand and implement that solution. Then take

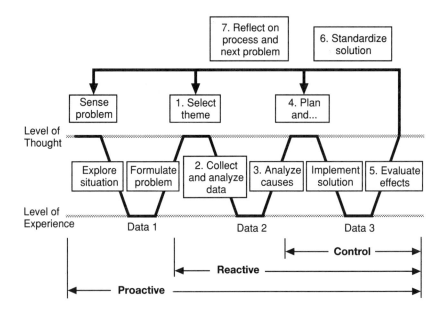

Figure 5-1. Proactive Improvement, Reactive Improvement, and Process Control

numeric data to make sure that the process is functioning as intended, evaluate the data, and if necessary correct the process so that it again functions according to standard.

The essence of the reactive approach is standardization of the problem-solving process, using, for example, the 7 steps and 7 QC tools.[1] The idea of a problem-solving process has been known since the Greeks, but has typically been practiced only by a gifted few. In our own time, the inventor Thomas Edison, well known for his creative genius, used and required his assistants to use an explicit standard problem-solving process.[2] In this era of rapid change, everyone needs the benefit of standardized problem solving. Figure 5-2 shows a model of the steps of reactive problem solving. The rest of this chapter and the next discuss these steps one by one.

Reactive improvement as a standardized practice became common in the 1970s as the process used by quality circles in Japan. In the 1980s, the use of reactive improvement spread

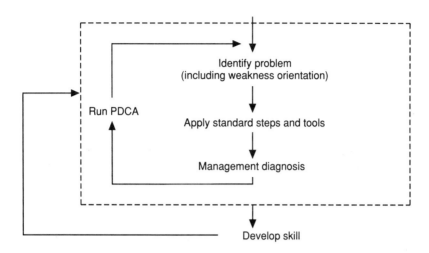

Figure 5-2. Model of the Steps of Reactive Problem Solving

throughout the corporate hierarchy. This use by top and middle management is discussed further in Chapter 15.

IDENTIFYING THE PROBLEM

How does one identify the area of the problem for a reactive problem solving effort? The 7 steps do not explicitly include the part of the WV model at the left side concerning sensing a problem, exploring the situation, and formulating the problem to be solved. But these steps are very important. Therefore it falls to managers to guide a quality team in identifying an appropriate problem. Otherwise, quality teams may take a very long time, fail to solve the problem, or perhaps spend time solving an insignificant problem. Most failures of quality teams occur because managers don't know how to guide the process, especially step 1 — identifying the problem.

Identification of the problem is the most important aspect of reactive problem solving. The process of identifying the problem may be divided into four parts:

- weakness orientation
- problem exploration
- careful selection of theme
- clear statement of theme

Weakness Orientation

For reactive problem solving, the first aspect of problem identification is using a weakness orientation (see Figure 5-3).

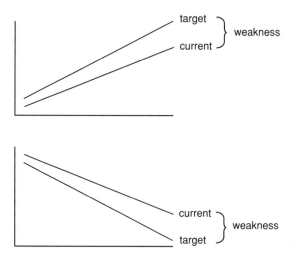

Figure 5-3. Identifying Weakness

From a TQM perspective, weakness can be defined as the difference between the current situation and the target. For instance, in Figure 5-3, the target is changing as time moves from left to right, and the actual performance starts weak and gets relatively weaker over time. The goal is to eliminate the weakness so you can move from the current level of performance to the target rate of performance. The weakness orientation focuses on closing the gap between current and target, that is, eliminating weakness as the basis of improvement. "Decrease delayed delivery rate from 25 percent to 15 percent" is a weakness orientation. Why is a weakness orientation preferable to a strength orientation? If instead of a weakness orientation you used a strength orientation, your goal would be to "increase on-time delivery rate from 75 percent to 85 percent."

The weakness orientation has several characteristics that are less likely to be present with a strength orientation:

- focus on facts — base actions on facts, not opinion
- focus on process, not results — results are the driven (effect) variable and you must focus on the drive (cause) variable
- focus on root causes, not solutions — encourages objective analysis of causes ("what caused the delays"), not jumping first to solutions ("what can we *do* to improve?")

The weakness orientation is the most important component of problem identification for improvement. For this approach to work, however, management (e.g., middle managers) must be supportive. Workers want to reveal weakness to improve quality; they may say, "Let's discuss last week's problem." However, managers may say, "Our factory is perfect," "Why not choose another problem?" or "When we have problems they are small and we can easily solve them." Also, senior managers see reality through the middle managers. Thus, if a middle manager does not encourage and support workers who want to reveal weakness, the weakness will remain hidden from senior management. Senior management, in turn, must encourage a weakness orientation. If a senior manager blames the middle manager for revealing a problem ("Why was that allowed to happen?" "Why wasn't that fixed sooner?"), the middle manager will never show another problem.

The key point is that workers should be encouraged by all levels to reveal problems. CEOs must be patient and refrain from blaming people about problems; they must encourage exposure of weakness. If CEOs don't encourage exposure of weakness, everyone will hide problems.

Many Japanese companies fail to implement TQM because they don't encourage revelation of weakness. For instance, if the CEO gets angry at a presentation of quality improvement teams (QITs), QITs can easily next time create a story and data to make the CEO happy. If they do this, improvement and TQM will fail.

In Japan when a weakness is discovered, they try to say, "This is very good." Say it again and again; constantly encourage a weakness orientation. To get permanent good results, you have to define the problem in terms of weakness when selecting a theme.

Problem Exploration

The second step in identifying the problem is to explore the problem thoroughly. There are many problems that you could work on. The question is how to select which problem to work on from among the many that could be worked on. The answer is to follow the chain of cause and result (see Figure 5-4).

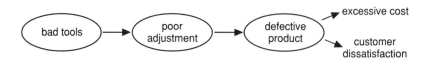

Figure 5-4. A Cause and Result Chain

For instance, suppose you find a situation where a process or machine is poorly adjusted. You could work on that problem, but instead you trace the chain of cause and result until you reach the immediate cause of customer dissatisfaction or excessive cost — for example, a defective product. Choose that immediate cause as the theme. You must choose a theme directly related to the customer or the next process. If you do not, you risk working on nonvital problems that don't improve the company's ability to satisfy customers, or reduce costs; you can't afford to spend time on such problems.

The 5 *evils* — defects, mistakes, delay, waste, accident/injury — are a device to focus attention on a theme directly related to basic satisfaction of the customer or next process — to focus on a market-in approach. Defects, mistakes, delay, waste, and accident/injury always cause customer dissatisfaction or excessive cost.

Thus, if you develop an initial theme, such as poor adjustment, you should trace it forward to one of the 5 evils, in this case, defective product that causes excess cost and customer dissatisfaction. Then you can use the rest of the problem-solving process to work your way back along the chain of result and cause to a find a root cause that really is related to customers and costs — in this example, we tracked backward from defective product to poor adjustment to the root cause of bad tools. You must make sure that people tackle these 5 evils, not other problems, to get a good result from quality improvement activities. The 5 evils are shorthand to help in TQM's mass movement approach to improvement. They are a good first approach to reactive improvement. People more experienced with reactive improvement may sometimes use the KJ method as well as the 5 evils to find problems that affect customer satisfaction or cause excessive cost (see Chapter 8).

Careful Selection of the Theme

The problem exploration step is likely to produce several themes to work on. The third step in identifying the problem is careful selection of the particular theme to use as an explicit statement of the improvement effort.

For continuous improvement it is necessary to repeat the problem-solving process. Thus, you don't have to select the most important, most difficult problem at first. Select one theme at first and then another later, both building problem-solving skill and finding a manageable path to solution of a large, difficult problem.

If you are to experience the achievement of problem solving, you must tackle a problem that can be solved with current levels of skill and that is important to solve. Often there is a trade-off to be made. In selecting the theme, consider these issues:

- sense of achievement to be gained
- difficulty of situation
- urgency/effect
- quickness of potential solutions

First, look at the difficulty of the situation as shown in Table 5-1.

Table 5-1. Evaluating Problem-Solving Difficulty

		Area of Problem		
		Equipment	Methods	Human Behavior
	Yourself	1	1	3
Data collection or potential solution implementation	Yourself and others	2	2	4
	Others	3	3	4

There are two dimensions in Table 5-1: Can you collect the data and implement the potential solutions by yourself, or do others have to do it? and, Is the problem area equipment, methods, or human behavior? The areas marked 1 are easiest for the beginner to work on. The second and third least difficult areas are also shown. Working on the human behavior of others is very difficult, as shown. You can use Table 5-1 to evaluate the difficulty of the situation in terms of both difficulty of data collection and difficulty of potential solution.

Next, having understood the difficulty of the situation, you might construct a theme selection matrix, which prioritizes problems for solution in terms of difficulty of the situation (data collection and potential implementation), urgency or impact, and

quickness of solution (see Table 5-2). Regarding quickness of solution, three or four months is good; one to two years is too long.

Table 5-2. Determining Problem-Solving Priorities

Rank 1-3 (1 is best)	Ease of data collection	Ease of potential implementation	Urgency/ impact	Speed of solution	Priority (lowest total is highest)
Problem 1					
Problem 2					
Problem 3					
Problem 4					

Fill in the matrix in Table 5-2 for each problem being considered. Vote 1 (high), 2 (medium), or 3 (low) in each box. Add
across the rows and put the total in the priority column to pick
the first problem to work on, that is, the problem with the lowest total.

Clear Statement of the Theme

The fourth step in identifying the problem is making a
clear statement of the theme. The following examples use this
process of refinement to illustrate various ways in which themes
are clarified.

Example 1

"Increase on-time delivery" is an initial attempt to state a
theme. *"Decrease late delivery"* is better. The key point is that because of its weakness orientation, the second statement does a
better job of directing the team toward the facts and causes of
the problem.

It is difficult to write a clear statement of theme. It is often best to write the obvious theme, *"Increase on-time delivery,"* first, and then iteratively refine it until you reach an effective statement of theme. The following examples show this process of refinement.

Example 2

"Understand customer delivery, quality, and pricing requirement."

First convert the above statement of partial solution to a statement of weakness; for example:

"We do not meet requirements of the customer in delivery, quality, and pricing."

But delivery, quality, and pricing are too much to tackle at one time, so let's focus on the delivery:

"We do not meet requirements of the customer for delivery."

Example 3 (for a Sales Group)

Start by exploring the problem. The first version of the theme is,

"Define the method to identify long-term opportunity customers."

You have already imposed the solution. What is the weakness?

"We don't know the long-term opportunity customer."

Suppose that in your company, there is already agreement on the following definitions: long-term = three to four years; opportunity = increasing sales; customer = big-volume customer. Therefore, rewrite the theme as:

"We don't have a good forecast of 3- to 5-year sales to big-vol-

ume customers."

This is not a theme, however; it is a problem. To convert this problem to a weakness orientation theme, write:

"Decrease misforecast of 3- to 5-year sales to big-volume customers."

The past may not predict the future, but it is all the data you have, so it is what you have to use.

Example 4

"Optimize face-to-face selling time."

This is not a weakness orientation. It anticipates a solution. Suppose experience tells you that you meet with the purchasing person 90 percent of the time and the user of your product only 10 percent of the time. What does "optimize face-to-face selling time" mean — with whom do you want to meet face-to-face? Suppose you believe that it is important to change the mix of face-to-face selling time so that more time is spent with the user. A better theme, then, would be:

"Decrease time spent with other than the end user."

That is an improvement, but now look for further improvement. What is the purpose of decreasing time spent with other than the end user?

"To sell more."

Time spent yields an order, which yields dollars. Decreasing time spent with other than the end user is one of the means to achieve the order. This leads us to think about what the real problem is. The real problem is to get an order. Thus the theme should be (using a weakness orientation):

"Decrease orders lost."

You should select a theme directly related to the customer or money. Spending time with people other than the end user and not getting an order is an example of one of the 5 evils — waste.

Example 5

"Decrease delay between the committed and actual date of shipment."

This initial theme statement is product-out; "delay" is not defined. Before the senior manager suggests a better statement of the theme, however, he or she should first encourage the quality team: "Very good — your theme is stated in terms of weakness. But there is a way to improve it. Have you thought about it from a market-in point of view?"

This leads to:

"Decrease the disparity between customer-demanded and actual date of shipment."

In addition to illustrating iterative refinement of a theme, the above examples suggest some of the characteristics of an effective theme:

- weakness orientation
- market-in orientation
- stated as a problem, not a solution
- stated in terms of results, not a solution
- stated as a single problem, not several
- every word well defined

Some managers worry that a weakness orientation will undermine morale. A weakness orientation, correctly handled, can coexist with high morale, for the weaknesses addressed are weaknesses of the system, rather than weaknesses of the people who work within the system. Weakness is a means to an uplifting and positive end — continuous improvement.

The manager needs to guide the team or provide facilitation or training to enable the team to select an effective theme. Having a carefully selected, clearly stated theme is essential to successful application of the 7 steps. Application of the 7 steps is the key to empowering teams to solve problems on their own without requiring constant oversight and management intervention.

STANDARD STEPS AND TOOLS

TQM is a mass movement. Thus the process of reactive problem solving must be

- easy to understand and learn
- easy to use
- easy to monitor

Therefore, you need standard steps for reactive problem solving, and TQM provides these. They are called the 7 QC steps, or 7 steps, and were previously listed in the description of the WV model. However, the individual steps and substeps require specific methods, for example, for collecting facts. This leads us to the need for tools, of which there are many, even just for collecting data and analyzing facts. Therefore, TQM has focused on the most effective and most frequently used tools, based on experience of real problem solving in real companies. The 7 QC tools listed below (and in Table 2-1) are described in more detail at the end of this chapter.

- check sheet/stratification
- Pareto diagram
- cause-and-effect diagram (also called an Ishikawa diagram or fishbone diagram)
- graphs
- control charts
- histogram
- scatter diagram

The previous section described how to identify a problem and select an effective theme. The essence of the 7 steps and 7 tools is *standardized reactive improvement*.

The number 7 in the 7 steps and 7 tools is an arbitrary number. It is a strategy for mass movement — easy to become familiar with, to learn, to use, and to monitor. The only thing important about the 7 is that it is not too many steps or tools to learn. In fact, some companies have six or eight steps in their standard reactive problem-solving process, and there is even variation among the seven standard tools themselves. Sometimes *stratification* is included as one of the 7 tools, for example, in place of check sheet. Process flowchart is also sometimes included in place of check sheet. Within each company each tool is well standardized, both in the process of application and the process of teaching the tool and its use.

In Japan most companies that implement TQM or QC circles choose a coherent set of standard steps and tools for use in their reactive improvement process. Even companies that use a standard set of tools are weaker without standard steps to connect them.

Table 5-3 shows the way the 7 steps and 7 QC tools are typically used together. The 7 steps define and clarify the problem-

Table 5-3. How the 7 QC Steps and 7 QC Tools Work Together

7 QC Steps	7 QC Tools
1. Select theme. 2. Collect and analyze data. 3. Analyze cause.	Check sheet, graph, Pareto diagram, histogram, scatter diagram, cause-and-effect diagram
4. Plan and implement solution.	
5. Evaluate effects.	Check sheet, graph, Pareto diagram, histogram, scatter diagram, cause-and-effect diagram, control chart
6. Standardize solution.	
7. Reflect on process (and next problem).	

solving process. The 7 QC tools provide the methods to execute the steps.

Most problems can be solved with use of only a few tools. For instance, graphs, Pareto diagrams, and cause-and-effect diagrams make up 60 to 70 percent of the tools used in Japanese quality circle activities. In the beginning, a company can focus on teaching and using these tools. It is not useful to teach a comprehensive tool set to beginners — they won't be able to make effective use of so much training before they have experience working on real problems. Teach the standard seven steps and these three tools, and teach your teams how to apply them to their own problems and selections of themes. Following the case study below is a brief description of all seven of the QC tools.

THE 7 STEPS: A CASE STUDY

The case study by the Broken Pellicle QI Team at Analog Devices illustrates the use of several TQM standards: the 7 steps, the most commonly used three of the 7 QC tools, and a standard presentation format called a quality improvement story, or QI story.[3] Following is the text that accompanied a presentation of the QI story by the Broken Pellicle Quality Improvement Team. This is a real story by a real team with all its strengths and weaknesses.

> Good morning. I would like to present to you the efforts of our quality improvement team, which we call the Broken Pellicle Team. Here are the members of our team. [See Slide 5-1.] Improvement teams at Analog Devices have specific members, usually cross-functional and chosen according to the nature of the problem being solved. Members are requested, but not required, to participate, and can be anyone with insight into the problem. Members remain

> **ANALOG DEVICES**
>
> **Broken Pellicle**
> **Quality Improvement Team**
>
> Marge Hendriks
> David Kneedler
> Cheryl McGee
> Paula Nowell
> Doug Smith
> Anne Spagnolo
> Julie Vinnacombe

Slide 5-1.

on the team throughout the problem-solving cycle. There are two production operators, one production supervisor, one production trainer, one engineer, one technician, and a facilitator on this team.

Step 1: Select Theme

Step 1 of the seven-step problem-solving process is theme selection. Each improvement team at Analog has a written theme — a specific, measurable goal. Here is the theme our team selected: *Reduce the number of broken and*

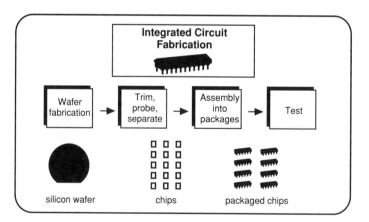

Slide 5-2.

scratched pellicles in wafer fab by 50 percent by the end of 2Q91.
I will now explain the theme.

Some of you may not be familiar with wafer fabs or
the steps used in producing our product, an integrated circuit or "chip." This slide shows the major steps in making a
chip. [See Slide 5-2.] In wafer fabrication — "wafer fab" — a
flat slab or wafer of silicon, a few inches in diameter, is
used. Through a complex sequence of hundreds of photolithographic and chemical process steps within a clean-
room environment, individual integrated circuits are etched
or imprinted into the silicon wafer. This is a cyclic process,
through which a multilevel circuit is built up within the silicon. After wafer fab, certain parameters of the circuits are
tested for functionality; good chips are taken out in the
"separate" step, are assembled into packages, and are sent
through a final test.

This team's theme addressed the "photo" area within
wafer fab. [See Slide 5-3.] This room imprints images of the
multiple levels onto the wafers in a process similar to taking
and developing a photograph. In the photo area, wafers from
other rooms are staged on a table. Some of these are baked in
an oven before further processing. All wafers are then sent to
the "coat" station, where a photosensitive polymer is spun

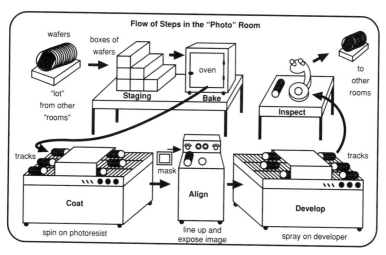

Slide 5-3.

on the wafers. The wafers are then sent to "align," where previous processing levels are lined up with a mask pattern containing the current level; the image of this pattern is exposed onto the polymer film on the wafers. The image is then developed, inspected, and sent on to the next step in another room.

Continuing with an explanation of our theme, this figure shows a drawing of a photolithographic "mask." [See Slide 5-4.] A mask is a clear glass plate, held by a plastic holder, and contains an image of the circuit being exposed at the current process level. The pellicle is a thin plastic film stretched across the glass plate to protect it from dirt and scratches. As shown in the figure, the image on the glass mask would be in the center of the mask holder, in the large circular area. The operator slides the mask holder into a groove on the loader arm, which protrudes from the aligner machine. The mask holder is held onto the arm via the groove at the bottom "finger" as well as by the mask holder slot on the side. The loader arm is then retracted into the machine and drops the mask into the proper position.

Teams are always asked to try to verify why their theme is important, so that they understand it better and have a feeling for its importance to the company. This team's verification is in terms of two of the 5 evils: waste

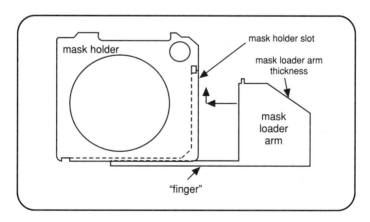

Slide 5-4.

(cost of repairs) and delay (increase in cycle time). [See Slide 5-5.]

Why is this theme important?

New vendor will replace ADS Mask fab:

- Cost to replace pellicle will be $400/mask, or $50,000 to $100,000 annually

- Delay will be 4 days/mask, or 500 to 1,000 additional days of cycle time per year

---

Slide 5-5.

Step 2: Collect and Analyze Data

Step 2 of the seven-step problem-solving process is to collect and analyze data. Teams at Analog are encouraged to examine existing data collection systems carefully; it is better to design a new system specifically for your problem-solving efforts rather than struggle with the flaws and assumptions built into someone else's system. Our team examined the old data system ("mask repair logbook") used when a pellicle was found broken, and decided that there was insufficient information as to causes and types of holders, and no ability for our technicians to give more information and more easily form check sheets and Paretos. The new data collection system devised by our team answers the questions: Who? Where? How? [See Slide 5-6.]

- Team member fills out logsheet with aligner operator
- Technician adds input
- Material control files logsheet
- QIP team analyzes/plots data

After collecting data for two months, we plotted our data with the use of a Pareto. Here is the data sorted by machine causes, handling (human) causes, and other (unknown; found broken) causes. [See Slide 5-7.] Our

Broken and Scratched Pellicle
Data Collection Check Sheet

Date: _____

Operator ID# _____

Machine # _____

Time SL/PA notified _____ SL/PA initial _____

Serial # _____

Operator inputs: _____

_____

_____

Circle one: scratched   broken

Circle one: machine   handling

Time given to tech. _____ Tech initial _____

Tech input: _____

_____

_____

Location of scratch: _____

Corrective action: _____

_____

Holder condition: _____

Holder type (circle):   black   white

Please return to Material Control upon completion

Slide 5-6.

conclusion is that over 70 percent of the broken pellicles were caused by the aligner machine, so we focused on machine causes.

In studying machine causes we found three categories. [See Slide 5-8.] The highest category included cases where the pellicle broke while the aligner was unloading

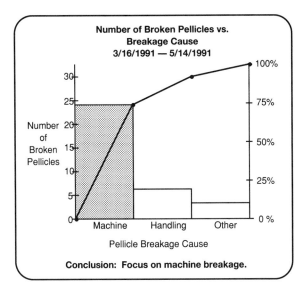

Slide 5-7.

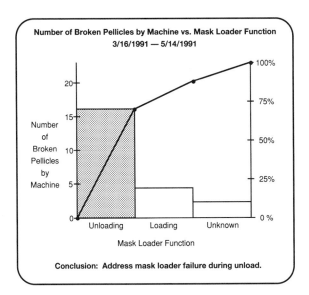

Slide 5-8.

the mask from the machine (over 70 percent); the next highest was when the aligner was loading the mask into the machine (20 percent of occurrences), and the rest of the causes could not be determined exactly. Thus, our conclusion was to study why the pellicles broke during unloading.

Step 3: Analyze Causes

We now felt we had sufficient data to move to step 3. This figure shows our "Ishikawa," or "cause-and-effect," diagram, answering the question, "Why does the mask unloader arm break or scratch pellicles during unloading?" [See Slide 5-9.] We addressed causes due to machine, materials, and people. We decided that the root causes were of two types: The finger on the loading arm was out of alignment with the mask holder; and the tolerance of the groove

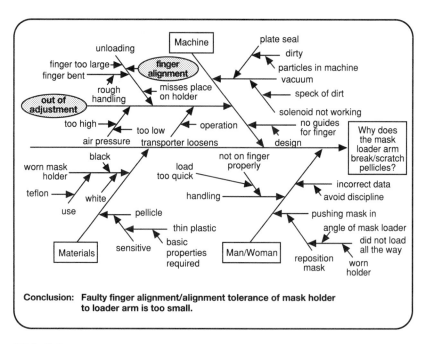

Conclusion: Faulty finger alignment/alignment tolerance of mask holder to loader arm is too small.

Slide 5-9.

on the side of the mask holder did not ensure consistent linkage with the loading arm. Thus, as the mask was withdrawn from the machine, it could shake or wobble, and the pellicle could be scratched or broken.

Teams at Analog Devices are asked to verify root causes discovered with the Ishikawa diagram. This team verified its conclusions by observing the machine in operation, examining the motion of the arm each time a mask was unloaded. They found that the next six times a pellicle broke, the finger was observed to be out of alignment. They then repeated the breakage under controlled conditions to verify the alignment problem and the tolerance problem. Thus, the team was confident that it had found the root causes.

The team also sorted the data for breakage during unloading into different types of mask holders. We were using two different types (made by different vendors), a "white" holder and a "black" holder. The figure shows that the white holders were in use for over 80 percent of the breakages. [See Slide 5-10.] The team measured the grooves on

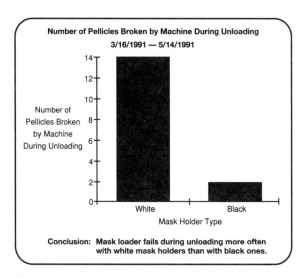

Slide 5-10.

the two holders and found that the white holders had slightly less tolerance than the black holders.

Step 4: Plan and Implement Solution

The team used a solution matrix to decide the effectiveness of various solution options. [See Slide 5-11.] The most effective solutions were to design and install a guide on the loader arms of each aligner machine, and to convert all the mask holders to the black type. The other factors making this an attractive solution were that the guide could be fabricated and installed by our own technicians. This team decided to design, install, and test guides on the ma-

Solution Matrix			
Solutions	Finger Alignment	Mask Holder Alignment Tolerance	Other Factors
1. To design and install a guide	3	3	Fabricate in-house by our technicians. Cost minimal. Equipment down for 1 shift. Need resources outside of QIP but within department.
2. Ensure carriage is home	2	1	Requires 100% operator attention.
3. Hit run/reset if mask starts to come out wrong	1	1	Depends on operator being there 100%. After-the-fact "fix."
4. Designate mask holders	2	2	Requires transfer of plates 100% of the time (increases handling).
5. Convert to all black push-button-type holders	1	3	Limits vendor? May increase price.

Ranking system: 3 Very effective
2 Somewhat effective
1 Low effectiveness

Slide 5-11.

chines with the most occurrences of breakage. In addition, all mask holders would be converted to the black type, since the data was so conclusive that this was a major cause.

These figures demonstrate the action of the guide, which is screwed to the mask loader arm and catches either side of the mask holder as it is inserted into the loader arm. [See Slides 5-12 and 5-13.] The guide holds the mask holder firmly so that it remains in alignment with the arm, tolerance is improved, and the mask does not shake when the mask is unloaded.

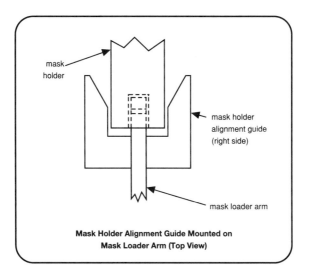

Mask Holder Alignment Guide Mounted on Mask Loader Arm (Top View)

Slide 5-12.

Step 4 of the seven-step problem-solving process continues with solution implementation. [See Slide 5-14.] The team used a matrix to indicate what needed to be done, who would do it, by when, and how the action would be performed.

Step 5: Evaluate Effects

In evaluating the effects of implemented solutions, the team plots its data following solution implementation. [See

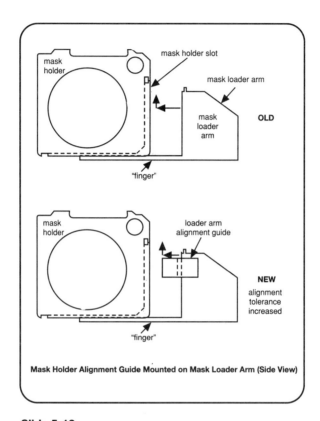

Mask Holder Alignment Guide Mounted on Mask Loader Arm (Side View)

Slide 5-13.

Slide 5-15.] The solution worked! Pellicle breakage caused by machines was reduced from 24 cases to 2 cases. In addition, handling breakage was eliminated because of increased operator awareness of the issue.

The team also evaluated the savings in terms of two evils, waste and delay, and demonstrated to management the significant reduction in costs as well as cycle time from their solution, as follows.

- Cost invested:
  - Mask aligner brackets $380.00
  - Black mask holders $31,620.00
  - Total invested $32,000.00
- Estimated annual cost to replace pellicles:

Solution Implementation			
Who	**What**	**When**	**How**
Dave Kneedler	Get first guide made.	5/22/91	Get commitment from Sonny and George.
Doug Smith	Install first guide as pilot on PE #5.	5/29/91	Doug/George to install. Anne will get priority on system.
Anne Spagnolo/ Doug Smith	Inform all shifts of pilot program.	5/29/91	Anne will inform the other supervisors and send a PROMIS message to Photo Mail. Doug will inform all Photo technicians.
Anne Spagnolo	Determine similiar amount of work thru PE #5 during data collection.	5/29/91	Via daily reports.
Anne Spagnolo	Ensure similar work load on PE#5 after installation.	5/29/91	Via daily reports.
Anne Spagnolo Julie Vinnacombe	Designate all black holders on PE #5 and PE #8.	5/29/91	Julie will inform all shifts and post a sign on PE's.

Slide 5-14.

- Before $52,800.00
- After $3,200.00
- Savings $49,600.00
- Estimated annual cycle time lost:
  - Before   528 days
  - After   32 days
  - Days saved   496 days

Step 6: Standardize Solution

The team again used a matrix to indicate what was to be done to standardize the solutions, who would do it, by

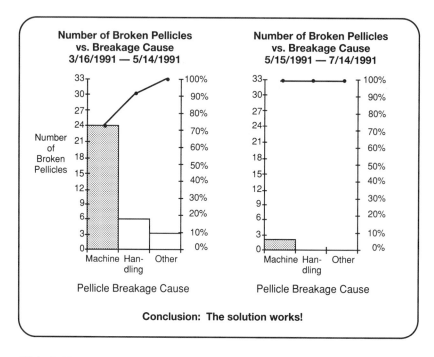

Slide 5-15.

when, and how it would be done. [See Slide 5-16.] The team decided to reset its specs for mask holders so that all would be of the black type in the future, and to install guides on all remaining aligner machines.

Step 7: Reflect on Process (and Next Problem)

The PDCA cycle for this team's efforts would not be complete without step 7, reflection on process and choice of the next problem. Upon reflection, we decided that we wasted the first few weeks of our problem-solving process by trying to utilize the old data system; we should have recognized its weaknesses immediately and designed a new one. We recommend that teams always consider designing their own data system very early in the process. Secondly,

Install Black Holders and Guides on All Machines

Who	What	By When	How
C. McGee	Reset spec black holders	6/30/91	Paperwork
C. McGee	Convert high runners to black holders	6/30/91	Order and install
C. McGee	Convert rest of holders	8/31/91	Order and install
A. Spagnolo	Continue monitoring "intangible effect"	perm.	Use same data system
D. Kneedler/ D. Smith/ T. Clark	Order and install remaining guides	8/31/91	Contract out

Slide 5-16.

we did not coordinate well with the other two shifts. Third, someone knowledgeable in mask fabrication should have been recruited to help from the beginning. For our next problem, we are considering working on the breakage caused during loading of the mask. Loading failure is now our most important pellicle breakage problem. Before we attack this problem, however, we will examine other problems within wafer fab to see if there is a more important topic to address with our team.

THE 7 QC TOOLS

In this section we say just a few words about each of the 7 QC tools, to clarify how each is used. In addition to these tools, other statistical tools, such as multivariate analysis and experimental design, are sometimes taught as part of reactive problem solving.

Check Sheet

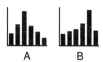

To analyze problems, you must collect data that represent the facts. Forms used for easy collection of data are called *check sheets*. Use check sheets to take data systematically regarding the frequency of various effects. They are much like a set of tally marks on the back of an envelope. However, they are usually marked on forms prepared in advance, according to expected effects. Also, they are calibrated so that when you take the data, you have a running plot of frequency of effects; the check marks create a histogram.

Stratification

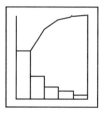

One of the practical ways to determine the specific cause is *stratification*. For example, when the diameter of the shaft of a rotor has too much dispersion, and it is made from two machines, you have to stratify or segregate the data corresponding to each machine. Thus, you can find the difference between machine A and B and easily make adjustments.

Pareto Diagram

At any given time there are many kinds of problems around you. It is not practical to attack all these problems at the same time. Therefore, arrange the problems in order of importance and attack the bigger problems first. A bar graph that shows the biggest problem on the left followed by the lesser problems is called a *Pareto diagram*. Pareto diagrams help one focus on the vital few effects or causes. The absolute totals of effects are always shown on the left side, and the cumulative percentages are always shown on the right side.

Cause-and-Effect Diagram

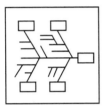

To solve a problem, it is important to know the real causes and the intertrelations among causes. You can then identify the major causes to solve the problem. Use a *cause-and-effect diagram* to guide data collection and analysis to find the root cause of a problem. A cause-and-effect diagram shows an effect at the right and the main causes of that effect off the horizontal axis. These main causes are in turn effects that have subcauses, and so on, down many levels. This is not basically a statistical tool; it enumerates the variety of causes rather than the frequency of events. However, it is a useful tool for noting the frequency of events, once one you have the data.

Graphs

Graphs display data. There are many kinds of graphs: bar graphs, line graphs, circle graphs, and radar graphs are some of them. Most people are familiar with the first three types of graphs.

A *radar graph* compares several items on multiple dimensions. Suppose that for three competitive products, *e1* is performance, *e2* is cost, *e3* is reliability, and *e4* is delivery — in all four dimensions, the good direction is out from the center. The example shows that one of the products is inferior in all dimensions. Of the other two products, one wins slightly in performance and delivery, and the other wins slightly in cost and reliability.

Control Chart

A *control chart* is a graph with limit lines to show the acceptable range of quality production. It is very helpful for spotting abnormal situations in standard manufacturing processes. Control charts are used to plot over time (left to right) the observed output or status of a process around the mean and between upper and lower control limits. In the figure, the circled dot is outside the control limits.

Histogram

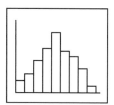

We produce a large quantity of products with a great number of parts and materials. Each of these products and parts cannot have the same quality but always has some amount of dispersion. A *histogram* is a graph that shows dispersion of the data. From this graph, we can analyze the characteristics of the data and the cause of dispersion. Typically, a histogram is a bar graph showing the statistical distribution over equal intervals of some measure of quality, such as defects. Histograms are used in analysis for *stratification* to create hypotheses for why defects are occurring.

Scatter Diagram

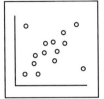

The relationship between cause and effect (for example, between illumination level and inspection mistakes) may be drawn on a graph called a *scatter diagram*. A scatter diagram plots many data points, typically with a measure of quality on one axis and a variable hypothesized to influence quality on the other axis. Used in analysis to test hypotheses on cause-and-effect relations, a scatter diagram is a visual representation of a two-dimensional correlation. A diagram such as this is often very useful because it illustrates patterns of data that are not otherwise obvious.

NOTES

1. Complete descriptions of the 7 QC Tools are found in many books, for example: Kaoru Ishikawa, *Guide to Quality Control* (Tokyo: Asian Productivity Organization, 1982) and *How to Operate QC Circle Activities* (Toyko: QC Circle Headquarters, 1985); Hitoshi Kume, *Statistical Methods for Quality Improvement* (Tokyo: AOTS Press, 1985); and Tetsuichi Asaku and Kazuo Ozeki, *Handbook of Quality Tools: The Japanese Approach* (Cambridge, MA: Productivity Press, 1990).
2. Unreferenced statement by Peter Drucker quoted in Spencer Hutchens, Jr., "Strategic Design: Key to Profit in the 21st Century," in Ross E. Robson, ed., *The Quality and Productivity Equation* (Cambridge, MA: Productivity Press, 1990), 293.
3. The case was prepared by Ira Moskowitz, Production Manager, Wilmington Wafer-fab, Analog Devices, Wilmington, Mass.

6

Management Diagnosis
of the 7 Steps
# of Reactive Improvement

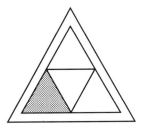

QI stories are the standard presentation format for the 7-step reactive improvement activities. The QI stories are presented to management, and managers have a standard way of responding, called management diagnosis of the 7 steps. There are several reasons for presenting and diagnosing the QI stories. For example, such a process

- diffuses good improvement practices throughout the organization by example
- acknowledges team accomplishment
- increases improvement skills of the team through management review and comment ("diagnosis")
- creates management buy-in to standardize the solution
- ensures legitimacy of conclusions

Ensuring legitimacy of conclusions is deliberately listed last. Employees following anything like the proper process will have acceptable results; reactive quality improvement at its most basic levels is not supposed to be difficult. It's a "mass movement" — everyone can use the 7 steps to create permanent improvement.

This diagnosis is an important way to help employees increase their problem-solving and improvement skills over time. Although ideally such coaching happens continuously, the one time when coaching is formally expected is when a team presents its results to management in the form of a QI (quality improvement) story.

GENERAL GUIDELINES FOR MANAGERS DIAGNOSING A QI STORY

Senior Management Attends

Presentations of quality improvement stories are not just for the managers who supervise the team members; they are for management at higher levels. At both Digital's Hudson semiconductor plant and Florida Power & Light's Port Everglades power plant, we saw the senior management, starting from the plant manager on down, attend the QI story presentation. At Florida Power & Light, where we had an opportunity to talk with the managers, the QI stories seemed to give the plant manager a surprisingly intimate knowledge of what goes on at his plant.

Comments Highlight Positive Lessons and Areas for Further Improvement

It is more important to highlight key positive lessons than to identify and eliminate weakness. People learn more from good examples than from being told what not to do. Therefore, 70 percent of management comments during a QI story presentation should address the positive aspects of the work, and 30 percent should be on the most important areas for improvement next time. The developmental status of the team should also temper diagnosis. A quality improvement team may be just beginning to use the 7 steps and related tools. Managers should praise such a team's use of tools rather than criticize the way those tools are used.

Furthermore, managers should restrict comment on both positive and negative QI stories to the vital few. A barrage of helpful or critical comments doesn't provide focus. Comments should be specific: Rather than saying, "good theme," for example, say what specifically was good about the theme selection. Again, the goal is to provide focus.

To highlight the appropriate lessons, the senior manager diagnosing a QI story might prepare a matrix such as the one shown in Table 6-1, listing the key strengths of the QI story the manager is about to see and improvements that need to be made next time. A few of these would be mentioned to the team after the presentation, and others might be mentioned to the team facilitator at a later time.

Table 6-1. QI Story Diagnostic Matrix

Step Number	Step Name and Comment	Strengths	Suggested Improvements
1	Select theme		
2	Collect and analyze data		
3	Analyze causes		
4	Plan and implement solution		
5	Evaluate effects		
6	Standardize solution		
7	Reflect on process (and next problem)		

Nonverbal Signs Show Management Interest

Because a major part of the function of QI story presentations is to diffuse positive lessons, the senior managers attending the presentation should give every sign that the work is important. Simple attendance is not as effective as visibly attentive listening. Holding conversations on the side, reading unrelated materials, or slouching and looking around the room send the message that the presentation is unimportant and uninteresting to the senior manager. On the other hand, facing the presenter, taking notes, and asking questions at the end of the presentation send the message that the work is significant and interesting. This evidence of enthusiasm and support is necessary to motivate further improvement activities.

Following are some specific examples of nonverbal ways to show interest, typical of Japanese practice.

- Senior managers are expected to attend these QI and quality circle presentations.
- Executives sit in the front row, with the CEO in the center, visible to the presenter in front of them and to the audience behind them. Senior managers have to show constant interest through their nonverbal behavior.
- During a TQM presentation, the senior manager must be present at all times.
- Senior managers must sit on the edge of their chairs and lean forward — expressing interest by behavior instead of words.
- In response to good points, they should nod their heads and say "very good."
- They should be seen taking notes; they should not interrupt the presenters.
- They should show attentiveness by asking questions at the end of the presentation.

Employees don't know what managers are thinking, just what they see them do. Sixty percent of communication is nonverbal; 40 percent is verbal. During QI story presentations, senior managers must be actors, in the sense of conveying interest through behavior.

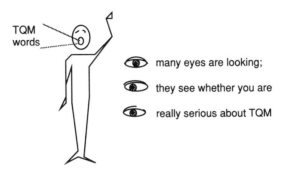

Don't Suggest Going Back

Diagnoses should be oriented toward doing better on the next turn of the PDCA cycle. While it is tempting to request redoing of data collection, analysis, and so on, it is important for team morale to keep moving forward. If redoing something is important, due process of theme selection will shortly bring the team back to it on a subsequent cycle.

The process being followed in the QI presentation is more important than the results. You have to teach this process to everyone. Ask people to follow the 7 QC steps process and they will get good results.

The Process Should Follow the 7 Steps Format

For improvement skills to diffuse through the organization, there must be a common language. QI stories in particular, because they are the medium for so much diffusion within a company, must use a standard format.

The step number and name of each step should be on the first slide of each step. The first slide should give the name of the team and the team members, to identify who undertook this improvement effort.

Each department says, "We are different, and we need our own version of Pareto." However, a common language throughout the company is needed; TQM is a mass movement that requires discipline.

DIAGNOSING STEP 1: SELECT THEME

Guidance from Management

Since the 7 steps start after problem exploration (left side of WV model), teams using the 7 steps need guidance from managers on problem selection. It is useful for the presentation to indicate how the team involved its management in theme selection.

Weakness Orientation

The theme should have a weakness orientation. Does it focus on the 5 evils (defects, mistakes, delay, waste, accident)? Beware of solutions masquerading as problems, such as "decrease lapses in worker discipline." Also avoid phrases like "improve," "upgrade," "create a better...," which indicate a strength orientation.

Working on an Ongoing Process

The 7 steps and 7 tools are best applied to an ongoing process — a process in which the problem repeats. If the problem will not repeat, there is little benefit in undertaking an improvement process. If the process has not repeated in the past, it is difficult to use the 7 QC tools to collect adequate data. If the problem does not repeat, it will be difficult to check whether the solution works.

If the problem doesn't repeat, it may make more sense to use processes and tools other than the 7 steps and 7 tools, such as proactive improvement, the 7 management and planning tools, or statistical analysis tools such as design of experiments and multivariate analysis.[1]

A problem that is stated in terms of future performance risks turning into a strength-oriented theme that focuses too quickly on solutions, without first dwelling on data and causation.

It is difficult to forecast the effect of a solution. Implementing the solution produces usable feedback. This is possible with an ongoing process.

Market-in and Results, Not Causes

Does the theme have a market-in concept (focused on customers or the next process)?

State problems in terms of results, not causes: customers dissatisfied, next process hurt, dollars lost, and so on. Problem statements cast in terms of causes short-circuit the process of gathering data and identifying causes.

Demonstration of a market-in theme should include the facts. These might take the form of a comparison of the company's error rates with those of a competitor, a plot over time showing a competitively important variable getting worse, or a customer survey showing that the problem area is a significant area of complaints. The more factual the ties to customer-related performance, the stronger the theme.

"My boss told me to do it" does not demonstrate understanding of the company's business or of customer satisfaction. Explaining the theme is a good way for employees to think about why they do what they do and who their customers are.

The philosophy of the dual function of work demands that the theme both make improvements and follow standard processes. Doing improvements simply because you were told to is just another form of following standard processes; it is not real improvement work.

Explanation of Theme for Audience

QI stories are an opportunity to teach the market-in orientation in two ways. One is the customer orientation discussed above. The other is the recognition that the presentation is a product and the listeners are customers. A product-out orientation results in presentations that plunge ahead without regard for who its listeners are and what they know about the technical terms, processes involved, people and responsibilities involved, and so on. A market-in presentation, on the other hand, starts from terms the audience knows, giving its listeners the context they need to understand the theme. It dispenses with details that fall outside the main theme. Making such a presentation requires great personal strength.

Good explanations are essential: Listeners must understand the situation and learn something new, and quality improvement teams (QITs) must understand their themes. They must know the real reason for making the improvement — it should not be just something they are told to do. The presentation process is a learning process for the QIT.

The presentation should not include nonessential explanations of what the team did. The transparencies or handouts for a QI story should be self-contained, conveying their message without the absolute need for a presenter. Also, the relationship between data and conclusion should be clearly drawn. Don't show information not relevant to the theme, for example, details of trial and error. That is indicative of a product-out orientation. The customer (the audience for the QI story) doesn't need to spend precious time and attention on nonessential issues. If you must show such details, leave them for step 7.

Good explanations have benefits that go beyond the team involved. They promote good improvement practices throughout the organization. If people from other teams can't understand the problem, they won't understand how the steps and tools might apply to their own themes as well. As Professor Shiba says, "One success story gives more effect than 100 lectures."

Finally, explanation of context is important for acknowledgment. How can team members be acknowledged if the presentation doesn't say who they are?

"Middle Ground" in Narrowness of Focus

Themes stated too broadly can cause a team to flounder, while themes stated too narrowly almost presuppose causes, and therefore solutions. An overly broad theme might be stated as "reduce manufacturing losses." Such a theme puts few bounds on the scope of the data collection and analysis. Should manufacturing losses include those whose root cause lies in product design? Should the team be addressing losses over all plants? All production lines? All processes? A narrower theme statement like "reduce scrap and rework on the B line" constrains a problem to the point where the analysis and solution are within the ability of a well-trained team.

Very narrowly stated themes fundamentally take responsibility away from the team and give it back to their managers. "Reduce tubing scrap generation at point 3 on line B" presupposes (correctly or not) that someone has done data collection and causal analysis to determine that point 3 tubing scrap is one of the "vital few" rather than the "trivial many." But if the team doesn't get to make that determination, they won't learn to do it. Such themes are throwbacks to the division of labor, that organizational structure in which one set of people does analysis and another set of people executes. A theme should take the middle ground of focus, neither so broad that the theme becomes diffuse or undoable, nor so narrow that it involves no creativity or skill development.

Schedule Included

A Gantt chart to show the planned schedule should be included. Leave space to compare the planned with the actual.

DIAGNOSING STEP 2: COLLECT AND ANALYZE DATA

Data Collection Process Described

Quality improvement uses the scientific approach, which requires that work be reproducible and reviewable, and particularly that the specifics of data collection be described: Where and when was data collected? How often was it sampled? What are the definitions of counting? and so on. Without such a description, "data" are not much different from opinion.

Data Collected and Stratified

You must collect and analyze data to understand the cause of the problem. For this there are three important techniques: stratification, graphing, and focus on deviation. For instance, graph the data in many ways — according to time sequence, type of product, location in the process, and so on. Then stratify the data according to the 4Ws (who, when, where, what). At each point along the way focus on deviation. For instance, suppose a given product costs too much to produce on average. You might graph the distribution of costs for making this product; see, for example, Figure 6-1. In this way, you see the distribution more easily.

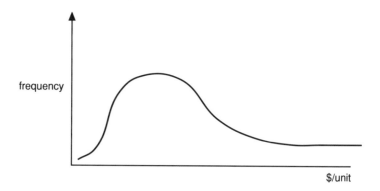

Figure 6-1. Graph

Next, stratify and graph the data in various ways (e.g., by plant that makes the product or by month in which the product is made) and continue to focus on the deviation (see Figure 6-2).

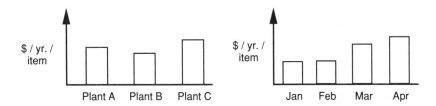

Figure 6-2. Graphs of Stratified Data

The graphs in these two figures show that average cost over the year didn't deviate significantly by plant but did deviate significantly at midyear, perhaps because of a midyear change in materials or process. Histograms, Pareto diagrams, scatter diagrams, and graphs are useful for highlighting deviation. A cause-and-effect diagram may be useful for considering possibilities. A Pareto diagram summarizing the relevant amount of problem by category is almost always a part of step 2 of the 7 QC steps.

Data Appropriate to Process

Was the data taken so that unusual factors don't cause misleading conclusions? Are an adequate number of samples taken? Are they taken far enough apart in time to represent independent samples (in the statistical sense)? Was there anything unusual going on while the data was being taken (e.g., recovery from a fire)?

Appropriateness of data is a significant issue for improvement activities. Be careful about using data collected for process control purposes (data 3), because it may not be appropriate for reactive improvement (data 2). Definitions can be skewed, and errors in collecting data continue for long periods of time if no one has actively tried to make use of it. Data taken before the improvement activity started is suspect — not necessarily wrong, just suspect.

Logic and Logical Consistency

There should always be a conclusion of the analysis. A flowchart of the logic leading to the conclusion is useful. In particular, make clear how conclusions follow from the facts. In cases where there were several rounds of data collection, for example, the QI story should visually show the logic by which the team progressed from one stage to the next — how it focused its investigation.

Standard Format of Tools

For the widespread diffusion of the 7 QC steps, use the tools in their standard forms. Here are some examples of standard forms to look for:

- Pareto diagram: no gaps between bars, a curve showing cumulative totals, scales on left and right, units labeled legibly, and conclusion written underneath
- Ishikawa (cause-and-effect) diagram: effect is a *why* question, in a box on right, cause to effect flows left to right, major cause categories in boxes above and below horizontal line, and ideally, five levels of *why*.

DIAGNOSIS STEP 3: ANALYZE CAUSES

Having focused on the cause of the problem (step 2), teams must analyze the detailed cause of the problem. For managers, it is more important to diagnose the process than the solution of the theme. Senior managers should not ask too much of a beginning team; the team will improve through repeated use of the 7 QC steps.

Cause-and-Effect (Ishikawa) Diagram Derived from Pareto

For analysis of causes to be a teachable, diffusible process there must be an explicit process by which you can consider possible causes of a given problem. That process revolves around construction of an cause-and-effect diagram (or possibly a relations diagram). Without such a diagram, there is no way to know how well or poorly the team considered the possible causes of a problem. The effect of the cause-and-effect diagram should be related to an important bar in the Pareto diagram of step 2 (see Figure 6-3).

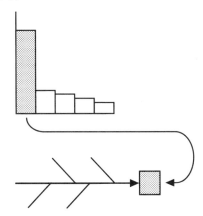

Figure 6-3. From Pareto to Cause-and-Effect Diagram

The head (right side) of the cause-and-effect diagram should be a result (effect), not a solution (cause). It usually takes the form of a *why* result, as in Figure 6-4.

Causes Investigated Thoroughly

The situation should be thoroughly investigated. Show the 4 Ms (man, machine, method, material), the 4 Ps (people, plant, policies, procedures), or other relevant categories (see Figure 6-4).

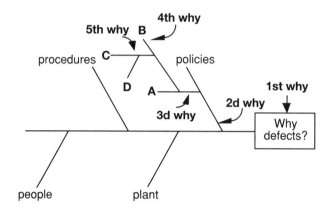

Figure 6-4. Cause-and-Effect Diagram

The cause-and-effect diagram reflects how thoroughly the team considered possible root causes for the problem. Superficial consideration usually yields a diagram with only one or two levels of branches. A thorough consideration, however, usually produces a diagram that traces back to potential root causes by answering "Why this result?" down five levels as shown in Table 6-2.

Table 6-2. "5 Whys" to Uncover Root Cause

Why?	Answer
Why defects?	Policies
Why policies?	A
Why A?	B
Why B?	C
Why C?	D

Managers can diagnose thoroughness just by seeing how many levels of branches the cause-and-effect diagram has. Having listed many possible causes on the diagram, you must find the root causes. This is done by eliminating improbable causes and by focusing on the causes that data show as most influential. Potential causes may be eliminated because they prove to be irrelevant, are disproven by prior knowledge, or are disproven through newly collected data. The remaining probable causes are hypotheses that should be tested against data to find the dominant root cause.

Understandable Conclusions

Make it clear how conclusions were reached and verified. This means that graphs should illustrate only one concept. Use separate graphs to illustrate separate concepts, each with its own conclusion at the bottom. The team may construct very complicated graphs while exploring the data. But the audience needs a simple, logically solid transition from the facts to a conclusion.

DIAGNOSING STEP 4: PLAN AND IMPLEMENT SOLUTION

Solution that Reverses the Root Cause

Steps 1, 2, and 3 are designed to make planning the solution straightforward. If the root cause has been found, the solution should be clear — reverse the root cause.

It is tempting to solve problems by redesigning the entire system. That approach is dangerous, however, for the team may not know why the rest of the process was designed the way it was. Redesigning the process therefore creates the risk of introducing new problems. It is safer to design very local solutions, sharply focused on eliminating the root cause, while leaving most of the system intact.

However, there may be several ways to reverse the root cause. The team should consider alternative methods and pick the solution that removes the root cause quickly for little cost.

Solutions Consistent with Causal Analysis

Surprisingly often, teams identify a major problem area and find the root cause, and then implement solutions that don't address the root cause, perhaps because of preconceived notions about the solutions.

In some cases, the team may think that the solution to the most important root cause is too difficult or beyond its authority to implement. In such cases, it makes sense to choose the root cause next in importance, gearing the solution toward that. Still, however, the most important root cause and its potential solution should be reported to the appropriate part of the organization.

Don't Try to Fix Everything at Once

Causal analysis may reveal many weaknesses of the present processes; fixing only the largest item on the Pareto chart is fine. Getting through the cycle

- brings quick improvement to the organization
- gets quick recognition and accomplishment for the team
- brings analysis and better planning to the next PDCA cycle.

This is continuous improvement, not only of performance but, more important, of improvement skills.

Solution Implementation Explained to the Audience

If other teams are to learn from the example of a quality improvement and apply the knowledge to their own situations, they must be able to understand how the problem was solved. Diagrams and graphics are helpful.

Implementation Facts Shown

As with data collection, a conclusion statement like "we implemented our solution" is little better than opinion unless accompanied by verifiable facts. The standard format for presentation of facts about implementation is a matrix as shown in Table 6-3.

Table 6-3. A Matrix of Implementation Facts

	Task	Who	When	Where	What	How
1						
2						
3						
4						
5						
6						

Use the following important checkpoints when implementing a solution:

- Were the people who will have to use the solution involved in planning the solution?
- Was there a pilot test of the solution?
- Was quick feedback obtained?
- Are there undesirable side effects that outweigh the advantages of the proposed solution?

Management Acceptance of Solution

If a team has proposed a solution and its managers have accepted it, implementation becomes a responsibility of the managers as well as the team. If an accepted solution hasn't been implemented, senior management must take up the matter later with the team's supervisors or managers.

DIAGNOSING STEP 5: EVALUATE EFFECTS

Resisting Temptation to Advance to Next Topic

The term *solution* connotes an ending point, which creates the temptation to turn to another topic. But a closer look at the facts suggests otherwise. Do you know the problem is solved? What have you done to ensure that it stays solved? Have you extracted the maximum amount of learning and improvement benefit from the work done thus far? The following steps should be taken after "solution."

Confirmation of Improvement

Having proposed and implemented a solution (step 4), you must next find out if the solution actually solved the problem. A graph showing the decrease in defects over time indicates improvement. Before-and-after Pareto diagrams confirm actual reversal of the root cause, as in Figure 6-5, where an improvement has clearly been made to problem A.

Evaluation of Consequent Effects

Do not evaluate only the direct effects of the solution. It is even more important to evaluate the consequent effects, such as more satisfied customers or increased staff morale. The pro-

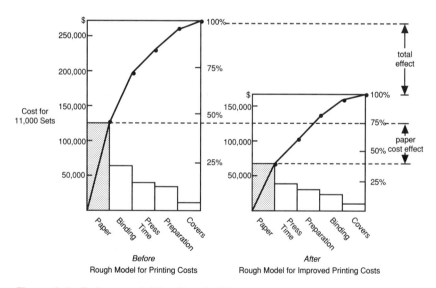

Figure 6-5. Before-and-After Pareto Diagrams

cess of selecting a quality improvement theme is based on the assumption that there would be consequent effects of solving the specific problem; the team will be frustrated if these effects are not noted.

Emphasis on Improvement Process, Not Results

Improvement work is more like an investment than an expense: it pays off over time rather than immediately, through the increase of problem-solving skills throughout the organization. Therefore, diagnosis should focus on following good practice more than achieving large results. Teams that jump to solutions without defining a problem or collecting or analyzing data do not improve their problem-solving skills because there is no repeatable process they can identify and reuse. Even if the solution is very good, without due process, it is difficult to learn from the example, leaving good solutions in the province of genius and inspiration rather than making them easily accessible to anyone.

DIAGNOSING STEP 6: STANDARDIZE SOLUTION

Facts of Standardization.

Standardization goes well beyond getting everyone to agree to do things in a certain way. To make clear to the audience that the solution has been standardized, the presentation must give the facts about what creates and maintains the new way of doing things. Specifically, it should answer the following questions:

- What manual or document describes the new procedure?
- Who trains people?
- How often do people meet to review?
- What happens to minutes of review meetings?
- Who is in charge of scheduling meetings?

- What is the standard reporting for the new procedures, and to whom do they go, and for what action?

Acid Test: If the People Go, Do the Procedures Stay?

An improvement must endure beyond the people who created it. One helpful heuristic for seeing whether something is standardized is to imagine what would happen if a key person got sick or got promoted. Would the new procedures still be followed? Are there sufficient materials or knowledge in place for a newcomer to learn? What if two or three people got sick or left — does the system survive?

Process to Detect Future Problems

Does the improved process include check and act steps so that corrective action can be initiated if the process slips out of alignment or doesn't work as well as expected?

DIAGNOSING STEP 7: REFLECT ON PROCESS (AND NEXT PROBLEM)

A Focus on Most Important Lessons Learned

The reflection step allows the team to do self-diagnosis, with exactly the same criteria senior managers use for diagnosis. The senior manager assesses the reflection step by checking the following:

- What were the difficulties during process, steps, and use of tools — does the team clearly understand the difficulties or not?
- Do team members clearly understand what they have learned and what the benefit was?
- Does the team understand what part of its process it is going to improve in the next improvement effort?

- Did the team leader keep the team motivated?
- Did the facilitator teach the 7 QC steps and the 7 QC tools?

Even if the team did a poor job on steps 1 through 6, it may learn enough through step 7 to do a better job next time.

CASE STUDY FOR DIAGNOSIS OF THE 7 STEPS

Read the following case study to practice the diagnostic process just described.[2] Construct a 7 steps diagnostic matrix as shown in Table 6-1, and read the case study, noting its strengths and weaknesses step-by-step. Then highlight the vital few strengths and weaknesses (remember the 70-30 rule). A filled-out matrix follows the case study (Table 6-4).

Improvement teams at Analog Devices have specific members, usually cross-functional and chosen according to the nature of the problem being solved. Members are requested, but not required, to participate and can be anyone with insight into the problem. Members remain on the team throughout the problem-solving cycle. Teams often choose a fanciful name (in this case, the Errorbusters, since they were to "bust" errors in wafer fab). (See Slide 6-1.) Teams sometimes have buttons, T-shirts, and other articles printed with their team's logo.

Step 1: Select Theme

Each improvement team at Analog has a written theme, with a specific, measurable goal, a metric, and a timeframe by which it intends to reach its goal. In this theme, the goal is to "reduce occurrences of incorrectly processed wafers in the photo area by a factor of 2," the metric is "misprocessed wafers per million processed," and the time frame is nine months. (See Slide 6-2.) Note that the team avoided the use of the word *errors*, which suggests that human error is the cause of the problem. Instead, it used "incorrectly processed wafers."

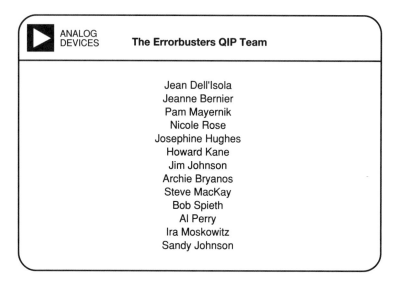

Slide 6-1.

Teams are often asked to try to verify why their theme is important, so that they understand it better and have a feeling for its importance to the company. This team showed with a

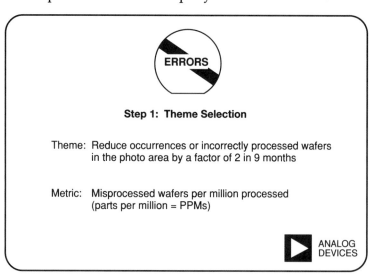

Slide 6-2.

Pareto diagram that of all the areas in the wafer fab, the photo room had the highest incidence of incorrectly processed wafers. (See Slide 6-3.) Since this affects yield and thus cost, the team demonstrated that the photo room was the right theme to work on.

Step 2: Collect and Analyze Data

When the team first began to collect data, it found that the existing forms used to report mistakes in wafer fab were not useful. Moreover, operators were reluctant to provide information out of fear that the data could be used against them. The forms were traditionally completed by their immediate supervisor. As can be seen on this actual form (recopied for clarity on Slide 6-4), the operator stated that the form is unfair and intimidating; the engineer's suggestion was to just "follow the spec."

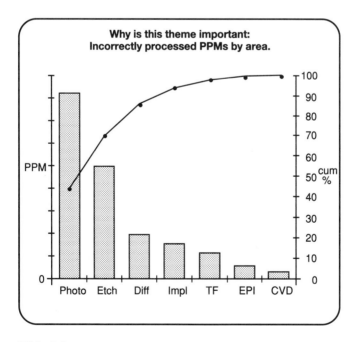

Slide 6-3.

Date: __12-12-88__

Product Type: __C841, C846,__   Lot Number(s): __5685, 5994__

__A848, A568__ (CB's)   __6031, 5683__

Process: Step: __M-NCONT__   Quantity Affected: __10, 10, 10, 10__

Supervisor: __J. R.__   Originator: __J. R.__

Operator(s) __9352__   Date

Shift: __3rd__   Misprocessed: __12-9-88__

Disposition: Waived: ___ Reworked: ✓ Rejected: ___ MRB: ___

Nature and Results of Misprocess:

These lots were passed through pre-etch inspection with no

pattern due to a developer problem.

Supervisor's Corrective Action to Avoid Future Misprocessing:

Operator will be contacted.

Operator Comments:

From now on I'll have the engineer check CB lots. I do not want to sign

this form because the lots could be reworked. If they were scrapped —

that's different. Should allow for human error which can be reworked —

I don't think it's fair. This is very intimidating.

Engineering Recommendation:

Follow the spec . . . please!

Sign Off

Area Supervisor: __J. R.__   Operator: ___

Area Engineer: __P. M.__   Production

Engineering   Manager: ___

Manager: ___

Slide 6-4.

The team decided to collect its own data and make the form more useful and friendly (Slide 6-5). In addition, it obtained a commitment from management that errors would not be held against operators unless the error rate was excessive.

Errorbusters SOS

Product Type: _537_   Lot Number(s): _9840_

Process Step: _Mask 1 pre-inspect_   Quantity Affected: _21_

Operator(s) _11643_   Originator: _JH_

Shift/Area: _2/photo_   Date of Error: _12-9-88_

Disposition: Waived ___ Reworked _✓_ Scrapped ___

What Happened:

Used wrong mask, ran lot #F537-1-9843 and then lot #537-1-9840.
The device numbers are close.

QIP Member/Operator Analysis:

Thought it was the same device type as the previous lot;
did not look close enough.

QIP Member/Operator Recommendation:

We should have a "mark" on the masks when the device types are almost the "same" ➞ "F537-1" "537-1"
This rework could have been avoided!!

Slide 6-5.

When filling out the new form, an operator on the team sat down with the other operators involved in the incident, discussed the incident, and jointly wrote comments. The form was then sent directly and in confidence to the production manager (that is, around the direct supervisor), so the operators would not have to fear recrimination for their comments.

With data from their new forms successfully coming in, the team was able to focus on leading types of problems. One cut of the data (Slide 6-6) shows the team found that wafers getting on the wrong track at the coat step and wafers receiving incorrect alignment at the align step were leading causes of incorrectly processed wafers in the room. The team moved on to step 3.

Step 3: Analyze Causes

Slide 6-7 shows one of the early Ishikawa, or cause-and-effect, diagrams the team created to determine the root cause of

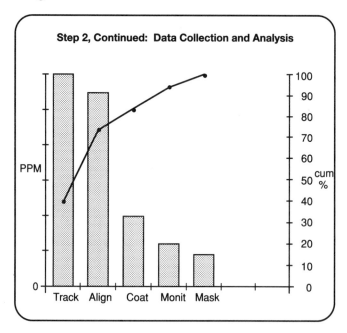

Slide 6-6.

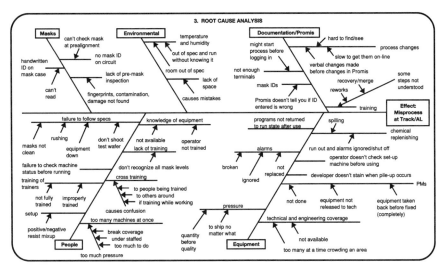

Slide 6-7.

incorrectly processed wafers at coat and align. Later diagrams focused on the "people," investigating why too many machines were run at once, and "environment," investigating why there was a lack of space.

After further discussion and data collection, the team agreed on the root causes shown in Slide 6-8, all dealing with either poor room setup and organization or poor task assignment. The team verified these conclusions by surveying all operators in the room.

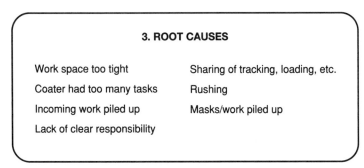

Slide 6-8.

Step 4: Plan and Implement Solution

The team moved on to step 4, solution planning and implementation, as shown in Slide 6-9. In their solution, the team borrowed concepts from just-in-time (JIT) methodologies, focusing on the use of kanbans to address the root causes found in step 3. The team also assigned responsibilities for each aspect of the implementation, and a timeframe for completion (not shown).

Step 5: Evaluate Effects

Slide 6-10 shows the team's evaluation of effects. The team was formed in March 1989, and implemented its solution during August 1989. There were two special cases of incorrectly processed wafers that were not related to the root causes at hand, as

---

4. PLANNING AND IMPLEMENTING SOLUTION
Kanbans

- "KANBAN" (signal)
  - squares with labels (bake, coat, develop) — OR —
  - racks numbered (inspect)
- Chain of steps (bake, coat, align, develop, inspect) analyzed for capacities, throughput, bottlenecks
- Quantities of kanbans chosen for each station
- "Incoming" racks moved out of room; coater controls incoming work via kanbans
- Coat, develop tracks:
  - "IN" kanbans: Full boxes waiting to start
  - "OUT" kanbans: Empty boxes waiting for wafers
- "Drybox" kanbans for align (coated lots)
- **Everything in room assigned a space**
  - taped areas for work being logged in to terminals
  - taped areas for tech tool boxes
  - taped areas for empty boxes waiting for wafers

Slide 6-9.

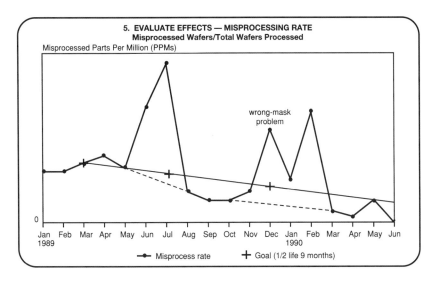

Slide 6-10.

shown by the peaks at July and December of 1989 and February 1990. However, the team continued to implement and improve its solution, driving down the rate of incorrectly processed wafers until the problem virtually disappeared by March 1990.

As shown in Slide 6-11, the room also reaped benefits from JIT methods in the form of queue time reduction.

Step 6: Standardize Solutions

The team recognized that the use of the JIT principles could decay over time unless the team performed step 6, standardization. As shown in Slide 6-12, the team instituted JIT meetings every shift to discuss problems or improvements for the system, with minutes of these meetings published daily. It also handed over the system to the supervisors and operators in the room to run, and agreed to meet only once per month as the Errorbusters to monitor progress and ensure that the gains were being held.

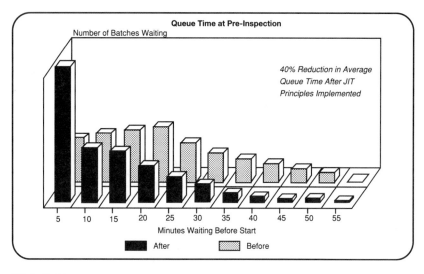

Slide 6-11.

Step 7: Reflect on Process (and Next Problem)

In step 7, reflection on the process and planning of future work, the team agreed that the main thing it did incorrectly was to focus on too many Pareto items during step 2, and thus on too many root causes in step 3 (Slide 6-13). Had it focused more closely when taking data, it would have solved the root causes one at a time and would have moved faster because its attention would not have been spread too thin. The team also decided to attack the next largest bar in the Pareto created during step 1, and thus work on incorrectly processed wafers in the etch room.

Sample Diagnosis of the Errorbusters QI Story

In the matrix in Table 6-4 is an example of notes that a manager might have taken while observing a 7 steps QI story presentation. The manager noted step-by-step the strong and weak aspects of the presentation. The "vital few" are highlighted. Such

6. STANDARDIZING THE PROCESS

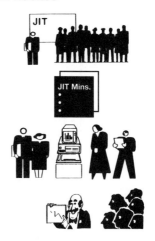

• JIT meetings held during each shift.

• JIT minutes published daily.

• Supervisors and operators given ownership for improvements.

• Errorbusters meet once/month to monitor misprocesses.

Slide 6-12.

notes will provide good preparation for a diagnostic statement at the end of the presentation, in which the manager can note strong points of the presentation and also key weaknesses.

7. REVIEW PROCESS AND PLAN FUTURE WORK

• **Review of Process:**

Team focused on too many Pareto items at the same time during Step 2. If team had focused on problems one at a time, the solution of each one would have been faster.

• **Future Work:**

Attack next largest bar on Pareto of occurrences of incorrectly processed lots (the etch room).

Slide 6-13.

Table 6-4. Errorbusters QI Story Diagnostic Matrix

Step	Strengths	Weaknesses
0.		• All the steps are not numbered with 7 steps number.
1. Select theme	• A weakness theme is used. • The process steps are shown. • The importance of working on a theme in the photo area is shown.	• It would have been better to use specific figures, e.g., decrease from 2,500 ppm to 1,250 ppm.
2. Collect and analyze data	• **The decision to collect their own data is the best point of this QI story [you want to collect your own data and the diagnosing manager should make a point of this].** • A Pareto diagram is used.	• The first slides of step 2 are not numbered. • The Pareto diagram on Slide 6-6 has spaces between its bars and the cumulative distribution curve is not to the same scale as the bars.
3. Causal analysis	• An Ishikawa diagram is used. • The head of the Ishikawa diagram is connected to the bars of the Pareto diagram in step 2. • There are 5 levels of "why" at many points in the Ishikawa diagram.	• Only one Ishikawa diagram is used for two characteristics (alignment and tracking); there should be a separate Ishikawa diagram for each. • The important root causes are not circled in the Ishikawa diagram. • **There was no focus on a single root cause.**
4. Plan and implement solution	• The team showed knowledge of the Kanban system.	• Too many solutions are attempted simultaneously. • It is not shown how the solutions are logically tied to the root causes.
5. Evaluate effects	• A run chart showing improvement is included.	• The run chart is not convincing. • "Before" and "after" Pareto diagrams are not shown. • A pilot test may not have been run.
6. Standardize solution	• The team has worked hard to standardize the improvement. • They have used nice graphics to show the various parts of the solution.	• The solutions are based on changes in human behavior and will be hard to maintain.
7. Reflect on process (and next problem)	• **The team understood that it was not focused enough.**	

Many groups ask why they must follow the 7 QC steps closely. The diagnostic matrix suggests an answer to this question. Assume that the team being diagnosed in this case, like most, was well intentioned and serious about its improvement efforts. Assume the team followed the 7 QC steps to the extent that members understood it. From this perspective consider the diagnostic comments in the matrix.

- Because the team did not know or follow the 7 QC steps completely, it did not get as good, tangible, and standardized improvement as it might have. Improvement skill is not automatic; it must be developed through practice and emulation of past successful methods. Even a well-intentioned, thoughtful team is unlikely to achieve excellent results with ad hoc methods.
- Even partial use of the 7 QC steps produced some useful results. However new a team is to the process, using it will provide insight into its value and also produce some good results.
- In diagnosing a 7 steps QI story, management must be careful to provide the necessary amount of encouragement for the team's level of expertise with the 7 steps and to minimize criticism.

RUN PDCA AND DEVELOP SKILL

Sometimes when you undertake an improvement effort you will get a poor or incomplete result. In such cases, you must simply try again. The concept of PDCA provides for such repetition.

PDCA teaches you to start again from step 1 of the 7 steps rather than going back to redo the last few steps of the previous PDCA cycle. You must build on what you did and learned during the previous iteration of the 7 steps. If during the previous iteration of the 7 steps the theme has not been completely addressed, the facts of the situation will lead to the same theme (from a new perspective) for the next iteration.

If the theme has been completely addressed, the facts will lead to the next most prominent and tractable theme to address.

In any case, iteration of the 7 steps or PDCA cycle will build a variety of skills: insight into the problem area, skill with the 7 steps improvement method, skill in working as a team, and skill at diagnosing the 7 steps process.

Table 6-5 adds a column to Table 5-3, showing the relationship of PDCA to the 7 QC steps and the 7 QC tools.

Table 6-5. Relationship of PDCA to the 7 QC Steps and 7 QC Tools

7 QC Steps	7 QC Tools	PDCA
1. Select theme. 2. Collect and analyze data. 3. Analyze cause.	Check sheet, graph, Pareto diagram, histogram, scatter diagram, cause-and-effect diagram	Plan
4. Plan and implement solution.		Do
5. Evaluate effects.	Check sheet, graph, Pareto diagram, histogram, scatter diagram, cause-and-effect diagram, control chart	Check
6. Standardize solution. 7. Reflect on process (and next problem).		Act

NOTES

1. See, for example, G.E.P. Box, J.S. Hunter and W.G. Hunter, *Statistics for Experimenters* (New York: John Wiley & Sons, 1978); and R. Gnanad Esikan, *Methods for Statistical Analysis of Multivariate Observations* (New York: John Wiley & Sons, 1977).
2. The case study was provided by Ira Moskowitz, Production Manager, Wilmington Wafer-fab, Analog Devices, Wilmington, Mass.

7

Proactive Improvement

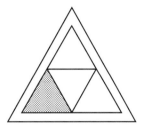

INTRODUCTION TO PROACTIVE IMPROVEMENT

Proactive improvement deals with situations in which companies, having headed in one direction, now face several directions that could be followed, but don't know which one to take. The proactive approach is used to find the upstream criteria upon which the rest of your improvement efforts are based.

The methodology of the proactive approach is not so well established as the 7 QC steps and 7 QC tools for the reactive approach or the standardization and statistical methods of process control. There is no one standard process (like the 7 QC steps) for proactive improvement; the most fully developed proactive process to date is quality function deployment (QFD).[1]

Senior managers are unlikely to use QFD themselves to design products; even so, they need to become familiar with QFD for product design so that they can understand and diagnose the processes used by their design team. Senior managers will use the proactive management and planning tools to do business and strategic planning very much as they are used in QFD for product development.

Market-in and the WV Model

Let us review the market-in model. When the work is done according to a standard or manual, the orientation is product-out.

The Product-Out Concept

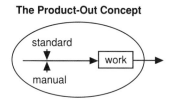

The real purpose of work, however, is to satisfy customers, either external or internal.

The Market-In Concept

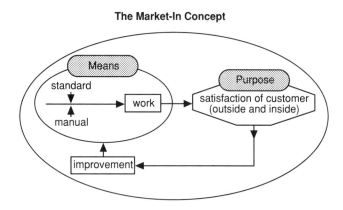

Keep the market-in model in mind when pursuing proactive improvement in order to direct your energies to satisfying the customers' explicit and latent requirements.

Whereas the market-in model keeps you focused on doing the right things, the WV model keeps you focused on doing things right. Its broad-based exploration of essentials and alternation between the levels of thought and experience defines key issues in ever-finer detail.

The WV model shows the problem solving moving between the level of thought and the level of experience (see Figure 7-1). You sense a problem, explore it broadly, formulate a problem to work on, state a specific improvement theme, collect data and analyze the situation, find the root causes, plan a solution and implement it, evaluate the effects of the solution, standardize the process to include the new solution if it is good, and then take on the next problem.

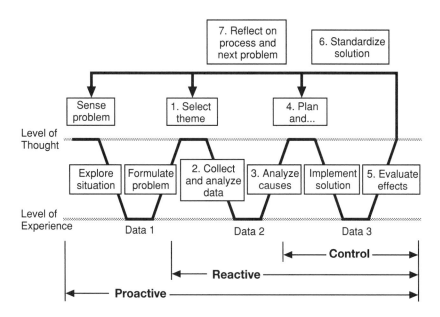

Figure 7-1. The WV Model

Sometimes a defect occurs during process control (*V* of WV model). You must eliminate it, following the manual for the process, to make the process work within specification again. Standard operating procedures are used to address the problem. This is described in Chapter 4.

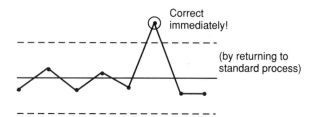

The key methods of process control are standardization, statistical process control, and inspection.

Moving left in the WV model, if you have a process but are not satisfying the customer, you must improve the standard and manual, using reactive improvement. In reactive improvement, there is a plan and an actual result, and the difference between them is weakness (see Figure 7-2). The 5 evils (defects, mistakes, delay, waste, and accident) are examples of weakness. The reactive approach is to eliminate the weakness through a structured problem-solving process, described in Chapters 5 and 6. The 7 QC steps and 7 QC Tools are key elements and methods of the reactive approach.

However, according to what criteria do you improve? How do you understand what customers perceive as weaknesses? An important purpose of proactive methods is to identify what the customer wants and what changes in society create those wants.

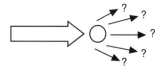

Collecting Data for Proactive Improvement

Although proactive improvement, like reactive improvement, is well described by the context of the market-in concept and the WV diagram, the details differ substantially from the reactive practices described in Chapter 5. Proactive methods are also newer and probably less familiar to most people than reactive methods. Therefore, we begin with a rather conceptual in-

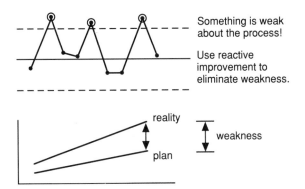

Figure 7-2. Discovering Process Weakness

troduction to orient the reader, both to the language and methods of proactive improvement and to the relation of proactive to reactive improvement. Case studies follow this introduction, at the end of this chapter and throughout the next.

Proactive problem solving begins at the left side of the WV model.

As explained in Chapter 4, the WV model refers to three kinds of data (see Figure 7-3):

- Data 1 is qualitative data used to design a product or to make other business direction choices. Data 1 is typically image or language data.
- Data 3 is quantitative data used to control processes. In order to control something, data 3 must be in the form of numbers and figures.
- Data 2 is used for reactive improvement activities. Data 2 falls between data 1 and data 3 — it uses both numbers and language. The aim is to move toward data consisting only of numbers, but sometimes this isn't possible — when, for example, an Ishikawa (cause-and-effect) diagram is used.

At the first data collection stage, look for qualitative intuition. As you move across the WV model, you increasingly seek

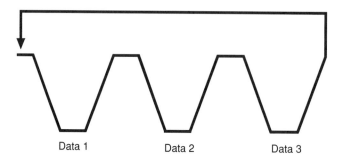

Data 1   Data 2   Data 3

Figure 7-3. The WV Model and the 3 Kinds of Data

quantitative data, focusing entirely on quantitative data by the last stage. Much theory and experience and many tools exist for collecting the numeric data 3. A different approach is needed for collecting qualitative data 1.[2] Jiro Kawakita, the inventor of the KJ method, has evolved five principles for collecting data 1.[3] These are summarized in the left column of Table 7-1 and described in the following text. The right column of the table contrasts these five principles with more structured approaches of traditional market research.

1. 360-degree View

Shoji Shiba recalls: "I have a friend who is a journalist. He says there are two kinds of journalists. One kind goes around and around the issue and looks at it from all different points of view. The other kind has a strong personal point of view and writes from that point of view." The latter is an approach for data 3, but not for data 1.

To create a new product you cannot believe your own ideas so strongly that you become blind to customers' needs. You cannot simply test a hypothesis. Starting with a predetermined hypothesis may prevent you from comprehending the customer's view. Like the first kind of journalist, you must look at the situation from all 360 degrees.

Table 7-1. Comparison of Kawakita's 5 Principles with Traditional Market Research Method

	Principles for collecting type 1 data	Traditional market research method
1	*360-degree view:* no hypothesis — walk all around reality — you want to find something new — forget your biased opinion	Focus: have hypothesis — look at reality through hypothesis testing
2	*Stepping-stones:* leave a flexible schedule — be able to step from one person/place to the next as the opportunity arises during the day	Rigid schedule: scheduled hours for customer focus groups
3	*By chance:* utilize chances (but you can create these chances; if you are sensitive about a problem, you can see the problem you couldn't see before; increase and amplify sensitivity) — concentrate on problem	Structured predetermined research plan that must be followed
4	*Intuitive capability:* logic may tell you certain data are unimportant, but if intuition says otherwise, then they are important — human intuition has great capability to find something new — for instance, something the customer is doing may be logically irrelevant, but may actually be the key to something new	Objective processes, e.g., statistical summaries
5	*Qualitative data:* numbers are not so important — cases, personal experience are important; e.g., different types of defects are more important than numbers of defects	Quantitative data

2. Stepping-Stone Approach

When crossing a river by means of stepping-stones, you step on one and then decide where to step next (see Figure 7-4).

A customer visit often demands the same approach. One person you see may say, "I don't know how to answer your question. Why not see Mr. A?" Therefore, you can't have a rigid schedule or agenda when gathering type 1 data.

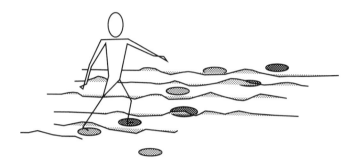

Figure 7-4. Stepping Stones

Keep a flexible schedule to pursue unanticipated opportunities — when you have no predetermined hypothesis there is no way to know in advance all of the people to see and things to be done.

Don't make a rigid schedule. Go from point to point, person to person to get data as people become more available. Be flexible enough to go anywhere at anytime to get data.

3. "By Chance"

When Professor Shiba was at a semiconductor company counseling staff on making customer visits, the question came up of which companies to visit. He puzzled over the question for several days. During this period he was invited to dinner by MIT professor Eric von Hippel, who spoke about his concept of lead user. Professor von Hippel studies user innovativeness, with categories ranging from active innovators to late adopters. This conversation enabled Professor Shiba to advise the semiconductor company on whom to visit. The opportunity was not totally by chance. By concentrating his attention and sensitivity, Professor Shiba recognized an opportunity to learn when it came along.

If you focus your interest, you will find the information you need. This is the *by chance* principle. Sensitivity to a problem, the result of concentrating on the issues surrounding it, enables you to notice and capitalize on obscure but valuable opportunities. Louis Pasteur said, "In the field of observation chance favors only those minds which are prepared."[4] There is also the old saw, "I believe in luck — the harder I work, the more of it I have."

4. Believe Your Intuition

Professor Shiba tells the following story:

> I had an opportunity to work in 10 countries (from 1 month to 6 months), working and living with workers. The data which I collected was logical, including such information as hourly output, etc. However, I had an intuition about style of eating. Different groups of people ate together, and although it wasn't originally planned, I collected this data. The data later proved very useful. In India hierarchy dictates completely who eats together. In Japan it was mixed.

Experience provides a wealth of knowledge, much of which is unconscious — when the intuition alarm rings, pay attention to it. As Poincaré said: "It is by logic we prove, but it is by intuition we discover." Even before logic proves something, one's intuition may understand part of it. Therefore, don't collect only the data that logic dictates are "needed" for the problem. Also collect information that intuition flags as important.

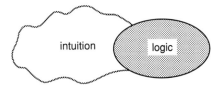

5. Collect Qualitative Data

Collect qualitative data, not quantitative data. Collect real cases and personal experiences. The customer may try to generalize, but you must ask for specific personal experience and history. Data 1 establishes the *dimensions* of a problem; later, data 2 will measure *along* such dimensions. For type 1 data, the diversity or spectrum of data is much more important than the amount of data about any one point. The number of "data points" isn't important yet.

Focus on the Vital Few

As shown in the rest of this chapter, proactive improvement begins with a broad exploration of the situation — for example, with conversations with a diverse set of customers, open-ended questions, and other means of examining the situation from 360 degrees. Then the tools of proactive improvement are used to structure and focus the data toward specific plans. Finally, there is a check to make sure that the vital issues have been handled. Throughout the stages of proactive improvement, work repeatedly to detect what is vital and to focus on it.

Focus on the vital few is a key principle of TQM. At no time is focus on the vital few more necessary than in proactive problem solving, where there may be nearly unlimited directions from which to choose. It is not sufficient to just focus on a few; *vital* and *few* are the key components of the phrase. Proactive improvement provides tools for both identifying the vital and selecting the few.

TOWARD STANDARD STEPS FOR PROACTIVE IMPROVEMENT

A single standard process for reactive improvement (the 7 QC steps) was described in Chapter 5. At this writing there is no consensus on a corresponding single model for proactive improvement. The standard version of the WV model shows the proactive process leading into reactive improvement (see Figure 7-5).

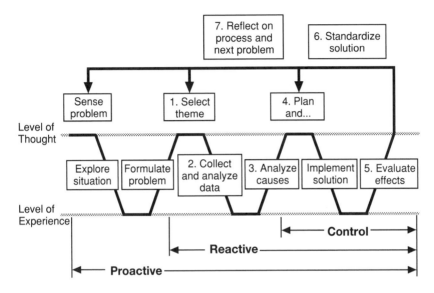

Figure 7-5. Proactive and Reactive Improvement

In this version of the WV model, proactive methods are used to explore the problem area thoroughly and to focus on a specific problem ("formulate problem") to which the 7 QC steps are applied. The WV model can be redrawn in expanded form as in Figure 7-6 to show clearly the roles of the proactive, reactive, and process control activities.

The sequence from proactive to reactive improvement described in Chapter 5 is shown in the expanded WV model, starting at A, with a proactive investigation of the problem. Once the problem is formulated, ending with E, the 7 QC steps are executed, starting at B. (Benchmarking often has such steps: proactively discover a weakness and reactively correct it.) When a new standard is available, C, the SDCA cycle can be executed starting at D. From then on the SDCA and 7 steps cycles are interleaved, as shown in the top two rows of the expanded WV model.

However, in a typical planning or product development situation the early stage of proactive improvement from A to E does not usually lead immediately to the 7 QC steps and reac-

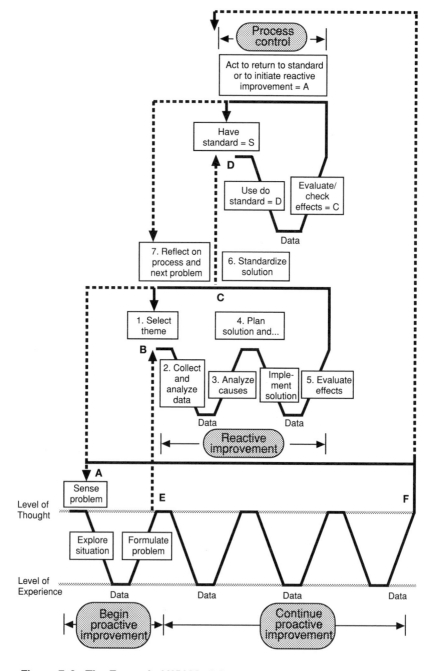

Figure 7-6. The Expanded WV Model

tive improvement. A product or system must be developed before it can be improved. In this case the flow goes from A to E and across the rest of the top line in the expanded model to F.

There are several proactive improvement processes that have standard steps. Chapter 8 explains the steps in operationally defining the voice of the customer in terms of the WV diagram. The frequent follow-on to voice of the customer, quality function deployment, likewise has roughly standardized steps. Practices oriented toward process design, like Motorola's 6 Steps to 60 or Xerox's Quality Improvement Process, are likewise standardized proactive methods. (Increasingly, both have reactive practices embedded within them as well.)

Although there are as yet no standard steps for proactive improvement in TQM, some very useful tools do exist. Some of those tools, which are used in the examples in this book, are described below.

Sketch of the KJ Method

The origin of the KJ method exists in Jiro Kawakita's early work with students doing fieldwork in the 1950s. Methods developed then for gathering and analyzing data evolved into the problem-solving approach now identified with his initials as the KJ method. A publication in 1964, *Partyship (Pati gaku)* described this early form of KJ and gained considerable recognition in the Japanese business community as well as the public sector. In 1967, Kawakita outlined this method in the publication, *Abduction (Hassoho)*, and developed a training system detailed in the 1970 publication, *Abduction: Part Two (Zoku Hassoho)*. Thousands of students from all sectors of Japanese society have since trained in this method.[5]

The scope of the KJ method includes four aspects: 1) a problem-solving model (the W model); 2) qualitative data formulation and analysis tools (the KJ method, etc.); 3) a new type of field research concept and method (MPM, Kawakita's Five Principles, etc.); and 4) teamwork concepts for creativity.

The steps of the KJ method are described below as adapted for use in the field of quality improvement.

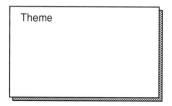

1. Agree on a topic. Begin with careful consideration and team agreement on the appropriate topic to be considered. For a 7-step reactive improvement activity, the "theme" is much more sharply focused and usually calls for numeric data, for example, "Reduce the percentage of line items delivered after promise date by 30 percent in four months." The "theme" to formulate a problem using the KJ method is fairly broad and calls for subjective language (rather than numerical) data, for example, "What do our customers dislike about our service?" In many other types of discussions or arguments, an entire meeting may be held without precise agreement on the topic being discussed.

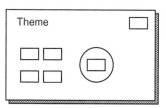

2. Write and understand the data. Next, each member of the team writes down several facts they know about the theme (you can use ideas also). Each fact is written on a separate label. Writing the facts makes them explicit so they can be examined by all team members. Then, one by one, each fact or idea on its label is clarified (in writing), using the rules of semantics (discussed shortly), until all members of the team understand what is meant by each item written by the team members.

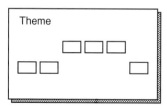

3. Group similar data. The team then works together to group facts that intuition says are similar to each other. Writing high-quality facts is difficult, although people new to this tool often don't recognize the difficulty. Grouping facts is also difficult, since people new to the tool find it easier to group by logical classification.

Such people ask, "Should grouping be done individually or collectively? What if people get in a loop, making and breaking the same groups?" The question is indicative of a two-valued mentality that needs to change to multi-valued thinking. The answer to the question is that each label has different distances from the others in the group of labels. Speaking is logical. Skilled users of the tool try to create an image in their heads. Intuition is image; they look at alternative grouping by physically moving the labels back and forth.

There is surprisingly little need for oral discussion, which in any case would be logical rather than intuitive. Shoji Shiba says, "Verbal statements such as 'I don't like this label to be part of this group' are counterproductive debate. Don't think with the brain — think with the hand. Listen to the facts — this is the voice of the customer. There is no methodology for hearing the facts. Skill must be gained through practice and experience." There is no right answer; there are just better ways. Consider how videos would show something — they would explain work by showing an image of a person sweeping a floor, a person standing at an assembly line, or a person sitting at a desk.

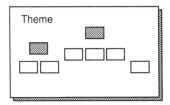

4. Title groups. The groups of similar facts are then given titles that express the same meaning or image of the group of facts, but at the next higher level of abstraction. Again the principles of semantics are used to refine titles. Grouping and titling continues until a hierarchy of no more than five groups exists.

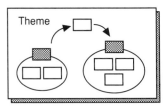

5. Lay out groups and show relationship among groups. The group hierarchies are then laid out on the page to show clearly the internal structure of the groups and the relationship among the groups.

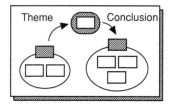

6. Vote on the most important low-level issues and draw conclusions. Once the team has reached a common understanding of the individual facts, their grouping and hierarchy, and the relationship among the groups, the team votes the most important low-level facts (one must think of action in specific, not abstract, terms). From the important low-level facts a conclusion is drawn. Finally, the team decides what next steps are appropriate, given the outcome of the KJ.

A Parallel with Numeric Data Analysis

Table 7-2 shows a parallel between analysis of numeric data (done with statistical tools) and analysis of language data (done with the KJ method).

With numeric data, first clean the data by eliminating data in incorrect formats, and so on. Then stratify the data into logical groups and perform average and standard deviation operations on the data in each group. Finally, use various analytical methods, such as regression and experimental design.

With language data, the same possibilities are available. First, convert the information written on labels into data by going through the "label-scrubbing" phase, in which you make sure each label is written so that everyone understands it. Next, find the underlying common message of the data by intuitively grouping labels. You must apply intuition to create something new in a grouping — recall Poincaré's words, "It is by logic we prove, but it is by intuition we discover." Then make titles for the groups one level of abstraction higher; this corresponds to calculating the average or standard deviation of numeric data. This is a process of summarizing original data. Laying out the diagram is analogous to analytic methods in statistics, such as regression, correlation, and so on.

Table 7-2. Parallel Between Numeric Data Analysis and Language Data Analysis

Steps	Numeric Data	Language Data
Convert information to data.	Collect original numbers. Eliminate errors in data.	Collect original facts. Make information have uniform quality.
Find the underlying common message.	Stratify data. Average and standard deviation.	Form groups of data. Make titles for groups.
Identify the structure.	Use analytic methods, e.g., regression, experimental design.	Make diagram.
Evaluate importance. Plan appropriate actions.		Vote on vital few problems, then use analytic methods, e.g., KJ, tree diagram, arrow diagram, etc.

The 7 Management and Planning Tools

Among the most popular proactive methods in TQM are the 7 management and planning tools developed by the JUSE Research Committee on the 7 Management and Planning Tools (chaired by Yoshinobu Nayatani).[6] The 7 management and planning tools provide the means for understanding complex situations and making appropriate plans. Six of these tools require an understanding of the concepts of semantics (discussed shortly) and type 1 data collection (see Figure 7-7).

Table 7-3 shows how the 7 tools for proactive improvement, or management and planning tools, often fit with PDCA, the 7 QC steps, and the 7 QC tools.

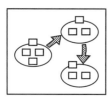

Affinity diagram (KJ method).[7] A tool that structures detailed data into more general conclusions. Used for providing initial structure in problem exploration. Often structures answers to "what?" questions, e.g., "what is going on in a complex situation?"

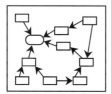

Relations diagram. A network of cause-and-effect relations. Often used to trace through answers to "why?" questions, e.g., "why is 'what's happening' happening?" A relations diagram is used when the situation is too complex for use of an Ishikawa diagram.

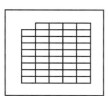

Matrix diagram. For relating multiple alternatives to multiple consequences of each. Often used to answer "which?" questions, e.g., "which things do we have to do to satisfy the customer's requirements?"

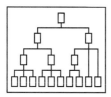

Tree diagram. A tool often used to relate means to ends, which in turn are means to more general ends. Often used to structure answers to "how?" questions, e.g., "how do we do the things that we have chosen to do?"

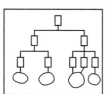

PDPC diagram (process decision program chart). A diagram of the flow of alternative possibilities and countermeasures for each. Often used to design responses to possible setbacks — answers to "what if?" questions?

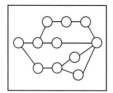

Arrow diagram. A simplified PERT chart, used for scheduling events and identifying bottlenecks ("critical paths"). Answers "when?" questions, e.g., "when do we have to do the things we have chosen to do?"

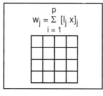

Matrix data analysis. Mathematical analysis of numerical data arranged as matrices, e.g., "where in the data do we find various patterns?" There are many methods, often called multivariate analysis, including cluster, multiple regressions, and principle component analysis.

Figure 7-7. The 7 Management and Planning Tools

Table 7-3. **The 7 Management and Planning Tools in Relation to PDCA, the 7 QC Steps, and the 7 QC Tools**

(A) PDCA	(B) 7 QC Steps	(C) 7 QC Tools	(D) 7 Management and Planning Tools
Plan	1. Select theme.		KJ method Relations diagram Matrix diagram
	2. Collect and analyze data. 3. Analyze causes.	Check sheet, graph, Pareto diagram, process flow diagram, histogram, scatter diagram, cause- and-effect diagram	
Do	4. Plan and imple- ment solution.		Tree diagram Matrix diagram Arrow diagram PDPC diagram
Check	5. Evaluate effects.	Check sheet, graph, Pareto diagram, histo- gram, scatter diagram, cause-and-effect diagram, control chart	
Act	6. Standardize solution. 7. Reflect on process (and next problem).		Arrow diagram PDPC diagram KJ method
(Provides repetitions)	(Provides steps)	(Provides tools)	(Provides tools)

As the table correctly suggests, there is a continuum between proactive and reactive methods. Even though it is probably inadvisable initially to teach the 7 management and planning tools as part of a "mass movement" reactive improvement curriculum, they are useful in the reactive context. Matrix diagrams for theme selection, solution selection, and action planning may be the fourth most useful tool, after Paretos, cause-and-effect diagrams, and graphs. One way to select a 7-steps theme is through unstructured customer interviews, KJ to create survey questions, and survey to identify what most concerns customers. Solutions that require coordination among several groups (e.g., redoing an administrative process) are natural applications for arrow and PDPC diagramming.

The preceding examples suggest that some reactive improvement activities (correcting currently existing, unambiguous defects) can in some steps have a distinctly proactive flavor (using richly available language data to pitch directions into as-yet-untried activities). Mechanically, this is revealed by the pattern of some of the 7 QC steps being well supported by the 7 QC tools (steps 2, 3, and 5), and the others (steps 1, 4, 6, and 7) having no QC tools but some management and planning tools.

MPM

Information often comes as language data from several sources: customer responses to surveys, transcribed notes from customer visitation or TQM visitation, or synthesized results from multiple KJ diagrams. Any of these can result in dozens or hundreds of statements. The multipickup method (MPM) is a methodology for winnowing these statements down to a manageable number.[8] Jiro Kawakita created it, along with the basic KJ method. Like the KJ method, MPM uses facts or ideas.

There are two principles by which to reduce the number of data: emphasizing strength, and eliminating weaknesses. MPM follows the former principle — focus on the importance or strength of the data in relation to the theme. The idea of MPM has some similarity to McGregor's Theory Y.

Table 7-4 outlines the MPM process. The first stage, preparation, includes a warm-up, discussion of the theme, and selection of leaders.

During the second stage, *unconstrained pickup*, team members mark the statements they consider likely candidates for final consideration. During each round of this stage, each team member marks all of the possibilities he or she thinks are important. At the end of each round, unmarked statements are removed from consideration. There are several rounds of unconstrained

Table 7-4. The MPM Process

Stage	Steps
Preparation	Warm up Discuss theme
Unconstrained pickup	Choose labels Count labels chosen
Focused pickup	Choose labels in turn

pickup, gradually reducing the number of choices. By repeatedly inspecting the list of statements at each round and marking them, team members reach consensus on the most important issues, without taking time for discussion.

The third stage, *focused pickup*, represents the final focusing. About 20 to 30 percent of the statements chosen in the previous stage will be weeded from the final selection. Each team member is given a limited number of choices to designate final candidates. By this time, every team member has considered all the remaining statements several times, so they are ready to focus on the most important.

MPM is not just voting. Each team member marks one statement in turn. If there are six members, each member makes a choice in turn so that there are six statements chosen. They may repeat this so that twelve statements will be selected.

After the MPM exercise, the labels are used for whatever purpose has been specified. For example, a KJ diagram may summarize the findings for presentation to a management group, or a tree diagram may structure the results if the labels were selected as, for example, customer requirements.

SEMANTICS

TQM for senior executives emphasizes direction setting and proactive methods, which in turn use language data. For instance, most of the data used in business, including that relating to proactive improvement, is image data ("I like the feeling of speed") or at best linguistic data ("I want a fast, inexpensive car"). Users and customers seldom specify in quantitative terms what companies need to do to satisfy their needs (you seldom hear, for example, "I want three liters of compression in the engine and 280 foot pounds of torque at the rear wheels").

Just as statistical methods root out the underlying facts from numerical data for reactive improvement and process control, so are semantics methods the basis for discovering the underlying facts from language data.[9] Semantics is the scientific study of the relation between language and reality. Semantics provides a set of tools that help clarify linguistic data. The concepts of semantics are used in many ways; they even clarify numeric data.

Semantics for Bridging the Dual Function of Language

The field of semantics distinguishes between two kinds of language: affective language and the language of reports. Affective language is that used to convey emotional information ("we've just begun to fight!"). The language of reports is that used to convey information that can be validated ("we shipped five computers before noon today"). Both functions of language are important.

In business, affective language is important for conveying enthusiasm and encouraging the staff ("leadership through quality"); for getting along with colleagues ("your idea is very good, but I have another suggestion"); for marketing ("Oh! What you do for me!"); and for achieving personal happiness ("I would enjoy spending more time with you"). However, to understand what is going on in a complex business or operational situation, you need logical, not emotional information. This is the language of reports.

Avoiding the "garbage in, garbage out" phenomenon requires realizing that much of the information available is initially in affective language ("I hate operating this machine"). Similarly, affective language is often used to express latent requirements ("I hate forgetting my car keys"). You must convert affective language into the language of reports if you are to understand the situation sufficiently to improve it ("The control lever is on the right and I am left-handed"). Table 7-5 compares several examples of affective and report language.

Table 7-5. Comparison of Affective and Report Language

Affective Language and Leading Question for Translation	Report Language
Accountants aren't concerned with the important aspects of our business. [What makes you feel that way?]	Accountants did not give us the accounting rules that the government requires us to follow.
Salespeople lie to customers to get orders. [What evidence do you have of this?]	Salesperson promised delivery without confirming whether the product could be delivered on time.
Engineers live in ivory towers. [What makes you feel that way?]	Product designer omitted features customers want four times.

The translations on the right side of Table 7-5 can still be improved (as will be seen shortly), but the first large step has been taken: translating emotionally charged affective language to the more objective language of reports. Making a legitimate translation requires the collaboration of the person making the statement. No mechanical translation will suffice; a mutual learning process takes place when one person translates the words of another. Especially when affective language is being removed, the refinement of language data is like a game of "find the hidden fact." A rich body of experiences is revealed, even in the restricted domain of a person's statement. The mutual learning process involves discovering how to express parts of that experience in a simple and purely informational way.

For example, to design a product to satisfy a customer, first get the person to verbally describe his or her image of the product. This verbal expression is likely to be in emotional or affective language ("I like fast red cars"). Next, this verbal language must be converted into measurable parameters that can be used in designing and building a tangible product. That is, the customer's verbal data must be converted into detailed specifications of components that the customer wants. These specifications are written in the language of reports.

Similarly, if a machine operator remarks that "this machine is awful to operate," or if an executive says, "I'm uncomfortable with the competitive analysis portion of this year's strategy document," you would use semantics concepts to convert this emotional language into the language of reports. Only then could you improve the machine design or operating process. Use semantics concepts to convert affective data into data that precisely represents reality, and describe reality in the language of reports.

Semantics concepts can also bridge from the language of reports to clear images in affective language. If the language of reports says that "we must decrease defects by 68 percent per year from 1988 to 1992 to catch up with our competitor," then you can say to the staff in affective language, "Six Sigma by 1993."[10] If the detailed design of a new car is expressed in the language of reports, it can be converted to affective language or to an image that can be used in marketing the new car (a sleek red car streaking, top down, across the plain under a clear sky with a beautiful couple sitting in the front seat, their hair blowing in the wind).

Keys to Clear Expression

Opinion versus Fact

Reports differ from one another in to how verifiable they are. Some statements are couched in terms of who, what, when, where, and how.[11] Such statements can be (or could have been) in principle corroborated by an observer; they are verifiable reports. Some statements represent assertions of facts not directly observed, but deduced from closely related observed facts; these are *inferences*. Finally, some statements represent opinion, approval, or disapproval, loosely, if at all, based on observed fact; these are *judgments*.

Refinement of language data replaces judgments with inferences and inferences with reports. It means eliminating judgment (approval/disapproval) and moving toward fact ("he is not a good operator" might actually mean "he did not operate his machine according to the manual"). Judgments often use evaluative words such as *poor, only, good, bad,* or *acceptable,* which imply comparison with the speaker's implicit standards. More subtle judgments are conveyed in comparative words, such as *too little* and *too much.*

The only acid test for inference is to ask whether what was said was literally observed. If it wasn't observed, it may have been an inference. Statements about states of mind ("he was melancholy") or potential ("he wasn't able to understand the design") are often inferences. Any statement about the future can't be a verifiable observation, so is most likely an inference ("the car won't start when we try again tomorrow"). Statements about hypothetical conditions ("if I had said so, he would have blown his stack") are often inferences.

In the appropriate context, judgments and inferences are both useful, but initially facts are more important. Inference must be converted to fact. "He doesn't know how to operate his machine correctly" might actually mean, "He turned the valve left when the instructions said to turn it right."

Like minimization of affective language, minimization of judgment and inference requires the participation of the person who made the original statement. Notice that a single judgment or inference may translate into more than one reported fact. But it is important for us to focus on the vital few important or symbolic facts.

Ladder of Abstraction

Understanding is very much a process of moving from low-level facts to higher-level concepts; well-understood concepts can be explained in terms of lower and lower levels of abstraction. If you speak at high levels of abstraction without having reasoned your way to them from lower levels, then what you say is unlikely to be founded in fact, or understood by others.

A semantics concept called the "ladder of abstraction" can help you find the appropriate level of abstraction. The ladder of abstraction is critical to clear thought. Hayakawa and Hayakawa provide an example of the ladder of abstraction in referring to a cow (start from the bottom):[12]

Wealth =	very abstract, omitting almost all reference to Bessie's characteristics.
Asset =	still more of Bessie's characteristics are left out.
Farm assets =	what Bessie has in common with other salable farm items.
Livestock =	the characteristics Bessie has in common with chickens, goats, and other farm animals.
Cow =	the characteristics that stand for the things we recognize as cows.
Bessie =	the name we gave to that particular object of our senses.
Cow we perceive =	what our senses abstract when we see the process that is a cow.
Cow known to science =	atoms, electrons, and so on = the physical process that is the cow.

Work at the appropriate level of abstraction. It is not useful to speak at too low a level of abstraction, saying, for example, "I am sitting on a geometric arrangement of sticks, each of which is made of certain chemical compounds" when you mean "I am sitting in a chair." It is also not useful to speak at too high a level of abstraction; for example, saying "I am sitting on a household asset" is unclear and ambiguous.

Controlling the level of abstraction is among the most difficult skills to acquire for effective use of the 7 tools for management and planning. Without an explicit clarification process, statements like "we've empowered our employees" often create the illusion that the senior executives share a common understanding. But one executive may mean "90 percent of my people's suggestions are implemented," whereas another may mean "I've officially told my people that I want them to make suggestions, and that should be enough." In terms of implications for action, these two understandings are very different. Without facts at a low enough level of abstraction, one can understand very little about important topics, whether they are customer needs or what the competition is doing.

In the initial fact recording, start low on the ladder of abstraction; only in later steps, when low-level facts are understood, should you build up to more abstract statements. Thus the initial clarification, or "scrubbing," process usually pushes facts down the ladder of abstraction. An example appears in Figure 7-8. The KJs in Chapter 8 provide many additional examples of statements at different levels of abstraction.

5 Ws and 1 H. TQM practice includes the concept of the 5 *Ws and 1 H* — who, what, where, when, why, and how.[13] One uses four of these Ws (who, what, where, when) and the one H to dig for detail, plow through emotion and dissect inference and judgment to get to the underlying facts and guide statements down the ladder of abstraction.[14] The following examples are taken from Imai.[15]

> *Who:* who does it, who should do it, who else can do it?
> *What:* what to do, what is being done, what can be done?
> *Where:* where to do it, where is it done, where else should it be done?

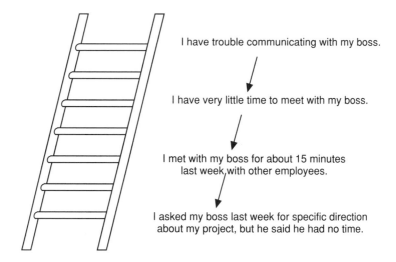

I have trouble communicating with my boss.

I have very little time to meet with my boss.

I met with my boss for about 15 minutes last week, with other employees.

I asked my boss last week for specific direction about my project, but he said he had no time.

Figure 7-8. The Ladder of Abstraction

When: when to do it, when is it done, when else should it be done?

How: how to do it, how is it done, how should it be done, how can this method be used elsewhere?

By asking *why* 5 times one can often get to the real facts of a problem.

Multi-Valued versus Two-Valued Thought

People have a strong tendency to use two-valued or 0-1 thinking ("It's a hot day," "Boston Harbor is polluted"). The two-valued scale is very gross, and it is unclear what the boundary between the two values means, as the following figure shows.

hot/cold scale

hot	cold

Two-valued thinking or speech, if used carelessly or deviously, can be a tool of rhetoric or demagoguery. It simplifies the situation to the point of nonreality, and people often use it for the purpose of dominating others or deluding themselves ("our product is the best on the market and doesn't need improvement").

Multi-valued thought and speech is the tool of those trying to understand a real situation and initiate effective corrective action ("our product has three features customers said they liked, two that they didn't like, and two to which they are indifferent"). Multi-valued thought uses a scale with fine gradations and precise locations of the values, as the following figure illustrates.

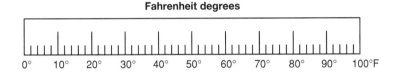

Fahrenheit degrees

0° 10° 20° 30° 40° 50° 60° 70° 80° 90° 100°F

Converting two-valued statements to multi-valued statements is especially useful because two-valued statements often contain the germ of observable facts. For example, consider Table 7-6.

Table 7-6. Converting Two-Valued Statements to Multi-Valued Statements

Two-Valued Statement	Refined, Multi-Valued Statement
The day is hot.	It was 78°F at noon.
Quality is not acceptable.	3% of the units were returned under warranty last year.
We don't follow our standard development process.	75% of projects reaching stage 3 didn't get stage 2 sign-off by the VP R&D, as our process requires.

AN EXAMPLE OF PROACTIVE IMPROVEMENT: CUSTOMER VISITATION

One of the most useful approaches to proactive improvement and hearing the voice of the customer was described by George Fisher, CEO of Motorola.[16] He gave us five principles of "customer visitation," a form of open-ended interview.

George Fisher's Five Principles of Customer Visitation

1. Start with the CEO. The customer visitation program must start with your CEO. It is an important, visible sign of respect to the customer. It is also a good signal for your employees.

2. Don't sell. Don't visit to sell, but to visit and listen to the customer.

3. Ask key questions. What does the customer like about doing business with your company? What does the customer not like about doing business with your company?

4. Meet the toughest customer. Motorola meets a certain demanding customer in Japan. If it can make this customer happy, it can satisfy any customer.

5. Meet customers you want to understand. If you want to see your product used, you need to see an end user. If you want to understand distribution channels, visit a dealer. If you want to understand the purchasing process, interview the participants in the decision to buy.

BBN Customer Visitation Program Case Study

In late September 1990, BBN decided to undertake a customer visitation program.[17] A number of the senior executives of BBN had heard George Fisher's presentation on Motorola's executive customer visitation activities. His ideas about customer visitation were compelling. BBN was beginning to think about planning its TQM implementation, and visiting customers seemed an important part of BBN's TQM program as well as an excellent way to gain insight into what the rest of the TQM program should be. BBN has historically been a technology push or product-out company to a considerable extent. The customer visitation program is one of several important steps being taken to shift the balance toward market-in.

Plan

The nine most senior managers of BBN, led by Chairman Steven Levy and guided by Shoji Shiba, spent about three-quarters of a day developing the customer visitation plan, using a variety of techniques and tools. At the planning session they started by using the KJ methods to understand the purpose of customer visits. The executives concluded they had three purposes for their customer visitation program:

- to get better understanding of customers and to build long-term relationships
- to demonstrate the importance of customers to the BBN staff
- to find out how BBN compared with its competitors

The next issue was to determine what the output of the customer visitation program would be. After considerable debate the executives concluded that the output would be a customer focus day on November 27, 1990, to which several customers and 175 BBN managers would be invited and at which the findings of the customer visitation program would be presented. In retrospect, the nine senior executives felt that selection of the specific day for presentation, slightly less than two months in the future, was one of the most important aspects of the customer visitation program execution: by declaring this date to 175 other managers, the senior managers made a public commitment to the customer visitation program and simultaneously constrained the scope of the program to what could be accomplished in two months.

Next in their planning, the senior executives made lists of the minimum output they desired from the program, the specific output, which customers to visit and why, and which executive would visit each customer. Categories of customer considered for visitation were

- lost customers
- customers with non-U.S. headquarters or focus
- U.S. government customers
- customers who are key to BBN's future
- companies who were targeted as future customers
- unhappy customers
- customers practicing TQM
- good current customers
- customers who buy multiple products or from multiple BBN divisions
- distributors.

According to Fisher's five principles of customer visitation, the goal in selecting nine customers to visit (one for each executive) was diversity — as much representation as was feasible from the categories shown in Table 7-7.

Table 7-7. Diversity of Customer Representation

Company	Key/ Target	Lost/ Unhappy/ Good	U.S. Government/ Commercial	International (Non-U.S.)	Multidivision	TQM	Distributor
A	key	good	commercial			yes	
B	key	good	government		yes	yes	
C	key		government			yes	
D	key	good	commercial	yes			
E	key	good	government		yes	no	
F	key	lost	government		yes	yes	
G	key		government				
H		lost	commercial	yes			
I		lost	commercial	yes			

A senior executive was assigned to visit each of the selected companies, and a list was made of which part of BBN had the background information on the customer to be visited, as shown in Table 7-8.

To prepare for the visits each senior executive, with the help of the people in BBN who normally dealt with the customer to be visited, collected all of the available background information on the customer (trip reports, open trouble reports, annual report, and so on — everything in the customer file). A set of five questions and subquestions was developed. The five main questions were intended to be open-ended and to encourage wide-ranging response. The subquestions were prepared as handy follow-up questions in case the answers to the main questions failed to convey as much information as was desired. The list of questions follows:

1. What would be the most effective way for BBN to improve its visibility to your company?
   - What is the single dominant characteristic of BBN's culture?
2. What will your needs be in three to five years, and what must we do to be a strategic supplier?

Table 7-8. Visit Assignments and Background Information

Company	Visit Assigned To	Systems and Technical Division	Communi-cations Division	Software Products Division	Advanced Computer
A	Levy		X		X
B	Walden		X	X	
C	Glabe		X	X	
D	Rampe			X	
E	Ide	X	X		X
F	Rankin		X		
G	LaVigna		X		
H	Barker	X	X	X	X
I	Goldwasser	X	X	X	X

- What is your company vision?
- What outside influence will affect your future?
- What is the biggest challenge facing you today?
- What is your expected market?
- Who is your primary competitor?

3. Who should we benchmark our products against and what benchmarks should we use?
   - Who will/did you buy from if not us, and why?
   - Why did you buy from us originally?
   - What is the key reason you may decide to buy from us?
   - Who do you think our competitors are for your business?
   - What is it you like about other companies' goods and services?
   - What do our competitors say about us?

4. How do our product weaknesses and other weaknesses affect you?
   - What are the weaknesses of our products, services, and administration?
   - How do you use our product?
   - Is our product/service quality the best in the world?

5. What problems can we help you solve?
   - What aren't we doing that you'd like to have us do?

In some cases, the people who knew the customer best constructed a KJ diagram of anticipated answers to the list of questions. This was done to further prepare the visiting senior executive, who in most cases was not deeply familiar with the customer's situation.[18]

The final planning steps consisted of the following three activities: development of an arrow diagram (like a PERT chart) to plan the schedule leading up to Customer Focus Day on November 27; two hours of instruction by Shoji Shiba for the senior executives on how to take notes and understand nonverbal communication (described in the text following this case study); and deciding who should go with each executive on the customer visitation to take notes and provide continuity with the customers.

Do

Seven of the nine senior executives were able to schedule and carry out their customer visits in the time allowed. In all cases the customers were very receptive to the visitors from BBN. The BBN people felt they gained insight into the customers' feelings about BBN that they would not have been likely to obtain in the normal course of communication with the customers.

In each of the visits, the senior BBN executive and note-takers visited the customer without a time deadline for leaving (in keeping with the stepping-stone principle for collecting type 1 data). The open-ended questions were asked and active listening was practiced. Everything that the customer said was written down as close to verbatim as possible.

Check

Back at BBN after the visit, the verbatim notes were transcribed onto KJ labels, with one thought per label. Typically this resulted in 50 to 200 labels. Then a group of people familiar with the customer (typically the relevant cross-functional customer support team) used MPM to pick out the most important voices from the large number of customer voices collected, and organize them into a KJ diagram. This process of picking out the most important customer voices and structuring them into KJ diagrams is shown at the left of Figure 7-9.

Two parallel courses of analysis were followed from here: dealing in the relevant division with specific issues brought up by customers, and finding the cross-customer, cross-company issues. Although it is not shown in the figure, dealing with customer-specific issues in a specific division typically entailed using MPM again on the KJ diagram for the customer. This step

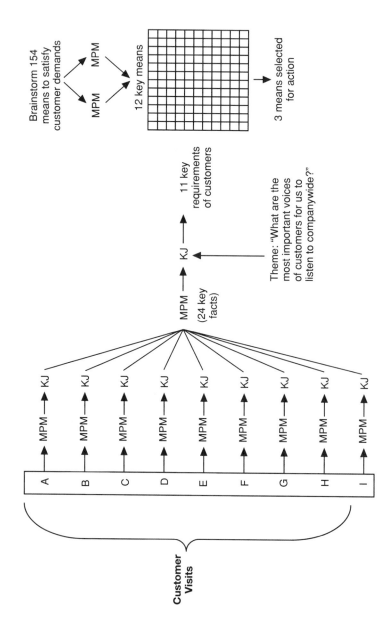

Figure 7-9. Using the MPM and KJ Method to Understand Key Customer Requirements and Key Means to Meet Them

enabled executives to find key problems, brainstorm to suggest possible solutions, and conduct feasibility and impact analysis to select the most powerful solutions.

The cross-customer, cross-company issues were analyzed in a two-day meeting of the nine senior executives. Each of the seven KJ diagrams from a customer visit was presented to all of the executives. As shown in the figure, the MPM technique was used then to select 24 key facts learned about the customers, and these were organized into another KJ diagram. The theme of this KJ diagram was, "What are the most important voices of customers for us to listen to companywide?" The KJ layout and evaluation process resulted in 11 key customer requirements. The general conclusion of the KJ diagram was that BBN had an incomplete understanding of its customers' requirements, and BBN's processes for meeting those requirements needed substantial improvement.

Through a brainstorming process, executives proposed 154 possible means of satisfying the 11 key requirements, and reduced this list of 154 to 12 key means, using MPM twice — once for high-impact means and once for high-feasibility means. They then constructed a quality table that correlated the 11 key requirements with the 12 key means.

Act

From the quality table correlation, it was possible to pick three near-term activities that would have significant effect on customer satisfaction, as follows:

- Institutionalize customer visitation activities.
- Implement a common product development process including core teams, phase review process, and product review board.
- Create a monthly scorecard of defects delivered to customers.

The customer visitation program, the analysis, and the above decisions were reported to 175 BBN managers at Customer Focus Day on November 27, 1990. After Customer Focus Day, senior management decided to appoint a cross-company team to plan how to implement each of the above decisions. These teams reported their implementation plans at BBN's second customer focus day, on May 1, 1991.

Seven Key Points of Customer Visitation

Seven key points of customer visitation emerged from BBN's customer visitation program.

1. Clarify the Purpose

The KJ diagram constructed during the planning phase clarified the purpose of customer visitation and why BBN needed it. Three dimensions of the purpose are shown in Figure 7-10.

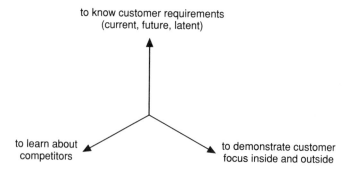

Figure 7-10. The Purpose of Customer Visitation

2. Set a Concrete Target

Always create a deadline and plan from the future to the present, instead of toward the future. This limits the scope of work and number of customers to visit, and works as a mobilization strategy.

3. Train for Visits

Training the people who will visit the customers is necessary. The BBN executives were taught how to ask questions and take notes. Visiting an internal customer first is a useful exercise. Don't bring a structured questionnaire; questionnaires are useful for testing hypotheses and controlling the quality of existing processes. For example, traditional marketing research has a scale for the answers — this is a structured methodology. Use open-ended questions, briefly listed for the interviewer's use, not for the customer to read.

Asking for facts, facts, and more facts is not good. People want to talk in generalities, not specifics. Customers often don't know the facts; they only have opinions. They may get angry if you press for facts like an inquisitor.

Anthropologists and field social scientists have well-developed methods of drawing out information. Their technique is to develop the skill of "triangulation." One finds the height of the mountain by triangulation, by looking at it from different viewpoints. Similarly, you have to ask in different ways and from different points of view to confirm facts. For instance, find ways of asking when, what, where (without sounding like an inquisitor).

Keep the 5 Ws and 1H (who, what, when, where, why, and how) in mind when asking these questions, but don't ask them directly. The goal is to get the data to move from the customer's affective language to the language of reports, at the appropriate level of the ladder of abstraction, and to convert two-valued thinking into multi-valued thinking. The triangulation principle elicits this data and ensures that it is interpreted correctly.

Professor Shiba does not recommend using tape recorders for customer visits. Sometimes these make customers uncomfortable. Also, mechanical problems may occur, transcribing tapes takes considerable time; and using a tape recorder does not increase one's note-taking skill for situations where taping is not possible.

The preferred alternative to tape recording is taking extensive notes. Two people should visit the customer. One should ask questions, focus on triangulation, and not take notes. The other should take notes full time, writing down everything that's said, exactly as said, without summarization. This may seem difficult. A helpful image in getting started is to think of what you see and hear going from your eye and ear directly to your hand, skipping your brain entirely. Trying to listen, interpret, summarize, and write all at once (eye to brain to hand) is more difficult and invites hasty interpretation.

When you take notes, write what the interviewee says, what you see, and what you think. Professor Shiba takes notes in Japanese. He writes the exact words of the customer, adding notes on what is intuitively interesting.

Training in semantics helps the questioner guide the inquiry. A customer's initial statements on a subject may be judgments ("it's good"), highly abstract, two-valued, or affective. Skill in gently clarifying meaning is needed to get factual data at a level of abstraction that can be acted on.

4. Respect the Customer

Demonstrating respect for the customer is not only an essential ingredient for information gathering, but is a fundamental purpose for visitation in its own right. Respect for the customer starts with deep study of the customer. Background information for a given customer is usually abundant. Annual reports, memos, trip reports — all flesh out background. In

Japan, it is proper form to get information on senior executives and CEOs — their management style, job history, current stature, future in the organization, and role in decision making. Study of the customer's organization and decision makers allows perceptive questioning and greater understanding of the answers. But in addition, knowing the facts demonstrates a commitment to that customer.

Visitors also demonstrate respect by preparing the customer about what to expect: what will happen during the visit; how the results will be used; and what follow-up will be needed with the person being interviewed.

The next aspect of respect is nonverbal behavior during the visit. Training and practice of nonverbal behavior become especially important when you are visiting a different country. This is not a logical issue. There are many good books on nonverbal behavior.[19] In Japan and the United States, arriving with an extra person to take notes signals the visit's importance and shows respect for what the customer says. By contrast, sprawling back in your chair indicates lack of interest. The most important nonverbal behavior is constant note-taking. It indicates that the company is paying close attention to the voice of the customer.

A final necessary aspect of showing respect for the customer, and the most difficult, is accepting what the customer says. Often, customers will say things about a product that are simply wrong. The first job of the visitor is not to attempt to correct or counter such misperceptions, but to receive them, acknowledge them, and triangulate on how such perceptions were formed and what they mean. BBN has found that telling visitors to "bite their tongue" isn't enough — people need to practice respectful listening. Eventually, customer misconceptions need to be resolved, but this can be done later, after the customer knows that the visitor has heard clearly. Make it clear that the visit's purpose is to hear the customer, and don't ruin it by going on the offense at the last minute.

One corollary of accepting customer input is keeping such informational visits strictly separate from direct-selling activities.

Even employees who ordinarily sell to the customer on other visits need to refrain. Attempts to convince a customer of one's own point of view tend to stop the customer from giving his or her true views.

One way to show respect for customers is to do something unusual. One famous episode (although it did not occur on a customer visit) concerns the CEO of Asahi Brewery. Asahi is the second-place beer company in Japan (Kirin is the first). The CEO was attending a TQM meeting at a resort in the mountains. During a break in the meeting before dinner, some CEOs drank beer and cocktails and some walked around the garden. The Asahi CEO went around the nearby village unannounced to see small retail shops that sold his beer. At these shops, he said, "I am the CEO of Asahi Beer. Thank you for selling my products. Are there any problems? What are the reactions of your customers?" This behavior on the part of the Asahi CEO was unexpected and memorable. Such serious interest in hearing the voice of the customer becomes widely known very quickly.

5. Learn PDCA

There is no way to initiate a perfect customer visitation program. There is considerable variation in company cultures, customer cultures, and the skills of individual visitors. These issues will be only partly understood in advance. The only effective way to proceed is to use PDCA. Plan the first visit as well as is practical. Make the visit (perhaps with a very safe customer), and later check on the weaknesses of the visit by debriefing, perhaps even asking the customer. Act on the weaknesses by analyzing them for root causes. Then develop countermeasures that become part of the plan phase of the next visit's PDCA cycle. Do PDCA with each visit, and soon the visits will be effective and comfortable.

Senior executives can use explicit TQM methods to do PDCA on customer visitation, such as KJ ("What were the weaknesses of the first customer visit?"). If done in a visible way, this PDCA is a fast, early opportunity for senior executives to lead the company's TQM through visible personal practice.

Organizations also need a longer PDCA cycle. After completing the plan and do steps of a customer visitation program, check the results. Have the results been acted on, and do the customers say there has been improvement? Act on the results in two ways. First, analyze root causes of weaknesses to incorporate into next year's planning. Second, standardize on measurement of customer-validated issues for overall corporate quality control. If there is a full cycle where customers identify a weakness, the company improves it, and the customers say they are more satisfied, then the next step is to institutionalize measurement and response to this issue so that it never grows to be a problem again. This is creating the SDCA cycle from PDCA.

6. It Is Not Necessary to Meet Many Customers

Data 3 (numeric data control) is quite different from data 1 (language data for direction setting). With data 3, more data gives better results. MIT research shows that with data 1, after about 20 visits you reach a point of diminishing returns, where virtually all of the new concepts have been identified. The MIT research showed that about 10 visits got 70 percent of the available data (see Figure 7-11).[20]

7. Apply the Fishbowl Principle

Traditional market research starts from a hypothesis, which is tested through data gathering. Shoji Shiba says that this approach is like standing outside a fishbowl and from that vantage point measuring behavior inside the fishbowl (see Figure 7-12).[21]

Customer visitation, contextual inquiry, and other TQM practices are all methods of jumping into the fishbowl (the market), swimming around and seeing what is actually going on,

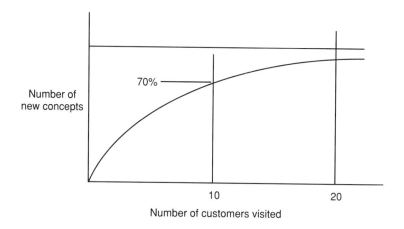

Figure 7-11. Diminishing Returns from Customer Visitation

and then jumping back out to reflect on what was seen and heard (see Figure 7-13). These TQM practices define systematic processes for exploration prior to creation of a hypothesis.

The best method for using the fishbowl approach is observation: it shows the product in context, it shows you the customer's voice in context, and it increases your sensitivity to the customer's requirements. If you visit the customer, ask to see the product in use where the customer really uses it. Often it is difficult to believe customers' answers, but you must recognize their validity; you must see and understand what is actually happening.

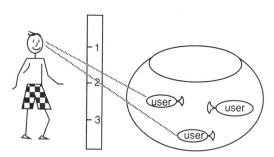

Figure 7-12. Looking from Outside the Fishbowl

Figure 7-13. Jumping into the Fishbowl

Take unobtrusive measures. Take notes on what you saw in a company. Collect the "jargon" (i.e., conventional wisdom, pat sayings) of the company (e.g., "Company A is hard to work with"). These are also the facts of the product. For example, in Japan, when a machine does not do its job well, a circle is drawn on the floor near the machine and the engineer must stay in the circle, watching the use of the machine for a half day. This is another application of the fishbowl principle.

NOTES

1. See, for example, Yoji Akao, *Quality Function Deployment* (Cambridge, MA: Productivity Press, 1990); John R. Hauser and Don Clausing, "The House of Quality,"

Harvard Business Review 66, no. 3 (May-June 1988); and Bob King, *Better Designs in Half the Time* (Methuen, MA: Goal/QPC, 1989).

2. U.S. researchers Barney G. Glazer and Anselm L. Strauss emphasized the need for methods of discovering new theories in addition to the orthodox methods for confirming theories in *The Discovery of Grounded Theory: Strategies for Qualitative Research* (New York: Aldine de Gruyter, 1967).

3. Jiro Kawakita, *A Scientific Exploration of Intellect ("Chi" no Tankengaku)* (Tokyo: Kodansha, 1977), 49-70.

4. Inaugural lecture as professor and dean of the faculty of science, University of Lille, Douai, France, December 7, 1854 in Houston Peterson, ed., *A Treasury of the World's Great Speeches* (New York: Simon & Schuster, 1954), 473.

5. See Jiro Kawakita, *The Original KJ Method* (Tokyo: Kawakita Research Institute, 1991); *The KJ Method: Chaos Speaks for Itself* (Tokyo: Chuo Koron-sha, 1991).

6. Shigeru Mizuno, ed., *Management for Quality Improvement: The Seven New QC Tools* (Cambridge, MA: Productivity Press, 1988); see also Research Committee on the 7 Management and Planning Tools, *Introduction to Seven Management and Planning Tools (Yasashi-shin QC7 Dougu)* (Tokyo: JUSE, 1984); and Michael Brassard, *The Memory Jogger Plus+: Featuring the Seven Management and Planning Tools* (Methuen, MA: GOAL/QPC, 1989).

7. The KJ method was developed by Kawakita before JUSE introduced the 7 management and planning tools. When JUSE introduced the 7 management and planning tools, they included a part of the KJ method in a modified form as one of the management tools and called it the affinity diagram.

8. Kawakita, *A Scientific Exploration of Intellect*, 153-162.

9. See S.I. Hayakawa and Alan R. Hayakawa, *Language in Thought and Action*, fifth edition (New York: Harcourt Brace & Company, 1990).

10. "Six Sigma by 1992" was Motorola's slogan, standing for its intention to reduce defects in all business functions to less than three parts in a million by 1992.

11. We exclude "why" from this list to highlight the frequent case in which causation, unlike other observable aspects of an event, is a matter of speculation or inference. Of course, apparent causation is sometimes directly observable, and can therefore itself be described in terms of who, what, when, where, and how.

12. Adapted from Hayakawa & Hayakawa, *Language in Thought and Action*, 85.

13. Even though they are introduced here, the five Ws and one H are not strictly part of semantics; they are used throughout TQM to get the facts and to explore possibilities.

14. *Why* is used primarily for cause-and-effect analysis, which may or may not move statements down the ladder of abstraction.

15. Masaaki Imai, *Kaizen* (New York: Random House, 1986), 235.

16. From a presentation by George Fisher to the CQM, Bedford, MA, July 10, 1990.

17. This case study was prepared by Steven Levy and Michael LaVigna, chairman and president, respectively, of Bolt Beranek and Newman Inc., Cambridge, Massachusetts.

18. This is in keeping with the principle (discussed in the next section) of becoming deeply familiar with the customer's situation before the visit both as a sign of respect and to better understand what the customer says; in doing this, one must be careful to keep an open mind (remember the 360-degree rule).

19. One is Desmond Morris's *Manwatching: A Field Guide to Human Behavior* (New York: Harry Abrams, 1977).

20. Abbie Griffin and John Hauser, *The Voice of the Customer*, MIT Marketing Center Working Paper no. 91-2 (Cambridge, January 1991). Jiro Kawakita also pointed out this fact in his books.
21. Shiba's fishbowl principle is described in the cover story of *MIT Management* (Fall 1991): 6-9.

8

Applying Proactive
Improvement to
Develop New Products

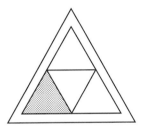

One of the most common uses of proactive improvement, and the one we will focus on in this chapter, is for product development. Proactive improvement clarifies vague customer requirements or unclear means for satisfying them. Customers often have only images of their needs and requirements. The proactive approach converts vague or invisible needs to physical specification for new products. The customer may also have clear requirements, but the path for converting them into a physical product may be unclear; you may not know how to solve the real problem. For example, a customer may want low price, but you don't have the technology to deliver it. Thus, as Figure 8-1 shows, proactive improvement clarifies a customer's unclear image or finds a clear path to a desired physical product.

Between the invisible needs of the customer and a new physical product there is a lot of work to be done.

There are common techniques for all the stages of product development, including product development, process development and production.[1] The earlier phases, which our col-

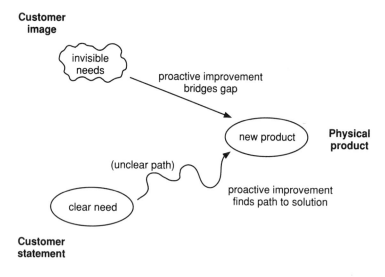

Figure 8-1. The Purpose of Proactive Improvement

leagues in the Center for Quality Management call "operationally defining the voice of the customer," "concept generation," and "concept selection," in many companies are the weakest parts of the product development process, particularly in making the vague customer requirements visible and explicit.[2] Therefore, this chapter will concentrate on "operationally defining the voice of the customer" — understanding in unambiguous terms what will satisfy and delight customers.

Defining customer requirements can be thought of as having three stages (as shown in Figure 8-2), which in turn can be divided into nine steps.[3] These steps demonstrate the principle of alternating between thought and experience, or checking theory with reality, in the extended WV model (discussed in Chapter 7). The steps with asterisks are at the level of thought.

> Stage 1: Develop an understanding of customers' needs and environment.
>
> > Step 1: Plan for exploration (decide how to broadly explore what customers may need).

*Step 2: Collect the voice and context of the customer (go hear what potential customers say they need and see what they are doing).

Step 3: Develop an image of the customers' environment (integrate and make explicit what you see customers doing).

Stage 2: Convert understanding into requirements.

Step 4: Transform the voice of the customer into customer requirements (on the basis of your understanding of what customers are doing, convert the possibly ambiguous statements of what customers need into unambiguous statements of customer requirements).

Step 5: Select the most significant customer requirements (from among all customers

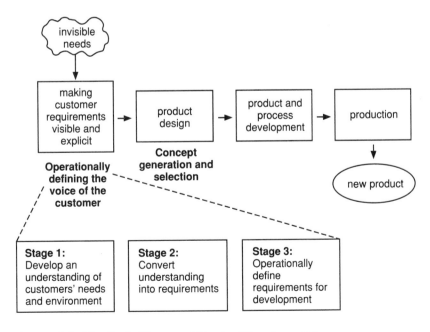

Figure 8-2. The Early Phases of Product Development

studied, select what seem to be the most important requirements).

*Step 6: Develop insight into the relations between requirements (organize the most important requirements so you can see possible relationships between them).

Stage 3: Operationally define requirements for downstream development.

*Step 7: Investigate characteristics of customer requirements (ask the customers to help you categorize and prioritize the most important requirements).

Step 8: Generate metrics for customer requirements (consider possible quantitative metrics and measurement plans that can be used to measure whether the product meets customer requirements).

Step 9: Integrate understanding about customer requirements (select the metrics that will best measure whether customer requirements are met, select the appropriate targets for these metrics on the basis of customer data and competitive product data, and document the learning for downstream use).

[STAGE 1] STEP 1: PLAN FOR EXPLORATION

Several issues must be considered as you plan how to explore broadly what customers may need.

Whom to visit. The first question is whom to visit. There are at least three dimensions to consider, as shown in Figure 8-3.

Do not neglect any segments of customers. Understand why customers move from being happy to being unhappy, and how to

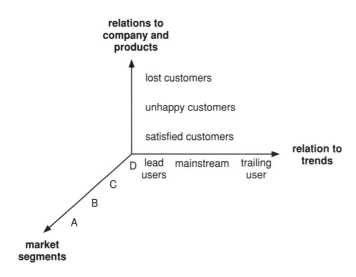

Figure 8-3. Dimensions for Considering Which Customers to Visit

position current offerings and predict future needs. The BBN customer visitation case study presented in Chapter 7 provided an example of listening to customers from a variety of market segments and in a variety of states of satisfaction. The stripping basket case study presented later in this chapter provides an example of predicting future needs by listening to lead users.

Eric von Hippel of MIT observes:

> Users selected to provide input data to consumer and industrial market analysis have an important limitation: Their insights into new product — process, and service — needs and potential solutions are constrained by their real-world experience. Users steeped in the present are, thus, unlikely to generate novel product concepts that conflict with the familiar.[4]

He suggests seeking out a special class of users, which he calls "lead users," from whom greater insight about future needs can be derived. He says that lead users have two characteristics: They (1) "face needs that will be general in the marketplace, but they face them months or years before the bulk of that marketplace encounters them," and they (2) are positioned to benefit significantly by obtaining a solution to those needs."[5] Von Hippel goes on to say that, unlike users who are "steeped in the present," lead users often have the ability to perceive or express future needs as a function of their experience. Von Hippel's research shows that in a surprising number of cases, innovative product ideas come from these lead users rather than the company that produces the product.

The idea of lead users is a powerful one. If you are trying to develop products today to meet the market's demands of tomorrow, it makes sense to interview the most innovative customers currently using your products or those of a competitor. These innovators represent a small percent of the entire market but constitute the leading-edge users. Their demands today are likely to be the mass market's demands tomorrow. Various researchers, including von Hippel, are working on how to identify lead users.

Who should collect the data. Von Hippel also provides insight into the important question of which staff member should visit the customer to collect data. The natural inclination is to have market research people make the visits and collect the data, and von Hippel's research confirms that they should participate because they are good at hearing what the customers have to say. However, his research findings also show that in a majority of cases lead users have already implemented something that will shed light on the requirements of the future market. Von Hippel therefore believes that people from the development organization must also participate in visits and help collect data, since they are better at seeing what customers have already done to address their needs.

How to visit. In Chapter 7, the seven principles for customer visits provided some basic guidance on listening to customers. In this section the theme is explored more broadly.

The voice of the customer is difficult to hear. Customers do not have the specific, quantitative data needed to design a product or make an improvement. Instead, they use vague images or affective language (see Chapter 7). In the case of future customers, even their identity is vague. Nevertheless, companies must hear the actual voices of customers if they are to develop products or make improvements that will satisfy the customers. Therefore, all available methods must be used to hear the voice of the customer.

Two of Kawakita's five principles (discussed in Chapter 7) are "by chance" and "use intuitive capability." To capture the benefit of these principles, you must spend time with the customer. For example, you must have a 360-degree perspective of the actual environment in which the product or service is used to discover something new. There are three ways to explore the market:

- through open-ended inquiry
- through process observation
- through participant observation

Figure 8-4 shows the degree of intervention with the user for each of the above methods and in what proximity to the user's actual environment the intervention takes place.

Open-ended inquiries are customer or user interviews in which open-ended questions are asked. They are not meetings in which a specific product hypothesis is being tested. Open-ended inquiries involve great interaction with the user and can take place near the user's environment or far from it.

Process observation involves watching users in their real environments and occasionally asking questions to clarify understanding.

Participant observation involves very little explicit intervention with the user. It can take place in a human performance laboratory, where the product is real but the environment is not, in an antenna shop (a store where "interviewers" wait on customers to watch them make purchase decisions), or by watching the behavior of users in their own environment.

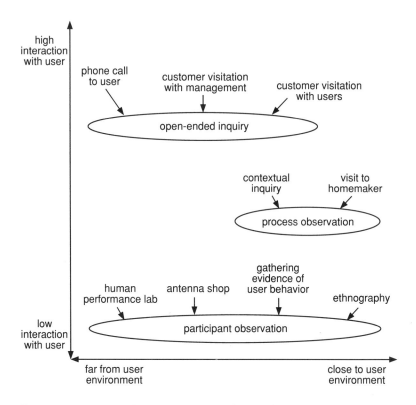

Figure 8-4. Degree of Intervention and Proximity to User Environment

[STAGE 1] STEP 2: COLLECT THE VOICE
AND CONTEXT OF THE CUSTOMER

The BBN customer visitation case study presented in Chapter 7 provided one illustration of open-ended inquiry. The stripping basket case study presented later in this chapter is another example.

Contextual Inquiry at Digital

The method of hearing the voice of the customer known as contextual inquiry is a form of process observation. Following is a case study of contextual inquiry at Digital Equipment Corporation.[6]

The voice of the customer is usually qualitative. To collect this type of data, one can use a questionnaire or do an interview. However, a particularly effective way to collect qualitative data is through process observation. Anthropologists have developed this technique to a high level. Digital uses a technique called contextual inquiry to do process observations. It is a method of "swimming in the fishbowl."

Digital's voice-of-the-customer initiative includes several programs:

- Contextual inquiry
- QFD
- Customer surveys (limited)
- Customer events (like DEC World)
- TOP mapping (Technology and Organizational Performance mapping, a process for "navigating the organization")
- User requirements analysis

Following is a description of contextual inquiry as an input to QFD.

The voice of the customer needs to include what customers don't say or can't say. Out-of-context inquiry methods such as surveys, focus groups, and human performance laboratories can miss such hidden sentiments or can change the meaning of the original voice. For instance:

1. Surveys ask about the customer's work and results, but
   - the customer tends to editorialize
   - the customer probably can't remember much — you get a three-line report for six months of experience
2. Focus groups give companies a chance to spend time with customers and discuss work and results; but
   - the information they provide differs from that given by surveys

- you still only get what they remember, and you don't see them in their real work environment
3. Laboratory work (for example, watching users through a one-way window as they attempt to use a product) might seem a logical method of observing and discussing the user's work and end results, but
  - the work done in such performance laboratories is often not real user work, and
  - the work is not done in the users' real work environment

Figure 8-5 indicates some of the environmental and real work issues, such as interruptions and purpose, that typically are missing in the laboratory situation. When such environmental and real work issues are not present, companies are unlikely to understand the needs of the customer completely, especially the implicit or latent needs.

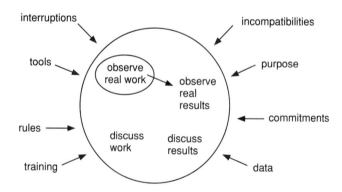

Figure 8-5. Issues Missing in Laboratory

Contextual inquiry provides what is missing in the figure. It is inquiry in the context of the user's real work environment. In contextual inquiry, engineers sit with the customers as they work. This permits observation and discussion of both work and results. Contextual inquiry also provides these advantages:

- It provides an opportunity to intervene when the customer is having a problem. For instance, an engineer watching a user run a program on a terminal might ask, "Why did you use the complicated command instead of a simpler one?" or "Why did you save the file before you gave that command?"
- It places the observer in the context of the customers' actual work, thus revealing unavoidable distractions that can significantly affect how customers use a product and what they need the product to do. Say, for instance, that the user receives a phone call alerting him to family problems at home, the person from the next office asks what he is doing, and the boss stops by to tell him that his report must be done by 4 PM.
- It permits the engineer to imagine and invent possible answers to the user's implicit requirements.

Contextual inquiry means living in the customers' environment and walking in customers' shoes to understand the customers' real situation. It requires time and travel to customer sites, so it should perhaps be done for only a few customers. From a few visits a great deal of information can be gathered and qualified as follows:

- With each customer visited, the engineer records a large set of observations.
- From the recorded observations of several customers, you can begin to deduce potential customer needs.
- Then, using traditional market research, you can size the potential market related to these potential needs.
- The confirmed customer needs become the input to QFD and product design.

Consider an example of the use of contextual inquiry. Suppose a systems manager responsible for a large computer center has multiple computers and many disk drives. The systems manager's task to manage and support such a system is very complex, difficult, and critical (for instance, a large money-center bank has several billion dollars in transactions every hour; downtime thus costs the center hundreds of thousands of dollars per minute). The systems manager needs software tools (software products) to manage such a system.

To design tools or products with the features and functionality that users really need, the designers need to understand the users' real requirements in their real environment. Surveys and focus groups cannot convey the full complexity of the users' environment and needs to the product designers, and performance laboratories are impractical.

To learn to do contextual inquiry, the Digital design group attended a workshop, where they learned about the concepts and methods of contextual inquiry. The engineers then tried the method, first in familiar territory, with a customer inside Digital. Next, a group of engineers went to a few selected customers to hold a series of interviews. At the customers' sites they explained the purpose and context of their visits and then observed specific users in their own offices. They suggested that the users continue normal work (not proprietary work), and they observed all activities, taking notes. They also noted which artifacts define the work environment; for example, they observed sticky notes on the wall beside a user's terminal. When it was necessary for their understanding of what was going on, they intervened in real time to ask the user clarifying questions, such as, "Why did you just do that?"

With prior permission, the engineers also recorded their conversation with the user. An example of one such recorded conversation follows:

> "What'cha doing now?" "I'm running the payroll program." [The sequence of commands the inquirer sees the user execute would not be seen in a focus group.] [The user then walks to a separate console.] "Why did you walk over there?" "I'm starting another program which checks the configuration." [The inquirer keeps track of the physical environment, logs interruptions of the user, and keeps an eye open for things that would facilitate the user's process.]

After such a session, the design engineers transcribe the tape recordings themselves, using the literal words of the user, and add annotations that only they, as observers, could make. Then, with the help of a facilitator, they transfer what they have learned during contextual inquiry to labels, which they post on the wall. These labels from contextual inquiry provide the input to QFD, which is a rational process for translating the voice of the customer into a product definition.

At this stage, as they begin translating the voice of the customer, the design engineers have gained profound understanding of implicit as well as explicit user needs, and they are better prepared to develop products that delight customers and provide the company with a competitive edge.

Stripping Basket Case Study — Customer Interviews

The stripping basket study, an example of open-ended inquiry, was provided by Lieutenant Commander Gary Burchill, Supply Corps, U.S. Navy, from a project he worked on at MIT.

A stripping basket is a device used by saltwater fly fishermen to collect their line before they cast it out. Typically it is a store-bought or home-constructed plastic container with four sides and a bottom, which is strapped to the chest or waist of the fisherman. While retrieving a cast, the fisherman lays the fishing line into the container so the line will pay out easily for the next cast. This process of placing the line in the container is called stripping.

The goal of Gary Burchill and his colleagues at MIT was to design a better stripping basket. They went to a major sporting goods retail chain and sought the names of lead users in the fly fishing fraternity whom they could interview.

Ofuji, Ono, and Akao suggest four open-ended questions and usage of images as a highly effective way to glean important information from open-ended inquiry of such lead users.[7]

Four Open-Ended Questions

1. "What images come to mind when you visualize this product or service?" This line of questioning both warms up the participants for the remainder of the interview and provides the interviewer with the necessary inputs for the "image KJ." From this question customer requirements can be developed in relation to actual use of the product.
2. "From your experience, what complaints, problems, or weaknesses would you like to mention about the product or service?" This line of questioning identifies factors that shape current expectations with respect to the product or service.
3. "What features do you think of when selecting the product or service?" This line of questioning determines factors that shape current perceptions.
4. What new features might address your future needs? This line of questioning identifies factors that can lead to increased customer satisfaction.[8]

Following is a sample script used to ask these four questions. Note that while the script appears to ask its questions in a straightforward manner, Burchill and his colleagues explicitly reviewed the principle of triangulation (see point 3 of the 7 key points of customer visitation described in Chapter 7). Thus, they attempted to approach the questions gently and from different directions in order not to appear too aggressive and to convert the affective language of the interviewees accurately into the language of reports.

Interview Script

Hello, my name is _____, and I am part of a design team at MIT working with the Orvis store in Boston on the redesign for stripping baskets. Pip Winslow gave me your name and number as a contact; has he been in touch with you about this yet? We would like fifteen minutes of your time to ensure that our design criteria are the right ones. Is this a good time for us to talk? (If not, emphasize that we'd like to have a prototype by May.)

Terrific! The discussion will consist of four sections:

1st: What scenes or images come to mind while you use a stripping basket?

2d: From your experience, what complaints, problems, or weaknesses would you like to mention about stripping baskets?

3d: What features do you think of when selecting a stripping basket?

4th: What new features might address your future needs?

All right, let's begin. The first area concerns the scenes or images that come to mind while you use a stripping basket. For example: Pip mentioned moving down the beach to where the birds were working. What images come to your mind?

That was terrific.

The second area involves the complaints, problems, or weaknesses with current stripping baskets (for example: water problems once the water level gets above the bottom of the basket).

Great.

The third area concerns the features you think of when selecting a stripping basket (for example: durability in a salt water environment). What features would you look for?

This has been wonderful.

The final area addresses the features that might address your future needs (for example: collapsibility for packing). What would you like to see in the future?

_____, the information has been extremely valuable and will definitely contribute to a better set of design criteria.

Are there any additional comments or observations you'd like to share with us?

Finally, we'd appreciate the opportunity to follow up in a few days with a very quick and easy questionnaire. The purpose of the questionnaire is to separate the most important design criteria from the useful many that we will receive from our interviews. If possible, we would like to telefax the survey to you.

Burchill and his colleagues interviewed 12 lead users; they were expert fishermen of the caliber seen on television sports shows. Altogether, Burchill and his colleagues collected about 200 individual statements ("customer voices") from these 12 lead users.

Following are a few examples of the customer voices of the customers that were collected during this interviewing process:

- adjustable belt is important; sometimes I wear a sweater and raincoat and sometimes a T-shirt
- quick-release basket so it doesn't get in the way when moving around the boat after a fish
- bungee cord is tight so the basket stays horizontal, thereby keeping the line from bunching and tangling
- fisherman don't like bright colors; any green or brown is OK
- it needs to wear like a good hat
- belt must keep basket in front of you
- 4-inch to 6-inch depth so loops don't fall out
- how the water spills out of it, drainage
- all lightweight plastic, no possibility of rust
- don't even feel it on your hip

- canvas doesn't last
- ease of carrying when not in use

Burchill and his colleagues followed the process described in the next subsection to interpret these voices of the customer.

[STAGE 1] STEP 3: DEVELOP AN IMAGE OF THE CUSTOMER'S ENVIRONMENT

If the voice of the customer is difficult to hear, it is equally difficult to interpret. Yet, interpretation is essential to discovery of the specific design criteria for developing new products that customers will buy and to improvements that increase customer satisfaction. Thus it is important to have a clear image of what the customer is doing and how the product will be used.

Stripping Basket Case Study — Customer Image KJ

The key reason for developing the customer image KJ is to tie the voice of the customer to the context of the product or service in actual use. The labels for the image KJ are obtained from the answers to the first of the four questions and from actual observations of the customer's environment. If explicit effort is not made to maintain an image of actual operation, company preconceptions of product use may speak louder than the voice of the customer.

Constructing a customer image KJ allows all the participants to have a common understanding or mental model of the product's use and environment as they collect the voice of the customer and discover the customer's specific needs. Interpretation of specific needs must be tied to the context of use if those interpretations are to provide any leverage for improving customer satisfaction. The customer image KJ for the stripping basket case study is included in Figure 8-6.[9]

What scenes or images come to mind when you visualize saltwater fishing?

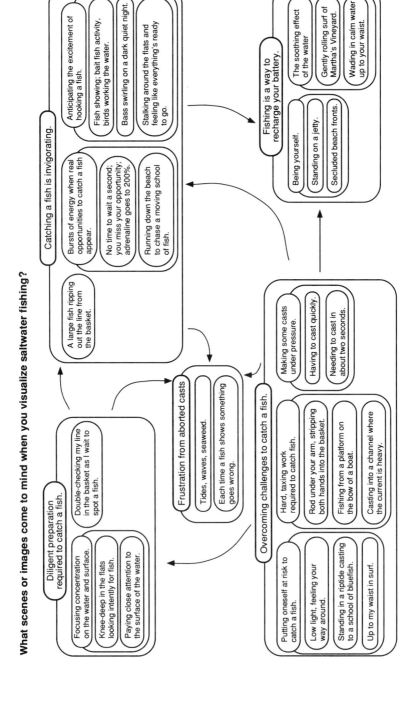

Figure 8-6. Stripping Basket Customer Image KJ

[STAGE 2] STEP 4: TRANSFORM THE VOICE OF THE CUSTOMER INTO CUSTOMER REQUIREMENTS

Customer requirements (CRs) are detailed, unambiguous, qualitative statements of customer needs. Since the original voice of the customer statement may be far from precise, you need methods to accurately translate the original customer voices into CRs.

The method used for transforming each voice of the customer to a customer requirements was developed by Ofuji, Ono, and Akao.[10] The process is shown in Figure 8-7.

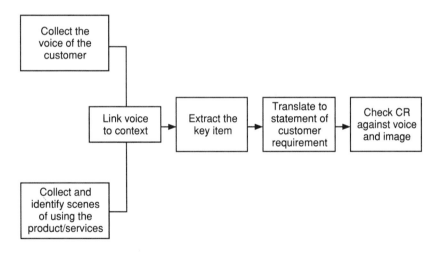

Figure 8-7. Transforming the Voice of the Customer into Customer Requirements

When visiting the customer, collect both the customer voices and images of use, for instance, using the four questions. Link the voice to the context by referring to the image KJ as you interpret the voices. Keeping the image in mind, for each voice of the customer identify one or two key items; from these key items, and using the seven translation guidelines given below, construct the customer requirements. Then go back and check the CR against the image KJ and the original voice.

Here is an example:

Voice: "big enough so you don't think about putting the line in the basket; you do it unconsciously"
Image: pressure to cast very quickly
Key item: basket doesn't change fishing style for casting or stripping

Customer requirements:

- basket is positioned at end of stripping motion
- casting motion is the same with or without basket on

Professor Shiba summarizes Ofuji's, Ono's, and Akao's suggestions into seven translation guidelines for converting the verbatim voices of the customer into customer requirements, as follows.[11] Examples of use of each translation guideline are provided for the stripping basket case. Each example illustrates one guideline rather than a totally perfect customer requirement. In each case, both poor ($-$) and better ($+$) translation examples are given.

Seven Translation Guidelines

1. *Avoid statements in a negative form* like "does not break when dropped." Instead, write from an affirmative, or positive, perspective. It is better to design for strength rather than to avoid weakness.

   Voice: "all lightweight plastic, no possibility for rust"
   Image: up to my waist in the surf
   Key item: no possibility for rust

   Translation:
   ($-$) The basket should not rust.
   ($+$) The basket is rustproof.

2. *Avoid two-valued (0-1) concepts* and use multivalued attributes. Use of the word *not* is a signal of two-valued

thinking — avoid it. The world is not black and white, but is mostly gray. Zero-one requirements inhibit the flexibility in addressing design trade-offs and conflicts in customer needs.

Voice: "how the water spills out of it"
Image: up to my waist in the surf
Key items: drainage

Translation:
(−) Water does not accumulate in the basket.
(+) Water drains quickly from the basket.

3. *Avoid abstract words* such as "reliable," "durable," and "appropriate to environment." Use words specific to the product and its use. Design requirements should be clear — the above words introduce ambiguity.

Voice: "durable — material made out of cane won't last; plastic will last longer than I."
Image: each time a fish shows something goes wrong
Key item: basket must last

Translation:
(−) The basket is durable.
(+) The basket is saltwater resistant.
(+) The basket withstands exposure to the sun.

4. *Avoid statements of "solution"* that indicate the product's implementation or construction (e.g., "frame is made of steel"). If the requirement is strength, then describe some situation that indicates the desired aspect of strength (e.g., "frame supports a large man"). Customer requirements that are stated as solutions can prematurely limit design options.

Voice: "quick-release basket so it doesn't get in the way when moving around the boat after a fish"
Image: fishing from a platform on the bow of a boat
Key item: basket can be released easily

Translation:
(−) The basket has Velcro fasteners.
(+) The basket fastener can be released with one hand.

5. *Avoid premature detail* such as "3 inches by 5 inches" before completing the customer requirements analysis. Customer requirements are not abstract; neither are they extremely specific (e.g., "power cord needs to run between unit and nearby plug"). Excessive detail can prematurely limit design options.

> *Voice:* "it needs to be designed as a truncated cone with a height-to-diameter ratio of one-third to one-half, so loops go to the outside of the basket; should be a parabolic dish"
> *Image:* double-checking my line in the basket as I wait to spot a fish
> *Key item:* bigger loops are better

> *Translation:*
> (−) Basket bottom is a parabolic dish with a height-to-width ratio of one-half.
> (+) Loops collect at the edges of the basket.

6. *Avoid the auxiliary verbs should* or *must*, which convey judgment. Instead, use present-tense forms of the verb *to be,* such as *am, is,* and *are.* Judgment-oriented statements draw premature conclusions about the necessity of those requirements. It is important to keep an open mind until all customer voices have been integrated. A later step will determine which requirements are necessary and which optional.

> *Voice:* "the basket needs to be lightweight; you can walk for miles along the beach"
> *Image:* running down the beach to chase a moving school of fish
> *Key item:* the basket must be light enough to carry easily

Translation:

(−) The basket should be easy to carry when transiting to the water.

(+) The basket is easy to carry to the water.

7. *Avoid intangible concepts.* Use terms that are more concrete.

Voice: "comfort: to wear it for hours and forget it is there; like a good hat"

Image: hard, taxing work required to catch fish

Key items:

• basket does not cause fatigue
• basket does not irritate the wearer

Translation:

(−) The basket is comfortable.
(+) The inner edge conforms to the body.

Stripping Basket Case Study: Translation of Customer Voices to Customer Requirements

Using the above techniques, Burchill and his colleagues translated the customer voices into customer requirements. Table 8-1 presents a selection of those translations.

Common Issues

During the conversion of customer voices to customer requirements, several issues commonly arise.

Successive refinement. The key item of the customer voice is often difficult to understand on the first attempt. A useful approach is to write down what appears to be the key item and customer requirement, then compare the customer requirement

Table 8-1. Voice of the Customer Translation

Customer Voice	Key Item	Quality Requirement
most baskets are jury-rigged	no commercial products are good	not able to determine
I have an Orvis basket on a bungee cord. Adjustable belt is important; sometimes I wear a sweater and rain coat; sometimes a T-shirt	attachment device is adjustable	basket belt is adjustable
bungee cord is tight so the basket stays horizontal, thereby keeping the line from bunching and tangling	• basket does not tip • line does not bunch • line does not tangle	• basket stays perpendicular to body • line in basket is evenly distributed • line is tangle-free
fisherman don't like bright colors, army-green or brown is OK	natural, not neon, colors	color is natural/neutral
belt must keep basket in front of you	belt must fasten basket securely	basket is stationary after fastening
4"- to-6" depth so loops don't fall out	line put in the basket must stay there	line remains in the basket until cast
how the water spills out of it, drainage	water can not accumulate in the basket	water is free to drain
all lightweight plastic, no possibility of rust	no possibility of rust	basket is rust-proof
don't even feel it on your hip	basket is comfortable	basket conforms to the body
big enough so you don't think about putting line in the basket; you do it unconsciously	basket doesn't change fishing style for casting or stripping	• basket is positioned at end of stripping motion • casting motion is the same with or without basket
I want it 8" off my front leg/hip	position of basket is important	basket is positioned at end of stripping motion
somehow comfortable on your waist; not cumbersome	basket is comfortable	basket conforms to the body

would not get away from core product; functionality is key	basic functions first	• line is cast tangle-free • line is cast without drag
canvas doesn't last	material must be durable	basket is able to last through several seasons of use
if it only goes out 5" from front of stomach, feeding line into it becomes another step in the process	basket should not change fishing style	stripped line is placed into the basket at the end of the natural motion

What new features might address your future needs?

stake or peg system to eliminate line shifting	eliminate line shifting	• line is stationary in the basket • line is free
ease of carrying when not in use	easy to transport	basket is easy to carry when transiting to the water
ease of packing	easy to store	basket should conserve space when not in use
possible dual functions	device should do more than hold line	other fishing functions are satisfied by the basket

From your experience, what complaints, problems, or weaknesses would you like to mention about the product/service?

soft "sack-like" construction causes line shifts	line shifts	basket does not allow line to tangle
adaptivity to varying conditions/positioning	the basket position is changed to meet conditions	basket can be worn in different positions
fastening system	fastening	• basket is easy to fasten • basket is easy to detach • basket does not shift position after fastening
belt/rim connection	too vague to work with	

to the voice and image. You then can improve on the key item and customer requirement through iteration (see Figure 8-8).

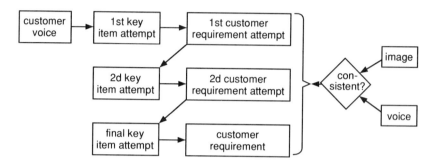

Figure 8-8. Refining the Key Item of the Customer Voice

Tip of the iceberg. Often the customers think they are being specific, when it is only the tip of the iceberg (see Figure 8-9). For instance, customers think and say they want a better manual for the appliance, when what they really want is an appliance simple enough to use without reading a manual.

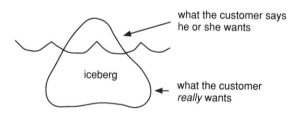

Figure 8-9. Tip of the Iceberg

A specific example of this phenomenon is given in one of the customer voices about the stripping basket: "stake or peg system to eliminate line shifting." The statement suggests that the customer is specifically asking for a stake or peg system. However, analysis revealed that the key item in this voice was "eliminate line shifting," which comprises two customer requirements — "line is stationary in the basket," and "line is tangle-free." The "peg or stake system" was only the tip of the iceberg. The customer really wanted the line to be stationary in the basket to prevent tangles so the line wouldn't foul when cast (see Figure 8-10).

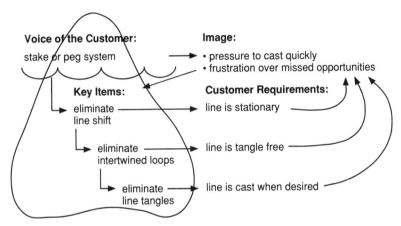

Figure 8-10. Iceberg Model for Stripping Basket Key Items

This process of delving below the waterline of stated customer requirements necessarily involves much interpretation. To ensure that the interpretations are identifying true customer needs, one must continually refer back to the image KJ.

Multiple thoughts. Another common situation is customer voices that have more than one thought in them. For example, one of the stripping basket customer voices was "Doesn't need to be deep. Only 3 or 4 inches. More depth is cumbersome. Only need 30 to 40 feet of line in the basket. Just deep enough so the line doesn't flop out." Although the customer apparently thinks he is addressing the issue of basket depth, there are really two key items in this voice: (1) line placed in the basket doesn't come out accidentally; and (2) smaller depth is less cumbersome.

These two key items lead to two customer requirements: (1) line placed in the basket stays there; and (2) depth is less than four inches.

Multiple interpretations per voice. Statements made in one context can have entirely different meanings in another context. When developing customer requirements, determine if the voice might be able to fit more than one image. If so, create requirements for each image.

[STAGE 2] STEP 5: SELECT THE MOST SIGNIFICANT CUSTOMER REQUIREMENTS

Usually, there are too many customer requirements to be manageable. In this case, the vital few must be selected from the trivial many. The multipickup method (MPM) is a tool to help with this.[12] Figure 8-11 shows how MPM may fit into the bigger picture.

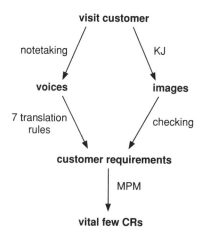

Figure 8-11. Selecting the Vital Few CRs

In the figure, note that MPM can be used after the voices of the customer have been converted to customer requirements.

Alternatively, the MPM could be done before the voices have been converted. The first method is preferable because it presupposes an understanding of all customer voices before any are discarded as weak.

Understanding the key item in the customer voice depends on the context of the statement; similar-appearing voices from different customers may actually mean different things; this is the reason for using the image KJ during the translation process and for converting the voices into customer requirements before eliminating apparently weak voices.

The second method, doing the MPM on raw voices, may be necessary if there are so many voices that interpretation of all of them is impractical. However, it is not necessary to meet a great many customers, as was explained in our discussion of the BBN case study (see Chapter 7). After exploring what was learned in the initial few customer visits, seek complementary information from subsequent customers. By doing this successively, you should be able to gather enough information without visiting too many customers or getting too much duplicate information.

[STAGE 2] STEP 6: DEVELOP INSIGHT INTO THE RELATIONS BETWEEN REQUIREMENTS

Having understood the voices of the customer and selected the vital few customer requirements, you now need to organize the selected CRs and characterize their roles in satisfying the customer. The first step in organizing the CRs is to construct a customer requirements KJ diagram (CR KJ), which can have several uses:

- It facilitates group understanding of the integrated results to date. Until this point, visits and translations may have been done by individuals or subgroups. Even if they have done all the visits and translations together, it is necessary to align everyone's understanding of what the group process has produced.

- The structure provided by the groupings in the KJ diagram provides the basis for detecting glaring omissions. Omissions can easily occur, either because there was so much data to process that something was overlooked, or because no customer articulated a real need.
- The synthesis of CRs shown in the KJ diagram may produce insight. For instance, the higher-level labels allow you to articulate the attractiveness of product features in the language of the customer
- The KJ diagram can be used as a tool for checking conclusions — by showing it to customers to make sure they have been heard, by letting customers vote on the importance of the CRs on the KJ, or by using the KJ votes to check against later steps.
- The structure and grouping within the KJ diagram may provide the basis for reducing the number of CRs to evaluate in later steps
- Knowing the structure of CRs is useful for sorting out apparent inconsistencies among the means of addressing the CRs.

Figure 8-12 is the CR KJ for the stripping basket case study. The votes on this KJ were by the eight fishermen interviewed earlier, and their remarkable consistency reassured the design team that it had accurately heard and interpreted the voice of the customer. For instance, with 3-2-1 voting, "line comes out of the basket easily" got 23 points out of a possible 24 first place votes; "accommodates casting, stripping, and movement" got 13 of 16 possible second place votes; and "line moves only when desired" got 9 votes for third place.

The KJ diagram in Figure 8-12 shows a hierarchy of customer requirements. The evaluation of the KJ diagram by lead users identified the following three groups of customer requirements as most important:

- when required, line comes out of the basket easily
- basket accommodates casting, stripping, and movement
- line moves only when desired

What are the customers' requirements for a stripping basket?

It should allow you to focus on fishing by eliminating line problems and discomfort.

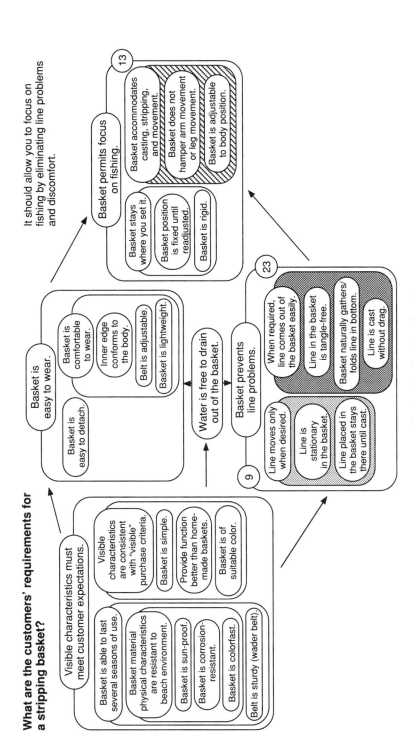

Figure 8-12. KJ Diagram of Customer Requirements (Stripping Basket Case)

The KJ diagram layout promotes understanding but is awkward for later use of the KJ data. However, since the KJ diagram is a hierarchy, it is easy to convert portions of the KJ diagram into a less awkward tree structure, using the parts of the diagram deemed most important (see Figure 8-13).

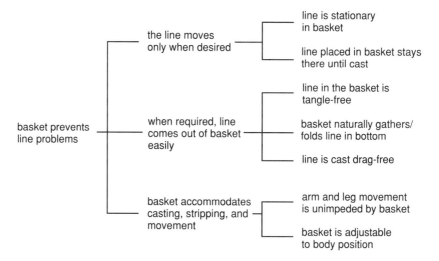

Figure 8-13. Customer Requirements Table

This tree structure of a portion of the customer requirements KJ is called a customer requirements table and will appear on the left side of the quality table, which will be described in stage 3, step 9.

The stripping basket case study started with a couple of hundred customer voices; then the MPM and KJ tools were used to extract from these voices seven key customer requirements. As mentioned earlier, it is not feasible to address a large number of customer requirements — the ones most important to the customer must be selected.

[STAGE 3] STEP 7: INVESTIGATE CHARACTERISTICS OF CUSTOMER REQUIREMENTS

There are many methods one can use to investigate the characteristics of the customer requirements that have been developed. One is to ask customers to rank-order them. The particular method we will discuss here is based on the work of Professor Noriaki Kano of Tokyo Rika University.

Professor Kano and his colleagues developed a set of ideas that we summarize as follows.[13]

Invisible ideas about quality can be made visible. Customer ideas about quality are often confused and difficult to see clearly, but they can be made clear. As the customer ideas of quality are made clear, many requirements emerge; and they fall into several groups. These groups can be represented in a tree structure of customer requirements (as shown in Figure 8-13).

Customer satisfaction for some customer requirements is proportional to how fully functional the product is with respect to a requirement. The *x*-axis of Figure 8-14 indicates how fully functional a product is, and the *y*-axis indicates how satisfied the customer is. Traditional ideas about quality were that the customer satisfaction was proportional to how functional the product was — the less functional the product, the less satisfied the customer, and the more functional the product, the more satisfied the customer. The line going through the origin at 45 degrees graphs the correspondence between customer satisfaction and product functioning. The customer is more satisfied with a more fully functional product and less satisfied with a less functional product. Such customer requirements are known as "one-dimensional" CRs. For the stripping basket, the rate at which water drains out is most likely a one-dimensional CR — satisfaction is probably proportional to the drainage rate. Some companies use the word "satisfiers" instead of one-dimensional CR — that is, the more fulfilled this requirement is, the more satisfied the customer is.

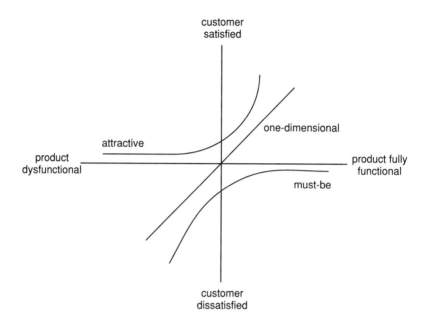

Figure 8-14. Identifying One-Dimensional, Attractive, and Must-Be CRs

Some customer requirements are not one-dimensional. These are indicated in Figure 8-14 by the curves labeled "must-be" and "attractive." The must-be curve indicates situations in which the customer is less satisfied when the product is less functional, but is not more satisfied when the product is more functional. For instance, having a flimsy belt on the stripping basket causes the customer to be less satisfied; however, having a sturdy belt does not raise the level of the customer's satisfaction. Some companies call these must-be elements "dissatisfiers"; they can dissatisfy but they cannot increase satisfaction.

The attractive curve indicates the situation in which the customer is more satisfied when the product is more functional, but not less satisfied when the product is less functional. For instance, a customer is not unsatisfied when the basket is not adjustable to different body positions, i.e., stomach, hip, or thigh, but he is more satisfied when the basket has this feature. Some companies call these attractive elements "delighters" — they do not dissatisfy if absent but they can delight when present.

Customer requirements can be classified by questionnaire.
Kano and his colleagues believe that the one-dimensional, attractive, and must-be customer requirements can be classified
through a customer questionnaire. This questionnaire has the
form of a list of questions, each having two parts: How would
you feel if that feature were present in the product, and how
would you feel if that feature were not present in the product?
To each part of the question, the customer can answer in one of
five different ways (see Table 8-2).

Table 8-2. A Customer Requirements Classification Questionnaire

If the water drains quickly out of the stripping basket, how do you feel?	1. I like it that way. 2. It must be that way. 3. I am neutral. 4. I can live with it that way. 5. I dislike it that way.
If the water drains slowly out of the stripping basket, how do you feel?	1. I like it that way. 2. It must be that way. 3. I am neutral. 4. I can live with it that way. 5. I dislike it that way.

The five choices in the table are those used in the stripping
basket case study. The following alternatives, however, seem to
differentiate better among the responses:

1. I enjoy it that way.
2. It is a basic necessity, or, I expect it that way.
3. I am neutral.
4. I dislike it, but I can live with it that way.
5. I dislike it, and I can't accept it.

Based on the responses to the two parts of the question, the
product feature (how fast the water drains, in the above example) can be classified into one of six categories: A = attractive, M
= must-be, O = one-dimensional, R = reverse, I = indifferent,
and Q = questionable. The first three categories were defined
above, and these are primarily what we are seeking in the Kano
analysis. The other three categories indicate the following situa-

tions: there is a contradiction in the customer's answers to the questions (= questionable); the customer is indifferent to whether the product feature is there or not (= indifferent); or your a priori judgment of functional and dysfunctional is reversed by what the customer feels (= reverse).

You can determine categories of customer requirements by comparing customers' answers about functional and dysfunctional aspects of product features (see Table 8-3).[13]

For example, if the customer answers "I like it that way"

Table 8-3. Kano Evaluation Table

Customer requirements → ↓		Dysfunctional				
		1. like	2. must-be	3. neutral	4. live with	5. dislike
Functional	1. like	Q	A	A	A	O
	2. must-be	R	I	I	I	M
	3. neutral	R	I	I	I	M
	4. live with	R	I	I	I	M
	5. dislike	R	R	R	R	Q

Customer requirement is

A: Attractive   O: One-dimensional
M: Must-be   Q: Questionable result
R: Reverse   I: Indifferent

about "water drains quickly," and "I dislike it that way" about "water drains slowly," you look at the intersection of the first row and fifth column and find an *O*, indicating that the customer views speed of water drainage as a one-dimensional customer requirement.

Stripping Basket Case Study — Kano Questionnaire, Matrix, and Diagram

A portion of the Kano questionnaire for the stripping basket case study is reproduced in Table 8-4.

Table 8-4. Kano Questionnaire (Stripping Basket Case Study)

8a.	If the line does not move around in the basket, how do you feel?	1. I like it that way. 2. It must be that way. 3. I am neutral. 4. I can live with it that way. 5. I dislike it.
8b.	If the line moves around in the basket, how do you feel?	1. I like it that way. 2. It must be that way. 3. I am neutral. 4. I can live with it that way. 5. I dislike it.
9a.	If line placed in the basket stays there, how do you feel?	1. I like it that way. 2. It must be that way. 3. I am neutral. 4. I can live with it that way. 5. I dislike it.
9b.	If line placed in the basket comes out, how do you feel?	1. I like it that way. 2. It must be that way. 3. I am neutral. 4. I can live with it that way. 5. I dislike it.
10a.	If line in the basket is tangle free, how do you feel?	1. I like it that way. 2. It must be that way. 3. I am neutral. 4. I can live with it that way. 5. I dislike it.
10b.	If line in the basket is tangled, how do you feel?	1. I like it that way. 2. It must be that way. 3. I am neutral. 4. I can live with it that way. 5. I dislike it.
11a.	If line gathers naturally in the bottom of the basket, how do you feel?	1. I like it that way. 2. It must be that way. 3. I am neutral. 4. I can live with it that way. 5. I dislike it.
11b.	If line does not gather naturally in the bottom of the basket, how do you feel?	1. I like it that way. 2. It must be that way. 3. I am neutral. 4. I can live with it that way. 5. I dislike it.
12a.	If the basket causes some drag on the line during casts, how do you feel?	1. I like it that way. 2. It must be that way. 3. I am neutral. 4. I can live with it that way. 5. I dislike it.
12b.	If line casts from the basket without drag, how do you feel?	1. I like it that way. 2. It must be that way. 3. I am neutral. 4. I can live with it that way. 5. I dislike it.

Table 8-4. *(Continued)*

19a. If the basket does not hamper arm or leg movement, how do you feel?	1. I like it that way. 2. It must be that way. 3. I am neutral. 4. I can live with it that way. 5. I dislike it.
19b. If the basket interferes with arm or leg movement, how do you feel?	1. I like it that way. 2. It must be that way. 3. I am neutral. 4. I can live with it that way. 5. I dislike it.
20a. If the basket is adjustable to different body positions, how do you feel?	1. I like it that way. 2. It must be that way. 3. I am neutral. 4. I can live with it that way. 5. I dislike it.
20b. If the basket is not easily adjusted to different body positions, how do you feel?	1. I like it that way. 2. It must be that way. 3. I am neutral. 4. I can live with it that way. 5. I dislike it.

The results of the Kano survey of customers were then tabulated, as shown in Figure 8-15. For the first customer, the classification of each customer requirement on the customer's questionnaire is determined on the Kano Evaluation Table.[14]

Every customer's questionnaire is similarly classified, and all are tallied on a tabulation table. Table 8-5 shows the results for the stripping basket case study.

For each row of the tabulation — that is, for each customer requirement — the dominant customer view is indicated by the highest tally. If two or more categories are tied or close to tied, it is an indication that more information is needed: you may be dealing with two market segments, or you may need to ask more detailed questions about customer requirements.

From the tabulation of customer response to the Kano survey for the stripping basket case study, the Kano diagram was derived; it shows the must-be, one-dimensional, attractive, and indifferent qualities for the stripping basket (see Figure 8-16).

All customer requirements are not created equal. Improving performance on a must-be customer requirement that is al-

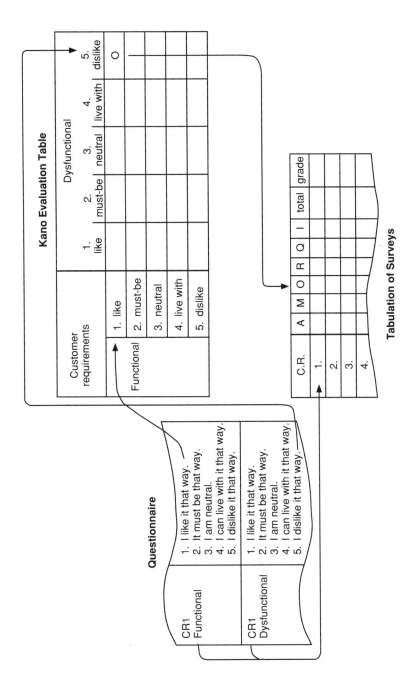

Figure 8-15. Tabulation of Kano Survey Results

Table 8-5. Evaluations of Customer Requirements (CR) for Stripping Basket Kano Questionnaire

C.R.	A	M	O	R	Q	I	total	grade
1.	3	6	14				23	O
2.	5	6	11			1	23	O
3.	2	5	13			3	23	O
4.	6	1	4	1		11	23	I
5.	1	9	6	1		6	23	M
6.	7		2	3	1	10	23	I
7.	1	2	16		1	3	23	O
8.	2	8	11	2			23	O
9.		10	13				23	O
10.		13	10				23	M
11.	3	4	14			1	22	O
12.		12	11				23	M
13.	9	1	2			11	23	I
14.	6	2	11			4	23	O
15.	6	4	11		1		22	O
16.	1	7	13			2	23	O
17.	1	3	18				23	O
18.		5	14	1		3	23	O
19.		8	15				23	O
20.	9	1	8			5	23	A

Customer requirement is

A: Attractive   O: One-dimensional
M: Must-be   Q: Questionable result
R: Reverse   I: Indifferent

ready at a satisfactory level is not productive compared with improving performance on a one-dimensional or attractive customer requirement. Insight into which CRs fall into which quality dimensions can improve one's focus on the vital few. In general, must-be requirements must be adequately covered, the set of one-dimensional requirements must be competitive, and some attractive requirements are needed for competitive differentiation.

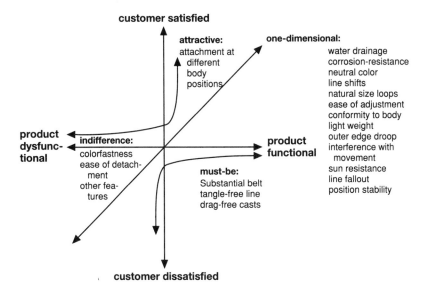

Figure 8-16. Kano Diagram of Customer Requirements

The Phenomenon of Quality Satisfaction Decay

Kano's diagram showing the relationship among the attractive, one-dimensional, and must-be customer requirements is useful for illustrating another phenomenon.

Experience has shown that in many instances customer satisfaction with a given product attribute decays over time. For instance, the Sony Walkman® was originally an attractive requirement. People were not unhappy without these portable radios, but they were delighted to have them. With time and widespread use, the Walkman ceased to be an attractive requirement and instead became a one-dimensional requirement. Not having one made people unhappy, and getting one made them happy — and the more features, the happier they were. It is arguable that the Walkman has now further decayed to the position of a must-be requirement. People get perfunctory appreciation for giving their children Walkmans; yet if those children don't have a Walkman, they tell their parents how deprived they are and compare their possessions with those of their friends. For many people having a Walkman is a given; they can't ride buses or jog without one.

In the computer industry computer reliability was traditionally one-dimensional, and customers were willing to pay for higher reliability and fast field service. Today customers increasingly expect their computer to run without breaking. Computer reliability is a must-be customer requirement, expected even of mail-order vendors.

The brakes on a car are always a must-be — having them does not make a customer happier, but not having them work at a specified level makes the customer very unhappy.

Notice the relationship between attractive, one-dimensional, and must-be and the four fitnesses described in Chapter 1.

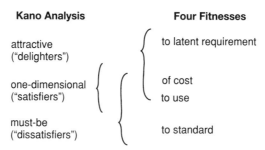

A product or service attribute that initially meets a latent requirement is a delighter. A product or service attribute that meets only fitness to standard is likely to be a dissatisfier — you get no points for meeting the standard, but you lose points for failing to meet it. Depending on the state of maturity of a product or service, meeting fitness to use could be one-dimensional or must-be, and meeting fitness of cost could be attractive, one-dimensional, or must-be.

This tendency of customer satisfaction to decay requires companies to try constantly to meet new latent requirements, decrease costs, increase usability and, of course, meet standards — in other words, to seek continuous improvement.

[STAGE 3] STEP 8: GENERATE METRICS FOR CUSTOMER REQUIREMENTS

Once you have characterized the CRs qualitatively and in the language of the customer, you must translate them into the quantitative language of the engineer. For example, if the CR is "line is cast without drag," the engineers need measurable physical targets for their design, such as "force needed to cast the line and fly a given number of feet." Such measured physical translations of CRs are called quality metrics (QMs). All of the vital few CRs must be mapped into such QMs.

The assumption is that if the measurement criteria and targets for each customer requirement are clearly identified, a good designer or engineer can find a way to implement the characteristic desired by the customer if implementation is in fact feasible. Thus, a clear specification is a key requirement for a satisfactory design.

There are several methods for deriving quality metrics. In the stripping basket case study, Burchill and his colleagues proposed quality metrics by brainstorming possible metrics for each customer requirement, then using the tree diagram method for organizing them and checking for completeness.[15] All of the proposed QMs for each CR are evaluated for validity to the CR and for feasibility. Validity is given precedence over feasibility, on the assumption that further thought will reveal a feasible way to measure a valid QM. From the set of all proposed QMs, those that are most valid and feasible for each CR are selected, and these selections are organized into a quality metrics tree.

Some of the proposed QMs will be valid measures of multiple customer requirements, while many of them will not be particularly valid or feasible.

Specifically, some customer requirements may have more ambiguity than others and thus require multiple measures to quantify them. For instance, the requirement that water drains from the basket is relatively unambiguous, and a single measurement unit — time to drain two gallons of water — characterizes how well the customer requirement is met. In contrast, "the basket is comfortable to wear" is more ambiguous. No one measurement unit captures the entire concept of "comfortable." Accordingly, it will take multiple quality metrics to assess comfort — body contour, the basket's inner edge, weight, force to secure.

[STAGE 3] STEP 9: INTEGRATE UNDERSTANDING ABOUT CUSTOMER REQUIREMENTS

A process is needed for focusing and selecting a powerful set of quality metrics that fully spans the customer requirements without redundancy. The central element in this process is a matrix called the quality table. It has customer requirements on the left vertical axis and a quality metrics tree on the top horizontal axis, as shown in Figure 8-17.

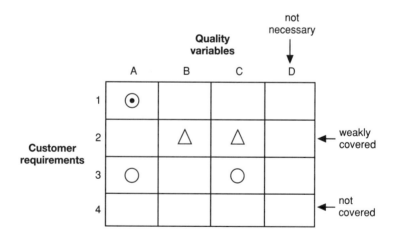

Figure 8-17. Quality Table

The quality table shown has four customer requirements, for which four quality metrics have been proposed. The circle with the dot means that quality metric A is an excellent measure of customer requirement 1. The circles indicate that quality metrics A and C are only good measures of customer requirement 3. The triangles indicate that quality metrics B and C are weak measures of customer requirement 2. Where there is no symbol at the intersection of the requirement's row and the metric's column, there is no cause-and-effect relation between customer requirements and quality metrics

Thus, the quality table provides a tool to ensure that each customer requirement is adequately measured by a quality metric and to eliminate redundant quality metrics.

In the above example, customer requirement A is well measured by quality metric 1, and measurement of customer requirement 3 requires a combination of the quality metrics A and C. Customer requirement 2 is poorly measured even by the combination of quality metrics B and C, and customer requirement 4 is not measured at all by quality metrics A through D. Furthermore, quality metric B is not very useful, and quality metric D is not useful at all. In this example, we would do well to replace quality metrics B and D with quality metrics that effectively measure customer requirements 2 and 4.

We now return to the stripping basket case study to show step-by-step use of a quality table.

Stripping Basket Case Study: Use of a Quality Table

The quality table for the stripping basket case study is shown in Table 8-6.

At the middle of the left side is a customer requirements table, immediately to the left of the column of priorities 1 through 7. The CR table was derived from the CR KJ, as shown in Figure 8-18. The KJ was converted to a tree and the tree converted to a table. The priorities were established from an evaluation of the KJ by eight of the lead users.

Across the top of Table 8-6 is a quality metrics table. In this case study, the quality metrics table was derived by a brainstorming session that produced possible quality metrics for each

Table 8-6. Quality Table of the Stripping Basket Case Study

Customer Requirements (1st / 2d / 3d level)	Priority	Measure the bend radius of the inner edge	Measure length of inner edge body contact in four wear positions	Count the number of adjustable parameters	Measure the maximum belt length	Measure the maximum belt length	Measure height of upward step that can be made without impacting basket	Measure length of largest stride that can be made without impacting basket	Measure height of bottom above knee of wearer	Measure distance from stripping motion start point to outer edge	Measure distance from stripping motion start point to top	Measure width of basket relative to width of wearer	Measure distance from top of basket to shoulder
Quality Metrics — 1st level		Measure how well basket can be adjusted to fit the worker					Test if basket facilitates body motions during fishing					
2d level		Measure how well basket fits against body	Measure how adjustable basket attachment is				Measure how the basket affects walking			Test if the basket accomodates stripping motion			
Basket prevents line problems / The line moves only when desired / Line placed in the basket stays there until cast	4												
The line is stationary in the basket	6												
When required line comes out of the basket / Line is cast without drag	1												
Basket naturally gathers folds line in the bottom	5												
Line in the basket is tangle-free	3												
Accomodates casting, stripping movement / The basket does not hamper arm or leg	2						◉	◉	△	△	△	△	△
The basket is adjustable to body position	7	○	△	◉	◉	◉							
Effectiveness		○	◉	◉	○	○	◉	◉	△	○	○	△	△
Feasibility		◉	◉	◉	◉	◉	○	○	◉	◉	◉	◉	◉
Measurement plan													
Technical Benchmarking Evaluation — Orvis													
LL Bean													
Surfcaster													
Other													
Target value													

◉ = high   ○ = medium   △ = low   (blank) = none

Check if basket prevents tangles/snags from occurring																				
Check if basket prevents line tangling				Check if basket prevents line movement in bottom of the basket				Measure how line covers basket bottom		Check if line falls naturally into the bottom of basket				Measure the drag during casts			Customer benchmark rating			
Count the number of perpendicular loops	Count the number of overlapping loops	Count fouled casts due to line problems as percentage of total casts	Count snags during casts and drops	Count the number of loops over the top of cones/stakes	Measure height of loops from bottom of the basket	Measure how much line falls out of basket when placed in it	Measure outer edge droop in four wear positions	Measure the distribution of loops in the basket bottom	Count the number of loops in each section	Count the loops that are not circular	Assess the geometric shape of the loops	Measure size of loops	Measure loop radii	Measure the effort needed to cast a given distance	Measure length of excess line paid out on a drop after impact	Measure time for line payout after drop	Orvis	LL Bean	Surfcaster	Ours
				△		◉	○													
△				◉	○	◉	○	△	△											
△	◉													◉	○	◉				
○		△	△		△			△	○	△	◉	◉	◉							
◉	◉	◉	◉											○	△					
△	◉	◉	◉	◉	△	◉	○	◉	◉	○	◉	△	△	◉	○	○				
○	△	◉	◉	○	◉	○	◉	○	◉	△	△	○	△	△	◉	◉				

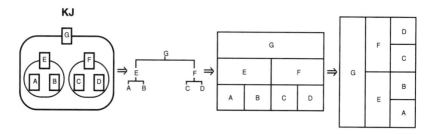

Figure 8-18. From KJ to Tree to Quality Table

item in the customer requirement table. Then a tree was constructed that classified the lowest level groups by common purpose. These groups were then grouped by common purpose, and so on. Finally, the tree was converted to a table.

As described in the example above, after laying out the quality table, make an assessment of the relationship for each customer requirement against each quality metric. In the stripping basket case study, an informal assessment process was used to determine the strength of the relationship using a four-level scale (see symbols).

At this point, the quality table identifies a minimal, comprehensive set of quality metrics that capture the important features of customer requirements. The feasibility row indicates the feasibility of measuring each of the quality variables. But the translation may still be ambiguous, because different people may understand in different ways how the metrics are to be measured. You need quality metrics that always give the same measurements regardless of who performs them. Thus, each quality metric requires a well-defined measurement plan. The measurement plan states what will be done when and by whom, and what will be observed in the process. The metric's measurement plans are indicated in the measurement plan row of the quality table. A quality metric with a measurement plan is said to be operationally defined.

Note the generality of the process of using a tree diagram to brainstorm metrics and a matrix to choose a set that will adequately measure multiple objectives. The same process can be used to define departmental or divisional nonfinancial performance measures, to define the needed capabilities of some process being redesigned, or to define internal corporate goals that assure satisfaction of external customers' needs (as in the BBN customer visitation case study described in Chapter 7). Using a visible process to define, refine, and choose metrics seems like a good way to reduce the consternation and conflict that the subject of metrics often engenders.

A quality table completed in this way provides an unambiguous way to communicate throughout an organization the most important customer requirements and how they will be measured; the quality table is a complete set of operational definitions for the design and development process. It specifies how to tell how good a product is. The next step is determining how good a product must be to provide customer satisfaction and to be competitive.

Stripping Basket Case Study — Benchmark Analysis

Customer benchmarking data, on the far right side of the quality table (Table 8-6) is used to assess the customer's relative satisfaction with respect to each competitor for each requirement along the left side of the table.

Table 8-7 shows the customer benchmark data for the stripping basket case study.

Design targets to meet or beat the competition are then established on the basis of technical benchmarking data, expressed in terms of operationally defined QMs (see bottom of Table 8-6.)

SUMMARY OF STAGE 3: OPERATIONALLY DEFINING CUSTOMER REQUIREMENTS

At this point we have unambiguous technical specifications of a product that will satisfy the customer and meet or beat

Table 8-7. Customer Benchmark Data (Shipping Basket Case Study)

Legend: ● Better ○ Equal △ Worse

Competitive Analysis	Demanded customer requirements	Customer Benchmark Rating				
		Product A	Product B	Product C	Product D	Burchill Product
Must-be	Substantial belt	○	○	△	△	○
Must-be	Tangle-free line	○	△	△	△	●
Must-be	Drag-free casts	○	○	○	○	●
Attractive	Variable attachment	○	●	△	△	●
One-dimensional	Water drainage	○	●	●	●	●
One-dimensional	Corrosion resistance	○	△	○	△	○
One-dimensional	Line shifts	○	△	△	△	○
One-dimensional	Loop size	○	△	△	△	○
One-dimensional	Ease of adjustment	○	●	△	△	○
One-dimensional	Outer edge droop	○	△	△	△	●
One-dimensional	Movement interference	○	○	△	○	○
One-dimensional	Position stability	○	○	○	△	○
One-dimensional	Conformity to body	○	●	△	○	●
One-dimensional	Light weight	○	●	△	●	●
One-dimensional	Line fallout	○	△	●	△	○

the competition. We have operationally defined the voice of the customer in the language of the engineer — each customer requirement derived from the voice of the customer is represented by at least one quality metric, and each quality metric has units of measure, a measurement plan, and a target. Figure 8-19 summarizes the process.

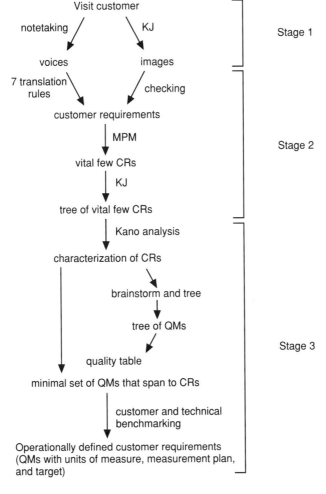

Figure 8-19. Translating the Voice of the Customer

FROM THE OPERATIONALLY DEFINED
CUSTOMER REQUIREMENTS TO A PRODUCT

Once the customer's requirements have been understood and made operational (in the form of quality metrics, targets, and measurement plans), you are in a position to deploy these operational customer requirements through the design, development, and production process. QFD may be the proper tool to provide an accurate deployment through the development process. QFD came to the United States from Japan in about 1984, and a number of United States companies have found it very effective for translating the voice of the customer into high-quality products. The process we have described here of listening to the voice of the customer, understanding what customers are saying, identifying key requirements, and operationally defining them is an excellent addition to the front end of QFD.

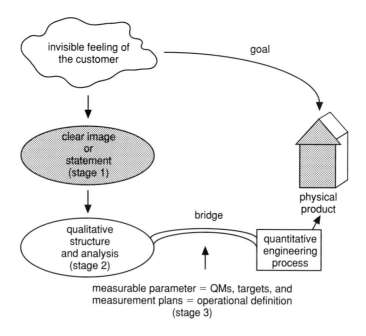

Figure 8-20. From Qualitative Customer Needs to Quantitative Engineering Process

The goal of the entire product generation process is to move from the invisible or vague feeling of the customer to a physical product or tangible service that serves a real customer need. The three stages of operationally defining customer requirements convert the invisible or vague feeling into clear statements of customer requirements. These in turn are structured into measurable parameters on which engineering design process can proceed. The operational definitions of customer requirements provide a bridge between the qualitative needs of the customer and the necessarily quantitative engineering process that realizes the physical product (see Figure 8-20).

Relating Proactive Product Development Process to the WV Model

In Chapter 7, we illustrated how the proactive portion of the WV model is extended to cover extensive planning and design processes. Let us look again at the WV model.

As shown in Figure 8-21, once upon a time it was possible to design a product, develop it, and then sell it. In the sense of alternating between thought and experience, this product-out approach first tested reality against theory when the company attempted to sell the product.

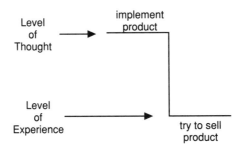

Figure 8-21. The Product-Out Approach

Figure 8-22 shows that as customers became more demanding, companies learned to use the techniques of market research to listen to the market before they finalized the product
design, developed it, and began to sell it.

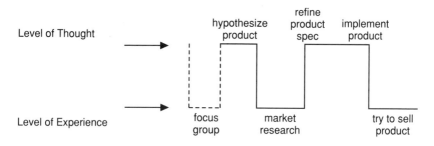

Figure 8-22. The Traditional Market Research Approach

The proactive methods described in this chapter increase
the number of alternations between theory and the reality of the
market before the product design is made final and the product
developed (see Figure 8-23). By repeatedly testing theory
against reality, the company minimizes the work it wastes as a
result of mistaken assumptions, and maximizes its chance of
bringing to market a product that customers will buy.

Many of these reality checks can be done within days or
weeks. Burchill at this writing is testing in real product development environments the hypothesis that early, thorough understanding of customer needs will reduce later changes that delay
development.

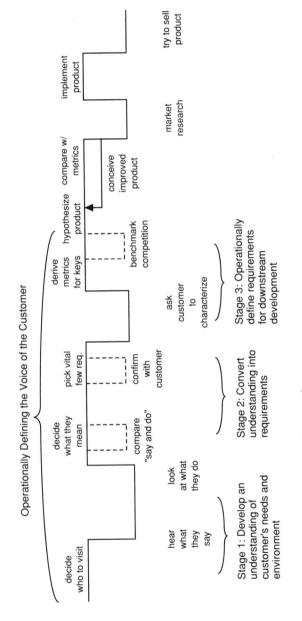

Figure 8-23. The Proactive Approach

NOTES

1. See Mizuno, *Management for Quality Improvement.*
2. For our discussion of this chapter, we are grateful to Yoji Akao, *QFD Manual 1: Hinshitsu Tenkai Niumon (Introduction to Quality Deployment)* (Tokyo: JUSE, 1990), and Tadashi Ofuji, Michiteru Ono, and Yoji Akao, *QFD Manual 2: Hinshitsu Tenkai-Ho (1) (Quality Deployment Method (1))* (Tokyo: JUSE, 1990).
3. The material described in these three stages is based on the research of our colleague, Gary Burchill, particularly the tight focus on "operationalizing the voice of the customer." Other practitioners and researchers in the CQM have worked with Gary to test and evolve these techniques. See Gary Burchill, et al., *Concept Engineering,* CQM doc. (Cambridge, MA: 1992). This manual also describes concept generation and concept selection, which are not covered here.
4. Eric von Hippel, *The Sources of Innovation* (Oxford, England: Oxford University Press, 1988); see particularly Chapter 8. See also von Hippel, "Lead User Analyses for the Development of New Industrial Products," *Management Science* 34 (May 1988): 569-582.
5. Eric von Hippel, *The Sources of Innovation,* 107.
6. This case study was presented in a 1990 session of a CQM course given by Yogesh Parikh, Digital Equipment Corporation, Maynard, Massachusetts; for a more extensive description of contextual inquiry see the chapter entitled "Contextual Inquiry: A Participatory Technique for Systems Design" by Sandra Jones and Karen Holtzblatt, in the book *Participatory Design: Principles and Practice* (edited by Aki Namioka and Doug Schuler), and see "Marking Customer-Centered Design Work for Teams" by Karen Holtzblatt and Hugh Boyer, *Communications of the ACM,* Vol. 36, No. 10, October 1993, pp. 93–103.

7. Tadashi Ofuji, Michiteru Ono, and Yoji Akao, *QFD Manual 2: Hinshitsu Tenkai-Ho (1) (Quality Deployment Method (1))* (Tokyo: JUSE, 1990).

8. Alternative forms of this question that have proved useful are "what future needs might you have?" or "what changes are you starting to experience?"

9. In this case, the KJ was prepared after the interviewers translated verbatim customer voices into quality requirements. However, during the translation and CR KJ process they had numerous discussions of context, and every selected quality requirement was tied to a commonly held image of the product's use and environment.

10. Tadashi Ofuji, Michiteru Ono, and Yoji Akao, *QFD Manual 2.*

11. Recently Burchill has consolidated the principles in these seven guidelines into three guidelines: *Concept Engineering* (Cambridge, MA: CQM, 1992).

12. MPM is described briefly in Chapter 7.

13. Presentations given at Japanese Society for Quality Control Annual Meetings, Noriaki Kano and Fumio Takahashi, "Hinshitsu No M-H Sei Ni Tsuite (Motivator and Hygiene Factor in Quality)," Oct. 1979; Noriaki Kano, Shinichi Tsuji, Nobuhiko Seraku, and Fumio Takahashi, "Miryokuteki Hinshitsu To Atarimae Hinshitsu (1), (2) (Attractive Quality and Must-be Quality (1), (2))," Oct. 1982; these presentations were published in *Quality, JSQC* 14, no. 2 (Tokyo: Japanese Society for Quality Control, 1984).

14. Ibid.

15. The construction of the tree approximately followed the Tree Diagrams method in the 7 Management and Planning Tools described in Chapter 7. The reader may also refer to *Tree Diagrams*, CQM doc. (Cambridge, MA: CQM, 1990).

The Third Revolution:
TOTAL
PARTICIPATION

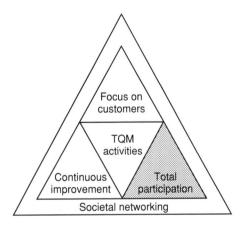

9

Teamwork Skill

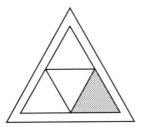

Everyone in a company must be involved effectively in customer satisfaction and continuous improvement activities. TQM is a mass movement. In today's world it is not sufficient to depend only on the few geniuses and highly effective people in a company. Today everyone in the company must be mobilized to improve the way they do their jobs and satisfy customers. To mobilize everyone to achieve these goals, companies must change the way they think about and organize work.

THE DUAL FUNCTION OF WORK

All organizations have two functions — their daily function or daily work, and their improvement function or improvement work. As stated in Chapter 3, the traditional method of organizing work within a company includes the division of labor between workers who do the daily work and managers who make improvements in the way daily work is done (see Figure 9-1).

However, this traditional organization does not react fast enough for the pace of change in today's world. Moreover, it

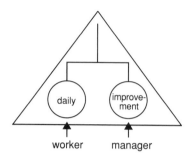

Figure 9-1. Traditional Division of Labor

kills human creativity. Few people are satisfied doing the same
thing every day according to standard. That is the job of
machines, not human beings. TQM aims instead to develop the
human capacity by uniting daily work and improvement work.
The TQM approach is to join the functions of daily work (D, in
Figure 9-2) and improvement work (I, in the figure) at each level
within the company and within each work unit so that quick
and correct reaction to change may occur.

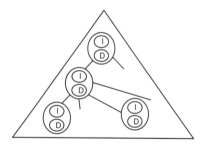

Figure 9-2. Joining Daily Work and Improvement Work

The joining of daily work and improvement work everywhere in the company is the idea of the dual function of work
that is illustrated in the market-in diagram (Figure 3-2), in
which everyone in the company does two jobs, daily work and

improvement work, in order to satisfy customers. Daily work is any repeated activity, however long or short the period of repetition. Examples of daily work include running a machine, typing memos, supervising staff, preparing a monthly report, doing a quarterly forecast, and preparing the annual hiring plan. In many instances the process for doing a daily work activity may not be explicit, especially for managers; but the process, however vague, repeats nonetheless.

Improvement work is aimed at improving processes for daily work and almost always involves discovering new things. Improvement work itself is more effectively done if a clear process is used.

In general, people want creative jobs. Nevertheless, when the concept of the dual function of work is introduced, most people view the improvement work as an extra burden for which they have no time. An underlying reason may be a natural human avoidance of change. Since the purpose of TQM is to address the need for rapid change, it is important to put systems in place to facilitate systematic improvement and change and eliminate the "not my job" attitude.

The interlinking SDCA and PDCA cycles first described in Chapter 4 provide a system for the evolutionary and continuous improvement of daily work. TQM practitioners commonly characterize daily work as following an SDCA cycle: *standard* (know it), *do* (the work as specified by the standard), *check* (the work against standard), and *act* (on any discrepancies between targeted and actual results, or return to S and do the work again). The SDCA cycle is shown in Figure 9-3.

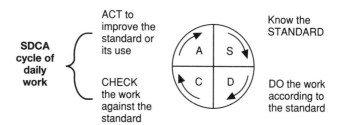

Figure 9-3. The SDCA Cycle

Reactive improvement — activities to improve qualities of conformance — arise from the SDCA cycle of daily work. Opportunities for improvement come from acting on non-conformance to standards in the A portion of the SDCA cycle. When there is clear evidence that something isn't working the way people want it to, improvement activities should begin, as Figure 9-4 shows. When improvement is verified, the remedies become new standards, which then become the new basis for the SDCA cycle of daily work.

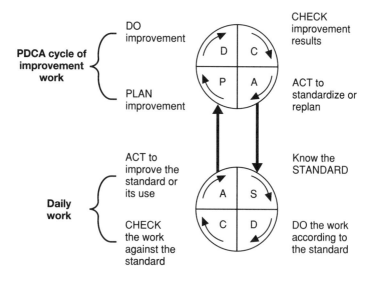

Figure 9-4. The SDCA/PDCA Improvement Cycle

Consider the application of the SDCA/PDCA model to a company just beginning to practice TQM. In the SDCA cycle, the standard (S) is the current process for doing something. It may be invisible or virtually nonexistent, but it is still the current daily work process. You do (D) the work according to this weak or almost non-existent standard (S_0). You accept the result and continue using the current process (C and A).

Eventually, however, during the check (C) stage of the SDCA cycle you may have some vague dissatisfaction with the results. Thus, you act (A) to initiate a PDCA improvement cycle.

The PDCA improvement cycle is used to improve the daily work SDCA process. For instance, the first improvement (A) might be to document the current standard. This in effect provides an improved standard, S_1.

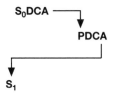

You use the new standard in the SDCA cycle for a while.

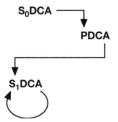

Eventually, at the check (C) stage, you are again (or still) dissatisfied with the result of the current process (S_1) and again you act (A) to initiate an improvement cycle, which again improves the standard process.

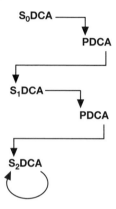

In this way, the TQM dual function of work successively improves the standard process.

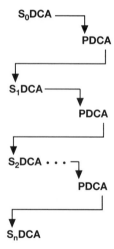

Improvement activities and daily activities are subprocesses of the larger process known as "the job" under TQM. Indeed, some companies refuse to distinguish between improvement work and daily work under TQM, thus discouraging the idea that there may be separate kinds of work done by separate people and stressing that improvement is everyone's job.

The balance between daily work and improvement varies, depending on where you stand in a company hierarchy. Higher ranking people get to do more improvement work than those lower down. The object of TQM is to increase everyone's improvement activities, as shown in Figure 9-5.[1]

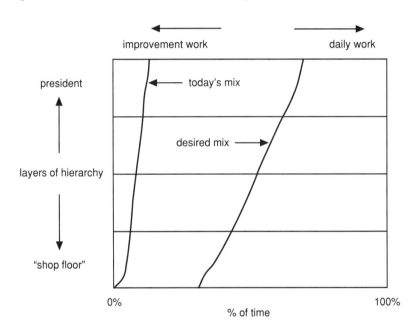

Figure 9-5. **Increasing Improvement Activities Companywide**

TEAMS AND TEAMWORK

In addition to embracing the dual functions of work, today's world requires a change in the way you organize work. Teams and teamwork are a fundamental component of the way TQM organizes work.

Teamwork activities are important to quality improvement for several reasons:

- Cross-functional teams are needed because complexity has increased.
- In the face of this complexity, you need to find your future strategy; this requires great creativity. The age of dependence on individual genius is over. It is a time of collective genius. To compete in the global market, companies need the collective genius of all their employees. They must have teamwork to obtain the collective genius.
- Companies must avoid division of labor. Teamwork provides a mechanism to avoid this division.
- Group learning has a greater effect on the organization than individual learning.
- People who learn together motivate each other to continue — one person learning alone finds it easier to stop.
- When a group of people has learned something together, that learning becomes a group asset, as well as an individual one.

Since teams and teamwork are a fundamental part of TQM, TQM must encourage practices that allow teams to function effectively. The most common symptom of dysfunctional teams is interpersonal conflict. A common approach to promoting effective teamwork is to provide methods of conflict resolution. The TQM approach is to provide methods that don't create conflict. It does this in three ways: by providing teams with a clear mission, requiring that plans be based on verifiable facts, and providing standard processes for analyzing the facts and reaching consensus. In addition, the team completes the PDCA cycle as a group of equals. This work of completion as a team creates an enhanced sense of achievement. Note, the TQM methods of fostering effective teamwork are not aimed at promoting collegiality, although that is useful to teams. Indeed, collegiality is often the result of practicing TQM teamwork methods.

Types of Teams

Traditionally, there were two types of work groups in Japanese companies: formal task forces and informal groups. These are shown in the top and bottom rows of Table 9-1.

Table 9-1. Types of Work Groups in Japanese Companies

	Set-up	Members	Problem to solve	Duration of work
Task force	ordered by superior	selected by management	work-related but given	duration of the task
QC circle	volunteers	all workers in same group	work-related but self-selected	to work continuously as long as the work group exists
Informal	volunteers	volunteers	not work-related and not given	to work continuously as long as the members exist

The QC circle was invented in Japan to fill the position between the traditional, too-rigid task force team and the traditional, too-flexible informal group. The goal in establishing the QC circle was to establish a work group that continuously works on work-related improvement, by bringing together all the members of a the group on a voluntary basis (more about "voluntary" later) for individual and mutual development.

Our definition of teams includes a mission of improvement of the organization. TQM has developed three main kinds of teams:[2]

- Quality circle, or quality control (QC) circle
- Quality improvement team (QI teams, or QITs)
- Cross-functional team (or cross-company team)

Each of the three basic types of teams functions at a typical place in the company hierarchy (see Figure 9-6).

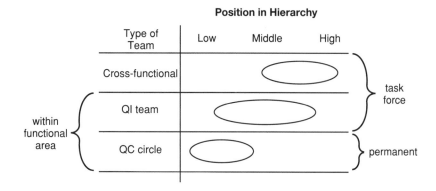

Figure 9-6. Team Positions in Company Hierarchy

QC circles are at a low level; cross-functional teams are at a reasonably high level, and QI teams are roughly in the middle. Quality circles and QITs function within a functional area; cross-functional, or cross-company, teams work across functional boundaries. Quality circles are permanent; QITs and cross-functional teams exist only for the length of the task.

QC circles are often made up of individuals who spend most of their time doing work according to standard, for example, workers on a manufacturing line or people doing standard processing of paperwork. The QC circle is a continuing activity that allows the group to work regularly to improve its performance. QC circle activities regularly address the reactive portion of the WV model and occasionally the proactive portion.

Quality improvement teams are established most often to accomplish a reactive improvement task, although occasionally QI teams address proactive tasks. We discussed examples of QITs in Chapter 5 on reactive problem solving. There may also be standing QI committees, permanently established to look for improvements in a particular area that direct QITs to specific issues.

Cross-functional (cross-company) teams are more usually established to accomplish a proactive improvement task, although they could also work on a reactive task.

Cross-functional teams allow all functions to meet multiple requirements. Close relationship between functions in an organization yields greater efficiency and faster cycle time. Such teams can coordinate all functions to make market-driven changes.

The principles for teamwork are nearly the same regardless of the type of team. Cross-functional membership teams have a larger inherent risk of conflict than other types of teams. We will discuss the types of difficulties and how to avoid them for these teams first, and will provide a case study of an effective cross-functional team. Then we will describe QC circles and provide a case study. Quality improvement teams were described with case studies in Chapter 5.

Cross-Functional Teams

There are at least three areas of potential difficulty with cross-functional teams.

1. Conflict among different functional business units
   - different unit goals
   - desire of each unit to run its own business
2. Conflicts among team members
   - representing home unit interests
   - different experience
   - personal goals
   - lack of respect for others on the team
   - different ranks of people on the team
3. Conflicts between team effort and home unit effort
   - insufficient time for cross-company efforts
   - home units don't trust team to take into account real business issues

We reviewed the cross-functional teams we'd participated in, including the CQM design study described next, to consider ways of addressing the problems. We sorted these ways into the three categories: setting up the team, during team activities, and at the end of the team effort.

Setting up the Team

Select a team with sufficient breadth and experience to develop an appropriate solution. Also consider adding one or two relatively inexperienced people to the team, primarily for their learning benefit rather than for their contribution. Avoid a charter that is too limiting so that the solution is not dictated by the charter. That way, the team will find the actual problem and an effective solution.

Ensure that the team takes the time to do its tasks. Set aside significant blocks of time for team effort — don't start if you can't get this commitment. Make team efforts the first priority (daily work will still get its share of time), and have an absolute near-in deadline that no one on the team can change.

During Team Activities

Reinforce the members' feeling that they are a team. Instruct them (explicitly or implicitly) that their obligation during team efforts is to the team (not to their home units) and its efforts to improve the company. Arrange to have the team members travel together at an early date — this is an excellent way to get them acquainted. You might even schedule some meetings that are purely social.

Design the process to avoid divisive debate. Steer away from topics that generate conflict during early team efforts or on the first revolution of PDCA. Start by focusing externally (on customers, success stories, authorities). Focus on weaknesses contrasted with best industry practices, and benchmark to learn best practice. In that way, you deal with goals and other divisive topics from the standpoint of fact rather than opinion.

Design the way the team deals with facts to minimize conflict without stifling insight. Give introductory TQM and problem-solving training (which also leads the team to root problems and effective conclusions). Leave little time for unstructured discussion in meetings. Stick to discovering the facts and using improvement tools — don't leave time for personal agendas and competitive instincts to emerge. Such an introduction means that all team members can speak the same language.

Of course, for the team to come to a firm conclusion, members need to have the same experiences and study the same facts. Even if subteams or individuals do their own investigation, they need to report what they uncover in a factual and nonevaluative way.

The focus of the team should be on process. The team facilitator manages the process and revises it as necessary (if the team accepts leadership in the process, great progress can be made). If the managers who created the team ask for an interim report, report process, not results. The focus on process eliminates the possibility that upper management will dictate a solution halfway through the study effort.

End of the Team Effort

The team as a whole should report its process and results: it needs acknowledgment and confirmation of management's receptivity to its efforts. Trust the team and its process — accept and implement its findings. Finally, use process diagnosis and PDCA to improve the process for the next time, and ask the team to include in its report recommendations for improvement. Demonstrating thoughtful analysis of possible weaknesses makes the recommendations more trustworthy and implementable. These techniques are illustrated in the following case study.

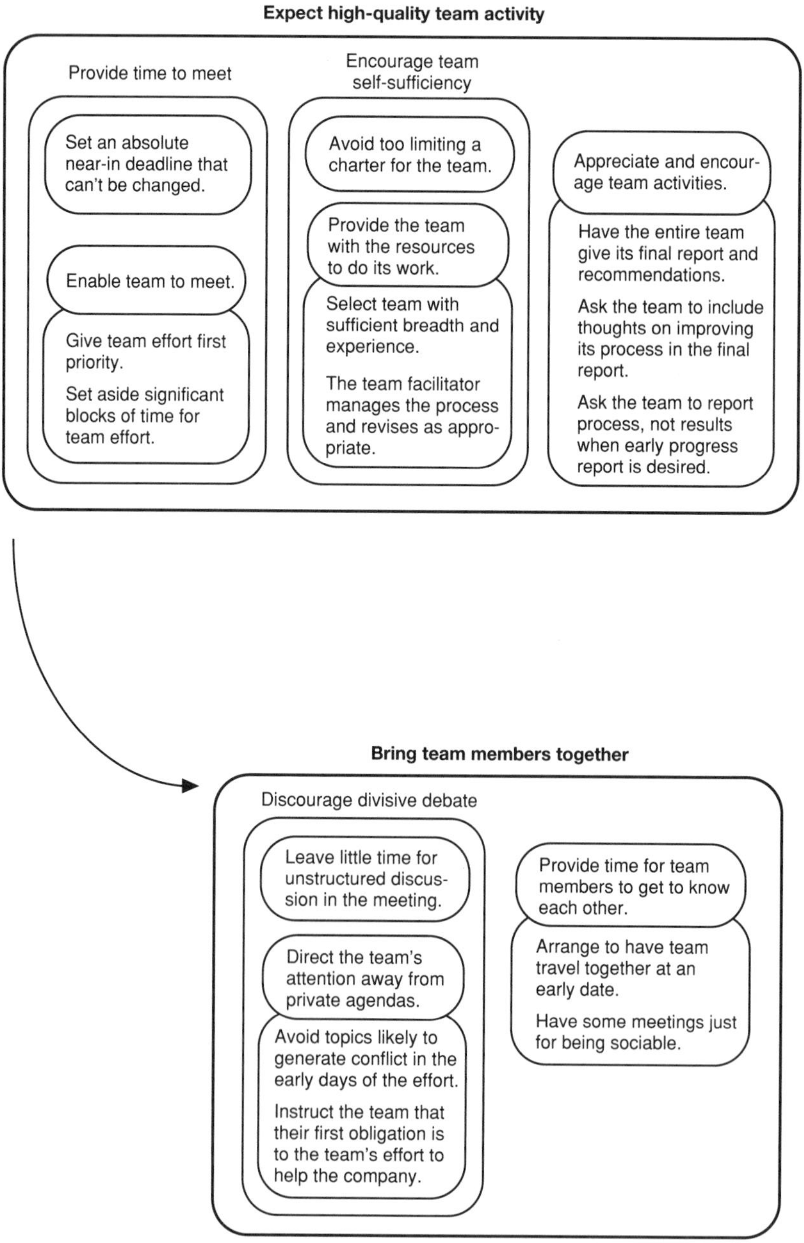

Expect high-quality team activity

Provide time to meet

Encourage team
self-sufficiency

Set an absolute
near-in deadline that
can't be changed.

Avoid too limiting a
charter for the team.

Appreciate and encour-
age team activities.

Enable team to meet.

Provide the team
with the resources
to do its work.

Have the entire team
give its final report and
recommendations.

Give team effort first
priority.

Select team with
sufficient breadth and
experience.

Ask the team to include
thoughts on improving
its process in the final
report.

Set aside significant
blocks of time for
team effort.

The team facilitator
manages the process
and revises as appro-
priate.

Ask the team to report
process, not results
when early progress
report is desired.

Bring team members together

Discourage divisive debate

Leave little time for
unstructured discus-
sion in the meeting.

Provide time for team
members to get to know
each other.

Direct the team's
attention away from
private agendas.

Arrange to have team
travel together at an
early date.

Avoid topics likely to
generate conflict in the
early days of the effort.

Have some meetings just
for being sociable.

Instruct the team that
their first obligation is
to the team's effort to
help the company.

Figure 9-7. Some Ways to Build Cross-Functional Teamwork

Improve staff and team activities.

Use team activities to train some team members.

Use process diagnosis and PDCA to improve the process for the future.

Trust the team and the process by accepting and implementing its findings.

Have team use same language and experience

Give TQM and problem-solving instruction at start.

Focus on root causes.

Avoid focus on goals.

Have team members see/hear same data.

Focus on facts.

Try to see the same things.

Give to whole team non-evaluative reports of things only some team members see.

Focus on weakness and best industry practice.

Focus externally (customers, success stories, authorities).

Teamwork Case Study: The CQM Design Team

The CQM design study took place in March and April, 1990 and is an example of cross-functional and cross-company teamwork.[3]

The Center for Quality Management has seven founding companies:

- Analog Devices
- Bolt Beranek and Newman
- Digital Equipment Corporation
- Polaroid Corporation
- Teradyne
- Bose
- GE Jet Engine Division

People from the first five companies plus MIT participated in the five-week design study. Shoji Shiba of Tsukuba University was our guiding adviser. The CQM design study team was thus cross-functional, intercompany, and international. Although we did not realize it at the time, Shoji Shiba was guiding us through an example of PDCA, as defined in Table 9-2. The following text and Figure 9-8 describe the flow of our activities.

Table 9-2. Activities in the PDCA Process

Stage	Activities	Weeks
Plan	Team building Basic education in TQM Preparation for fact finding	1
Do	Fact finding through company site visits in Japan and the United States	2, 3
Check	Consolidate facts, identify requirements (test by Deming and Baldrige benchmark), identify means, and construct quality tables of requirements vs. means and company weaknesses vs. requirements	3, 4
Act	Prepare first-year plan; outline future plan	5

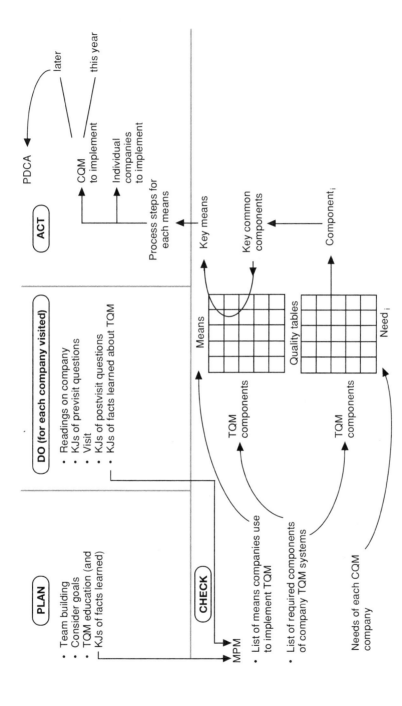

Figure 9-8. CQM Design Team's PDCA Process Activities

As part of the planning phase (plan), we did team building, considered our goals, and were given basic TQM education. We did a KJ diagram on what we learned about TQM (see top left of Figure 9-8).

In the visit stage (do), we read about the companies we were to visit when reading materials were available. For each company we visited, we prepared a KJ diagram of questions we wanted to ask. For the Japanese companies, Shoji Shiba translated our KJ into Japanese and faxed it ahead to them so they would know what questions we wanted to have answered. Then we visited the company. At the end of the visit, we checked our KJ of questions to make sure that all questions had been answered, and asked for further information on questions that had not been answered completely. After our visits, we prepared KJs of post-visit questions for each company. These would have been useful had we visited again, but we did not. However, it was helpful in thinking about questions for the next company. We also prepared a KJ on the facts we learned and reduced this to a manageable group of facts using the MPM method (see top middle of Figure 9-8).

In the check phase (bottom of figure), we studied what we had learned during our visits and from formal training in TQM as recorded on our KJ diagrams. From these important facts, we constructed a tree of components of a TQM system, which we then checked against the Deming and Baldrige criteria. We also constructed a tree of means of implementing a company TQM system. We did a correlation of these components and means to find the means that were most relevant to each component. Then the individual participants of each of the five participating companies studied the needs of their own company and correlated these with the components of a company TQM system to find the components most relevant to each of their needs. We then identified the key components that met the common needs of all five companies. We used the key components to select the key means via the components/means correlation table (bottom of Figure 9-8).

In the act (or standardization) phase, we sketched the process steps for implementing each of the key means and divided them into two categories: those that each company had to do for itself and those that the CQM could do for all the companies. The latter we divided into a group to be implemented in the first year and a group to be left to later years and future PDCA cycles (top right of Figure 9-8).

As we did our studies and analysis, Shoji Shiba taught us to use some of the QC tools, the KJ method, relations diagrams, tree diagrams, matrix diagrams, and quality tables. He demonstrated that with an experienced facilitator, a cross-functional team without previous experience can simultaneously learn new problem-solving techniques and apply them usefully to an important and urgent problem. Figure 9-9 shows the principles by which we worked.

Inside the big rectangle of Figure 9-9 are the elements of our work process that enabled us to do a thorough job: we focused on facts, stratification of the data, multi-valued thinking, working at a low level of abstraction, and capturing words on labels — all of which enabled us to get the detailed facts. We obtained our raw data by focusing on process and using analytic tools to handle non-numeric (language) data from which we developed concepts and models that we could test. These were our group norms. However, with these norms alone, one risks getting mired in detail.

Around the big rectangle are the elements that led to quick, high-quality work. First, we felt great urgency. We were on a high-level assignment from our respective companies and we had a five-week deadline. The urgency required that we eliminate debilitating differences in perspective and language. Second, therefore, we made great efforts to learn and see the same things — we learned a common language and experienced the same things. This gave us logical and intuitive homogeneity, which enabled us to quickly build upon each other's ideas rather than spend time trying to understand what the others were saying. Third, we adhered to the concept of continuous improve-

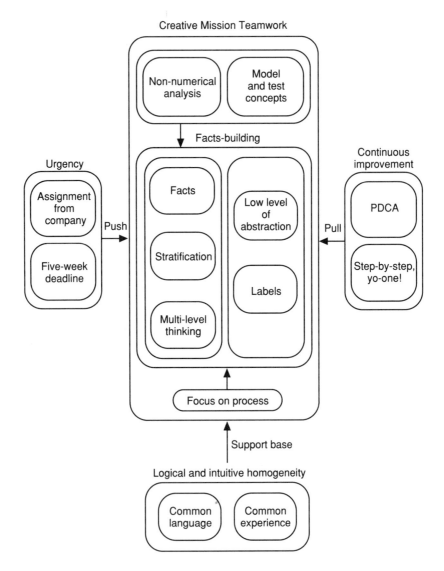

Figure 9-9. Principles Applied by the CQM Team

ment. We didn't fix our mission concretely at the beginning of our study. Instead, we turned the PDCA cycle many times in the five-week period, moving step-by-step with plenty of opportunity for feedback and reflection. This enabled a reasonable five-week goal and solution to emerge. We resisted the impulse to try to seek a perfect answer or unattainable quality of answer, assuming more PDCA in the future.

The design study report concludes with the following observation from the team:

> The team worked in a very process-oriented way, following the tenets of TQM, and found these practices to provide a quantum leap in productivity of the planning and decision-making process. The team used the KJ Method of analyzing qualitative facts as a substitute for less structured discussion. By agreeing, as a team, on each process to follow before embarking on it, the team was able to work rapidly and achieve consensus on both substance and presentation of these complex issues within the five-week time frame.[4]

Team Activities in a Functional Group — QC Circles

The description of cross-functional teamwork focused on mechanisms for avoiding conflict and gave an example of how to quickly develop a team that needed to be effective over a task of limited duration. QC circle members are from within a single functional group, which reduces the potential for conflicts and promotes long-term development of individual and team skill.[5]

In Japan, a quality control circle is a small group of about three to ten workers in whose activities all members participate. If seven employees work together in the same production line (i.e., form a natural work group), all seven participate in the circle activities; no one is left out. The circle has a twofold work-related objective: quality control to minimize the quality fluctuation in products and services, and improvement of quality in products and services. In achieving these objectives the group hopes to work toward the development of the individual worker, which is its main goal.

Two principal features enable the QC circle to reach its goal. First, it applies appropriate process improvement methods, which its members have to learn and apply to the problems they take up. Without this methodology, it would be difficult to improve the quality of a product. Second, QC circle activities are voluntary. The workers decide whether they want to set up a circle or not.[6] If they do organize a circle, the choice of problem to focus on is also theirs: they decide on the manner of data gathering, on the planning of countermeasures, and on other matters. Every step of the way, it is they who decide. In a true QC circle, there is no such thing as an order from above.

However, someone in management must remain responsible for a team's improvements. Otherwise the organization could lose control of its activities and adversely affect customer satisfaction. A system for providing permission from a team's management is very important, but maintaining control without disempowering a team is a delicate business. Several CQM companies have found it effective for management to suggest the initial problem areas (but not the theme), or to review the theme together. Management also may need to review the implementation plan, especially if it affects others. The trick is to maintain awareness of what the team is doing without guiding the team too much, trusting good improvement process to produce useful results and then standing behind those results. Of course, if a team is at risk of going seriously astray, management must provide more guidance.

Problem solving in the QC circle is a continuous process. Often a group will begin by tackling simple problems — such as cleanliness in their workshop or miscommunication between workers — and move on to more complex ones, especially problems in product quality, productivity, and those that affect multiple groups. This continuity is possible because the company supports the group. The company gives permission for QC circle activities to be held during work hours and provides conference rooms for meetings. This support, without which the QC circle cannot function, provides the group with an institutional framework.

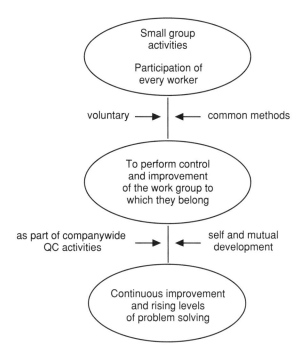

Figure 9-10. QC Circles

The QC circle also gives workers the opportunity for self-development — this is one of the most important aspects of QC circles. Through the problem-solving process as well as meetings, workers learn from each other's strengths; during QC circle conventions, circles share with one another the processes (not the results) they have discovered to be beneficial to their workshops. Finally, QC circles can expand the improvement area by including suppliers, multiple circles, and the like.

From a company viewpoint, the most important function of QC circles is to institutionalize the dual function of work for the participants.

The invention of the QC circle was the invention of a new kind of teamwork. Since Ishikawa's original work with quality control circles in 1962, there are now five million participants in

Japan, and QC circles in 60 countries. Perhaps one-third of the companies in Japan that have more than 30 employees have QC circles. Japan has enormous experience in establishing QC circles and using them for the long-term development of individual and team skill. Let us therefore study a famous example from Japan — the Ladybug Circle.

Teamwork Case Study: Evolution of a Japanese Team

The following description is excerpted from the translation of a paper and presentation by Yoshiko Fujino and Kimiko Kimura.[7]

Kobayashi Kosei is a leading cosmetic maker whose products are used throughout Japan. Our Sayama plant is located in Sayama City, Saitama Prefecture. At this plant, situated on a 110,000-square-meter site and surrounded by greenery and the fragrance of tea, 950 workers work, full of vigor. At the production headquarters to which we belong, 150 circles are energetically engaged in QC activities daily, under the overall headquarters policy of "building groups that learn and that struggle actively. . . ." All the QC activity organizations are defined as parts of the TQC-promoting organization. Wider linkages to sustain the activities are provided by the leaders' meetings (for circle leaders) and instructors' meetings (for instructors who provide support "from the rear").

At our specific workplace, our assigned work is the filling, packing, and finishing process for cosmetic products, which ranges from putting the cosmetic materials into containers to packing the products in boxes. The work force is divided into specialized squads, such as the Cream Squad, the Milky Lotion Squad, and so forth, but depending on the product, a squad may become short of personnel. Our squad's particular mission is to fill such personnel shortages, for we are the Relief and Reinforcement Squad. . . . Each morning after the chores (morning meeting), we disperse among the different squads; such has been our life and work as wandering workers.

Our circle consists of seven middle-aged female part-timers whose average age is 45.[8] As soon as I joined the company in 1979, my life as a wandering worker started. As a trainee, I could barely handle half of the volume of an average worker, and regular employees young enough to be my children would shout out: "Old lady, don't be so slow! You are really more of a hindrance!" If there were some defective products, then it was always the fault of us older part-timers: "It's your fault." I was getting rather dissatisfied with life as a wandering floater, and my footsteps were dragging as I commuted to work each day.

On top of all this, there was another large burden of QC circle activities. Our circle was formed on the recommendation of our superiors, but our feelings were that as part-timers who just worked slotted hours we could not have meetings delay our returning home. We took a stand of "didn't do it, don't know it, and can't do it," and so ours was a circle without even a shred of motivation or energy.

In 1981, there was a change in our squad leader, and we got a new woman chief who was full of motivation and energy toward her work and the work of the squad. Seeing that we were lacking in vitality and cheerfulness, she suggested that we have some interviews and social activities with her, in order to brighten our workplace. After we had interviews and meals together several times, it became much easier for us to talk about our families, discuss our problems at work, and so forth. Thus, these occasions served as opportunities for cleansing our hearts.

Next came the study sessions. Studying after work, when we were exhausted, was not always effective. Then she assigned material that we could not absorb as our homework, and she conducted tests on top of all that! It got to the point that we wanted to scream at her "You devilish chief!" On just such an occasion, the chief gave a notebook to each one of us, saying, "It's a present. If there is anything that you cannot understand, please write it down, okay?" When we wrote down things that we did not understand, she would write comments in response to them and would encourage us, "Please keep it up! A little more to go." We were moved by the chief's enthusiasm, and now it was our turn to show our true mettle. So we began to talk about the problems that existed in the different squads to which we were assigned, and as we made contributions in those squads, our work in those squads (with which we were also fed up) became that much more enjoyable. We, who had no motivation for work, began to desire to use what we were learning in our work.

In 1982, a large-scale production of small-sized products was planned for execution in a short time period. Since specialized squads alone were not sufficient to meet the delivery dates, it was decided that the people in the relief squad would also be assigned to production work. All members of our circle grasped onto "An Operation to Annihilate Shortcomings in Work Stages for Product A" as an ideal chance for us to apply what we had learned, together.

However, this production period was going to last for only one month. To be able to make improvements in this short period, we decided to collect information on shortcomings related to work stages from the specialized squads who had been engaged in production from an earlier period. From the data we gathered, it became clear that the preparatory work was very important, so we put this insight into practice with the motto, "Eight minutes to set up for work." As a result, we exceeded the goals we set and made significant improvements in a short period of time.

This QC theme was honored with an Award of Excellence at the Women's (QC) Meeting in the company, where it was decided that we would take part in the company-wide quality control contest. We felt good that we had tried so hard. This feeling gave us additional motivation for further progress. . . .

Because of our meetings and our efforts to gather data, we were often late in getting home, which caused much inconvenience for our husbands and children. Dissatisfaction grew accordingly.

Around this time, the husband of one of our members was hospitalized, and the family was in distress because they could not harvest their crop of citrons. So we invited members of our families to join us in helping this family; it was a great success, and our support was greatly appreciated. With this as the ice-breaker, we began to have singing contests, with a *karaoke* (a music-accompaniment tape player) and other events, and our family members gradually began to develop a better understanding of the good qualities of QC circle activities.

In this way, we prepared for, and participated in, the companywide quality control contest and won the Cattleya Gold Prize. We took turns taking the award certificate and the tape recording of our presentation home, and we shared the joys of receiving this award with our family members.

The presentation goes on to specify more of the specific improvements the Ladybug Circle created, and describes various appraisals of the successful improvement of the circle's activities from 1979 to 1984. Note the balance of various factors in the overall assessment of the circle's activities over the five years. The factors were

- extent of applications
- study
- recreational activities
- extent of family cooperation
- meeting conduct
- themes completed
- number of suggestions for improvements

At least two conclusions can be drawn from this list of criteria. First, team activities clearly support human values in the workplace. Teams that sacrifice all personal life for productivity will not win any awards or respect. Second, the process of improvement activities is valued more than the output of those activities, the improvements themselves. Evaluation of QC circle activities is detailed in the bible of QC circle activities, *QC Circle Koryo*, and its working manual, *How to Operate QC Circle Activities.*[9]

Small Group Dynamics: Evolution of Enthusiasm and Effectiveness

Let's analyze the development of the Ladybug Circle by examining Figure 9-11, starting from the top. A team is formed. The team views improvement as an extra job. The new chief, an enthusiastic change agent, begins encouraging the team and fostering closer communication. This gives the team some feeling of belonging.

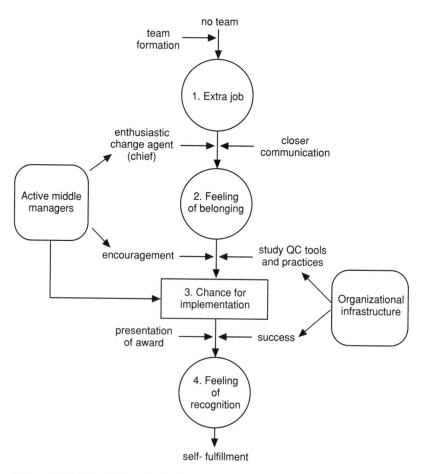

Figure 9-11. Evolution of the Ladybug Team

Additional encouragement is provided. Eating together is a basic methodology of starting teamwork in Japan (men often start with drinking). Eating together and having face-to-face conversations are standard management practice to encourage workers to feel good about QC circles. It is okay to focus on socialization and have personal discussions in this situation.

Study is encouraged, with notebooks distributed, and so on. Individual counseling and encouragement are provided. Also, only a few tools are taught at first. These are used three to four times, then studied or learned again, and then applied to three to four themes. Shiba's experience in European QC circles suggests that middle management support is lacking at this stage. The managers say "teaching is not my job" or "I taught them everything at the beginning." This isn't teaching, it is initialization.

Next comes an opportunity for implementation — being allowed actual use of improvement skills in one's real job.

Next, the team must have success. If the QC circle fails to solve a problem, it won't use the tool again. So choosing the right theme is important. The rewards of success are the sense of accomplishment that comes from solving a problem and the chance to present the team's story at a QI story meeting. The team is also given a tangible award or prize. Success and reward lead to a feeling of recognition and, eventually, to a sense of fulfillment.

The organizational infrastructure to implement the above will be discussed later.

Triggers for Improvement

Shoji Shiba and his graduate students have studied winning QC circles that appear in the proceedings of the All-Japan QC Circle Conferences and polls of work unit supervisors and circle members.[10] Most teams that perform at award-winning levels develop in the pattern described above. There is also a startling contrast between performance progress in daily work and performance progress in improvement activity. In daily work, improvement in performance in both physical labor and engineering activity is closely related to the length of career, shown by the straight sloping line in Figure 9-12.

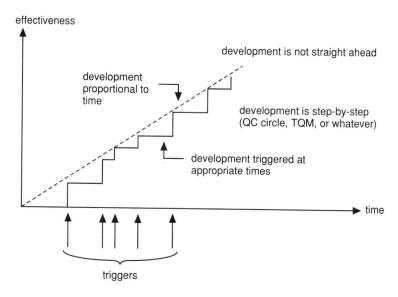

Figure 9-12. Pattern of Improvement in Daily Work

By sharp contrast, in QC circle activities the development of the team is not a function of time but is a function of developmental triggers. QC circles rise through a series of plateaus, shown by the irregular steps in the figure. There are identifiable "triggers" that move teams to higher stages of performance:[11]

- enthusiasm and communication
- encouragement of study
- opportunity for application
- success and recognition

Just as managers diagnose QI stories to determine what skills a team needs to perform better next time, so must they diagnose teams to determine when they are ready to move to the next level of development. It is their responsibility to monitor the developmental status of teams and to see that these triggers are present at the right time for each team. One of a manager's most important jobs is to educate subordinates, providing proper levels of training at proper times.

Triggers are created by management (the arrival of the new chief, in the Ladybug case), teaching new advanced tools, and the chance to apply the tools and achieve success. The manager must stay aware of the team's stage of development and give necessary triggers and support.

Let's review the details of Professor Shiba's research relating to Figure 9-11, which diagrams the evolution of the Ladybug team.[12] The initial condition is one of no team as such. The first phase is willingly initiating QC circle activities but viewing them as an extra job, something that employees aren't obligated to do but do anyway, for whatever reason. For example, 125 corporate QC circle facilitators were asked what the reaction was when QC circles were introduced into their companies.[13] Reaction was distributed as follows:

- 44 percent: "I can't understand why QC circle activities are necessary. Therefore I don't want to do it."
- 25 percent: "I don't like to sacrifice my free time for QC circle activities."
- 12 percent: "I don't know how to start QC circle activities."
- 8 percent: "There are no good teaching materials in our work group."
- 6 percent: "The leader of the circle has no capability."
- 3 percent: "We can't find a good theme to solve."

Almost 90 percent of the responses were, "It's not a necessary part of my job and I don't want to do it." About 30 percent were identifying excuses for not doing QC circle activities well. Of course, the perception that QC circle activities constitute an "extra job" is directly related to people's perceptions of their job. If "job" means only the SDCA cycle of daily work, then the PDCA cycle of improvement activities does in fact add to the job as seen by the worker.

Remember, this is the typical response of most of the teams that later become the best teams in Japan. Empirically, then, there is no cultural magic that enables first-level Japanese workers to form effective improvement teams instantly. Or, if there is such a thing, it resides at higher levels: within middle management, within organizational infrastructure, or within regional and national facilities.

In the second phase, the team members feel that they belong to a true team, whose members feel a special closeness to each other. The third phase involves working on a theme/problem area felt to be both important and improvable. In the fourth phase, the workers have made the improvement, have been recognized for it before their peers, and feel fulfilled by the team's continuing work. In the words of Yoshiko Fujino of the Ladybug Circle:

> Even though we started as wandering birds, with the cooperation of the circle members and consideration from others, we found out that even middle-aged "old ladies" can do a good job, and we have grown more self-confident as a result. In this process we have been able to get a tangible sense of the wonderful nature of QC activities as well. This year we are tackling with even greater energy the job of eliminating defective work processes and waste, and we have broadened the scope of our activities. As for the future, we are determined to polish our capabilities still further to create quality that will be appreciated, and to overcome all difficulties and obstacles through resolve and resistance. In this way, we firmly intend to continue to burn the light of our QC circle.

Throughout an organization, teams are constantly being formed, reconfigured, and dissolved. Therefore, even in the most supportive of corporate environments, there will be teams in all phases of enthusiasm and effectiveness. For example, when members of the leading QC circles in the Japanese steel industry, where QC circles have long been successful, were surveyed by the labor union on the extent of their interest in doing QC circle activities, they answered as follows:[14]

- 19.2 percent: very enthusiastic to do it
- 53.1 percent: so far, somewhat interested
- 23.0 percent: don't want to do it, but will tolerate it
- 2.4 percent: absolutely no interest in doing it
- 2.3 percent: other

Similarly, the effectiveness of teams shows a distribution.[15] Effectiveness, as compiled in Table 9-3, is indicated by the speed with which problems are solved. (Presumably, this population of contest winners excludes teams that move quickly because the themes are trivial.) Meetings per month and attendance are probably more indicative of enthusiasm, or perhaps of the effectiveness of the organizational infrastructure and a middle management that creates both the enthusiasm and the time and willingness to meet.

Table 9-3. Stages of Team Development and Their Characteristics

Stages of development of the QC Circle	1	2	3	4
Themes completed per year	2.5	5.2	7.7	10.2
Number of meetings per month	2.0	4.6	4.6	6.6
Attendance	59.2	77.5	86.3	ʙ100

QC Circles in the United States versus Japan

Are there cultural factors that make implementation of team improvement activities in Japan different from their implementation in the United States? There is perhaps a more constructive and focused way of approaching this subject. When the CQM design team visited a variety of U.S. and Japanese companies, its subjective impression was that differences between company cultures overshadowed differences between national cultures. If one were to consider companies according to national stereotypes, Hitachi would probably be described as being like an American company (one of their primary company values, known by everyone from the bus driver on up, is "frontier spirit"), and Florida Power & Light would be described as being like a Japanese company for the discipline and structure of its improvement activities at all levels of the company.

The implication for Western managers is in planning and publicizing implementation of work-group teams. Immediate competence and enthusiasm in 100 percent of the work force are just never seen. Founding an implementation on an expectation to the contrary is a mistake that can lead to abandonment of goals and actual failure by default. It would be well to establish realistic expectations regarding responses, enthusiasm, and performance.

To facilitate the design of implementations, we present a distinctly American case, that of quality circles in Digital Equipment Corporation's Hudson semiconductor facility.[16]

Case Study: Employee Circles Program
at Digital's Semiconductor Facility

Digital's Semiconductor Interconnect Technology Division has 5,000 employees at seven sites worldwide. Its semiconductor facility in Hudson, Massachusetts, is an engineering and manufacturing facility employing 2,130 people, with 800 employees in manufacturing. All nonexempt employees and 30 percent of the exempt employees at this site are involved in employee circle teamwork activities. Employee circles at Digital's Hudson facility are similar to quality circles in Japan.

The employee circles at the Hudson facility have worked on the following types of improvement activities:

- simplifying specifications and developing consistent format for spec writing
- reducing fumes in photo and etch area
- decreasing rework rate
- increasing efficiency of room layout

Digital has attempted return-on-investment analysis of its employee circle activities, but has found that many projects are not measurable in financial terms (which would be expected of initial QC circle activities). For these it has done force field analysis to highlight the benefits of improvement efforts. For the 20 percent of the improvement efforts that were financially quantifiable, return on investment increased about fourfold in absolute dollars over the period from fiscal year 1989 through fiscal year 1990.

The 1990 objectives for the Hudson facility's employee circle activities are to:

- improve quality
- reduce errors
- inspire teamwork
- create problem-solving capabilities
- improve communications

The graph in Figure 9-13 shows the number of employee circles at the Hudson facility.

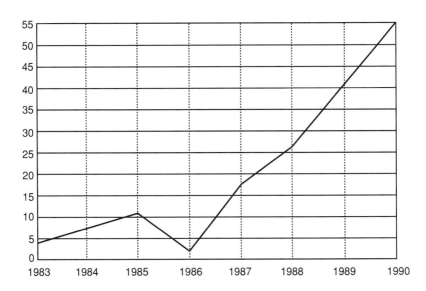

Figure 9-13. Number of Circles at the Hudson Facility

Managers of the employee circle program attribute its growth to three features: mandatory participation for nonexempt employees; visible support from upper management; and a training and support structure.

Mandatory Participation for Nonexempt Employees

The employee circle activities began on a voluntary basis with the nonexempt employees in 1983. Five years later, employee circles became mandatory for nonexempt employees. For each nonexempt employee, 39 hours of daily work and a 1-hour employee circle meeting are required. The employee circle meeting is held at the same time each week for a given employee circle. The goal of the Hudson facility is 100 percent involvement of all employees in five years.

It was necessary to make the employee circle activities mandatory instead of voluntary because use of employee circle activities became an integral part of the business and not a one-time program; it included all shifts, and there is less individual and team development if the activities are voluntary.[17]

Visible Support from Upper Management

Upper management provided visible support by designating certain rooms and times for employee circle meetings and promotional and recognition activities. Promotional methods include leader certificates, member certificates, and circle T-shirts. Management recognition methods include (1) a management presentation recognition; (2) an annual circle recognition day for a recognition of best circles and best projects in the categories of "most improved quality of worklife," "most opportunity for financial savings," and "best processes and procedures"; and (3) a recognition wall.

Training and Support Structure

Nonexempt employees train for 10 days every year. Employee circle facilitators get eight weeks of training. Basic training modules exist for brainstorming, data gathering, data format and graphs, Pareto analysis, and presentation skills. Advanced training modules exist for histograms, control charts, and scatter diagrams. A support structure for employee circles is also provided, as shown in Figure 9-14.

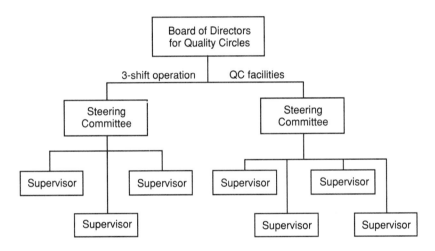

Figure 9-14. QC Circle Support Structure

The staff support for employee circles is four full-time people. Employee circle activities exist in the United States, South America, Europe, and Asia. The equivalent activities for exempt employees — small group improvement activities (SGIA) — are just beginning in the United States.

Voluntarism and Motivation

If QC circle activities are to reap benefits, management must systematize all the necessary elements. It must provide the necessary infrastructure for encouragement, space, scheduling, training, team formations, facilitators, recognition, and so forth. Without these, QC circle activities simply won't last. Many U.S. companies with QC circle programs have seen them die. To create the necessary infrastructure, management must be keenly aware of the need for management support and experience. In particular, it must deal with three key issues: participation, real results, and diagnosis.

Participation

The ideal in TQM is 100 percent voluntary participation. In the United States and Europe, the starting position is often completely voluntary, which may give only 20 or 30 percent participation (see Figure 9-15). From there it is difficult to move to 100 percent participation without a systematic and comprehensive approach to TQM that emphasizes motivation and support, senior management involvement, and organizational infrastructure.

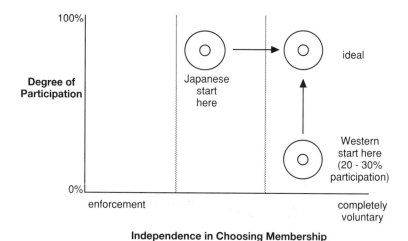

Figure 9-15. Building Voluntary Participation

In Japan and in many notable TQM companies in the United States, high initial participation is encouraged through indirect pressure, influence, and incentives. From there it is relatively easy to move to completely voluntary participation. Indirect pressures might take the following forms: managers persuade people to attend QC circles at other companies and to study QC circles; managers are rated by percentage of participation in QC circles; QC circles are not allowed to function unless all members participate.

Why not just tell people to form QC circles? The answer is related to why QC circles are necessary at all. You need teamwork not only for improvement but also to develop human capacity. The idea is to develop staff abilities and facilitate innovation. However, enforcement means making improvement part of daily work — working to standard and not creating something new. Improvement work needs to be creative and motivating. Without significant participation of work groups in QC circles, QC circles won't work, and the company will lose major improvement possibilities.

Real Results

It is up to management to ensure the success of QC circle activities. QC circles need to gain a sense of achievement. They need to work on something that makes a difference to the company financially. Remember the diagram of the dual function of work. It is management's job to focus the QC circle on the vital few activities that directly increase the customer's satisfaction (see Figure 9-16).

Next come the actual improvement activities — problem-solving steps, the weakness orientation, and the use of market-in concept.

Another team — a QIT or cross-functional team — may be needed to pinpoint the vital few activities that need to be improved. Management needs either to articulate the vital few

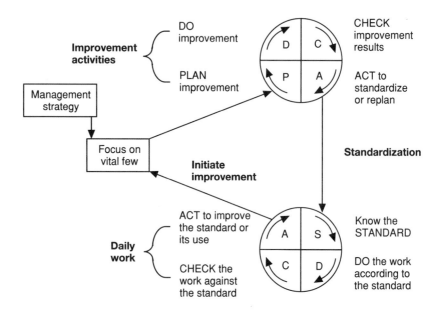

Figure 9-16. Focusing on the Vital Few for Successful QC Circle Activities

directly or to form teams that do. In fact, the extent of (voluntary) QC circle activities can be an indicator of a manager's ability to motivate his or her subordinates.

Diagnosis

The final key strategy is assessment and diagnosis. You must do assessment and diagnosis to find opportunities for further development and the way to future success. Whether you do a QC circle first or later, or use some other type of team, depends on the history and culture of the company. For example, Digital has long had a culture of quality and teamwork; therefore, its QC circles will survive.

According to Shoji Shiba, however, starting TQM with QC circle activities is often not a good idea for U.S. companies. The circles frequently die out for lack of real results because they aren't given a real problem or because middle managers and supervisors don't truly support them. It is very difficult to change the attitudes of middle managers through short-term training or courses. On the other hand, workers and senior managers are quite capable of changing in a short period. One's approach to QC circles must be diagnosed company by company. One of the founders of QC circle activity, Professor Ishikawa, said that QC circles account for one-third to one-fifth of the TQC activities, in a Japanese company.[18] Don't start with QC circles unless middle management is "on board." Even if QC circle teams are inappropriate for your company, you can nonetheless learn the fundamental elements of teams from QC circle activities.

PRINCIPLES FOR ACTIVATING TEAMWORK

Figure 9-17 illustrates seven principles for activating teamwork based on Shoji Shiba's observation of QC circles in Japan.

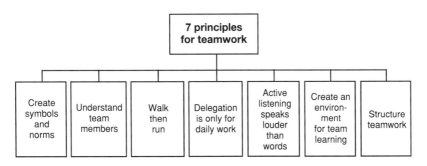

Figure 9-17. Principles for Activating Employee Teamwork

1. Create Symbols and Norms

Symbols and names give a team its external and internal identity. A team name is a first step; for example, the QI team discussed in Chapter 6 called itself the "Errorbusters." Flags, banners, and logos are helpful symbols.

The team leader can be a symbol, as when the CEO leads a team. Behavior norms facilitate teamwork. "Speak from the facts" is a good team norm. It is useful to develop a common language, as the CQM did when its cross-company team met for a week at the start of its five-week study to learn the language of TQM.

2. Understand Team Members

People need different kinds of motivation from leadership at different points. Think in terms of the hierarchy of needs and theory of self-actualization developed by Abraham Maslow (1908-1990) (see Figure 9-18):[19]

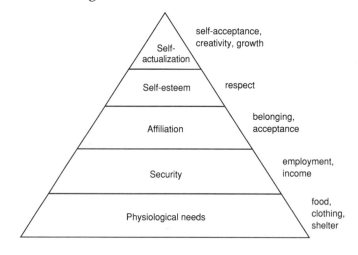

Figure 9-18. Maslow's Hierarchy of Needs

We all have physiological needs, such as food and air. Next in urgency are security needs — a person who fears for his or her job can't think about much else. Beyond that, we want to be affiliated with a group, earn the esteem of the group, and finally achieve self-actualization. The Ladybug case study illustrates the development of a team as it ascends the hierarchy of needs Maslow describes. Team leaders must be aware that fulfillment of team members' needs for affiliation and esteem strengthens the members' personal identities within the team and the organization, as well as their relationships with other team members.

Maslow provides a theoretical framework for understanding needs through his theory of self-actualization, which has four basic elements:

1. Motives are highly complex — no single motive is at work at one time.
2. Hierarchy of needs — in general, lower-level needs must be satisfied before higher-level needs become motivators.
3. A satisfied need is not a motivator — we are always "wanting beings."
4. There are more ways to satisfy higher-level needs than lower-level needs.

To go about understanding team members in a systematic way, leaders are advised to keep a notebook with one page for each team member. Write down the home address of each and impressions of each member's hopes and needs.

3. Walk, Then Run

Teams need early success. Start each team on a problem that is significant but can be solved easily. Choose a problem theme just slightly beyond the team's current knowledge and ability. Provide support for analysis and solution. If there is a big problem to work on, chop it into smaller pieces. As illustrated in Figure 9-19, successive rotations through PDCA make progress possible and teach teams how to be successful. By contrast, a single effort to solve a large problem is likely to be an unmanageable burden, as shown in Figure 9-20.

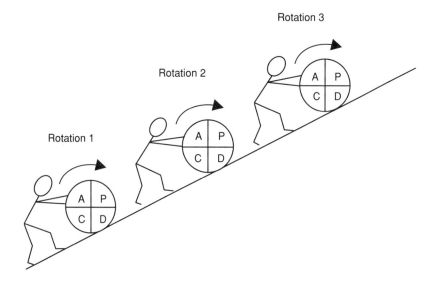

Figure 9-19. Successive Rotations Through PDCA

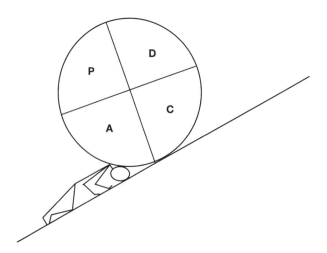

Figure 9-20. Tackling a Large Problem with a Single Effort

4. Delegation Is Only for Daily Work

Do not delegate downward — team members must do the work themselves. Neither should you delegate upward — team members are responsible for finding the solution. The job of improvement cannot be delegated. The need to delegate is a symptom that the wrong people are on the team.

Everyone is equal within a team. The team members themselves have to gather supplies, take meeting minutes, and participate in the problem-solving processes of the team. Some people protest that "my job is making decisions, not doing detailed work." This attitude is incompatible with improvement work. Daily work implies standardized and therefore well-understood work. The purpose of improvement work, however, is to discover new ways of doing things; the issues surrounding improvement work are therefore not well understood beforehand and therefore not delegable.

5. Active Listening Speaks Louder than Words

Psychotherapist Carl Rogers (1902-1989) studied the importance of listening and affirming while listening.[20] Rogers was internationally known for his study and practice of nondirective psychotherapy. Recognizing that a creative problem-solving capacity resides in every individual, he developed techniques for releasing that capacity. These included active listening, unconditional positive regard, empathy, and appropriate nonverbal behavior.

Rogers advised the following principles of active listening:

- Listen with empathy — understand both feeling and content.
- Clarify by restating, paraphrasing, or summarizing.
- Question and explore.

Active listening has the following benefits:

- It reduces defensiveness.

- It enhances self-esteem.
- It encourages cooperation.
- It identifies problems and solutions.

Active listening also involves nonverbal communication. For instance, slouching, looking away, or doing other things says "I don't care" to the speaker.

6. Create an Environment for Team Learning

Creating an environment conducive to team learning involves attending to three elements: the setup of meetings, the physical arrangement of people at meetings, and the psychological rhythm of meetings.

Setting up Meetings

In our experience, actually meeting is the most difficult part of teamwork activities. If you can get all the team members to all the meetings, you've had major success. Half the skill of successful QC circles in Japan (and maybe more so in the United States), is getting the group to meet. The tree diagram below outlines a number of techniques for getting teams to meet reliably.

Prepare. Scheduling is very important. Schedule for the same day every week or month. Consider having meetings at the same time factorywide. Schedule a half-year or year in advance. The agenda must be detailed and plausible. Without a day-by-day, hour-by-hour, minute-by-minute plausible plan for accomplishing all steps of a task, it will be difficult to finish the task in the meeting. Minutes from previous meetings must be available. Flip charts, markers, data charts, and other materials to be used by the teams in the meeting must be prepared in advance.

Don't postpone. This is a most important principle! There are two elements to it: First, schedule the meeting to take place sooner rather than later — teams can't make good progress if meetings are held off for times that are optimally convenient for everyone. Second, once a meeting is scheduled, never postpone it. Once you postpone, that time is irretrievably lost, and there's a good chance the team will not meet again.

Take minutes. Follow up with absentees face-to-face; just sending them the minutes isn't good enough. The leader is responsible for keeping all team members up to speed.

Find substitutes for meetings. One way to deal with the problem of finding time to meet is to do some of the meeting work outside the meeting. Bulletin boards and answering machines (e.g., voice mail) are useful for collecting ideas and comments from team members. We have seen good success in posting Ishikawa diagrams on a bulletin board and having team members stop by individually to brainstorm and add more items. E-mail and computer bulletin boards allow team members to have dialogue without meeting.

Finish effectively. Start and finish on time. Check against the agenda to make sure everything was accomplished and to improve planning for the next meeting. Agree on responsibilities for the next meeting.

Always end with an assignment and fun. Be sure people know their assignments for the next meeting. Consider starting the meeting at a time that permits informal discussion and fraternization at the end of the formal meeting — in Japan this frequently includes a move to a wine shop. We have come to call this the application of "eating and drinking methodology."

These techniques work in Japan. Team leaders must find techniques that work for their own country, company, and team. As the summary in Figure 9-21 suggests, a tree diagram is one tool for identifying such techniques.

Physical Arrangement

The physical arrangement of people in a meeting can be used to focus their attention on the activities of the meeting.

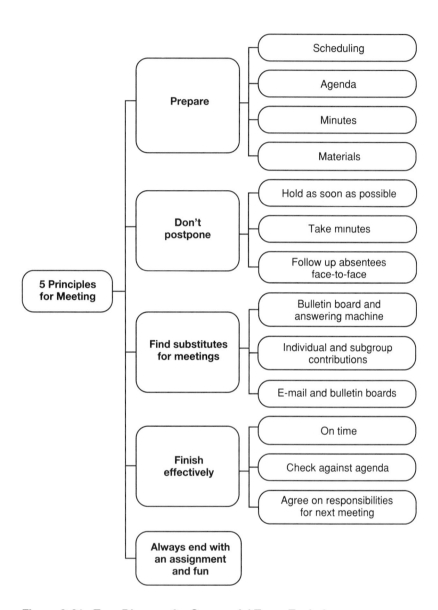

Figure 9-21. Tree Diagram for Successful Team Techniques

Consider, for example, the physical arrangement of people who are meeting to create an Ishikawa diagram or tree diagram, or to use other tools. There are three things to note. First, the participants sit along a table facing a nearby wall on which paper is posted. With this arrangement it is difficult to avoid concentration on the paper. No one should be allowed to sit between the table and the wall.

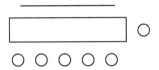

Second, the physical arrangement includes writing the theme of the session in letters two inches high, so that everyone in the group can see the theme all the time. This prevents confusion and lack of concentration. At no time is the theme out of sight; therefore, it should not be out of mind.

Third, the size of the table is such that people are forced to sit shoulder-to-shoulder facing the paper. This arrangement promotes participation in the group process and discourages side conversations.

If the participants sit as shown in the following figure, people will naturally talk across the table to each other, except for the one person who has distanced himself from the proceedings.

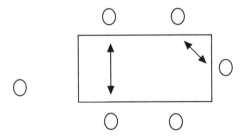

The distance between people in the way seating is arranged affects their sense of relationship to each other. Edward T. Hall's research on the subject is relevant to the physical setup for TQM group activities.[21] Hall has defined four types of distance between people:

1. One foot is an intimate distance; this is the distance between husband and wife, mother and child, sisters and brothers. TQM group work seeks relationships that are closer psychologically and more participatory than most normal business relationships.
2. Four to five feet is the distance between business colleagues and friends.
3. Ten to twelve feet is the distance at meetings and seminars. In a meeting or a seminar situation, try having the speaker first stand about 15 feet from listeners and then stand 30 feet from listeners. Moving farther away from listeners noticeably changes the speaker's relationship to the audience. During a meeting the instructor should be about 10 to 12 feet from most of the participants. After the formal session, the instructor can move to the 4-foot distance for an informal discussion and refreshments.
4. Twenty-five to thirty feet is the distance of ceremony, used for example, when a CEO gives a prize to a staff member or when the president of the United States presents the Baldrige Award.

Psychological Rhythm

Human beings have a difficult time concentrating for very long (one reason why TV commercials are so short). Accordingly, some of the 7 management and planning tools have been broken down into steps that better match people's span of concentration.

However, even with the step-by-step process (as shown in the following figure), the participants' concentration goes down over time.

Therefore, it is helpful to do something periodically to reenergize the team. Yo-one, with its standing and cheering (see Preface), is intended to reenergize members and restore their concentration to original levels (shown by the larger jump in the center of the following figure).

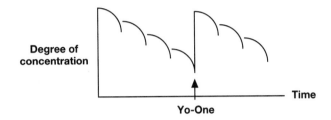

Part of being a team leader or facilitator is considering physical arrangements and psychological rhythm and how to structure them for effective team meetings.

7. Structure Teamwork (Group and Individual Work)

Many people misunderstand teamwork. Teamwork is not just work done in a group. Teamwork requires two kinds of effort: group work and individual work. In group work, consensus is sought on targets (tasks to be done) and the methods of accomplishing the tasks, and then tasks are allocated to individuals or combinations of individuals for execution. Much of the work of the team is actually done as the work of individuals or combinations of individuals. Thus teamwork combines group work and individual work, as shown in Figure 9-22.

For example, making a cause-and-effect diagram or a KJ diagram can alternate individual work and group work. Writing the theme, warming up, and distributing labels are group work. Writing labels is individual work. Scrubbing (clarifying the labels so that everyone can understand them) is group work. Even within steps, individual work and group work can be alternated.

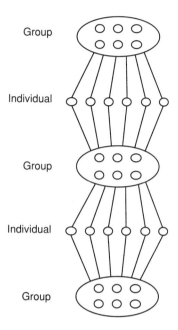

Figure 9-22. Group and Individual Components of Teamwork

As stated earlier, the purpose of group work is to decide on the target (purpose), decide how to do it, and then to allocate jobs to individuals. Individuals do their assigned jobs, which constitute much of a team's work. Then the group evaluates the results and decides on new targets, allocations, and so on. A QC circle follows this alternation. Such groups meet only one or two hours every two to four weeks. If people work only as a group, they can't get the job done even if they meet more often. Coordination of the group disturbs individual efforts, thus hindering creativity and decreasing the team's effectiveness. The most effective system balances individual creativity with group consensus. The group work makes its creative contribution through its task selection efforts.

CREATIVITY IN TEAM PROCESSES

American culture places much emphasis on individual heroes. Many people see the group aspects of TQM as a hindrance to creativity. This concern perhaps reflects an unawareness of the differences between

- creating an entirely original idea and creating an original arrangement or form of existing ideas
- individual creativity and team creativity

Much of team creativity involves creating new forms of existing ideas. In fact, few people ever create an original idea that is profound and important. How many have come up with revolutionary concepts of marketing, math, physics, music, or home repair? Some do, of course, but even these original thinkers often have only one or two new ideas in a lifetime.

Yet creating new arrangements or forms of existing ideas can be very powerful. This is what engineering is all about, the application of scientific ideas. This is what the human resources staff does, and what the sales management staff, the marketing staff, and the manufacturing staff do. We all take existing learning and practices we learn from others and apply them to our own situation. We do this in school, we do it at work by seeking out wise supervisors, and we do it by simply watching others to learn what works.

An important but underused word in English is *apperception,* the combining of two or more known ideas to come up with a new idea. Apperception is the predominant (and perhaps only) form of human creativity. The question is: Are you more apt to exercise such creativity alone or in a group? Keeping in mind that TQM is a mass movement and companies have but a few geniuses, you see why companies get their best leverage out of teamwork.

Most important work done is done as part of a team. This is one of the great powers of a company. Teams of people can work together for mutual benefit on any problem too large or too complex for one person to solve. This advantage is missing from a university, where tenure is individual.

In any case, team creation of new arrangements or forms of ideas is nothing to be ashamed of.

The important issue is how to harness group creativity to the task of building on existing ideas. The answer may cause discomfort to some because it flies in the face of conventional practice. Some of the most effective results of group creativity come from copying existing practices that are known to work. Yet people often excuse themselves from doing this by saying things like, "It has to be adapted to our culture," or, "Our problem is unique," or, "I don't learn that way." In an attempt to create something new, they change the methods in a way that has an unknown effect. The other way of getting good results from group creativity is by organizing the group so that it works harmoniously, with everyone's individual quirks subordinated to the smooth running of the group. Again, however, people avoid using process to facilitate group harmony and eliminate time wasted on individual foibles by saying "We can't blindly apply process," or, "I have a right to speak my mind"; then they go on to disrupt the group process with their own concerns.

In most cases in almost any field of business, science, or art, a person with great creativity is a person of great skill acquired through individual discipline (systematic study, analysis, practice). Groups are an ideal environment for cultivating such discipline. Creativity is not just surprising activity; creativity is the inspired application of skill.

A team also offers opportunity for synthesis. The role of synthesis is often undervalued, when in fact it is a major element of TQM. Great synthesizers perform their own acts of magic, bringing meaning to disparate ideas, absorbing, reordering and translating. But companies do not have to wait for the arrival of individual synthesizers. Teams and team processes offer a more ready source of synthesis.

Creativity comes about with teamwork, which, as you recall, includes both group work and individual work. There is room for creativity at all levels. Teamwork increases the possibilities for creativity.

NOTES

1. This figure is an adaptation and extension of Masaaki Imai, *Kaizen,* 7 (Figures 1-3 and 1-4).
2. A fourth type of team, recently introduced as an innovation in daily work, is the self-managed work group, where members of the team decide who leads and who does what. Since teams are part of daily work, rather than improvement work, they will not be discussed further here.
3. This case study was prepared by David Walden (Bolt Beranek and Newman, Inc., Cambridge, MA), who participated in the study. The design study is comprehensively documented in *The CQM Design Study* (CQM report).
4. Ibid.
5. Union of Japanese Scientists and Engineers, *How to Operate QC Circle Activities* (Tokyo: JUSE, 1985).
6. In Japan, a QC circle is officially organized when it is registered with QC Circle Headquarters (in the Union of Japanese Scientists and Engineers). Company management is not involved directly; however, as will be seen shortly, management can nurture growth of QC circles in many ways.
7. Yoshiko Fujino, "QC Circle Activities Which Were Put Up by the Iron Will of Part-Time Oba-Chan (Aged Ladies) and Kimiko Kimura, FQC no. 265 (Toyko: JUSE,

1984). The case was presented in English at the IC QCC convention, Toyko, 1985.

8. Part-time employees work full-time but are employed for one-year terms.

9. Union of Japanese Scientists and Engineers, *QC Circle Koryo: General Principles of the QC Circle* (Tokyo: JUSE, 1980); and Idem., *How to Operate QC Circle Activities* (Tokyo: JUSE, 1985).

10. *All Japan QC Circle Conference Proceedings*, Tokyo (annual).

11. Ichiro Nakajima, "Analysis of Development Process of QC Circles," Master's Thesis, Management and Policy Science Program, University of Tsukuba, Japan, 1983.

12. Note that the model of evolution in the figure describes a single work group teaming voluntarily. Evolution of cross-functional teams brought together by management may follow a different course. Joiner's *Team Handbook* describes a sequence of "forming, storming, norming, and performing." Peter R. Scholtes, *Team Handbook* (Madison, WI: Joiner Associates, Inc., 1988), 6-4 to 6-7.

13. Masaaki Inoue, "Effectiveness of Promotional Activities," Master's Thesis, Management and Policy Science Program, University of Tsukuba, Japan, 1984.

14. *Research Review* 130 (Japan Federation of Steelworkers, Jan. 1982).

15. Nakajima, "Development Process of QC Circles."

16. The case was prepared by Dr. Del Thorndike (Digital Equipment Corporation, Maynard, MA). Dr. Thorndike gave a presentation and showed videotapes of the activities of quality circles at Digital's Hudson facility in a 1990 CQM course.

17. One DEC observer, however, notes that the question of whether to mandate QC circle participation is still being debated, given the success of "voluntary" but

heavily promoted and supported QC circles like those at Milliken.

18. Kaoru Ishikawa, "The Current Situation in Exporting the Japanese Style of QC," *Communicators*, vol. 9, no. 16.
19. Dr. Phillip Gulley (Bolt Beranek and Newman, Inc.) prepared this material on Maslow.
20. Dr. Philip Gulley prepared the material on Carl Rogers.
21. Edward T. Hall, *The Hidden Dimension* (New York: Anchor Books, 1990). Hall calls these four distances intimate, personal, social, and public. An illustration similar to the preceding figure can be found on page 109 of Hall's book.

10

Initiation Strategies

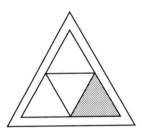

TQM is a mass movement — it is intended to reach everyone in the company. But TQM is also new to most companies, and it is difficult to figure out how to mobilize everyone. A mobilization strategy is needed. An effective strategy must have three parts: CEO involvement, strategies for introduction, and organizational infrastructure. The first two parts are the subject of this chapter; the last is the subject of Chapter 11.

CEO INVOLVEMENT

The most important aspect of a mobilization strategy is CEO involvement (see Figure 10-1).[1] Successful introductions of TQM in Japan, Europe, and the United States start from involvement at the top. Later sections give fuller definition to "involvement."

The next most important criterion is the absence of strong opposition from the workers (e.g., trade union resistance). But opposition of the workers' organization can be slowly reduced by the efforts of the CEO to build trust and create a role for the union in TQM implementation.

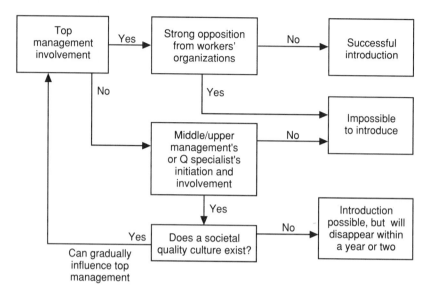

Figure 10-1. The Importance of CEO Involvement in TQM Mobilization

The middle or upper management of a company may try to introduce TQM without the CEO's involvement, but the long-term success of such an approach depends on a strong societal quality culture. Sufficiently strong societal learning of TQM might provide the necessary impetus in the absence of CEO impetus. Societal learning, described in Chapter 16, refers to the set of practices and institutions that allow companies to learn TQM from other companies. This approach sometimes works in Japan, but since societal learning is presently weak in Europe and the United States, TQM is unlikely to succeed outside of Japan without strong CEO leadership.

It is conceivable for a plant manager or division manager to create an island of TQM, if this manager is in effect the CEO of his or her operation. In such cases, a manager must control the operation and have no interference from above that negates divisional TQM efforts. However, when the sponsor moves or departs, such TQM islands tend to disappear.

A company should hesitate before trying to introduce TQM without strong motivation on the part of the CEO. Without CEO involvement there is a strong chance of failure, and once a company fails, success becomes more difficult; the initial failure creates a belief within the company that TQM doesn't work, which will make the retry difficult.

Shoji Shiba has collected Japanese data indicating that if the CEO is involved in QC circle implementation, additional levels of management and workers can be involved in turn.[2] The CEO can bring on board the upper managers and facilitators (people who help with the detailed planning of the QC circle implementation). If the CEO can make upper managers and facilitators enthusiastic, then middle managers can be convinced. Finally, the middle managers and facilitators bring in workers from the shop or individual contributors. This might be called the domino theory (Figure 10-2).

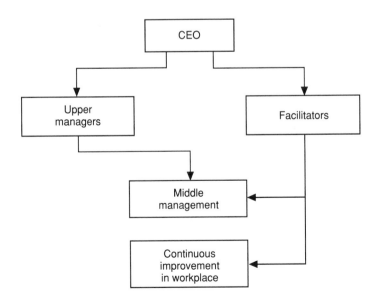

Figure 10-2. Domino Theory of Implementation

The data supporting the domino theory are shown in Figure 10-3. Shiba measured levels of promotion of QC circles at various levels within many companies. He then sorted companies into groups according to how actively the CEO was involved.

In Japan, many companies are subsidiaries of parent companies, and these parent companies put pressure on their subsidiaries to implement QC circles. If the CEO is very involved, the facilitators can be highly effective and other functions (such as managers' involvement and education) can be high. If CEO involvement is low, the facilitators still may try to implement (as in the bottom curve), but quality activities will remain weak. Empirically, the CEO's level of involvement is an upper limit on the other quality activities of the company.

What does CEO or top management involvement mean? In world-class companies the authors have visited, it means hands-on participation in TQM, as is shown in Table 10-1. This table also characterizes unsuccessful cases; note that simply approving and delegating, which is standard management practice, didn't work.[3]

We have provided empirical evidence of the necessity for CEO leadership of TQM. There are also theoretical bases for CEO leadership. First, as both military and business strategists observe, a two-front war is much more difficult to fight than a one-front war. Splitting CEO attention and resources is more difficult than focusing them. It is more difficult to lead simultaneous crusades for cost reduction, ubiquitous adherence to standards, faster design, and so on, than it is to lead a crusade for quality, which can encompass all of these.

Second, because true charisma is rare, most leaders need a leadership style that depends on visible participation and articulation of values and strategies more than sheer force of personality.[4] TQM has evolved many standardized opportunities for CEO involvement: from initial visits to TQM companies to involvement in planning and piloting, running the corporate quality committee, goal setting, taking and then teaching the

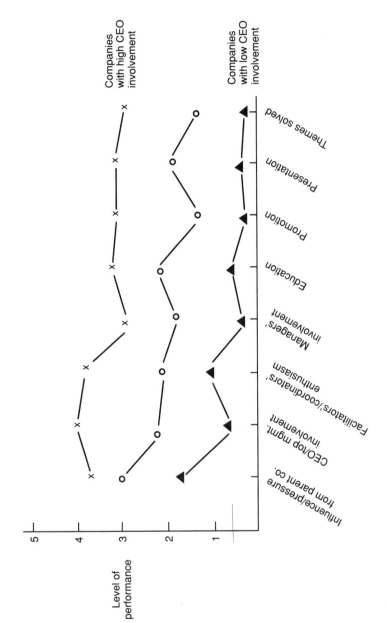

Figure 10-3. CEO Involvement: Domino Effect

Table 10-1. CEO Activity in Successful and Unsuccessful Cases

Type of Activity	CEO Activity in Unsuccessful Cases	CEO Activity in Successful Cases
Decision to implement TQM	Approve decision	Make decision
Plan	Appoint those in charge, i.e., delegate to quality specialist	Initiate planning for implementation
Do		Participate in improvement activities
Check	Evaluate results	Evaluate process/results
Act		Initiate next phase

first courses, diagnosing QI stories at events, and the presidential audit.

The next question, then, is what motivates the CEO to lead? The CEO's motivation has two parts. The first part is learning. Most of the CEO's learning comes from outside the company. Examples of external sources are seminars, pressure from the parent company, communication with other CEOs, and personal experience. Personal experience is particularly influential. The CEO of Xerox saw Fuji Xerox. Marshall MacDonald of Florida Power & Light saw the Kansai Electric Company. At least in Europe, Shiba's surveys indicate that only about 20 percent of the information that motivates a CEO toward TQM comes from inside the company.[5]

However, learning alone is not enough to provide the necessary motivation to the CEO. Learning only creates interest in actually doing TQM. Another trigger is needed. That trigger — the second motivator for a CEO — is fear, or crisis: increased costs, reduction of worker motivation, decreased sales or market share (market pressure for change), or even bankruptcy.[6]

That is not to say that the crisis itself is the motivator. Actual crises are clear to everyone. But delaying action until a full-blown crisis occurs may be acting too late. The CEO's job is to focus on the latent crises that others in the company may not yet see. In about half the cases in Japan, TQM is started because of a latent crisis. The CEO must be able to visualize the latent crises and bring them to the company's attention.

The example of Xerox, though often told, bears repeating:

> "In 1980 we were horrified to learn that the selling price of the small Japanese machines was our manufacturing cost," Kearns (the CEO) says. "We were not tracking the rate of speed of their improvement. We tended to put a peg in. By the time we thought we were up or thought we were close, we found ourselves still off the mark." Kearns began paying even more attention to Fuji Xerox, the company's Japanese partner. There, total quality control was the focus of its New Xerox movement, so the New Xerox movement became the model for Xerox Corporation's own focus on quality.[7]

Kearns used the rate of improvement information, the cost information, and one year's poor profit to identify a latent crisis and create a powerful and lasting source of change throughout the organization.[8]

Case Study: CEO Involvement at Teradyne

Alex d'Arbeloff, CEO of Teradyne, one of our CQM companies, provides a useful case study of CEO involvement in a company's TQM implementation.

Teradyne, which develops and sells electronic test equipment, has six operating divisions, each with about 30 managers. As part of Teradyne's TQM kick-off, d'Arbeloff met personally with the 180 managers of the six divisions, in 12 groups of 15. (A full description of Teradyne's TQM introduction strategy is given later in the chapter.) In August 1990, before he spoke to each of these groups, he sent each manager a videotape entitled "Getting Ready for the 90s." In the videotape, d'Arbeloff reflected on the need for Teradyne to implement TQM.

The videotape shows d'Arbeloff in his shirtsleeves, looking informal and down-to-earth. The image is that of the man all company managers know — engineer, company founder, and concerned colleague.

D'Arbeloff begins his videotape presentation with a story about the company's receipt of an order from a new customer.[9] Following is a paraphrased version of d'Arbeloff's video statement to his managers.

> I said something to the customer about being glad to have them as a new customer, and the customer said that the issue was not about there being a new customer but about there being a new Teradyne — a Teradyne that wanted to satisfy customers. Teradyne is changing, and the customers are seeing it. However, it takes a while for customers to see change; and until the customer sees the change, the change does not exist for the customer.
>
> Teradyne's business has been and will be a good business. However, in the last five years growth has slowed. This has resulted from the recession, the high dollar value, and the Japanese gain in market share. Teradyne has to do better, and I will explain how I think we can do much better.
>
> I predict that our market will grow in the next decade, and that our business will be global and highly competitive. We must find a way to win. There are good competitors, but we also lose some orders to rinky-dink companies. We need more business to support our programs and your ambitions. Some will come from growth of our industry, but we can also take orders from our competitors. We need to find a way to be a lot better in everything we do, so that there is no question in the customer's mind that we are the company to deal with. We must be better in everything we do — administration, sales, development, and so on.
>
> There is a method I have been studying and that we have used a bit, with spectacular results. I have been spending lots of time studying this. The method is TQM. I am not now training you in TQM. I am just telling you what we are thinking and why.

TQM is focused on everyone's satisfaction. TQM is an unyielding, continuing, improving effort by everyone in the company to understand, meet, and exceed the expectations of customers. TQM is not just a quality control program. It is a different way to manage. I have visited Japan, and I thought their culture was different, but I now think I'd just given myself an excuse. Japan's good companies have found a new and better way to manage. In the United States we believe "if it ain't broke, don't fix it" and in "management by exception." The Japanese have processes that they define; then they improve them to make them better and better. Event-driven management jumps around and sets our priorities. TQM is a different way to set priorities for what we see needs to change. There are many good things about Teradyne's culture:

1. We have open communications.
2. We have integrity: we are honest with customers and each other; we let our actions speak for us.
3. We have high respect for people.
4. We have participation of people in decisions (and sometimes consensus).
5. We are an informal company; we have the minimum structure to get the job done.
6. We focus on real values: what we add to make customers satisfied; actual business rather than formalities or mechanics of business.

What do we need to change? There are four things that we have to bring into the company. Everyone must be involved in each of these.

1. Work Is a Process

I'll give you an example of a sales manager and five sales people who want to communicate better, so they have a meeting at 8 a.m. on Monday. At the first meeting only three people showed up and no one was prepared. They worked hard so that on the next Monday everyone came, but they still weren't prepared. The next week they worked to make sure everyone was prepared, but the meeting wasn't very focused. The next week they scheduled one hour for management of the general sales situation and the other hour to focus on two accounts. For the next week, the sales manager provided further focus by making a list of what to discuss about the two accounts to be discussed that week. And so on. After six months of incremental improvements, they will have much better meetings.

2. Management by Fact

We must get real data; statistical process control fits here. The ineffective way is management by anecdote ("I feel . . . ; I think . . ."). For example, the Japanese board-test market is a fraction of the U.S. market. Why? We have never found out the facts about this. Another example: from 1980 to 1985 testers shipped was 4 percent of semiconductors shipped; since 1985 it was 2 percent. Why? No one knows why. Is this important to us?

3. Teamwork

Typically we glorify people who bail out failing projects, but we don't glorify groups that just do solid work and don't screw up. We have to reverse this behavior, to reward and recognize groups whose work is under control.

4. More Training

Our training is inadequate. In proportion to Texas Instruments, Teradyne would have to give 15,000 hours of training per year. We are far short of that today.

I'll review what I've been saying:

- Testing is good business.
- We must be better by a lot in everything we do.
- TQM is a method to make the 1990s the most exciting decade in the history of the company.

We have to win for the sake of our company and the sake of the electronics industry. The best of times is now!

Case Studies: CEO Crusades

In the United States the CEO crusade is a typical approach to CEO involvement and leadership in TQM.[10] James Houghton of Corning said,

> Communicating the total quality imperative [to 28,000 people in 19 countries] means me yelling about it all the time. Management committee members keep talking about it, and so do all managers. You almost have to have a messianic view of this. You must be willing to travel, to go and see people, and talk. You can't communicate or show your commitment on a videotape or in written form all the time. You have got to believe.[11]

Investigations of the CEO crusades at Corning, Federal Express, Florida Power & Light, Globe Metallurgical, Milliken, Motorola, Wallace, and Xerox (among these were six Baldrige Award winners and one Deming Prize winner) revealed the following common structure shown in Figure 10-4 and the seven common elements of CEO crusades discussed below.

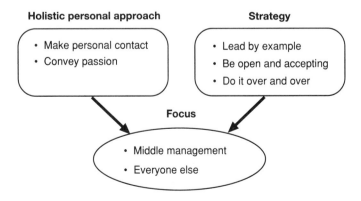

Figure 10-4. Common Structure of CEO Crusades

Make personal contact. The president or CEO must do the executive audits and site visits. Personal contact is required; 10 to 20 percent of the time should be spent in the field. James Houghton of Corning makes 40 to 50 trips per year to Corning locations; these are full-day visits with dinner and open forum meetings for questions. In 1990, Houghton made 35 to 40 speeches outside the company, of which over 50 percent were on the topic of quality and all included quality themes. David Luther, quality VP at Corning, made 37 speeches on quality. At Milliken, executives Roger Milliken and Tom Malone attend all two-day "sharing rallies."

Capture the imagination and convey passion through conviction. Symbolism and folklore can be important tools of leadership. Bob Galvin at Motorola established the procedure whereby quality progress is reviewed before financial results at monthly senior management meetings. After the quality review, Galvin would leave the room, to demonstrate his conviction that financial results follow from quality improvements. James Houghton at Corning approved a plant manager's decision to scrap hundreds of thousands of dollars of slightly out-of-spec TV glass at Corning's State College plant rather than seek a customer waiver of specification. In 1981 Roger Milliken stood on a banquet chair at a managers' conference, raised his right hand, and asked all managers to pledge to learn to listen and to recognize that management is the problem. John and C. S. Wallace of Wallace Company attended every one of the company's 51 training classes.

Lead by example. Practice what you preach, "walk the talk," and become a quality expert. At Milliken, Roger Milliken and Tom Malone reported working until 10:00 at night studying design of experiments. Arden Simms and Ken Leach at Globe Metallurgical worked all through the Christmas holidays on quality procedures. David Kearns at Xerox first was educated about TQM and then trained the top management. Galvin at

Motorola sent executives out on month-long customer visit trips.

Listen to people, work in teams, and open up. Methods like KJ and cross-functional teamwork required by TQM help executives break out of traditional power relationships. At Florida Power & Light, the executives learned the QI story, which taught them how to listen. At Xerox, David Kearns established Team Xerox. At Milliken, Tom Malone took down the fourth wall of his office — a "structural change." Houghton of Corning says,

> It must start at the top; there's no getting away from it. If top-level management is not really committed to quality, it can't work. I've heard about lots of companies where there are words, but not true commitment, and the employees see through it. They won't pay any attention to it. Along with pressure from the top, the second key area of pressure is from the folks at the bottom of the organization. If there is commitment at the top, the people at the bottom quickly become committed themselves. They're saying, "Where have you guys been all my life? We know how to do the job. Give us the tools and let us get on with it.". . . Once you've got commitment at the top and bottom, the big problem is then getting commitment in the middle. That takes a lot of effort. Eventually, commitment must exist throughout the organization. But it goes top-down, bottom-up, and then eventually hits the middle. It doesn't just go one way.[12]

Repeat yourself, and use all communication channels available. At Corning, James Houghton blitzed messages along all company channels — memos to the staff, speeches, newspapers, videos for company news, and training videos.

Work with middle management. TQM is tough for top management, and just as tough for middle management. Teach teamwork. Theory meets practice at the supervisor level. Openness is more than a feel-good principle — it is fundamental to TQM success. Removal of Tom Malone's fourth wall at Milliken was on target for middle managers. Again, Houghton of Corning says,

> The hardest people to reach are middle managers, and specifically first-line supervisors, because it means a very significant change. Instead of saying "do this, do that," first-line supervisors are now being asked to be coaches, to be part of a team, and to listen to their employees on how things could be done better. That takes away some of their management prerogative, which is very hard to deal with. It's very hard for someone who's been doing things the same way for three years to be told, "you're still the boss, but you're a different boss."[13]

From Globe Metallurgical comes the following story.

> When it came to empowering workers with statistical tools, however, the biggest stumbling block was the supervisors. Said Leach, "These were the middle management that Dr. Deming would call 85 percent of the problem. They already knew how to make silicon metal and they didn't need SPC or Dr. Deming or employee involvement or whatever." . . . In addition, there was an adversarial relationship between management and labor, represented in Beverly by the United Steelworkers of America. The last thing the supervisors wanted to do "was go out there and empower hourly people to start calling shots on the shop floor based on a control chart, which they really didn't have any confidence in anyway." . . . Leach, in retrospect, would call the resistance of middle management "the most difficult bridge we had to cross."[14]

Educate everybody. Education develops a language for top-to-bottom and bottom-to-top communication. Education enables improvement. At Xerox, Kearn's cascading education system was seen as the greatest evidence of his commitment. Motorola spends $50 million per year on education of its 100,000 employees. Globe Metallurgical educated its hourly workers in statistical process control and gave them calculators.

EXAMPLE STRATEGIES FOR TQM INTRODUCTION

"Introduction" is here used in a narrow sense: as the phase coming after senior management learning and occurring during or after initial pilot improvement projects, goal setting, and establishment of governance and organization. Introduction happens before rolling out widespread education in improvement skills. Following is a case study of Teradyne's introduction strategy.[15]

Case Study: Teradyne Strategy for Introduction

Until 1985 the automatic test equipment industry in which Teradyne works grew well and the company prospered. Its company systems were predicated on continuing growth.

Teradyne had quality programs before. It trained approximately 2,000 people in Crosby programs, the Teradyne staff has knowledge of statistical process control (SPC), and one division held a quarterly zero defects day. These programs continued up to 1989. They made good improvements from these programs.

However, during this period Teradyne CEO Alex d'Arbeloff was more of an observer and supporter than an active participant in Teradyne's quality programs. He had supported quality programs for some time. Procter and Gamble chairman Edwin Artzt, a long-time practitioner of quality improvement, sat on Teradyne's board and was instrumental in steering toward TQM. And, like many CEOs in the electronics business, d'Arbeloff had traveled often to Japan, and seen first-hand the results of TQM. He was also close to Ray Stata, CEO of Analog Devices, another Boston-area company that had been contemplating implementation of TQM.

As of 1990 Teradyne faced a crisis. Its industry experienced excess capacity, difficult price competition, and difficult product and service competition. Teradyne itself was not growing, was having difficulty sustaining profitability, and was dealing with a geographic shift in its market: nearly 50 percent of its customers were now in Asia.[16]

The basic strategy of TQM implementation at Teradyne has been to involve successively more people. The CEO got involved and first spoke to his seven-member management committee (see Figure 10-5). Their objective was to have the management committee educated and poised to implement TQM starting in July 1990. Then they involved the 42 upper managers from the company.

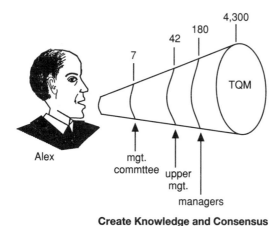

Create Knowledge and Consensus

Figure 10-5. Progressive Involvement of Management and Employees

All of these senior people read and discussed six books at the same time and in the same order. The books were

- Scherkenbach, *The Deming Route to Quality*
- Deming, *Out of the Crisis*
- Ishikawa, *What is TQC? The Japanese Way*
- Mizuno, *Company-wide Total Quality Control*
- Juran, *Juran on Leadership for Total Quality*
- Crosby, *Quality without Tears*

When others in the company heard that the senior managers were reading these books, they also wanted to read them. Many read at least three of them.

The managers also attended three seminars — a four-day seminar by Deming, a one-day seminar at Texas Instruments, and a one-day seminar from American Supplier Institute, which they brought in-house.

From their study, the Teradyne managers concluded that they would adopt a new management method based on three principles:

- process versus event-driven
- continuous improvement versus "if it ain't broke don't fix it"
- customer satisfaction instead of assuming they know what the customer needs

Teradyne has a "Teradyne Values" book that reflects the "culture" of the company. The managers decided that this culture under TQM was going to change in four key ways:

1. While we still have a need for quick reactions to crisis situations, we will move toward organizing and managing our work as a process, whether in sales calls, service response, design, or order processing.
2. We will base our decisions on facts and move away from reactive or instinctive management, in which decisions are based on "I think" or "I feel."
3. We will structure our efforts to develop and take advantage of teamwork as well as rewarding team versus individual performance.
4. Training will become a more conscious part of how we run our business.

The time had come to talk to the next 180 managers. Between August 22 and September 6, Teradyne carried out its

CEO crusade. It scheduled six sessions in which CEO Alex d'Arbeloff, held two two-hour meetings with the 180 supervisors. The crusade was planned carefully:

1. *Homework was assigned before the meeting to create readiness.* People were invited by letter and then asked to watch videos, read the old values book, preview the new values, and be prepared to speak out in the meetings. Participation in the meetings was required.

2. *The PDCA cycle was run after groups of meetings.* Teradyne managers sought feedback on weakness after the meetings (two labels from each participant — one thing learned and one weakness; see Figure 10-6). For instance, some of the weaknesses reported were

   - agenda/objectives — lack of structure
   - participation — not speaking out
   - lack of implementation plan

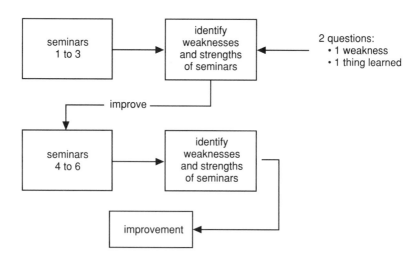

Figure 10-6. Post-Meeting Feedback and Improvement

After the first meeting, the managers took corrective action. For instance, they

- opened with an explanation of meeting's purpose
- issued follow-up agenda
- called on people who didn't speak out
- removed the video camera, which was inhibiting response

After meetings 4 through 6 the managers again made improvements, shifting their attention to later weaknesses as they corrected earlier weaknesses.

3. *They planned the diffusion of TQM beyond the 180 managers to all employees.* Each manager was asked to meet with his or her direct reports and send a written report on that meeting to Alex d'Arbeloff. The purpose of these meetings was to explain that it was right to change the company culture and that they would do so.

Teradyne decided it needed a parallel organizational structure for quality. Its companywide quality council is the same as its management committee (i.e., its highest-ranking management group). While the companywide quality council and management committee have the same members, the agendas for the two parallel entities are very different. The quality council sets quality priorities and controls the company's quality agenda. For instance, it deals with TQM implementation issues (e.g., training and deployment) and improvement issues. There is also a small companywide, or corporate, TQM office (two managers and an administrator). Each division has a similar structure, with its own quality council and TQM office (one part-time or full-time person as shown in Figure 10-7).

D'Arbeloff decided that for Teradyne TQM is the seven steps and market-in, implemented by quality improvement teams addressing three goals: increase in market share, reduction in cost, and reduction in cycle time (see Figure 10-8). Each division business plan for the year is to address these issues with action plans.[17]

Teradyne has a program to take this message to its 4,300 people. The program includes meetings for all employees and

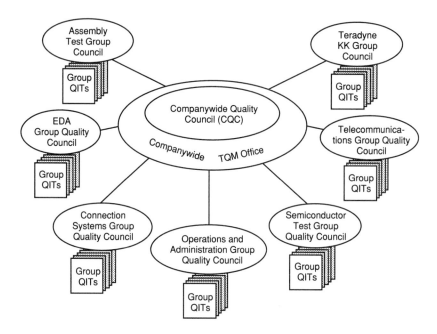

Figure 10-7. Teradyne Quality Organization

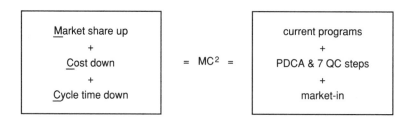

Figure 10-8. Teradyne's 1991 Goals and TQM Initiatives

development of a TQM brochure. D'Arbeloff himself led a KJ to decide the content of the brochure, which will include the following points:

- Explain why TQM is the method chosen.
- Jobs will change with the implementation of TQM.
- On-the-job examples are the basis for market-in.
- Explain market-in to the staff.

An outside agent from Procter & Gamble initially piqued Teradyne's interest in TQM. Teradyne now has 200 to 400 QITs. D'Arbeloff is now deeply personally involved in Teradyne's quality activities.

In summary, Teradyne's strategy involved three phases:

1. Consensus among the 42 top managers
2. The CEO crusade strategy to reach the 180 supervisors
3. A strategy to reach 4,300 employees

To reach this many numbers and levels of people, a company needs a system and structure. It requires management. If a company were only 42 people in total, it would just need communications. With 4,300, a company requires strategy.

Teradyne's initial crusade was followed in a few months by cascading and expanding training in the 7 QC steps and 7 QC tools for teams already formed and working. It took this approach even though its top management was trained in the 7 management and planning tools and customer visitation. With established systems for forming QI teams, measuring quality, and monitoring customer complaints, use of the 7 QC Steps was practical and sufficient for the initial wave of education. This strategy contrasts in detail but not in spirit with the next case study.

BBN Strategy for TQM Introduction

Another CQM company, Bolt Beranek and Newman (BBN), used a strategy somewhat different from the Teradyne strategy. Like d'Arbeloff, BBN CEO Steve Levy faced a company crisis and had learned something about Japanese TQM practices.[18] As chairman of the American Electronics Association, he had studied Japan's competitive practices, and he later heard Shoji Shiba speak on TQM, which convinced him that BBN should implement the system.

Unlike Teradyne, BBN as a company had no experience, either positive or negative, with TQM. From a core of contract research in computers and communication, BBN had spun out several divisions to commercialize the results of research. For many years, BBN's standard American management system and its practice of hiring very capable people had created success and growth, but in 1989 and 1990 several factors caused a major business reversal.

Over the course of nine months, BBN's CEO, chief operations officer, chief financial officer, and division presidents began study of TQM and initial use of some of the TQM tools. They attended a six-day course on TQM for senior managers, offered by the Center for Quality Management, which consolidated their thinking and gave them a common understanding of TQM.

Because customer focus was a weakness in the corporate culture, BBN first adopted the principle of customer focus and carried out the senior executive customer visitation program described in Chapter 7. Analysis of the data from the customer visitation program suggested that three companywide TQM initiatives should be undertaken to institutionalize the following:

- customer visitations and customer focus
- awareness of defects delivered to customers and efforts at defect reduction
- product development methodology based on concurrent engineering, a product review board, and a phase review process

BBN appointed cross-company teams to plan how to institutionalize each of these activities. Like Teradyne, BBN made explicit the concern for quality at the senior management level. At BBN, the equivalent of Teradyne's management committee and quality council is the Policy and Quality Council (PAQC), which consists of 10 people. This entity addresses key policy and quality issues, and an expanded group (including another five senior managers) addresses operations issues. BBN also established a group of employees, called the Companywide Quality Committee (which includes the leader of its one-person corporate TQM office and representatives from each operating part of the company and the Training and Education Department — 10 in all), to help senior corporate and division management plan and implement TQM and to coordinate TQM activities and disseminate information throughout the company. Figure 10-9 shows these relations.

With review by the Policy and Quality Council and other senior managers, the Companywide Quality Committee planned and wrote a pamphlet, *TQM at BBN*, which was given to the entire 2,350-person staff. The brochure was accompanied by a presentation on *TQM at BBN* by 50 to 60 senior division managers who had been trained by the Companywide Quality Committee to give the presentations and to answer typical staff questions about TQM. Within three months of completing his or her training, each senior manager had given presentations to every employee at BBN. Typical questions were generated from early presentations, and answers were discussed, then written by the PAQC. With these answers as guidelines, the training sessions could then include oral rehearsal of answers to typical questions.

Thus, the BBN approach did not include a CEO crusade, although the CEO did lead the introduction. Rather, the BBN approach is one of incremental education: first the top 9 managers, then the next 50 managers, and then an introduction to the staff at large. Furthermore, the practice of TQM at BBN has spread throughout the company in a number of incremental ways, as appropriate education is made available. All of the corporate (and most of the divisional) presidents and vice presidents have taken the CQM's six-day course for senior management. Derivative internal courses have been given on an ad hoc basis. Courses in customer visitation are spreading as people gain experience and thus the ability to teach. BBN is now following up this period of incremental education with an aggressive companywide rollout of 7 steps/7 tools training, loosely modeled on Teradyne's earlier rollout.[19]

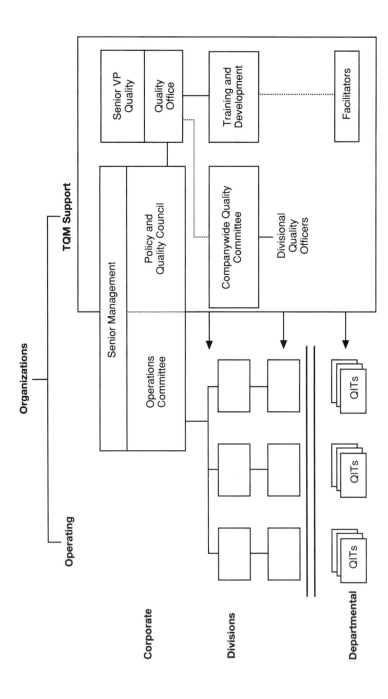

Figure 10-9. Bolt Beranek and Newman Quality Organization

Digital Strategy for TQM Introduction

The two examples given above are for companies employing a few thousand people. For bigger companies — those with tens of thousands or more than 100,000 — introducing TQM is a different problem. Large companies are too diverse and "the troops" too distant from top management to follow a completely uniform, top-down TQM practice. Instead, successful large companies standardize a core of practices and leave the rest to the discretion of the divisions. Corning teaches a unifying model of TQM: everyone is taught 4 principles, 6 strategies, and 10 actions; but the manner of implementation is up to the divisions.[20] Similarly, Motorola standardizes goal deployment (as embodied in everyone's "5 up" charts) but does not insist on standardizing problem-solving practices. Xerox standardized such practices as benchmarking but (at least initially) left goal deployment much looser. While Teradyne and BBN can plan how to get the message and education from the CEO to the few thousand employees, big companies are organized as if they were several companies, each with many thousands of people. Big and medium-sized companies like Digital need an internal organization similar to the CQM, to share experiences and resources within the company.

Digital is a CQM member that has approximately 100,000 employees as of 1990. Accordingly, there seem to be four core elements to Digital's corporatewide efforts:

- A model of TQM that explicitly includes a large variety of practices
- Increasingly centralized courses and internal consultants for TQM practices
- Relatively intense networking activities, including heavily used electronic bulletin boards/message exchanges, regular corporatewide meetings of quality educators (about 20 people), day-long "quality forums" for sharing

results across functions and product groups, and membership in many multicompany consortia

- Emphasis in the core initial course on a "TQM roadmap," based on Juran's work, that details the steps in implementing TQM, regardless of specific practices chosen

Digital's TQM activities were not launched with an explicit CEO crusade. Its organizational structure and tradition of consensual management and leadership work against such crusading. In the terms of Figure 10-1, Digital has undertaken the middle path, relying on middle and upper management to develop and spread pockets of quality culture. In its favor, Digital has a long tradition of focusing on quality. The following quality policy was given by Ken Olsen, Digital's founder and long-time CEO many years ago and remains in force today.

Growth is not our primary goal. Our goal is to be a quality organization, and do a quality job, which means that we will be proud of our work for years to come. As we achieve quality, we achieve growth.

Digital has also been aggressive in joining with other companies to become part of a greater quality culture. For instance, Digital is a founding member of the CQM and is a member of a quality consortium with several other *Fortune* 500 companies as well.

Important aspects of Digital's TQM initiative, illustrated in Figure 10-10, were adopted from the TQM activities of these other large companies (e.g., benchmarking from Xerox and six sigma from Motorola.)

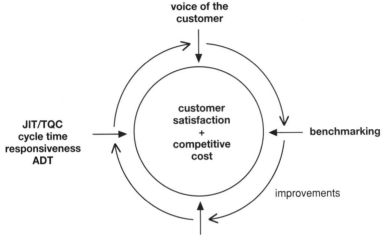

People Drive Quantum Improvements

Figure 10-10. The Digital TQM Strategy

NOTES

1. Shoji Shiba, "How I Have Observed Quality Management in European Countries," Proceedings of the 6th EOQC European Seminar on Education and Training, 1988.

2. Seiji Kojima, "Analysis of the Factors Disturbing Promotion of QC Circle Activities," Master's Thesis, Management and Policy Science Program, University of Tsukuba, Japan, 1989.

3. The chart derives from a three-year study of implementation described in more detail in Shiba's "How I Have Observed Quality Management."

4. For example, see Warren Bennis and Burt Nanus, *Leaders* (New York: Harper & Row, 1985), for typical strategies. Another study, David A. Nadler and Michael L. Tushman, "Beyond the Charismatic Leader: Leadership

and Organizational Change," *California Management Review* 32, no. 2 (Winter 1990): 77-97 classifies leadership style into charismatic, instrumental, and institutional. The latter two classifications can be thought of as the highly involved style of TQM leadership, which will be explored throughout this chapter.

5. Shiba, "How I Have Observed Quality Management," 5.

6. Empirically, major organizational change of any kind seems almost always to be precipitated by clear crisis. This is demonstrated by studies of companywide organizational change in general, and for Deming Prize winners in a survey by Professor Noriaki Kano.

7. Gary Jacobson and John Hillkirk, *American Samurai* (New York: Macmillan, 1986), 172.

8. Kano and Koura's research supports the model that visible or latent crises plus CEO leadership trigger TQM implementation; Noriaki Kano and Kozo Koura, "Development of Quality Control Seen through the Companies Awarded the Deming Prize," *Reports of Statistical Application Research, Union of Japanese Scientists and Engineers* 37 (1990-91): 87.

9. Professor Shiba, who has been active in video production, notes that video is particularly appropriate for a CEO presentation such as d'Arbeloff's. By contrast, video is not the medium for logical diffusion, or what takes place in a classroom lecture. You use video to convey affective language, to speak personally to individuals, not formally to a classroom. For instance, Alex d'Arbeloff momentarily fumbled with a couple of items he was holding at the beginning of the video, and this conveyed an informal feeling. Backlighting and close-ups would increase this feeling.

10. This case study was researched by Ron Butler of Teradyne.

11. Nancy Karabatsos, "The Chairman Doesn't Blink," *Quality Progress* (March 1987): 19.

12. Ibid.

13. Ibid.

14. Mary Walton, *Deming Management at Work* (New York: Putnam, 1990).

15. This case study was prepared by Owen Robbins of Teradyne and presented in December 1990 at the CQM's first senior executive courses.

16. Note that the Teradyne case study matches the model, in which the crisis plus information leads to CEO involvement in TQM. The crisis plus information about TQM prompted Teradyne's CEO to become directly involved in the company's quality activities.

17. Teradyne's TQM efforts and QIT activities are building on the company's previous study and implementation of Crosby's methods. Teradyne is changing vocabulary over time and letting teams evolve how they work rather than disbanding them.

18. Again, this matches the model in which information plus crisis leads to CEO involvement in TQM.

19. BBN's rollout is described by Cliff Scott in "BBN's 7 Steps Implementation," *The Center for Quality Management Journal* 1, no. 1. (Autumn 1992): 19-27.

20. These are described in the *Corning Total Quality Digest* 2 (Director of Quality, Corning, Inc., HP-CB-06-4, Corning, NY 14831).

11

Infrastructure
for Mobilization

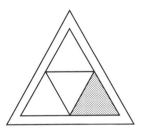

When a company has only a few dozen people, they can talk to each other, read the same books, and in general communicate with each other about how to implement TQM. With thousands of people, however, a company needs a strategy and structure for introducing TQM.

There are seven elements of organizational infrastructure for implementing TQM (see Figure 11-1):

1. Goals must be set for the company's TQM implementation and for the company's business.
2. An organizational setting must be provided — people in corporate management and in the operating divisions to help plan and mobilize the company's TQM implementation.
3. Training and education must be provided.
4. TQM must be promoted throughout the company.
5. Operational (not TQM) success stories resulting from the implementation of TQM must be diffused through the rest of the company.
6. There must be appropriate awards and incentives to mobilize TQM.

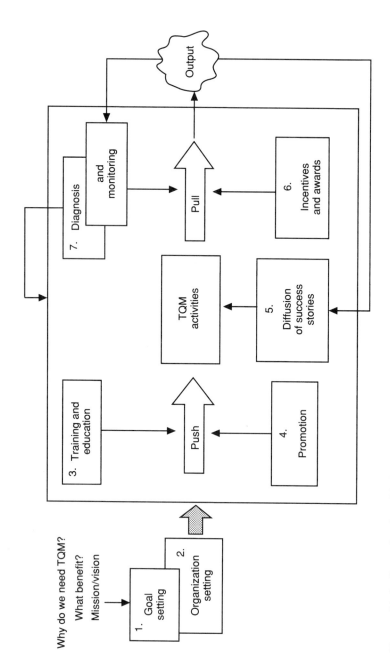

Figure 11-1. Organizational Infrastructure for Implementing TQM

7. The implementation effort must be monitored and diagnosed by top management.

Note that the description of infrastructure above applies to suborganizations as well as the larger organizations. Managers of suborganizations must support their people in TQM by having clear goals and improvement organization, promoting and giving training for improvement activities, widely publicizing success stories, recognizing improvement achievements, and doing PDCA on the operation's TQM activities. For a small unit (or a small company, for that matter), these elements of infrastructure will be executed less elaborately and more informally and personally.

The following sections detail the seven elements of infrastructure.

GOAL SETTING (VISION/MISSION)

There are three types of goals — noble goals, intermediate goals, and annual goals.

Noble goals. Noble goals are abstract and are aimed outside the company; they include ideas such as "contribute to society" or "benefit the customers." Alex d'Arbeloff of Teradyne gave a noble goal in the videotape described in Chapter 10 when he said that the company must succeed for the sake of the electronics industry. NEC, in its position as a computer and communications company, also has a noble goal: to "advance societies worldwide toward deepened mutual understanding and the fulfillment of human potential." Noble goals motivate people; long-term goals of profit or growth are not noble goals.

Intermediate goals. A company also needs intermediate goals stated in a language common to everyone in the company. Noble goals motivate people but are too abstract to guide them on strategy for attaining the company's goals. In Japan the intermediate goals are ideas such as "management by facts," "focus on the vital few," "PDCA," and so on. These goals encourage the processes necessary to accomplish the noble goals.

The authors' impression of American market performance-oriented intermediate goals in non-TQM companies is that they are primarily longer-term quantitative goals, such as market share, sales, or profits. TQM exemplars vary. Florida Power & Light and Xerox seem to publicize Japanese-like process and customer-focused goals. Motorola deploys quantitative longer-term goals, focused on quality and cycle time results.

Annual target and goals. A company also needs a specific annual target, for example, cost down 10 percent (or CD10) from the previous year. In Japan, a company might monitor several annual targets, but focus on one target for mobilization purposes.

NEC Shizuoka provides good examples of all three types of goals.[1] Shizuoka has a noble goal in common with all of the NEC companies, as given above. A management philosophy and slogan provide intermediate goals. Shizuoka's management philosophy has three parts:

1. Management that places top priority on quality
2. The customer comes first
3. Creation of a workplace where individual potential can be realized to the fullest

Shizuoka's slogan is "immediate response when quality is at stake." If quality is at stake, the company pours in every resource. Finally, each manager has yearly targets for quality assurance, profit, and manufacturing lead time, which are selected on the basis of the prior year's results. Incidentally, when we asked Michio Ikawa, Shizuoka's president, the reasons for the company's good results, he cited (1) having a process for systemizing improvement activities and other business processes, and (2) lowering costs via factory automation.

U.S. Company Value and Mission Statements

As the following examples show, U.S. company value or mission statements often fall somewhere between the definitions of noble and intermediate goals.[2]

Xerox. Quality is the basic business principle for Xerox. Quality means providing our external customers with innovative products and services that fully satisfy their requirements. Quality improvement is the job of every Xerox employee.

3M. Continuous improvement in all businesses and support services at a rate of change that attains and sustains global leadership in chosen markets.

Florida Power & Light. During the next decade, we want to become the best managed . . . in the United States and an excellent company overall, and to be recognized as such.

Ford Motor Company. Our mission is to improve our products and services continually to meet our customers' needs, allowing us to prosper as a business and to provide a reasonable return for our shareholders, the owners of our business.

AT&T. Quality excellence is the foundation for the management of our business and the keystone of our goals of customer satisfaction. It is, therefore, our policy to consistently provide products and services that meet the quality expectations of our customers . . . and to actively pursue ever-improving quality through programs that enable each employee to do his or her job right the first time.

N.A. Phillips. We . . . are totally committed to achieving lasting corporate-wide quality excellence. This means that each of us must understand and meet the requirements of our customers and co-workers. We all must continually strive for improvement and error-free work in all we do . . . in every job . . . on time . . . all the time.

Shell. Our objective is to supply products, services, and technology that meet the customer's requirements every time without error.

Hewlett-Packard. Our intent is to provide products and services of the highest quality and greatest possible value to our customers, thereby gaining and holding their respect and loyalty.

There are three main threads in these value and mission statements:

1. Quality improvement is a basic business principle and is everyone's job.
2. Our goal is to attain global leadership as a best-managed company, to gain the respect and loyalty of our customers, and to provide a positive return to investors.
3. Our methods for doing this are
   - to fully satisfy the customer's expectations
   - through innovative products and services
   - by doing it right the first time

As we have seen, in U.S. companies the noble goals are perhaps a little less noble than in Japanese companies, but not so down-to-earth that they become intermediate goals. Japanese companies are process-oriented, and their intermediate goals are process-oriented: manage by facts, manage by process, focus on the vital few, and use the PDCA cycle (see Figure 11-2). In Japan, if the annual goals are not met, then the next year redoubled attention is paid to the intermediate goals. TQM needs these intermediate goals.

The United States is more results oriented than Japan; most of its goals, like annual goals, are short term and focused on dollars. However, a results orientation is not the best way to achieve improvements. Some form of process-oriented intermediate goals are needed. Since TQM is a mass movement, its language must be geared to the company culture. Process-oriented intermediate goals are best, but a company must be realistic and find a compromise that includes as much process focus as is tol-

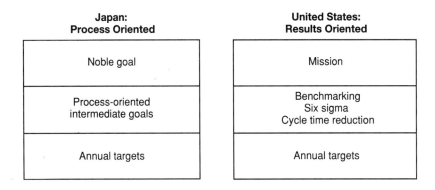

Figure 11-2. Japanese and U.S. Approaches to Goal Setting

erable. The U.S. inventions of benchmarking, defect reduction, and cycle time reduction provide serve as a useful compromise. They provide process-related intermediate goals in a results-oriented environment.

Cycle time reduction permits a simple focus on numeric improvement objectives (reduce cycle time by x percent) that directs companies to analyze and to change process. Six sigma permits a focus on numeric improvement objectives, but the goal of extreme reduction of defects forces companies to significantly change the process. Benchmarking usually starts with a look at the numeric results of another company but then leads into a study of the processes by which they achieve those results.

Benchmarking is especially useful in the United States. In Japan, imitation is the first step for learning. In the United States, however, people don't like to imitate. Benchmarking is a way for U.S. companies to encourage intelligent imitation without incurring the stigma often attached to imitation.

Benchmarking is an intermediate concept (see Figure 11-3). It falls between the Japanese process-oriented intermediate goals and the U.S. inclination to results-oriented goals. By focusing on the results and methods of performance of the best companies, benchmarking provides the targets the United States likes so well along with processes to imitate to achieve these targets.

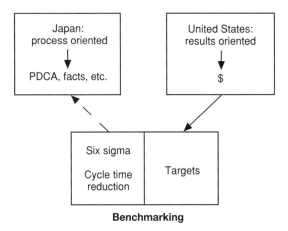

Benchmarking

Figure 11-3. Benchmarking as Intermediate Goal Setting

ORGANIZATION SETTING

There are two essential components to a TQM organization: the TQM committee, and the TQM office. The TQM committee is the group responsible for leading, diffusing, and managing TQM; it is the management group of the organization, convening with TQM as its agenda. The TQM office is a small office that assists the CEO and the TQM committee. These components typically are both used at the corporate level and the divisional level.

Joe Junguzza of Polaroid has looked into the organizational setting for TQM at Hewlett-Packard, Corning, Xerox, Texas Instruments, and Henry Ford Health Care. In each case, the company had a quality organizational structure roughly similar to that described here.

The TQM office reports to the top manager, or CEO (see Figure 11-4). It helps the CEO, who will lead the TQM implementation but will not have time to do all the detailed planning. Most of the people in the TQM office are not quality specialists, particularly not in the corporatewide TQM office. The TQM office must not have a narrow attitude about quality.

These people don't have to know TQM, but they must ha√e strong motivation to learn about quality. In Japan, sometimes a respected strategic planner takes responsibility for the quality office, but more often it is a line person, not a quality specialist. The person leading the quality office is typically on assignment from a line management position and has five qualifications: he or she is a strategic thinker, respected throughout the company, is a good communicator (particularly a good listener), has hands-on capability (such as dealing with real data), and has a strong personality.

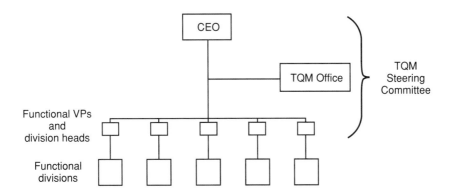

Figure 11-4. The TQM Office

There is no job description for the TQM office. The TQM vice president, like the president, has to create the job (see Figure 11-5). The primary role of the quality office varies from company to company. In some, the primary role is teaching and coaching the senior management, or even just the CEO. In other companies, the VP of TQM is the "leading learner," and the TQM office mostly designs and starts courses. The job may be promoting and organizing events and courses. By analogy, VPs of finance in some companies drive financial planning, in others cost cutting, and in still others organizational change. Similarly, VPs of quality (or, more generally, the head of the TQM office) address whatever needs the company has.

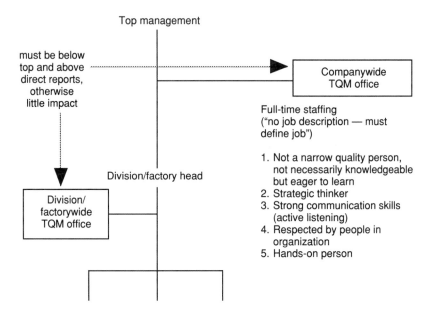

Figure 11-5. Structure of the TQM Organization

The person in the quality office has no formal authority over most of the organization; he or she relies on persuasiveness, ability to articulate issues, and particularly active listening. The TQM VP needs the respect of the rest of the organization from the start; potential future presidents come out of the quality office. As said earlier, the quality office should be relatively small. However, one person has a hard time doing things alone. Therefore, two or three people in the quality office is about right for a company of a few thousand people. Divisions of such a company would have one full-time person or a part-time person, depending on the size of the division. The full-time quality office staff for a 100,000-person company might be 10 to 20 people. More people are needed for the initiation phase than later, when a stable TQM system is in place.

TQM steering committees are made up of the people across the divisions who have the job of diffusing TQM. Basically these people need the same qualities as the person in the quality office

— a strategic mind, good communication skills, the respect of others, broad-mindedness, and hands-on quality practice. At Xerox each operating unit top executive has at least one quality officer, a broad-minded person able to make TQM happen.

The form of a company's organizational structure for quality depends on the company size. Companies of a few thousand people can have the quality organization described immediately above. A company of 100,000 people needs its own internal "Center for Quality Management" to oversee planning and sharing among divisions just as the CQM facilitates sharing among companies, through special events, networking, promotion, and TQM development (see Figure 11-6).

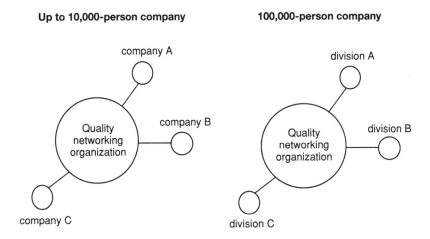

Figure 11-6. Intercompany and Internal Networking Organizations

TRAINING AND EDUCATION

Ishikawa, in many ways the father of modern Japanese TQM, is widely quoted as saying "TQM begins with education and ends with education."[3] That education in TQM is important is now a widely espoused belief, to the point where Corning Glass, when supplying other companies with its courses, explicitly and repeatedly warns that TQM is not just education.

Less widely acknowledged are the differences between world-class TQM education and traditional classroom methods. These differences can be illustrated in a simple model of TQM training and education containing seven observations on world-class TQM (see Figure 11-7).[4]

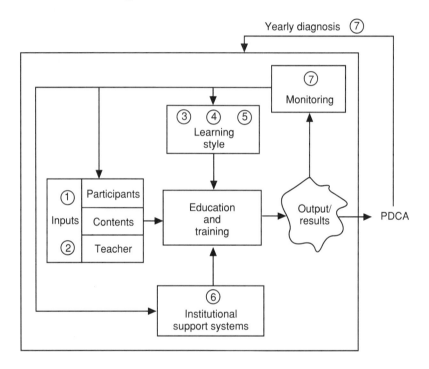

Figure 11-7. A TQM Training and Education Model

At the left of the model are the inputs to education and training; the participants, contents, and teachers. At the center top and bottom of the model are the environmental issues affecting education and training; the learning-style environment and the institutional support systems. The learning-style environment refers to the environment in which learning is provided — in the classroom, on the job, through study groups, via one-on-one situations such as reviews, through visiting other divisions or companies, and so on.

The institutional support system consists of the company's policies, funding, and administrative structure for education and training. Toward the top right of the model is the normal monitoring of effectiveness, which goes on within the education and training system; this feeds back to modify the inputs and environmental situation. Finally, at the far right of the model is the yearly diagnosis by senior management. (Their job is to create the education and training system and diagnose it, not to plan the course content.) The components of the model are discussed more fully below.

Seven Observations on World-Class TQM Education

Our seven observations are offered merely as aids in designing an appropriate education system for one's own company. There is nothing magic about them.[5] As TQM education (and corporate education in general) advance, we hope some of the observations will become well known and will no longer have to be stressed. Furthermore, there are undoubtedly more commonalities to be discovered.[6] However, the ones offered here should be helpful in breaking through the traditional classroom mind-set. They are the following (numbers correspond to the circled numbers in Figure 11-7):

1. Plan the inputs to training to reduce variance of output.
2. Don't use education professionals to teach.
3. Use mutual learning, not the traditional teacher-student roles.
4. Create opportunity for learning in daily routine work.
5. Create environmental influences for learning.
6. Create institutional support structures.
7. Manage education with PDCA.

Plan the inputs to training to reduce variance of output. To reduce the variance of the output of a course, you must reduce the variance of the inputs. This is basic quality control. The inputs are the participants, the learning contents, and the teacher.

Stratify the participants by background and needs. This means giving classes for specific function, management level, or prerequisite training. Stratification may involve giving separate sessions with "open enrollment" for interested individuals versus management-mandated training of entire teams together. Stratification means teaching serious learners, and ejecting those who miss a class. Stratification allows adaptation of teaching (pace, nature of group work, types of examples and cases, and relative emphasis on subjects) to produce uniform learning.

Stratifying by needs often means organizing courses by some means other than topic. See, for example, Figure 11-8, which shows one example of a training curriculum for a medium-sized Japanese company. In this organization companywide trainings are given for particular *roles* (e.g., QC for technical staff), while only specialist training is given for particular *subjects* (e.g., design of experiments).

Uniform learning of TQM concepts requires uniformity of teaching materials. Teachers must be taught what they can change (examples, emphasis, homework) and what they cannot change (the steps and formats for problem solving and tool use, the vocabulary, basic concepts such as *the four revolutions*).

In this book we have deliberately used a variety of terms to encourage liberal translation among different company TQM programs. But within a company, a core of TQM practices and concepts must be standardized to facilitate communication between specialists and managers, superiors and subordinates, and one function and another. A company can enforce these standards naturally by supplying and mandating the use of materials (overheads, manuals, cases) that conform to the standards.

Uniform learning requires uniform quality of teachers, which in turn implies an effective process for recruiting, training, preparing, and diagnosing teachers. For managers rotated into quality offices as facilitators, consultants, or teachers, "train the trainer" courses are common. For example, see the intensive "basic courses" for specialist training in Figure 11-8.

	Object			Course Name	Hours	Instructor
Compulsory training	Directors		All	Executive course (within company)	1.5 days 11 H	External instructor
	Department and section managers		All	Department and section management course	4 days 38 H	Specialized instructor
			Mgrs with 5+ yrs. experience	Refresher course	2 days 19 H	
	Staff	Technical	All	QC (staff) course	4 days 32 H	Instructor in each plant, division, and office
		Clerical	All	QC (staff) course	3 days 24 H	
	Line	Supervisor	All	Supervisor course	3 days 24 H	
		Group leader and circle leader	All	Group leader course	3 days 32 H	
		Worker	All	QC worker course	1 day 8 H	
	New employees		All	New employee course	1 day 8 H	
	Part-time employees		All	Part-time employee course	1 day 8 H	
Specialist training	Staff		Selected Staff	1. Basic course (A)	4 mo 5days/mo 192 H	Specialized instructor
				2. Basic course (B)	3 mo 4 days/mo 114 H	
				3. Reliability	4 days 39 H	
				4. Design of experiments	4 days 36 H	
				5. Multivariate analysis	4 days 36 H	
				6. Others		

Figure 11-8. Example of Training Curriculum for a Midsize Company

Even in situations where much less structured preparatory work is possible, planning the inputs and the process can still yield uniformly good results. For instance, the CQM has CEOs teach most days of its six-day course. The CEOs who are invited to teach have already taken the course and have personal experience in the general area being taught. The course design emphasizes real cases and group work. Only about a third of the course is lecture, and most of the lectures are accounts of diverse examples. CEOs are called on not to teach theory but rather to share personal experiences.

Leaders for each day (the CEOs are not called "teachers") are given videotapes, full classroom materials, and analysis/diagnosis from previous offerings to support preparation.

The course format requires preparation of overheads, which ensures a certain amount of preparation. The overheads are checked to provide advance warning of major problems of pace or omission. Always in attendance in each course is an administrative support person and a course committee member (i.e., someone familiar with both TQM and the course), over and above the people brought in by the leader to facilitate, present cases, and otherwise supplement instruction. The process ensures effective education without dictating how a CEO goes about preparing.

All of these strategies are designed to ensure that all those participating in a course have in fact learned what they need to learn about TQM. Contrast this with the typical "Darwinian model" of public education, where students who do poorly just get poor grades.

Don't use education professionals to teach. All but the most specialized topics in world-class TQM companies are taught by managers. The CQM design study team *never* saw training done by people whose professional training and job function was in education.

Xerox, in cascading its initial quality awareness course, had every manager teach his or her subordinates, as part of its LUTI (learn, use, teach, inspect) cycle. At Florida Power & Light plants, the person who reviews a team's work and teaches methods when necessary is simply a manager well trained in methods who then becomes a part-time teacher. At Motorola and IBM, TQM teachers are managers rotated into teaching jobs for no more than two years.

There is a misconception that teachers must have professional qualification in education. This furthers the old division between teacher and learner, professional teacher and consultant, teacher and doer — a division that has proven ineffective. All must teach and learn. As the Japanese say, "all teach." There are many advantages to designing a management system that demands that everyone teach, especially busy line managers. The managers learn better by teaching. Subordinates learn better from a teacher with the authority of rank and personal practice in what is taught. Finally, having managers teach provides one more reality check on the curriculum: Is it necessary? Is it simple enough?

Consider the opposite strategy of selecting teachers who are not managers. Imagine the cost of hiring and training professional instructors to develop and deliver a curriculum tuned to the examples of every nook and cranny in the corporation. Imagine the difficulty of getting instructors to understand the issues of every particular function well enough to teach authoritatively and create understandable examples. The strategy of simply buying instructors and a fixed curriculum is obviously ineffective. So, the only real question is which training and how far to cascade down from the top versus rotating managers into either part-time or full-time instruction.

Teaching is the best way to learn. For instance, members of the CQM Operating Committee helped teach a six-day TQM course to the senior managers of the CQM companies. The Operating Committee members and the senior managers all learned from this effort. At present, CEOs and vice presidents teach most of that six-day course and uniformly say they learned much from the experience. "I didn't know how much more I had to learn until I taught it," is a typical comment.

From the viewpoint of a professional educator, the "all teach" strategy represents a major role shift. Professional educators need to create, adapt, and perhaps buy curriculum materials.[7] More subtly, professional educators need to collaborate with the TQM office in designing and executing the "delivery management system" that translates business strategy into educational strategy and then into curriculum development processes, trainer training, monitoring, diagnosis, and PDCA.

Use mutual learning, not the traditional teacher-student roles. The traditional image of the teacher is one of a "master" who imparts wisdom by talking to students. This image belies the kind of learning that takes place within modern organizations. No teacher comes anywhere close to "knowing it all." All students are functioning adults. A model of learning that recognizes these facts can be called *mutual learning*, in which a community or group of people share what each has learned and learn from others.

An environment for mutual learning is necessary even in the classroom, and there are many ways to create one. Homework can be posted on the wall so that the students can study each others' efforts, both strong and weak. Another example is using a workshop to roll out initial 7 QC steps training: participants "retrofit" problems they've solved into the 7 steps format and present them in a workshop. The participants discuss each other's work and formulate guidelines to improve 7 steps problem solving. This mutual learning format eliminates the need for omniscience in a teacher.

Mutual learning extends learning well beyond the classroom, if work groups rather than individuals can be trained together. Such training promotes a common language and teamwork and makes it easier to implement the results. Don't send just one person to a course; always send at least two. People in teams teach each other better practices. Indeed, it is not uncommon to put one or two people on a team primarily to learn, rather than because of special expertise or position.

Presentation meetings diffuse success stories. Exchange visits with other work groups, divisions, or companies (even competitors) provide opportunities for mutual learning and knowledge of the customer or new process. One need not be a world-class authority to provide learning to others. It is sufficient to be a practitioner of a specific good practice. Indeed, it is continually a pleasant surprise to find how much world-class TQM can be taught through the sharing of individual cases among CQM member companies, even though most have not yet achieved overall world-class TQM performance. This is the great strength of mutual learning.

Create opportunity for learning in daily routine work. To quote Ishikawa,

> Formal education is less than one-third of the total educational effort. Education does not end with assembling workers to receive formal instruction. At best, this instruction can represent only a small portion of their total education. It is the responsibility of the boss to teach his subordinates through actual work.[8]

The concept "learn first and apply later" must be avoided. An argument can be made, however, for "apply first and learn later." By trying to use a technique before learning it, students will better understand the issues involved when they do learn the technique. The idea that a new technique must be learned perfectly before it can be applied must be squelched.

Avoid one-shot learning. At the minimum, students should alternate learning with practice. For instance, before a course, participants can register a theme from their job that they have to solve during the course, and courses can be given in several sessions, with several weeks between sessions for on-the-job use of the new learning. After all, the purpose of the training is to get improvement on the job. Students may also write up their own monographs on what they learn. In Japan it is common for participants in a course to take detailed notes and then write up what they learned.

Avoid thinking that theory is above reality. The idea that the tool has to be applied in the theoretically correct way is mistaken. In fact, reality (daily job) is above theory; what is needed for the real situation is what should be learned. "Force-fitting" a

problem into either a purely reactive or purely proactive framework is a mistake; instead, do whatever creates permanent
improvement and learning. Reality is a teacher. A method can
be applied, the weakness in the method found, and the method
improved. In particular, real customers are the best teachers.

Managers can create numerous opportunities for learning
as part of normal work outside class. Linking class work to the
job as described above is a start. So is on-the-spot teaching or
seeing improvement teams' work-in-progress. Any review processes, whether personnel reviews or budget reviews, are opportunities to show where improvement methods can be used.

Create environmental influences for learning. The idea
that education and training should be passed only from the top
down is wrong. Education and training are available from
many sources (see Figure 11-9). Presidential audits, QI story
diagnosis, and customer visits are all ways that a TQM environment teaches senior executives.

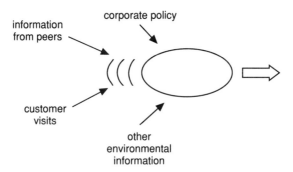

Figure 11-9. Environmental Influences for Learning

One indirect influence on learning is a teaching assignment. Monetary and nonmonetary incentives are another indirect influence. A monetary incentive may be nothing more
than footing the bill for refreshments at team meetings. Visits
outside the company can be a very good incentive.

Create institutional support structures. Just as most companies have institutionalized the process of planning, acquiring, and monitoring the use of capital equipment, so have TQM companies institutionalized the process of planning, delivering, and monitoring the use of TQM education.

Therefore, normal business planning would establish annual goals for training and education. Course content and participants must be related to annual corporate goals, and targets must be related to choice of company strategy and business goals. For example, if cost reduction is a target, course content should include training on reducing costs, and participants should be chosen for their ability to apply cost reduction techniques successfully.

Another support structure that Motorola uses is a nonrefundable training and education budget. For instance, if a division does not spend the money on training and education, it loses the money — it cannot spend it for any other purpose.

Standards should be established and performance monitored and measured against the standards. The process described in Chapter 8 for translating the "voice of the customer" into metrics can be used to translate weaknesses and potential problems in TQM education into appropriate metrics.

Manage education with PDCA. As with many business processes, long-term success in the TQM training process depends much less on where it starts than on how well it improves over time.[9] For example, the first companywide quality education course at Corning Glass did not cover standardized methods for problem solving, such as the 7 QC steps and 7 QC tools. At the time, the company believed that its people were too smart to need such instruction. (This was more than a decade ago, when TQM was virtually unknown in the West.)[10] After Corning taught the introductory quality course to everyone in the company, little happened. Quality didn't change. But here is the point: *Instead of declaring TQM a failure, Corning diagnosed the weakness (difference between plan and actual) and eliminated the root cause.* These were the *check* and *act* phases of PDCA.

The Corning senior management and quality officers recognized after the fact that their people did need formal instruction in problem solving, and they quickly relabeled the initial course as Phase 1 and instituted a Phase 2, which taught the needed tools and practices.[11]

The *plan* phase happens at several levels in the organization. Senior management derives the design for courses directly from business needs. For example, consider BBN, whose senior management studied TQM and decided that the company needed to learn more about TQM (call this "need 1"). Senior management's customer visitation program, described in Chapter 8, convinced them that the company needed to do a better job of keeping in touch with customers (call this "need 2"), and to ensure that products always worked in the field as specified ("need 3"). We are simplifying the internal discussions and learning that led to the educational responses, but it is a matter of record that the three hardest pushed and most widely diffused courses at BBN are: (1) a TQM awareness course, "TQM at BBN" (meeting need 1); (2) a course on the procedure for customer visitation (meeting need 2); and (3) a 7 steps course (meeting need 3). As of this writing, a course is still being designed for the final item in the initial customer visitation results, standardization of product development process ("need 4"), even though the standardization efforts are already well started.

Planning deployment of courses is done by the TQM office and sometimes by professional educators, as is designing the actual curriculum materials. Similarly, the *check* phase of PDCA happens at several levels and time horizons. Following the new standard training practice, participants give daily feedback; some aspects of courses can be improved overnight by instructors. The use of course content in improvement work is monitored by the TQM office or corporate education staff on a three- to six-month time scale, and corrective actions are taken. For example, Teradyne's TQM office in 1990 rolled out a

7 steps course very rapidly. After several months, it discovered that teams were going through the steps more slowly than expected. It found that the primary cause was that the managers to whom team members reported (called sponsors in Teradyne terminology) didn't have clear ideas on how to monitor and encourage team progress or on what constituted appropriate progress. So the TQM office instituted a short course for team sponsors, and teams started to solve problems more quickly.[12]

Finally, on a yearly basis senior managers diagnose (check and act on) strategic issues: determining whether business needs have changed and whether improvement goals are being met. Often changes or additions in courses or their deployment result from senior management diagnosis. At Motorola this has become such a regular process that part of the quality goal for quality educators is quickly putting together a set of courses responding to newly identified business needs.

PROMOTIONAL ACTIVITIES

Promotional activities create a fertile environment for TQM. Figure 11-10 shows the three dimensions of TQM promotion: logic, events, and image.

Logical activities include newspapers, flyers, and other written material. However, people often don't read written material, which makes image all the more important.

Image activities include videos, visual displays, (such as QI story boards), quality flags, and symbols. The manager of one Japanese steel factory always greets QC circle leaders with a hand sign that means "what is the progress of your QC circle?" At the Hitachi factory front gate, big thermometer charts indicate the progress of various quality activities.

Promotional events include events such as the CEO Crusade described at Teradyne, the customer focus day described at BBN, presentation ceremonies (of QI stories and to reward

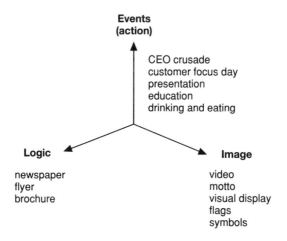

Figure 11-10. Three Dimensions of TQM Promotion

individual and team TQM activities), educational events, and eating and drinking events used to build teamwork.

Promotional activities often integrate with other activities. For example, BBN's initial customer visitations culminated in a customer focus day. The presentations that day not only promoted TQM, but also showed how the goals were set and how to use some of the 7 tools for management and planning, thus pushing ahead on goal setting, education, promotion, and diffusion.

DIFFUSION OF SUCCESS STORIES

TQM is not a theory. It is a mass movement. There is much genius in the masses — collective genius. If someone has a good idea, it should be used, standardized, and diffused. TQM developed a system of regular presentations of QI stories to help with this diffusion. QI stories are always like those described in Chapters 5 and 6, with a standard story format that shows process and tools. These stories teach the "how-to" of improvement by example and also promote improvement activities.

Milliken's presentation system is based on two-day quarterly "sharing rallies" at which improvements are shared. Milliken believes that to succeed the company depends on the experience and innovation of its employees (whom Milliken calls associates). Milliken goes by the slogan "Shared knowledge — shared success." Many kinds of presentations are given over two days, to peers and to upper management. Each participant gets a small award, which is presented by Milliken's president, Tom Malone.

Each presentation is rated by the audience for its use of the Milliken six-step improvement process — specifically, for problem identification, use of techniques, course of solution implementation, and evidence of lasting results. (Note that indirect learning occurs as each audience member studies the six-step method of each presentation.) The best presentations get awards. The presentations are grouped in several categories: corrective action teams, success stories, customer/supplier stories, innovative improvement, and so-called quick picks (small improvement actions). Although Milliken uses no standard formats for the presentations, it does use a standard evaluation form that diffuses the standard problem-solving process. Teams use slides, computer graphics, skits, costumes — whatever they want to make their points. These sharing rallies are very popular; there are usually long lines to the auditorium where presentations are given.

Japanese companies have developed a nationwide presentation system in which the best QI stories from each region are presented. (The system for choosing QITs to present is important and will be described later.) Tokyo Electric Power uses such a presentation system. Tokyo Electric has about 40,000 employees and 4,000 QC circles. Nine circles are selected for the company's annual presentation day at the largest auditorium in Tokyo. There is a long queue of executives waiting to get in to see it. Two thousand staff members come together to hear the presentations of the nine teams. Documents for each presentation are handed out to attendees.

These presentation days are also documented with videos that are distributed throughout the company. The CEO is involved in presentation day, sitting in the front row, attentive at all times. The presentations document success stories and detail how the 7 QC steps were used. The 7 steps format is strictly followed to ensure the diffusion of process skill. Teams use graphics, comics, and color to clarify the presentations. Each presentation is 15 minutes long and clearly organized, with a five-minute discussion session.

In Japan, separate presentation systems exist for workers, engineers, and managers. In general, there are two types of presentations — those on improvement processes and those on supporting processes. Workers mainly give presentations on improvement processes, while engineers and managers give presentations both on improvement processes and on the processes they use to support workers in their improvement processes. When presenting improvement processes, workers, engineers, and managers all use the 7 QC steps format. The engineers and managers try to follow the 7 steps but don't necessarily limit themselves to them because there is no standard process for proactive problem solving. The separate presentations also allow people to hear their peers in language they can understand. Worker presentations are the easiest to give, so companies should start with these. Worker presentations tend to deal with actual improvements, while manager presentations deal with focusing workers' activities.[12]

QI stories are judged by 8 to 15 judges. The teams use a standard presentation format, and the judges use a check sheet, which lists several items to check for, to score each step.[13]

Seven Benefits of the Japanese Presentation System

We have mentioned that some Japanese companies have a highly developed system of QI stories presentation. More detail on this system and its seven benefits follows. Of the seven, the first three — diffusion of success stories, mobilization, and deadline effects — benefit the company; the fourth and fifth — reflection and motivation — benefit individuals; and the last two — cases for societal learning and exchange between companies — benefit society.

1. Diffusion of Success Stories

A thoroughly done QI story represents an appreciable amount of work for the team. Therefore, people should extract maximum benefit from their improvement activities. The presentations and written documents widely communicate the success stories. They communicate not just the idea that improvement can happen, but the specific means by which it is accomplished.

2. Mobilization

Some Japanese companies have many branches or divisions; Tokyo Electric Power is an example. In October, each branch or division has its own presentation day, at which each QC circle in the branch presents its QI story. One QI presentation is selected from each branch or division for regional competition. All the circles in a branch or division are given modest awards, so that no one feels like a loser.

The QC circle selected from each branch or division attends a regional presentation day in November. From each division one is selected for a companywide presentation in December. This hierarchical presentation system is important, for it creates a motivating force for improvement activities at every location of the company. Indeed, the preliminary events in the branches are more important than the companywide event.

3. Deadline Effects

Everyone in the company knows a year in advance the days of the branch presentations in October, the regional presentations in November, and the companywide presentations in December.

These well-known dates provide pressure for all QC circles to finish their work by October. Without such a deadline, there are many reasons not to finish.

4. Reflection

Quality improvement is a trial-and-error process. It doesn't go smoothly through the 7 QC steps. For instance, the following figure shows an unimpeded progression from step 1 to step 4. At that point, however (perhaps because the solution didn't work well enough), the team repeated steps 2, 3, and 4, before going on to step 5, at which point it had to return to step 3 before completing the process (see Figure 11-11).

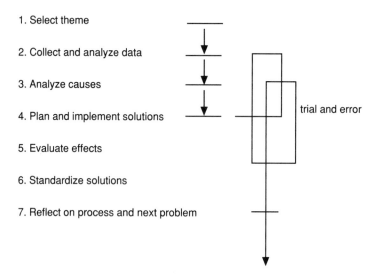

1. Select theme

2. Collect and analyze data

3. Analyze causes

4. Plan and implement solutions

trial and error

5. Evaluate effects

6. Standardize solutions

7. Reflect on process and next problem

Figure 11-11. Quality Improvement Through Trial and Error

The presentation lets the team reflect on its trial-and-error process, and on how to improve. Most serious weaknesses and failures of the 7 steps process, as well as the successes, are presented. However, the presentation should basically show forward progress and only hint at problems. The focus should be on the use of the 7 QC steps and improvement through use of the steps. The presentation also enables the team to reflect on how well the members worked together. The presentation should show the real process, acknowledging loops in the process but not showing so many that it confuses listeners.

5. Motivation

Many QIT members have a fear of public speaking or simply don't like making public presentations. The presentation system motivates such people to overcome their resistance. Giving presentations often rewards workers with a sense of fulfillment and achievement. It also reveals hidden worker skills such as skill at drawing, speaking, or data collection, which may be recognized and used.

6. Real Cases for Societal Learning

The sharing of real cases furthers societal learning. The presentation materials must be gathered in a document and distributed to nonattendees. These documents accumulate and in time create a body of standard methodology.

7. Exchange and Networking Between Companies

Even at company events, other companies are invited to share their stories. Many companies invite listeners from subsidiary or sister companies, for example. In this way the presentation system disseminates knowledge not only through documents (point 6), but through live presentation and personal contact.

AWARDS AND INCENTIVES

Joe Junguzza of Polaroid has looked into the awards and incentives a variety of U.S. companies use. The companies studied had activities in two areas: improving environment for quality, and praising quality. Quality environment-improving activities include those listed in Table 11-1.

Table 11-1. Quality Environment Improvement Activities

Management Leadership	Creation of vision Communication Motivation Behavior
Focus on customers	Information systems Customer visits Behavior
Participative management	Total involvement
Extensive training and education Respect for people	Teamwork
Extensive use of benchmarking to establish "stretch" goals and metrics	Xerox Motorola Corning Henry Ford Health Care 3M

TQM companies use many forms of rewards and recognition to reinforce appropriate behavior. Such rewards may be individual or team oriented, and monetary or nonmonetary. Tables 11-2 and 11-3 show some examples of individual versus team awards.

Xerox, Motorola, Hewlett-Packard, Corning, and 3M all use awards in various forms. Corning uses the following:

1. Individual outstanding contributor award
   - six in total
   - private
   - $3,000
2. Division cash award
   - 10 to 1,000 per division ($25 to $2,500)
   - division-administered

Table 11-2. Individual Awards

Xerox	President's Award
	Xerox Achievement Award
Motorola	CEO Quality Award
Hewlett-Packard	Use of internal publications to recognize individual contribution
NA Phillips	Breakthrough Award

Table 11-3. Team Awards

Xerox	Team excellence award
	Excellence in customer satisfaction
Hewlett-Packard	Group awards
	Group presentations of awards
Motorola	Division awards
NA Phillips	Breakfast/dinner awards
Florida Power & Light	QIT competition
Henry Ford Health Care	Team recognition

3. Division team award
   - 10 to 20 awards per year
4. Quality person of the year award
   - two per location
   - nonmonetary
5. Each location holds dinners, picnics, and formal award ceremonies all year long, and these are heavily stressed.

Xerox uses rewards to put a major emphasis on team recognition, for the traditional Xerox culture rewarded individuals almost exclusively. The rewards include:

1. Team excellence award (the premier award for the Xerox "leadership through quality" process)
   • $8,000 to $12,000 per team
   • process allows for many teams to be recognized
2. Many local awards
   • monetary awards
   • recognition awards
3. Trend toward giving awards to first-line employees (50 percent)
4. Gainsharing being piloted

MONITORING AND DIAGNOSIS

Monitoring and diagnosis represent PDCA for a company's overall TQM activities. In companies that have progressed to the Deming Prize level, monitoring and diagnosis of TQM activities are fully integrated into the PDCA of all the company's business processes.

Monitoring QITs

Florida Power & Light (FPL), the first non-Japanese winner of the Deming Prize, provides a good example of monitoring the subsystem of QI teams and their education and management.[14]

When QI teams are formed in FPL, a standard form and process are used, as illustrated in Figure 11-12. The team registration goes to FPL's Information Central, the companywide database of quality improvement activities. The team registration also goes to the team's supervisor (if it is a work group, which FPL calls a "functional team"), to the plant manager, and to the plant's facilitator. The facilitator, we were told, is typically a normal manager or engineer with greater-than-average methodology training, whose job includes part-time monitoring of methodologies used by QI teams in the plant.

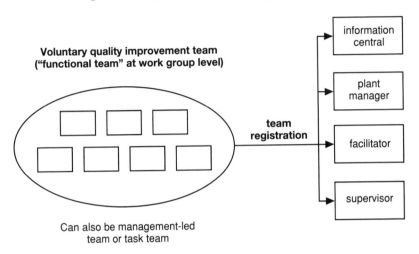

Figure 11-12. FPL Team Formation Process

Each time a team begins a new theme, there is a formal notification process for the same four parties, as illustrated in Figure 11-13.

After each meeting of the improvement team, the team writes up minutes and distributes them to the same four parties, as shown in Figure 11-14.

Machinery is clearly in place for hierarchical supervision of the improvement effort. The supervisor has first-line responsibility for seeing that the team makes progress and follows good process. The plant manager and the plant facilitator both ensure, via the minutes, that the supervisor is doing that job well. For example, if a team misses an opportunity to use a scatter diagram, or misuses an Ishikawa (fishbone) diagram, the supervisor and the facilitator make sure that the situation is corrected, either by simply pointing out the error, by training through coaching, or by recommending formal training.

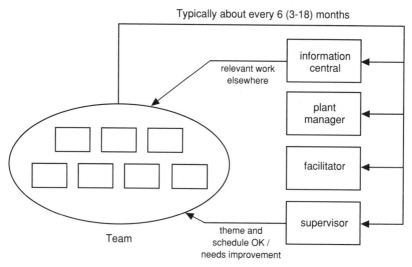

Figure 11-13. Registering Themes for Improvement

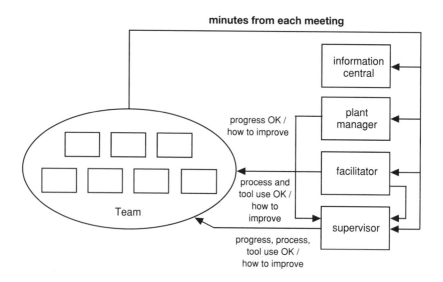

Figure 11-14. Distribution of Meeting Minutes

Part of the daily work of the plant manager and the plant facilitator is monitoring the activities of improvement teams and taking corrective action as needed. They know and follow the company standard for training people, encouraging formation of teams, and so on. They check the improvement activities against the standard, both for quantity and quality of improvement activities. They act when there are discrepancies. But if there are persistent discrepancies, continuing SDCA alone is inappropriate. If teams keep bogging down, improvement is called for, on the theme of teams missing schedules. This is PDCA. What are the root causes for the teams' difficulties? What changes in training or management can reverse those causes? and so on through the 7 QC steps or their equivalent. Note that our information was mostly about monitoring; the descriptions of diagnosis and root-cause correction were almost offhand. Nonetheless, the machinery for monitoring is firmly in place, and either formal or informal diagnosis and improvement would be straightforward.

Diagnosis by External Assessment

Another way companies monitor and diagnose their TQM activities is by assessment. Rather than check against goals and process standards a company has created internally (as in policy deployment), assessments use generic categories applicable (somewhat more loosely) to a wide variety of companies.

The original TQM assessment is Japan's Deming Prize. Though it was originally intended as a national promotion device (see Chapter 16), Japanese companies uniformly "challenge the Deming" in order to get the insights and improvements that come out of the examination process.[15]

America's Malcolm Baldrige National Quality Award was likewise intended as a promotional and diffusion device. So that it is less arduous and less open to the criticism of subjectivity, the Baldrige Award examination process is done according to 7 major categories, some thirty examination items, and approximately 100 areas to address.[16]

However, a new use of the award process has appeared. Companies use the Baldrige categories to assess their TQM programs, without any firm intention to apply for the award. Motorola very publicly required all of its suppliers to have plans for applying for the Baldrige Award. IBM has gone further and required at least some of its suppliers to have a "Baldrige-like" self-assessment system in place.[17]

One variation of external assessment is normative phase-, or maturity-based, assessment, which scores an organization relative to other organizations of comparable overall TQM maturity.[18] The outcome of such assessments is a profile of weaknesses relative to comparable organizations. Of course, the usefulness of such a profile depends on the quality of the organizations being compared. Another important category of monitoring and diagnosis is embedded in hoshin management (described in Chapter 14).

NOTES

1. Michio Ikawa, "TQC Activities at NEC Shizuoka," *Reports of Statistical Application Research, Union of Japanese Scientists and Engineers* 37, no. 1-2, 1990-91, 67-68.
2. This research was done by Joe Junguzza of Polaroid Corporation.
3. Ishikawa, *What Is Total Quality Control? The Japanese Way*, trans. David J. Lu (Englewood Cliffs, NJ: Prentice-Hall, 1985), 37-39.
4. Created by Shiba and Graham on the basis of the CQM design study of eight world-class TQM practitioners, Shiba's visits to Japanese and European companies, and visits by representatives from Florida Power & Light and Corning Glass to the CQM.
5. For a perspective on such codifications, consider the history of Philip Crosby's "four absolutes of quality," as described in his *Let's Talk Quality* (New York: McGraw-Hill, 1989), 51-52: "The Absolutes, as they now stand,

were laid out as a teaching aid for the first Quality College course. . . . There had been five Absolutes originally. They were listed in *Quality Is Free*. I eliminated two and replaced them with one. The two were designed for quality professionals. Therefore, they did not mean much to managers. They are both still true, but we teach them in different ways."

6. Some candidates for additional generalities: (1) Senior managers get longer classes in TQM than junior people; (2) the first course is TQM awareness — what it is, its importance, its vocabulary — and the second course is basic problem-solving methods (7 QC Steps or the equivalent). Bear in mind that these are all observations of companies that have ascended rapidly (three to five years) in TQM. Companies that have been practicing TQM since its inception, such as Toyota, may have different characteristics.

7. Purchased or licensed curriculum materials make PDCA and diffusion difficult. Typically, licensees may not alter materials, which makes continuous improvement difficult and education therefore less effective and more costly. Also, companies usually cannot share licensed materials with other companies. Without the ability to share successful practices, the evolution of TQM practice regionally or nationally is impaired. Chapter 16 discusses such issues further.

8. Ishikawa, *What Is Total Quality Control?* 37-39.

9. The authors are aware of the sharp distinction often made by education professionals between education (broad and conceptual knowledge learning) and training (focused, results-oriented skill learning). We consider this to be unnecessary 0-1 thinking, and advise against even speaking in ways that separate improvement skill from the surrounding conceptual context. Here the terms are used interchangeably, to reinforce the notion that training and education are united and balanced.

10. This story was told to us by Don Hopkins, the business manager of Corning Quality Systems at Corning, in a talk to the Center for Quality Management in Cambridge, October 9, 1990.

11. The idea that often does not sit well is that capable managers or engineers need instruction in problem-solving and improvement skills in general. As has been observed throughout this book, improvement differs from daily work. Perhaps we should not expect immediate transferability of skills between the two any more than between, say an airplane pilot and an aeronautical engineer. The two have many common elements, but each requires different training to function effectively.

12. This assessment of the 7 Steps rollout was done formally as a 7 Steps exercise, and is reported in Michael Bradley's and John Petrolini's "7-Step Case Study: How a 7-Step Process Reduced Roadblocks Impeding Quality Improvement Teams at Teradyne," *Center for Quality Management Journal* 2, no. 1 (Winter 1993): 7-17.

13. Masao Nemoto gives a very useful discussion and examples of checklists for evaluating QI stories in Chapter 5 of his book, *Total Quality Control for Management* (Englewood Cliffs, NJ: Prentice-Hall, 1987).

14. Florida Power & Light, *FPL Quality Improvement Program Team Guidebook* (1984). See also Eric D. Dmytrow, et al., "QIP — FPL's Continuous Improvement Process," in *ASQC Quality Congress Transactions* (Toronto: ASQC, 1989), 359.

15. John Hudiberg, chairman of FPL when it sought and won the Deming Prize, describes the preparation and examination process in his *Winning with Quality: The FPL Story* (White Plains, NY: Quality Resources, 1991).

16. The central document for the Baldrige Award is the "Application Guidelines" (including the application forms), which is available free of charge from the Malcolm Baldrige National Quality Award Office, National

Institute of Standards and Technology (NIST), (formerly the National Bureau of Standards), Administration Building, Room A537, Gaithersburg, MD 20899. A good synopsis of the usefulness of the award and discussions surrounding it appear in two articles in the *Harvard Business Review*: David A. Garvin's "How the Baldrige Award Works" (Nov.-Dec. 1991): 80-93; and "Does the Baldrige Award Really Work?" (Jan.-Feb. 1992): 126-47, in which several noted commentators respond to Garvin's article.

17. Other assessments, such as ISO-9000-1, may provide somewhat greater emphasis on quality maintenance than the Deming or Baldrige assessments do.

18. Examples include the Software Development Process Maturity Assessment, described in Watts S. Humphrey, "Characterizing the Software Process: A Maturity Framework," in *IEEE Software* (March 1988): 73-79; Sematech's "Detailed Organizational Assessment," *Total Quality Guidebook* (Austin, TX: Sematech, 1990); and Hewlett-Packard's Quality Maturity System (QMS), which is described in Brad Harrington's "Hewlett-Packard"s Quality Maturity System," *Center for Quality Management Journal* 2, no. 1 (Winter 1983): 44-47.

12

Phase-In

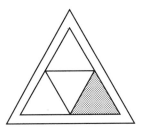

The discussion of initiation strategies in Chapter 10 has broached the topic of how to mobilize everyone in a company to practice TQM. We took an apparent detour in Chapter 11 through elements of infrastructure, because empirically, TQM prize-winning companies tend to implement TQM by emphasizing various elements of infrastructure in turn. Or more accurately, they formulate the elements of infrastructure to reflect phase-in sequences found to be typical.

Shoji Shiba and Masanobu Abe created a general description of TQM phase-in from research on Japanese quality circles activities and from a document of Deming Prize-winning presentations, which includes synopses of reports by companies that won the Deming Prize from 1982 to 1988.[1] The CQM design team found the same sequence in American companies we visited, and in fact Shiba's sequence is consistent with empirical descriptions of implementation from Juran, Corning Glass, and other American companies.[2] Figure 12-1 reproduces the seven elements of infrastructure divided into the three most typical phases of TQM phase-in. The idea of push and pull, introduced in the figure, are derived from the ideas of Lillrank and Kano.[3]

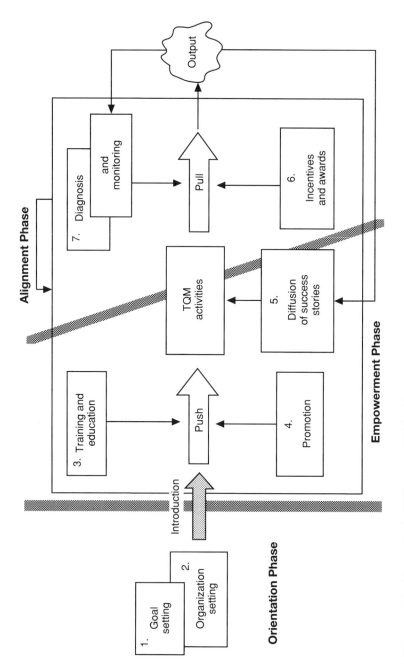

Figure 12-1. Three Typical Phases of TQM Phase-In

1. *Orientation.* When you introduce TQM, it is necessary to set goals and set up new organizational structures. Tell the staff of the company what TQM is and why it must be implemented (point 1 in the figure). Then create a new TQM planning and facilitation organization within the traditional organization (point 2).

2. *Empowerment.* You must create "pushing power" for TQM activity. The staff must be given the tools to practice TQM (point 3) and encouraged to use the tools and be involved in the quality effort (point 4). This must be reinforced by diffusion of improvement success stories (point 5).

3. *Alignment.* Once TQM has started and is moving ahead, you need pulling power to direct the activity — to synchronize and align the TQM and business goals and practices of the company (points 6 and 7).

These three phases are unlikely to be executed in a strict 1-2-3 order. It is typical to start with orientation and then move on to empowerment. However, you usually can't wait for full empowerment within various functional areas before beginning cross-functional and intrahierarchy alignment. Thus, you cycle back and forth across the three phases, advancing in each phase as necessary to support the activities of the other phases. This may take four to five years.

TQM "implementation" always takes place over periods of several years, and in several discrete stages that differ from company to company. It is better to avoid the overly simplistic and 0-1 term *implementation.* It is too easy to speak of TQM as "implemented" at one company and "not implemented" at another. A more precise term is *phase-in,* as in "what phase the company is in on its journey toward TQM." A discussion of each typical phase follows.

ORIENTATION PHASE

The orientation phase emphasizes goal setting and organization setting. The activities necessary to do these tasks effectively are senior management learning and middle management exploration and piloting. Effective goals require articulation of latent or actual crises, which in turn requires that senior management acquire convincing facts. Motorola and Xerox set goals by benchmarking competitors. Corning set goals in response to being outperformed in quality and cost, and losing entire markets. Motorola executives started regular customer visits.

Senior managers need to learn about TQM more extensively than those below them, in order to design and lead the company's program. Motorola senior executives uniformly take longer courses than mid-level managers. Florida Power & Light started its involvement with numerous trips by its senior management to Kansai Electric in Japan. (See Chapter 16 for more discussion about learning from other companies.)

The orientation phase involves exploration and experimentation. Bill Smith, VP for quality in Motorola's largest division, Communications Products, says, "We tried everything; but what worked is six sigma." It is common for entrepreneurial middle managers to attempt smaller-scale improvement activities, from which the company can learn what works and what doesn't work. Large companies may draw on successful experiments by entire divisions, as IBM did with its Baldrige Award winning AS/400 operation in Rochester, Minnesota.

The role of the senior executive learning in the orientation phase motivated the order of presentation in this book. Step 1 of successful "implementation" is always learning about the basics of improvement and the organizational systems needed to support them, which were covered in the first part of the book. Numerous choices are available for phase-in strategy. Without knowing what those choices are and how to fit them into the culture, strengths, and needs of a specific organization, it makes little sense to discuss phase-in strategy.

During the orientation phase, the other elements of infrastructure are likely to be informal, done primarily by senior executives and a few pioneering managers lower down. Training and education mixes classroom work with much visitation among peers from other TQM companies. Promotion is likely to be person-to-person, as is diffusion of success stories. Incentives and awards are personal satisfaction and the high regard of people engaged in orientation. Diagnosis and monitoring are likely to consist of informal assessments of knowledge: Do we know enough yet to be able to create an effective companywide program based on PDCA?

EMPOWERMENT PHASE

The empowerment phase is marked by initiation of training and promotion unequivocally intended to reach everyone in the company. This phase often begins when training cascades from managers to their reports, when "train the trainer" graduates move to active teaching, and when widespread diffusion of successful stories begins. Empowerment is working when training creates more training and success creates more success. This can be called the "snowball model" of phase-in (see Figure 12-2). Having a system for diffusing success stories — publicizing the detailed methods by which workers create improvement — is the key to creating a "snowball" effect.[4]

By contrast, any strategy in which a limited group of people expends more money or effort to train and engage the larger organization might be called the "Sisyphus model" of phase-in, after the Greek mythological figure condemned to push a large rock uphill forever (see Figure 12-3). Examples include hiring outside trainers or sending all managers to an outside course. These strategies are expensive and don't build on success.

The empowerment phase, then, is a period when new concepts and the practice of TQM are spreading throughout the organization.[5] During the empowerment phase, the orientation-

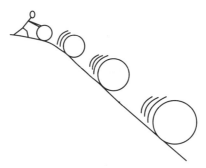

Figure 12-2. The Snowball Model of Phase-In

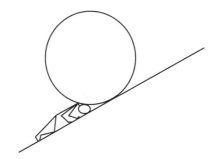

Figure 12-3. The Sisyphus Model of Phase-In

phase activities of goal setting and organization setting change character as they penetrate the organization. Goals are deployed as managers figure out how their respective functions contribute to the overall corporate goals. The goals become a focus of promotional efforts both through regular communication channels and through the "why" questions posed in TQM courses.

The choice of methods taught and how they are taught also embed goals into the training programs. For example, the 7 QC steps can be focused on specific company goals such as cycle time reduction or reduction of product defects.

The quality organization also extends further into the company during empowerment. Divisions and sites create their own TQM office and TQM steering committees. Early training goes to TQM officers, facilitators, or trainers, who may or may not be the same people. Also, cross-functional activities begin to happen more regularly.[6]

During the empowerment phase, the alignment activities of incentives and awards, monitoring, and diagnosis take place on a larger scale. The incentives and awards are likely to be recognition coupled with QI story diffusion.

ALIGNMENT PHASE

The transition to the alignment phase is difficult to define sharply. However, there are general themes. Some form of improvement activity has spread to almost every part of the organization. With the ubiquity of standardized problem-solving methods, it becomes possible to incorporate PDCA into all planning processes, which is to practice hoshin management (explained in Chapters 14 and 15.) This is a new emphasis on the monitoring and diagnosis element of infrastructure.

With most of the "low hanging fruit" of early improvements already attained, further improvement corresponds more closely to the quality of individual or team efforts, and to the methods they use in making the improvements. Therefore, awards, incentives, and recognition can more reliably reflect individual and team merit, which causes them to become more widespread. This is a new emphasis on the incentives and awards element of infrastructure.[7]

During alignment, the focus of TQM changes. Dominated in the empowerment phase by the addition of more systems or activities, it now shifts to integration, standardization, and customization. As will be seen, hoshin management can be thought of as managers integrating individual and team improvement activities throughout the company by working toward consistent goals and minimizing inconsistencies in means (such as excess resource demands) by planning. *Means planning* and *control by measurement* are standardized processes that managers use to carry out improvements. Integration and standardization capitalize on synergies among different processes. For example, hoshin management can yield information about which markets to target for product R&D. Florida Power & Light even linked medical practice to TQM; every visit to a plant's nurse or doctor for job-related medical problems mandated a QI story to improve the safety or health issue involved. In even a medium-sized corporation, there are many opportunities to find synergy among processes. As one FPL plant manager told us, "TQM isn't a separate activity anymore; it's the way we do business."

A final theme is customization. With several years of experience in TQM, companies typically improve their methods (sometimes in ways that would not have been feasible earlier). The companies create unique TQM policies. For example, Akao's books on hoshin management and QFD reveal many different variations in these practices.[8] Companies may deemphasize some of the 7 QC tools and add others (often a process flowchart, for example).

EVOLUTION OF THE PARALLEL ORGANIZATION

The form of organization changes with phase-in of TQM. Organizations begin with a standard formal organization, as shown in Figure 12-4.

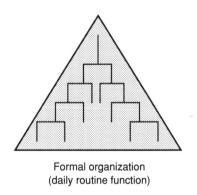

Formal organization
(daily routine function)

Figure 12-4. Standard Formal Organization

A company goes from where it is to where it wants to be in a few years by applying the PDCA improvement cycle, as illustrated in Figure 12-5.

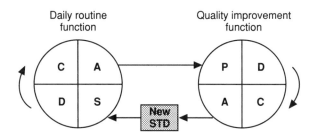

Figure 12-5. Using the Improvement Cycle to Create a New Standard

The improvement cycle is applied to the conventional or formal organization in two ways. First, it is applied within functional groups at every level, as shown in Figure 12-6.

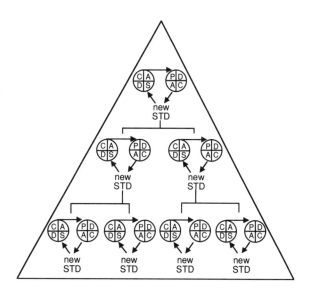

Figure 12-6. Applying the Improvement Cycle within Functional Groups

Second, the improvement cycle is applied in a cross-functional way to cross-functional systems by the improvement organization parallel to the formal (daily work) organization, as shown in Figure 12-7.

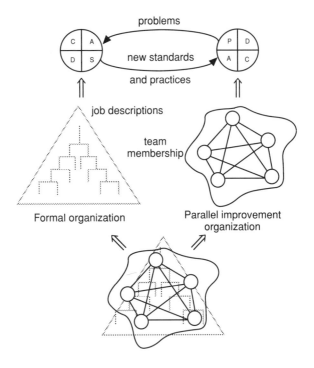

Figure 12-7. Applying the Improvement Cycle Cross-Functionally

The formal organization evolves for control of daily work processes — divisionalized for some companies, functional for others, and so on. Likewise, the parallel organization evolves to support improvement activities. The permanent committee structure may parallel the organization for daily work, as at Florida Power & Light. There may be permanent cross-functional committees directed at long-standing goals like cost, quality, and delivery. Companies as varied as Toyota and the

Ion Implant Division of Varian use this approach. One interesting experiment is IBM's establishment of permanent worldwide ownership by 14 committees, each for one fundamental business process. In all cases, the permanent organization spawns initiatives for individuals and task teams.

It is essential to have a parallel organization to do improvement.[9] The daily work organization, shown on the left of Figure 12-7, is constrained by job descriptions and operational pressure to do ad hoc and one-shot improvements. The daily work organization generates improvement problems. The parallel quality organization (QI teams, the TQM office, the TQM committee) has the flexibility to do what needs to be done to make permanent improvements. The parallel quality organization develops new practices and standards for the hierarchical daily work organization.

The parallel organization also develops behavioral norms and practices for itself that differ from those for daily work, even though the same people participate in both. Table 12-1 summarizes these ideas.

Table 12-1. Comparison of Organizational Principles

Functions	Elements of Infrastructure	Principles of Organization	
		Formal organization	Parallel organization
Orientation	Goal setting	Regulation	Philosophy
	Organization setting	Hierarchy	Networking
Empowerment	Training	Discipline	Mutual learning
	Promotional activities	Top-down exhortation	Permeation
	Presentation	Penalty	Praise
Alignment	Companywide mobilization	Mandate	Support
	Diagnosis	Supervision based on result	Diagnosis based on process

NOTES

1. Shoji Shiba and Masanobu Abe, "TQM as a Strategy for Societal Learning Process," *Quality, JSQC*, 20-1 (Tokyo: Japanese Society for Quality Control, 1990).
2. Juran's "Quality Roadmap" as adapted by Digital Equipment has five phases: decide, prepare, start, expand, integrate. Corning's implementation sequence is roughly described by its "Principles, Structure, and Strategies" *Corning Total Quality Digest* 2 (1990): 15-17. A description surprisingly similar to Shiba's appears in Dan Ciampa's "The CEO's Role in Time-based Competition," in Joseph D. Blackburn, ed., *Time-Based Competition: The Next Battleground in American Manufacturing*, (Homewood, IL, Business One-Irwin, 1991), 280-91. For more detail, see Ciampa's *Manufacturing's New Mandate: The Tools for Leadership* (New York: John Wiley, 1988).
3. Paul Lillrank and Noriaki Kano, *Continuous Improvement: Quality Control Circles in Japanese Industry* (Ann Arbor: Center for Japanese Studies, The University of Michigan, 1989).
4. No doubt our colleagues in the field of system dynamics would have us explain the same phenomenon as increasing the gain of a positive self-reinforcing feedback loop, as described qualitatively in Peter Senge's *The Fifth Discipline: The Art and Practice of the Learning Organization* (New York: Doubleday, 1990).
5. Which functions start TQM most aggressively differs from company to company. Japanese companies typically emphasize manufacturing and "move upstream" during empowerment phase to bring in R&D and marketing. (Even NEC Integrated-circuit Microcomputer Systems, a purely R&D operation, started "downstream" with design reviews and moved upstream with design plan reviews.) By contrast, Xerox's strategy for cost reduction focused as much, or more, on its product development process as it did on manufacturing as such.

6. Here the American and Japanese practices may differ. In contrast to the Japanese QC-circle-like emphasis on forming work group improvement teams first, the CQM design team saw a general American tendency to encourage cross-functional improvement teams right from the start. And, unlike Japanese companies, which according to Shiba formed permanent cross-functional committees in the empowerment phase (like Toyota's committees on quality, cost, and delivery), the American companies we visited made no mention of such permanent committees; functions cross only high up, where they meet in the normal hierarchy. Even at Florida Power & Light, which has a very highly structured TQM system (even by Japanese standards), cross-functional problems could be highlighted by goals set and deployed by high-level "lead teams" (TQM steering committees). Creating specific cross-functional teams, however, was apparently left to lower-level functional managers. Motorola's Bill Smith takes pride in the company's ability to easily form teams that not only cross functions horizontally, but also cross ranks vertically. Such teams, as Analog's Arthur Schneiderman points out, may be an American countermeasure to the classic difficulty of middle management resistance.

7. W. Edwards Deming has been a vocal opponent of performance-based pay schemes, contending that most variations in individual performance are outside the individual's control and many are simply random. Certainly Deming's objections apply with a vengeance to rewards for improvement in the absence of ability to identify cause and effect. Until a Pareto in step 5 can demonstrate that observed improvement comes from the changes made, rewarding improvements is equivalent to flipping a coin. For awards to be motivating instead of becoming a source of contention, 7 QC steps or the equivalent should already be widely used.

8. Akao, *Hoshin Kanri: Policy Deployment for Successful TQM* (Cambridge, MA: Productivity Press, 1991); and idem., *Quality Function Deployment*.

9. The concept of parallel organization originated in Rosabeth Moss Kanter, *The Change Masters* (New York: Simon & Schuster, 1983); also Lillrank and Kano, 112-116, develop the idea of the "hybrid parallel organization."

13

U.S. Strategies
for Phase-In

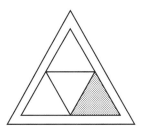

Organizations differ from one another in their TQM needs because they differ from one another in their history, culture, and business needs. Each company must find a TQM phase-in strategy (or strategies) that works for it. For instance, Alcoa Aluminum drove its successful TQM program with safety as the primary focus, which not only embraces a noble goal explicitly but also points out shortcuts that are being taken because of inefficient standard processes or inadequate tools for daily work.[1] Safety is a theme that company unions can embrace more readily than, say, cost cutting.

Table 13-1 shows a number of successful strategies for TQM phase-in, organized according to the three phases discussed in the previous chapter.

Although we have noted the country in which each of these strategies originated, companies in the United States and Japan have used various of these strategies.

In Japan, such concepts as market-in, fact-based problem solving, and focus on the vital few are used to orient the company to what must be done, by focusing on customer satisfaction as the purpose of the work people do in the company. QC

Table 13-1. Successful Strategies for the Phases of TQM Phase-In

Orientation phase (what must be done)	Customer satisfaction; Benchmarking (best performance)
Empowerment phase (how to do it)	Benchmarking (best practice); Six sigma; Cycle time reduction
Alignment phase (getting everyone to do it)	Customer satisfaction; Baldrige assessment

circles, improvement activities, and managers teach people how to improve their process to improve quality and customer satisfaction. Market-in provides alignment along the chain of suppliers and customers to the ultimate customer. Hoshin management and cross functional quality assurance activities focus all of the managers in a company in an annual cycle aimed at realizing the vital few breakthrough improvements the company must make. Finally, challenging the Deming Prize is used in Japan to focus the company on achieving the highest levels of quality practice.

U.S. companies also use customer satisfaction (Chapter 4) to orient the company to what must be done. As in Japan, customer satisfaction aligns everyone in the chain of suppliers and customers, and in recent years the Baldrige assessment has been used to focus the company on achieving superior levels of quality. In the rest of this chapter, we briefly describe three additional phase-in strategies — benchmarking, six sigma, and cycle time reduction — that are important U.S. innovations.[2] Benchmarking formalizes the idea of learning from others by first measuring the performance level of best-in-class companies — this orients the company to what must be done to be competitive — and then understanding the processes best-in-class companies use to achieve their superior levels of performance — this shows the company how to reach these competitive levels. Six sigma shows a company how to improve its processes to eliminate defects, and cycle time reduction shows a company how to improve its processes to reduce the number of steps and amount of time for processes.

In the following sections we describe benchmarking, discuss the synergies it achieves (which often expand beyond the associated phase shown in the above chart), and follow a similar procedure for six sigma and cycle time reduction.

BENCHMARKING

The place to start in any study of benchmarking is the book *Benchmarking: The Search for Industry Best Practices that Lead to Superior Performance* by Robert C. Camp of Xerox Corporation. Camp gives the following two definitions of benchmarking:

> Benchmarking is the continuous process of measuring products, services, and practices against the toughest competitors or those companies recognized as industry leaders. (David T. Kearns, chief executive officer, Xerox Corporation)

> Benchmarking is the search for industry best practices that lead to superior performance.[3]

We italicize some important aspects of these definitions. Benchmarking is a *process* (a process orientation is the way to learn and implement the methods of lasting effectiveness), and it is *continuous* (because the environment keeps changing). Benchmarking includes *measurement*, both inside the company and outside the company (i.e., it is based on objectively defined, consistently collected facts). Benchmarking looks at *products, services, and practices* (it is not just aimed at competitive analysis). Benchmarking also looks at those *companies recognized as industry leaders* (not just competitors). Benchmarking is a *search for best industry practices*; in other words, the aim in benchmarking is to learn from others, whether or not they are within your own industry. Camp's book describes Xerox's process for carrying on benchmarking activities. It contains a chapter on each of the following steps, with many implementation hints.

- Planning phase
    1. Identify what is to be benchmarked.
    2. Identify comparative companies.
    3. Determine data collection methods and collect data.
- Analysis phase
    4. Determine current performance "gap."
    5. Project future performance levels.
- Integration Phase
    6. Communicate benchmark findings and gain accep-
    tance.
    7. Establish functional goals.
- Action Phase
    8. Develop action plans.
    9. Implement specific actions and monitor progress.
    10. Recalibrate benchmarks.
- Return to step 1

One of our CQM companies, Digital, is implementing a benchmarking activity. It describes benchmarking as a search for industry process and procedures leading to superior performance. Benchmarking is not a competitive analysis of products, according to Digital, but rather a driving force for continuous quantum improvements. The company offers the following advice:

- Look for the best in class. For example, for distribution look at L.L. Bean and Hallmark Cards.
- Don't focus too hard on the financial numbers of the company you benchmark (they probably don't apply to your company). Look at the process it uses, and the operationally defined numbers for the business process or function you are benchmarking.

Digital is moving to benchmarking because its previous continuous improvement goals (for instance, 10 percent per year) are smaller than it now wants — it seeks breakthroughs. Digital presents a four-step benchmarking process:

1. What to benchmark? What are the critical success factors for the function being benchmarked?
2. How do we do it? What is our process?
3. Who/what is best? Who performs our function at world-class levels?
4. How do they do it? What are the "enablers" that create world-class performance?[4]

Steps 1 and 2 are internally oriented, while steps 3 and 4 are externally oriented. Steps 2 and 3 focus on "enablers" for improvement; steps 1 and 4 focus on critical success factors.

Digital cautions that one must be careful not to benchmark things that shouldn't be done at all — you want to eliminate waste, not improve it. Digital (as well as Xerox) notes that it is easier to get benchmarking data from noncompetitors than competitors, but this is all right since the best in class may not be competitors.

Benchmarking as one focus for an organization's TQM activities can fulfill several functions. We discuss them here not to praise benchmarking, nor to advocate its use for every company situation, but rather to show how a TQM program can be designed to be simple and effective by achieving synergy.

Goal Setting

At Xerox, you may recall, benchmarking was instrumental in establishing that a crisis existed, and therefore establishing both the need for and the feasibility of the aggressive goals Xerox pursued to survive.

Benchmarking, even if it does not become a companywide focus for TQM activities, can be important when initial goals are being set. For example, it was essential when Motorola established its six sigma and cycle time goals (to be discussed in more detail shortly). To remain competitive Motorola decided it needed a factor of 100 decrease in defects between 1988 and

1992 and a factor of 16 decrease in cycle time in the same period. Starting in 1988 it set these four-year goals:

- 68 percent reduction in defects each year for four years ($100 \times .32 \times .32 \times .32 \times .32 = 1$, i.e., a 100-to-1 decrease)
- 50 percent reduction in cycle time each year for four years ($100 \times .5 \times .5 \times .5 \times .5 = 6.25$, i.e., a 16-to-1 decrease)

Means Planning

For small-scale problem solving by quality improvement teams, planning the means for improvement is straightforward: reverse whatever is the major cause of the defect being pursued. For larger-scale improvement efforts such as automating production or speeding up product development, the means of accomplishing improvements are less straightforward.

For many years, the United States has used the concept of benchmarking products and services to provide targets based on competitive market analysis. However, this use of benchmarking did not provide U.S. companies with the means to achieve these targets. The extended concept of benchmarking being popularized by Xerox and others includes those means — the "enablers."

Customer Focus

Teaching people throughout an organization to act on a market-in philosophy is difficult. Companies need to find ways of putting a customer focus into operation. The design of the benchmarking process is one such way: before going out to find how best-in-class performance is achieved, benchmarkers following good process define what the customers of their function (internal or external) want.

Sometimes customer focus and even benchmarking can be built into common practices. For example, Motorola's "six steps to six sigma" improvement process integrates these concepts into the mechanics of improvement:

1. Identify the work you do (i.e., the product).
2. Identify who you do it for (i.e., the customer).
3. Identify what you need to do your work and from whom you need it (i.e., the suppliers).
4. Map the process.
5. (a) Mistake-proof the process and (b) eliminate delays (including non-value-added time).
6. Establish quality and cycle time measurement and improvement goals.

Steps 1 through 3 are the concept of market-in. Steps 4 and 5(a) are the defect reduction or six sigma concept. Steps 4 and 5(b) are the cycle time reduction concept. Step 6 is the benchmarking concept.

Promotion

As opposed to pure goal setting, benchmarking provides a solid factual foundation on which to set goals. Benchmarking gives you specifics on how competitors and best-in-class companies are outperforming your own. Such information has considerable value in promoting the need for TQM activities.

Diffusion of Success Stories and Learning from Others

In Japan imitation is considered laudable. On a recent trip to a major Japanese company, we were given the analogy of climbing Mt. Fuji. "You can drive or take a bus to the fifth station, but from there you must walk. Our goal in developing our products is to build on what we or others have done before, and thus conserve our scarce resources to reach the top, rather than walking all the way from the foot of the mountain." In the United States, imitation is not admired. Benchmarking provides an acceptable guise for imitation, enabling U.S. companies to learn demonstrably useful practices from each other without losing face, and thereby preventing wasted efforts on rediscovering (or never discovering) the wheel.

Benchmarking could be considered as an interesting variation on systems for sharing success stories. The standard QI story presentation event outlines a standard problem-solving process and how it created operational improvement. Presenting benchmark results outlines the standard benchmarking process, describes operational excellence in other companies, and shows how to implement such excellence in one's own organization. Moreover, the process of benchmarking requires enough creativity and effort that it is not difficult to get a sense of ownership and commitment to implementing the results. So benchmarking is a way of defusing the "not invented here" (NIH) syndrome.

Proactive Methods Balanced with Reactive Methods

Chapters 5 and 6 suggest that reactive problem solving can be universal within a company because it involves very tangible, unambiguous activities. Reactive methods have a disadvantage in that they work with defects or other preexisting "evils." Reactive methods generally imply step-by-step change in existing systems. Proactive methods, aimed at designing better products and processes from the start, are more demanding of skill and background knowledge, and so are more limited in terms of who can use them effectively. Proactive tools call for skill developed by continued use and substantive expertise in the product or process being designed or planned.

Benchmarking offers a middle path. It identifies problems (opportunities for improvement) before they become obvious in a company's operations. Benchmarking identifies opportunities for large improvements. It asks for moderately demanding effort to identify customers and their needs. And yet benchmarking involves steps that are less ambiguous and less

demanding of skill — in the sense that beginners are less vul-
nerable to making mistakes that significantly distort results —
than purely proactive approaches for many functions.

Results Focus Balanced with Process Focus

Companies differ in orientation to and understanding of
results versus process. Japanese TQM companies understand
that if the results are important, then the focus should be on the
processes for achieving those results. (Chapters 14 and 15
describe the process and results issue in more detail.) One must
go through all seven steps of the 7 QC steps. But this orientation
is foreign to many American managers and companies. Results
are the be-all and end-all: "I don't care how you do it, just do
it!" is the attitude. Benchmarking provides a results-oriented
way of introducing process orientation into management (see
Table 13-2).

Table 13-2. Benchmarking as a Results-Oriented Way to Introduce Process Orientation

Results-oriented surface appearance	Process-oriented experiences
Select benchmarking subjects. Set aggressive goals. Finish the benchmarking study.	Understand your job in terms of a business process that has customers. Identify most of the means for achieving those goals. Go through the steps. Repeat the steps.

The discussion above can be summarized by the matrix
diagram in Figure 13-1. Recall that generally speaking, a matrix
diagram is used to identify the least number of means to accomplish the requirements.[5] Across the top are options for means of

accomplishing TQM activities and infrastructure. Only bench-marking is shown; to use such a matrix to make choices about a companywide TQM program, one would include 7 QC steps and 7 QC tools, proactive improvement and the 7 tools for management and planning, customer visitation, and the other elements of TQM described throughout this book. Along the left side are requirements that a company might have for a TQM program to succeed. Listed are the issues described in the pre-ceding table. These issues will vary from company to company.

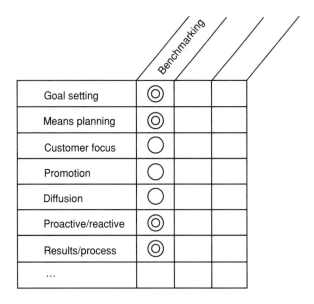

Figure 13-1. Matrix of Means for TQM Requirements (Benchmarking Example)

As Figure 13-1 indicates, if the profile of requirements was the same everywhere in the company, benchmarking would seem to be an effective focus for TQM because that single focus would accomplish a multiplicity of necessary functions.

Benchmarking requires considerable effort, however. As with any single TQM practice, companies should decide whether benchmarking is a permanent, companywide focus for

TQM (as it is at Xerox), something that top management and quality specialists do to set goals (as happened at Motorola and Analog Devices), or something not necessary to get started (as happened at BBN, where customer visitation and "near-benchmarking" proactive scrutiny of world-class engineering processes gave managers sufficient information and motivation to set goals and proceed with TQM introduction).[6]

SIX SIGMA AND CYCLE TIME REDUCTION

Six sigma (defect reduction) and cycle time reduction are the dual focus of Motorola's TQM. The purpose of cycle time reduction is to do things faster and more efficiently throughout the organization; it will be discussed shortly. Six sigma focuses on defect reduction. It is meant to imply a statistical concept; however, it is also a slogan calling for a several-year reduction in defects in all products and company processes to a very low level. In fact, the complete Motorola slogan is "Six Sigma by 1992," (i.e., within four years). The specific 1992 goal is a defect rate of no more than three parts per million. The following sigma levels are defined by Motorola (according to mathematics discussed in various Motorola publications):[7]

2 σ	308,700 ppm
3 σ	66,810 ppm
4 σ	6,210 ppm
5 σ	233 ppm
6 σ	3.4 ppm

Motorola defines sigma levels in terms of defects per million *opportunities for defects or errors*. This mathematical normalization establishes a metric that applies uniformly across products and processes, from making bread to making pocket-pager networks.

Motorola did extensive benchmarking while the six sigma concept and program were being conceived. Perhaps the most interesting finding was that once processes were normalized with the appropriate definition of sigma levels, most processes created errors or defects at around the four sigma level. Product manufacturing, payroll processing, airline baggage handling, doctors' prescriptions, orders written, journal vouchers, wire transfers, restaurant bills, and purchasing materials all tended to run around four sigma for processes not subject to world-class improvement efforts. Note that the list includes doctors' prescriptions, indicating that defect rate doesn't depend on intellect or level of education. Rather, it depends on process. The airline flight fatality rate is 6.4 sigma (.43 ppm), showing that with correct training and procedures, six sigma is achievable. Conversely, IRS tax advice is worse than two sigma, perhaps indicating the difficulty of attaining quality when the underlying standard is ambiguous.

Motorola's best-in-class competitors tended to run processes around six sigma. So "Six Sigma by 1992" became a matter of demonstrated competitive necessity.

Digital is adopting six sigma, which they call "Design for X" (x = reliability, manufacturability, maintainability, etc.) and which has the following characteristics:

- a disciplined approach to active leadership in design, marketing, manufacturing, selling, service, sourcing, and administration
- common measurement systems across the company
- a 60 percent per year defect reduction rate
- applicability to everyone — everyone provides added value, has suppliers, and has customers
- six steps, like the Motorola six-step process
- applicability to all types of work — administration, development, manufacturing, engineering, sales, marketing
- a common focus for all functions — the starting point is customer satisfaction, then improvement and streamlining of the process; and the common metric is total defects per unit

Note that Digital's explanation of six sigma includes diffusion of the concept we have called market-in.

The other major focus in the Motorola program, now widely emulated, is cycle time reduction. Digital gives the following definition of cycle time reduction: "a structured approach to review all implementation times against the theoretical optimum — the basis of elimination of all wasted time." This company uses a fairly pragmatic definition of the word "theoretical" in the above definition; it means the "calculated optimum" based on analysis of the current situation, as is shown by its four-step process for cycle time reduction:

1. Describe the actual process.
2. Identify the theoretical.
3. Analyze and eliminate the difference (or Δ) between the actual and the theoretical.
4. Challenge the theoretical.

Step 1 includes flowcharting the existing process, with each person analyzing his or her own job (and others looking from higher levels to make sure they eliminate unnecessary processes). At step 2 people think about which steps in the process are unnecessary and how long the remaining steps should take if everything goes smoothly. At step 3 they modify their processes. With their newfound experience, they begin again and reanalyze what the theoretical optimum should be.

Goals must be aggressive to get people energized and prepared to achieve the goals. A 10 percent improvement goal may attain a 10 percent improvement. People rationalize existing structures. A 50 percent improvement goal may attain 50 percent improvement. However, the theoretical calculations must be done at a low level, not centrally; the staff will reject centrally determined goals.

Many companies report similar observations, that is, factors of 5, 50, or 500 of waste in many company processes. George Fisher (chairman of Motorola) told an audience of CQM

members that perhaps 25 percent of the value of a good
company's revenue is waste. In one example from Digital, the
actual waste was 332 minutes and the theoretical waste was 57
minutes, showing potential waste of up to 570 percent.

Cycle time reduction is applicable in the factory and elsewhere:

- Shigeo Shingo, the Japanese guru of JIT, converted setup
  activities in factories that used to take many hours into
  ones that take only a few minutes by eliminating unnecessary motion.[8] For instance, he eliminated the step of the
  mechanic going to the tool room to get the right wrench
  by permanently welding the wrench onto the nut.
- At the Indianapolis 500 car race, mechanics change four
  tires and refuel the car in 20 seconds. They achieve this
  speed by closely studying the process, eliminating
  waste, and improving what has to be done; they film
  themselves and look frame-by-frame for what they can
  cut out.

There is a great deal more to Motorola's six sigma and
cycle time reduction programs than just articulated measures
and goals. For example, there are benchmarking processes to
establish meaningful goals for each functional area. There are a
multitude of training courses available on use of improvement
tools, team management, goal setting, and the technology of
daily work. But for the present discussion, we address the
advantages of six sigma and cycle time reduction as a dual focus
for the program.

Primary Drivers for Most Business Goals

As Bill Smith of Motorola puts it, making large improvements in defect levels (six sigma) and cycle time will make
large improvements in every single one of your business goals.
Figure 13-2 uses a matrix diagram to suggest how this can be
so. Motorola factually determined this for its businesses. For

example, field failure rates and fail-after-installation rates for semiconductor parts are well correlated with failure rates measured in the factory for outgoing products.[9]

	Six sigma	Cycle time			
Defects seen by customers	◎				
Waste	◎				
Overhead costs	◎	◎			
Production costs	◎	◎			
Responsiveness to customer orders	◎	◎			
R&D productivity		◎			
Product innovativeness and performance		◎			
...					

Figure 13-2. Impact of Defect Level and Cycle Time Improvement on Business Goals

Applicability to Diverse Functions

Defect levels and cycle time are drivers not only for the most important business goals; these improvement methods are applicable to nearly any process. We have heard stories of defect reduction in bread baking, and cycle time reduction in closing and auditing the accounting books. Like the 5 evils, defects and cycle time are applicable to a wide range of activities.

Simplicity of Goal Deployment

Motorola's TQM involves extensive and explicit goal setting in the fashion of policy deployment (discussed further in

Chapters 14 and 15). This involves setting overall corporate goals, then going through a planning process to deploy goals down to the individual manager and worker. If each individual and unit meet their goals, the corporation meets its goals. Sigma levels and cycle time turn out to be relatively easy to deploy in this scheme. If the defect goal for an assembled device is six sigma, the goal for each of the components and for the assembly process is likewise six sigma. Cycle times in a sequential process simply add, so if the cycle time is to be cut in half, one deployment of that goal is for the cycle time for each of the processes to be cut in half.

Balance of Process versus Results Orientation

The most visible physical manifestation of six sigma and cycle time reduction is a "5-up" chart that summarizes goals. But to produce such a chart you must have defined a customer-serving process and have data to back up the feasibility of accomplishing those goals. Motorola's planning process requires an understanding of process. Such an understanding of business process is especially important for your cycle time reduction.

An alternative explanation we heard was that if goals are set aggressively enough, people have no choice but to make permanent improvements to processes; anything less will cause them to fail to meet next year's goals. The business world is full of examples of aggressive goals not met. One must recognize what there is about Motorola's system for change — its TQM — that enables the company to consistently meet aggressively set goals.

Balance of Proactive and Reactive

Motorola is a highly automated high-tech company. Much of its improvement effort focuses not on long rows of assembly-line workers, but rather on engineering teams, or cross-functional teams involving both line workers and engineers. In that way, knowledge and experience usually exist on a team so that the process being considered can be substantially redesigned. And certainly the pace of change in the electronics industry should make design-oriented, proactive improvement more desirable than the reactive style. Indeed, Motorola's six steps to six sigma are design oriented rather than "fixing" oriented.

Step 5 of Motorola's six steps is to mistake-proof the process and eliminate delays. Buried in the detail of step 5 is the task of checking to see if improvement actually happens, and if it doesn't, using what amounts to the 7 QC steps and 7 QC tools — in other words, using reactive methods. Xerox also explicitly embeds a reactive methodology within a proactive framework. Analogously, step 4 of the 7 QC steps is to plan a solution. A solution involves knowing the present process, its customers, and their needs, and then designing a new (though similar) process to better meet those needs — in other words, using proactive methods.[10] Figure 13-3 summarizes the synergies created by the dual focus on six sigma and cycle time reduction.

	Six sigma	Cycle time	...	
Primary driver for most business goals	◎	◎		
Applicability to diverse functions	◎	◎		
Simplicity of goal deployment	◎	◎		
Balance of process versus result orientation	◎	◎		
Balance of proactive versus reactive methods	◎	◎		
...				

Figure 13-3. Synergies from Six Sigma and Cycle Time Dual Focus

NOTES

1. Thomas A. Stewart, "A New Way to Wake up a Giant," *Fortune* (October 22, 1990): 90-103.
2. Benchmarking was developed by Xerox and six sigma and cycle time reduction by Motorola. Readers may wonder why so popular an activity as benchmarking hasn't received more attention in this book. The authors believe that such ideas are best understood as unified, synergistic approaches to the design of a TQM system. Such systems may be appropriate for some companies but not for others. Therefore, treatment of this topic has been delayed to this point, when TQM can be considered as a designed system for company-wide improvement.
3. (Milwaukee: ASQC Quality Press, 1989), 10, 12. A brief introduction to benchmarking is also provided in Karen Bemowski, "The Benchmarking Bandwagon," *Quality Progress* (January 1991): 19-24; it discusses the benchmarking experiences of Alcoa and AT&T. Finally, GOAL/QPC (Methuen, MA) has published a research report that in effect synopsizes the Camp book in a monograph-length paper.
4. Benchmarking evolved separately from proactive problem solving, "voice of the customer," and QFD, so the vocabulary differs. Critical success factors can be described as important unmet quality requirements of the internal (or external) customers of the function being benchmarked. Enablers are the means for satisfying quality requirements at world-class levels. Benchmarking customer satisfaction directly as well as operationally defined quality variables is a standard part of full-blown QFD, as taught by (for example) the American Supplier Institute.
5. Those who have read Chapter 7 thoroughly know that this statement encompasses a considerable number of

variations. Sometimes the "means" are "means of measuring the extent to which the requirements are being met." In addition, the requirements may be all requirements, the ones rated important by Kano ratings, only those important and currently weak, and so on.

6. Because of the aggressive learning about competitors' products and processes that happens in Japanese TQM companies, American-style benchmarking is not widely practiced in Japan.

7. See, e.g., Mikel J. Harry and Reigle Stewart, "Six Sigma Mechanical Design Tolerancing," Publication no. 6θ-2-10/88, (Scottsdale, AZ: Motorola Government Electronics Group). These defect ratios are different from the ratios for various multiples of 1 standard deviation because Motorola's use of 6 in six sigma includes the possibility of a shift in the mean of the distribution.

8. See *A Revolution in Manufacturing: The SMED System* (Cambridge, MA: Productivity Press, 1985), Shingo's seminal work on setup reduction theory and methods.

9. Students of metrics know that focusing on only one or two metrics often leads to decreased performance in those areas not measured. Operationally, managers at Motorola (and the companies using the Motorola system such as IBM) have not two but five metrics upon which they are themselves measured. Typically there are one main defect measure, one main cycle time measure, and three other measures that round out the description of how well someone is meeting customer needs.

10. A similar yin-yang phenomenon happens between, for example, Motorola's six steps and benchmarking. Doing step 6 (goal setting) intelligently implies at least consideration of benchmarking. For example, Analog Devices used benchmarking to set goals, but determined that reactive methods would suffice to attain them reliably,

so that benchmarking did not need to be an ongoing, pervasive activity. ("Setting Quality Goals," *Quality Progress* (April 1988): 51-57.) In the other direction, DEC teaches that the goals that are being benchmarked, called critical success factors, should eventually become consistent top-to-bottom in an organization, as in hoshin management and six sigma.

14

Hoshin Management

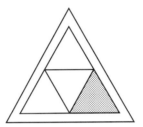

Hoshin management aligns the activities of people throughout the company so that the company can achieve key goals and react quickly to a changing environment. Hoshin management involves all of the managers in a coordinated way in the annual planning cycle of the company. Thus it provides an important strategy for total participation as well as fulfilling its obvious purpose of company alignment.[1]

WHAT IS HOSHIN MANAGEMENT?

Aspects of what has become hoshin management were tested by a number of Japanese companies in the second half of the 1960s. Among these companies were Toyota, Komatsu, and Bridgestone Tire Company. By the late 1960s and early 1970s, hoshin management had taken shape. It spread rapidly and became one of the major components of TQM. The Japanese called it *hoshin kanri*. Other English speaking authors have called it management by policy or policy deployment. We will follow the current convention of calling it hoshin management.[2]

Hoshin Management for Alignment

Hoshin management has three alignment purposes:

- It aims to align *all* the people throughout the company toward the key company goals, using indirect rather than direct enforcement — creating a sense of urgency; thus, even hourly employees are influenced to choose activities with strategically important objectives.
- It aims to align all jobs and tasks, whether daily work or improvement work, toward the key company goals in order to create *breakthroughs* — focusing and coordinating efforts and resources.
- It aims to quickly and effectively bring the company's goals and activities in alignment with rapid societal or environmental *changes*.

The following figures illustrate the power of alignment. In the following figure, the people and jobs are poorly aligned; the result is a total force that is limited and possibly ill-coordinated with key company goals.

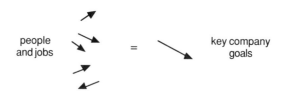

In the next figure, people and jobs are properly aligned; the result is a strong force aimed toward company goals.

The following figure shows that as environmental changes occur, company goals must be changed quickly and people and jobs realigned to these new goals.

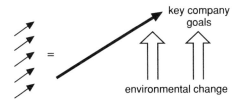

Hoshin management also has another purpose (discussed in greater detail in Chapter 15) — to force managers to run the PDCA cycle themselves as part of their daily job, and thus to develop themselves as managers.

Components and Phases of Hoshin Management

The main components of hoshin management are shown in Figure 14-1.[3]

As shown at top left of the model, the company's long-and mid-term vision and plans must be adjusted in consideration of environmental changes. From the mid-term plan, annual *hoshins* are developed.[4, 5] Hoshins are statements of the desired outcome for the year, plus the means of accomplishing the desired outcomes and measuring the accomplishment. Each hoshin ideally will include the following five elements:[6]

Hoshin = statement of desired outcome for next year
+ focused means
+ metrics to measure progress
+ target value for metric
+ deadline date

Here is an example of a hoshin:

Statement of desired   daily practice of
outcome for next year   =   market-in concept

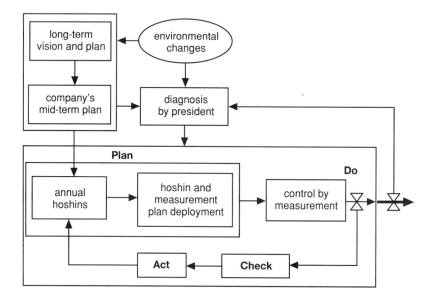

Figure 14-1. Hoshin Management

Focused means = Create attractive product by
improving market research;

Increase customer satisfaction of
our product by using quality tables;

Assure on-time delivery by improving
processes;
Improve quality of
production process by using
statistical process control.

Metric to measure progress   = On-time delivery rate

Target value for metric   = 100%

Deadline date   = March 1993

The primary, or top-level, annual hoshins are then deployed
(or cascaded) throughout the organization. In other words, a hi-

erarchy of subgoals and means for accomplishing and measuring them is developed, all in alignment with the top-level hoshins. At each lower level the hoshins have the same format but are more specific.

Next a *control by measurement plan* is made for monitoring month-by-month whether the goals and subgoals are being accomplished and the planned means for accomplishing them are being carried out, and for taking corrective action if they are not. Once the hoshins are deployed and the control by measurement plan is in place, these plans are executed. When it is time to plan for the next year, the data on which means were carried out and what was accomplished are analyzed (check) to discover what needs to be improved for the next cycle, and decisions are made on appropriate actions (act). This information is fed into the planning for the next year. Also on a yearly basis, the president does a diagnosis of the hoshin management system and suggests improvements relating to the system's effectiveness, any environmental changes that have occurred, and the company's long- and mid-term plans.

Proactive, Reactive, and Control in Hoshin Management

Hoshin management includes the problem-solving approaches enumerated in the WV model — proactive, reactive, and control, as shown below.

In the proactive phase the long- and mid-term vision and plans are adjusted in consideration of environmental changes, and the hoshin management system is itself managed, diagnosed, and improved.

The reactive phase is best thought of as a year-long PDCA cycle:

- Plan: develop annual top level hoshins, deploy the hoshins down the organization, and develop the control by measurement plan.
- Do: carry out the hoshins over the course of the year.

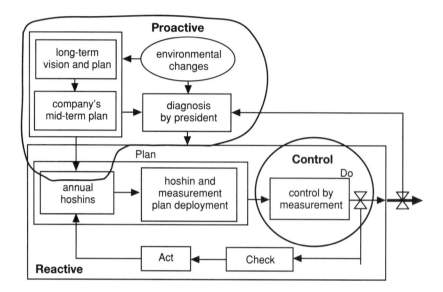

**Figure 14-2. The Proactive, Reactive, and Control Phases in
Hoshin Management**

- Check: analyze why hoshins were not accomplished —
  did the planned means not work, or were the planned
  means not carried out?
- Act: decide what to improve for next year.

The control phase is carried out over the course of the year.
The company uses the control by measurement plan to monitor
the results and controls the results and the means so that the
planned means are in fact carried out and corrective action is
taken when the means and results are not as planned.

As Figure 14-2 shows, there is overlap among the proactive, reactive, and control phases of hoshin management. Proactive and reactive overlap at the top-level annual hoshins.
Reactive and control overlap where the control by measurement
plan is used to monitor things over the course of the year, and
the control phase is the *do* part of the reactive phase.

Thus, PDCA cycles exist in hoshin management. First,
there is an inner PDCA cycle in the control portion of hoshin

management. Second, there is an annual reactive PDCA cycle. Third, there is an outer PDCA cycle that starts from the long-term and mid-term *plan*, goes through the annual deployment and execution *do*, and then does the diagnostic *check* and *act* to improve in the hoshin management system. These three PDCA cycles are consistent with the overall goal of the company.

We'll now describe the phases of hoshin management in terms of Figure 14-2.

PHASE 1 — STRATEGIC PLANNING (PROACTIVE)

The current daily management system of a company and the way people are currently doing their work should ideally provide a continuing degree of improvement in, for example, customer satisfaction (see top left of Figure 14-7).[7] However, analysis of circumstances may reveal that greater rates of improvement are needed. In such cases companies must analyze the difference between what the existing management system can provide and what is needed. They can then pinpoint the root factors that prevent the current system from improving fast enough and plan a solution. Solutions will employ standard tools and analogues of the 7 QC steps (described in Chapter 5). The 7 tools for management and planning (described in Chapter 6) will also be used. When the solution is deployed it may have two parts. First, it may be necessary to improve what people are currently doing or, second, it may be necessary for people to do new things. In either case, a revised system of daily work should provide the needed rate of improvement of customer satisfaction.

Hoshin management provides a systematic mechanism for calculating the difference between what a company can do and what it must do. It determines what improvements are necessary, and insures that solutions cascade through the organization so that people's daily work actually changes. Consider the schematic representation of the annual hoshin planning process in Figure 14-4.

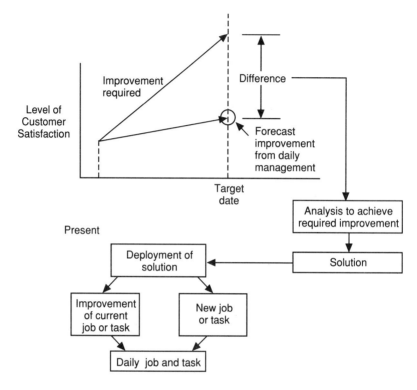

Figure 14-3. Analyzing the Gap Between Forecast Improvement and Improvement Required

What a company needs to do is dictated by the past (what it has been doing), by the environment, and by its vision of the future. To address the past, a company has the facts (what is), if it has the discipline to use them. The reactive, PDCA, portion of the hoshin management model deals with what is. The proactive portion of the hoshin management model addresses the environment (a given which the company needs to discover and address) and future vision (what is wished to be or will be). Once a company knows what is needed, it must focus people and jobs throughout the company according to what they can contribute to those needs. The hoshin plan and its deployment does this — it gives people the tools they need to change the way they work.

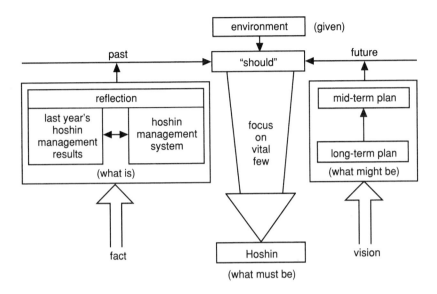

Figure 14-4. The Annual Hoshin Planning Process

The part of the hoshin planning process that deals with the past will be discussed later in this chapter. The section below addresses that part that deals with the future, an essential phase in strategic planning.

A Process for Creating a Mid-term Plan

Russell Ackoff has proposed some interesting methods for developing a vision for the future. He calls it backward planning. Ackoff's methods are compatible with the mid-term plan in hoshin management.

Ackoff's planning method, which he outlines in his book *Creating the Corporate Future*,[8] has five steps, three of which are described below.

Stage 1: Situation analysis. Situation analysis, or "formulating the mess," as Ackoff calls it, is identifying problems and opportunities. During this stage all current aspects of the company and its people are analyzed, the sources of obstruction are listed, and past and current performance is extrapolated assuming things stay as they are.

Stage 2: Ends planning. Ends planning means designing the desirable future. This step includes designing organizational structure and management systems. But its most interesting aspect is what Ackoff calls *idealized design*.

Idealized design is a powerful method of stating the desired future and planning efficient and practical means of accomplishing it. Idealized design does not design the company for some future circumstance. Idealized design designs the company you wish you had now.

Idealized design has the following properties:

- Work from the assumption that there is no system but the same environment.
- Design a technically feasible new system (consider the feasibility of the new system once it exists, not the feasibility or cost of bringing it into existence).
- Make sure that the new design is operationally viable in the current environment.
- The new system dissolves the mess.
- The new system allows for rapid learning and adaptation.

To do an idealized design you need a mission statement that says something useful about the business the company wants to be in, how it wants to operate, and what it wants to accomplish. You also need to specify the desired properties of the design. Examples might include:

- What products or services the company should provide and what its distinguishing characteristics should be
- How the products should be sold (where, by whom, on what terms, pricing)
- How products should be serviced
- Where and how products should be manufactured
- Which support services should be provided internally and which externally

- How the company should be organized and managed
- Personnel policies
- Methods of financing company activities
- Environmental and regulatory responsibilities

The next step is to figure out a design that has the desired properties. This design starts with a blank piece of paper. The designers assume the old system does not exist. This frees them from figuring out how to get from where they are to where they want to be, constraints that usually impede change.

The key value of the idealized design is that the designers can see the differences and similarities between the existing system (analyzed in stage 1) and the ideal system (designed in stage 2). Once they understand those points of comparison, they can plan the means for getting from where they are to where they want to be.

Stage 3: Means planning. Means planning is creating the means by which one effects the desired future. With the information on what design (rather than just the market share, revenue, and profit goals) a company wants to have, the planners can approximate a path from the new to the old. One method Ackoff suggests for finding this path this is to successively apply existing constraints on the new until the old is reached. This is illustrated in Figure 14-5.

At this point the designers have a map for undoing the constraints on the current system that prevent it from being the new system. They call this means planning.

Ackoff believes that the activities carried out in stages 1 through 3 will result in a plan that is much more feasible and focused than one created with the reverse strategy (starting from the present and moving toward future goals).

The typical company planning process goes something like this: The company decides on the goals it wants to achieve in 10 years and then plans toward them; the planners lay out a plan for achieving one-tenth of the goal per year (or project a hockey stick effect in which most advancement toward the goal is made

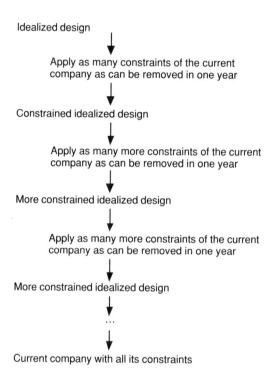

Idealized design

Apply as many constraints of the current
company as can be removed in one year

Constrained idealized design

Apply as many more constraints of the current
company as can be removed in one year

More constrained idealized design

Apply as many more constraints of the current
company as can be removed in one year

More constrained idealized design

...

Current company with all its constraints

**Figure 14-5. Means Planning by Applying Constraints to the
Idealized Design**

in the later years); the planners don't provide a detailed plan of
the year-by-year changes that will have to be made in the company to achieve the goals; the planners don't understand what
the company will have to become in order to achieve the goals.
Thus, the typical company planning process assumes a 10-year
effort to reach goals without really understanding what those
goals imply about the changes that the company will have to
make, and without making a plan for making those changes.[9]

In Ackoff's system of planning, the planners do situation
analysis to make explicit where the company is, where the company will stay unless it changes, and what is preventing change.
Then the planners do idealized design to figure out what they
would want their company to be like *now*, if they could create
an ideal company for competing in today's world. Then the

planners figure out a path from the ideal company to the current company. By simply reversing this path, they have a demonstrable path from the current company to the future company, and one likely to be shorter than 10 years.

Ackoff's methods fit nicely into the hoshin management methods of TQM (see Figure 14-6).

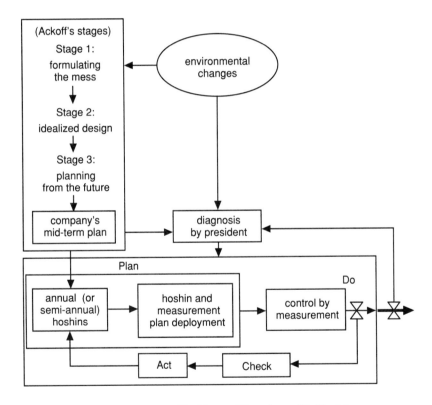

Figure 14-6. Meshing Ackoff's Means Planning with Hoshin Management

Goal Setting — Case Study of NEC Shizuoka

We learned the following details about goal setting in NEC Shizuoka's hoshin management system from a presentation given by Michio Ikawa, president of NEC Shizuoka.[10] The presentation was striking in its description of the NEC Shizuoka hierarchy of corporate mission and long- and mid-term objectives, which are so different from what we are accustomed to in U.S. corporations.

NEC Shizuoka was formed in 1969; by 1991 it had 1,350 employees and sales of $4.8 billion. Its main products are modems, facsimile machines, pagers, sophisticated telephone handsets, personal computers, and portable terminals.

The company has the following characteristics:

- a wide range of machine types, from communications to computers
- unification of design and manufacturing by product line
- realization of "2.5 industry" through operation of unmanned product lines
- corporate activities closely linked with the local community

A "2.5 industry" is an adaptation of economics jargon, where by the primary industry is agriculture, the secondary industry is manufacturing , and the tertiary industry is service. NEC Shizuoka is seeking to be a 2.5 industry, or to be between manufacturing and service.

NEC Shizuoka's goals are strongly influenced by those of its parent company. NEC's corporate philosophy is the following: "NEC strives through its slogan, Computers & Communication, to help advance societies worldwide toward deepened mutual understanding and the fulfillment of human potential." This is a noble goal, in the sense of the three levels of goals introduced in Chapter 8. Following from the corporate philosophy NEC also has what it calls the NEC commitment:

- Giving top priority to customer satisfaction through relentless efforts to provide better products and better services
- Creating value for society through the active exploration of new frontiers in science and technology

- Tapping the individual uniqueness of each employee and bringing out his or her fullest potential
- Fostering the autonomous spirit of each group and affiliate, which adds to the integrated strength of the organization as a whole
- Fulfilling its responsibilities as a corporate citizen
- Increasing profitability to facilitate dynamic growth internally and to contribute to society at large

Within the context of the NEC corporate goals and commitments, NEC Shizuoka has adopted the following management philosophy:

- Management places top priority on quality.
- The customer comes first.
- Make the workplace a place where individual potential can be realized to the fullest.

NEC Shizuoka has the slogan: "Immediate response when quality is at stake." Or, according to the president of NEC Shizuoka, when quality is at stake, the company pours in every resource.

NEC Shizuoka began its TQM implementation in 1983 in response to changes in the market: diversification of customer needs, major technology innovations and shorter product life cycles, and intensification of price competition to boost market share. In the face of these market changes, the company concluded it had insufficient systems for incorporating quality into the design and manufacturing processes and a passive business stance due to excessive reliance on NEC.

The TQM objectives of NEC Shizuoka state its desire to become:

- A company that can vertically handle everything from development and design to shipment, and that supplies products that meet customers' needs
- A company that incorporates higher quality and cost reduction both in design and in each process stage

- A company that can positively challenge and achieve management objectives
- A group of people with a consciousness of problems and the will to solve them

To these ends, NEC Shizuoka initiated the following main activities:

1. Implementing QCD (quality, cost, and delivery) focusing on source control
   - strengthening and expanding design capability
   - improving quality assurance in design and manufacturing stages
   - improving comprehensive production control that responds flexibly to changes in orders
2. Achieving management targets through promotion and improvement of hoshin management
3. Nurturing human resources

To summarize, NEC Shizuoka is a part of NEC, and all NEC companies have the same corporate identity: "Computers & Communication."[11] Based on the NEC corporate identity, NEC Shizuoka developed its company philosophy. From its company philosophy, NEC Shizuoka developed its Vision 2001, or mid-term plan. Vision 2001 is the basis of the annual plan. All of this goal setting can be charted as shown in Table 14-1, which includes the annual goals derived from the longer-term goals

PHASE 2 — HOSHIN DEPLOYMENT

Once a company has obtained the annual hoshin through analysis of the future and past, it is time to deploy the hoshin throughout the organization.

There are three fundamental aspects to hoshin deployment: moving down and up the ladder of abstraction, basing the deployment on facts and analysis, and deploying metrics to measure how well the means have been carried out and the targets achieved.

Table 14-1. NEC Shizuoka's Goal-Setting Process

Corporate Identity	Computers and Communication
⇓	
Company philosophy	1. quality first 2. customer first 3. development of employee capabilities
⇓	

Vision 2001
(mid-term plan)
	1. total sales $1.4 billion
	  • company to focus on office automation
	  • convey quality-first attitude to all employees
	  • accelerate new product development and
	    factory automation
	2. etc.
	3. etc.

⇓	

Annual plan (1990)	1. most important policy
	  • full implementation of quality-first attitude
	  • quick introduction and adaptation toward
	    small volume and large variety production
	    system
	  • etc.
	2. target (goal)
	  • cost down
	    – implementation of factory automation
	      requires pre-analysis
	    – with no people production system
	  • etc.
	3. guideline for management's behavior
	  • role was production only
	  • role should be planning design and production

Moving Down and Up the Ladder of Abstraction

There are several ways hoshin management moves down and up the ladder of abstraction. For instance, you can move from a long-term vision to an annual plan and deploy down the management hierarchy (see Figure 14-7).

You can also move down and up the hierarchy of processes to understand the targets and to analyze the root causes of

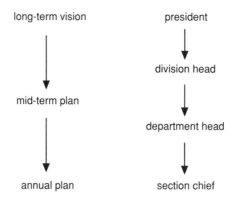

Figure 14-7. Deployment Down the Hierarchy

worse-than-expected performance.[12] For instance, as Professor Kogure showed us with Figure 14-8, the machine is a higher-level process which is in turn set up by a lower-level process, consisting of operators, materials, machines, and methods.

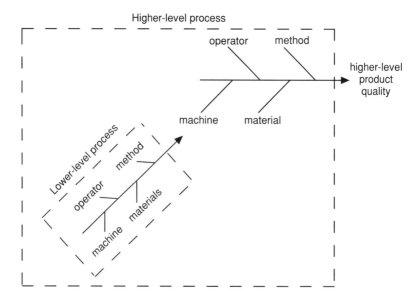

Figure 14-8. Deployment from Lower-Level to Higher-Level Process

Basing the Deployment on Facts and Analysis

There will follow a simple example of the deployment of hoshins from the president to the functional organizations. Each of the hoshins has the standard form

Outcome by Means: Metric: Target

For this example we'll not include the deadline. It is typical that the units of the metrics change at every level in the deployment and may differ from one hoshin to the next at the same level. Deployment will go down many levels in the organization, perhaps to the section level.[13]

Suppose, through analysis of the past, the environment, and the vision for the future, the president concludes that an annual hoshin should be "reduce costs 20 percent by decreasing the length of business cycles." The next step is to deploy relevant hoshins to each of the functional divisions below the president (see Figure 14-9).

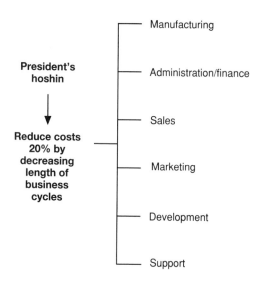

Figure 14-9. Deploying Hoshins to the Functional Divisions

Facts and analysis are essential to the deployment of a hoshin from one level down to the next. Analysis of the facts about key goals focuses hoshin deployment on the vital few.

The president and division heads must determine what prevents the company from achieving the key goals, and the president's subordinates must do the same. In other words, to deploy the targets and means sensibly, you must stratify the market, customers, products, sources of possible cost reduction, and so on. For example, you analyze which products have the biggest sales, which products grew most last year, and where cycle time can be reduced (see Figure 4-10).

The President and the division heads gather the data, stratify them, and then select the biggest problem at the next level for hoshin deployment.

At the lower levels, this analysis begins with the question, "What in our division prevents us from addressing our superior's proposed hoshin?" For instance, in the above example, the manufacturing division leader might ask, "What prevents us from decreasing the length of our business cycles?" Once again, a systematic, fact-based analysis is done, using, for example,

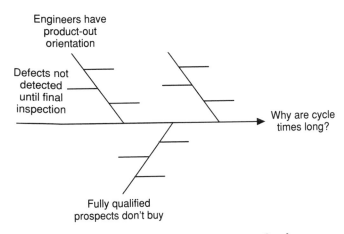

Figure 14-10. Analysis of Facts About Key Goals

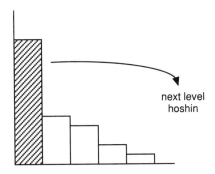

Figure 14-11. Stratifying to Select Problems for the Next Level Hoshin

Pareto diagrams, Ishikawa diagrams, and a seven-step PDCA process. As a result of this analysis, the manufacturing director might conclude that the root cause of manufacturing's inability to achieve the president's hoshin is "unresponsive procurement and inventory system." Similarly, each functional area would determine what prevents its own achievement of the president's hoshin.

Figure 14-12 shows what might result from each function's analysis of what prevents achievement of the president's hoshin.

From this analysis, each functional manager can draft appropriate hoshins deploying the president's hoshin to the functional area. Facts and analysis are also used to develop the hoshins, as well as the means and targets. Table 14-2 shows hoshins that might be developed on the basis of data given in Figure 14-2.

The system of hoshin deployment described here focuses on finding the process to achieve the desired outcome. In this sense it is very powerful. However, it has a weakness in that it fails to make clear what each means contributes to the higher-level outcome. Hoshin management as it has developed in Japan has a remedy for this weakness. We will return to this issue at the end of the chapter.

Let's take this deployment down another level, for instance, in the sales function. The sales hoshin in the example

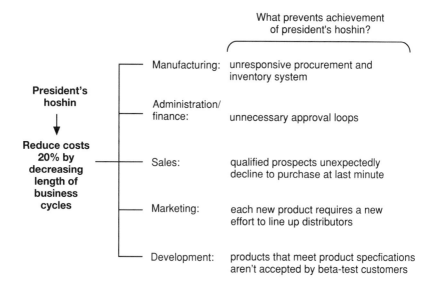

Figure 14-12. Function-Level Analysis of Barriers to Achieving President's Hoshin

Table 14-2. Development of Functional Division Hoshins

Function	What Prevents Achievement of President's Hoshin	Functional Division Hoshin
Manufacturing	unresponsive procurement and inventory system	decrease manufacturing cycle time 50% by implementing JIT
Administration/ finance	unnecessary approval loops	decrease key administration and finance cycles 40% by flowcharting processes and eliminating NVA work
Sales	qualified prospects unexpectedly decline to purchase at last minute	decrease average sales cycle 30% by decreasing qualified prospects who dont' buy
Marketing	each new product requires a new effort to line up distributors	decrease average time to release a new product 50% by creating strategic alliances
Development	products that meet product specifications aren't accepted by beta-test customers	decrease average time to successful product release 30% by increasing engineers' understanding of customer context

we've been following is "decrease average sales cycle 30 percent by decreasing qualified prospects who don't buy." Within the sales division there are two departments — direct sales and sales support. Each of these departments must gather the facts and analyze what prevents them from achieving the sales hoshin. Their analysis might resemble Figure 14-13.

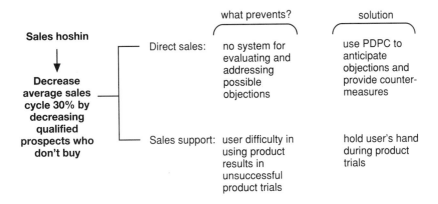

Figure 14-13. Analysis of Barriers to Achieving Sales Hoshin

You also use facts to align the deployment process. At a given level in the deployment, the manager's hoshins indicate a desired outcome and the means deemed appropriate to achieve the desired outcome. These hoshins are passed to the manager's reports, who draft hoshins supportive of those received from above. However, there may be disagreements. Between levels, managers use facts to verify the validity and feasibility of hoshins or to adjust them. These facts are conveyed back and forth on standard data sheets and through face-to-face discussions. This process of aligning the hoshins through the use of factual analysis is known as "catchball" in Japan. Catchball is indicated by the following symbol: ⓪. Catchball is not a negotiation of conflicting desires; it is a reconciliation of the plan with facts. The catchball occurs throughout the hierarchy (as shown in Figure 14-14).

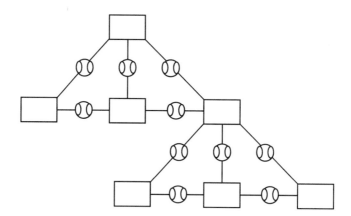

Figure 14-14. Aligning Hoshins Through Catchball

Once the analysis of facts and catchball is complete at all levels, a deployment like that shown in Figure 14-15 results.

How much guidance should a manager provide to subordinates in deploying hoshins? In his book *Total Quality Control for Management*,[14] Masao Nemoto gives the following guidelines for managers' deploying hoshins:

- Targets should be challenging but persuasive.
- Local issues need not be included as hoshins.
- Include as hoshins the few issues that will get special attention.
- The superior must provide implementation plans (means) for key hard items.
- The superior provides "points to consider" for a few items.
- Subordinates develop the rest of the means themselves.

While we have shown the deployment above as a tree, it is typical for the deployment to be documented in an alignment matrix such as that shown in Figure 14-16.

In the figure, the dotted circles indicate that hoshins a and b of the subordinate are aligned with hoshin B of the superior, and Hoshin c of the subordinate is aligned with hoshin C of the

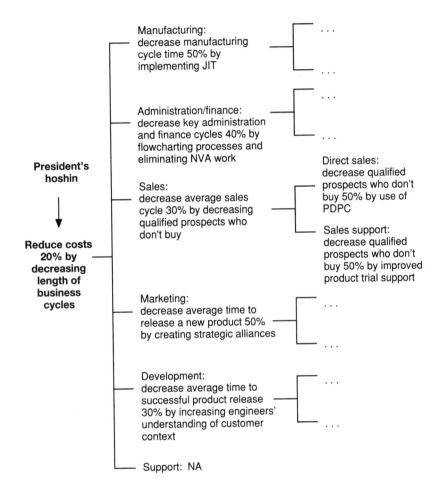

Figure 14-15. Deployment to the Next Level

superior. In this case, the subordinate does not have a hoshin related to the superior's Hoshin A. Focusing on the vital few at every level may mean that subordinates do not address all of the superior's hoshin goals.

Such alignment charts can easily be extended to summarize the hoshins of all of the subordinates of a manager, as in Figure 14-17. In this example all three subordinates have hoshins that

Superior's Hoshins

	Hoshin A	Hoshin B	Hoshin C
Hoshin a		⊙	
Hoshin b		⊙	
Hoshin c			⊙

Subordinate's Hoshins

Figure 14-16. Hoshin Alignment Matrix

Superior's Hoshins

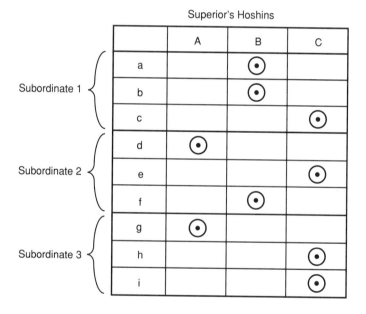

	A	B	C
a		⊙	
b		⊙	
c			⊙
d	⊙		
e			⊙
f		⊙	
g	⊙		
h			⊙
i			⊙

Subordinate 1 { a, b, c
Subordinate 2 { d, e, f
Subordinate 3 { g, h, i

Figure 14-17. Extended Alignment Matrix

are aligned with the superior's hoshin C, and subordinates 1 and 2 have hoshins that are aligned with the superior's hoshin B. Subordinate 1 does not have a hoshin related to the superior's hoshin A, but that may not be a concern because subordinates 2 and 3 do have hoshins that are aligned with A.

Deploying Metrics

A third critical element of the deployment phase (along with moving down and up the ladder of abstraction and use of facts and analysis) is use of metrics on execution of the plan and its results. The nature of these metrics can be made clear only through an examination of their use in the third (and next) phase of hoshin management.

PHASE 3 — CONTROLLING WITH METRICS (CONTROL)

Each of the hoshins deployed includes a metric and target. The metrics are monitored and compared against the target. Although the metrics and targets may also be shown in alignment matrices, the next figure shows them as little meters superimposed on the deployment tree. In addition to the meters representing metrics to monitor the outcome, the illustration also shows meters (metrics and targets) on the means to control execution of the means.

These metrics and targets permit the results and means to be monitored over the course of the year and corrective action to be taken as appropriate (see Figure 14-19). This is SDCA, where the "standard" is the planned means. Also, the metrics and targets tell you at year's end (or sooner) whether the failure to achieve the desired outcome was due to malfunctioning of the planned means or to a failure to carry out the planned means. If the means were carried out, then the process capability (planned improvements to product results) is inadequate and discrepancies between planned and actual results should initiate PDCA. In other words, the metrics allow you to monitor and control processes, even the process of changing other processes themselves.

The measurements of means and targets are monitored monthly, and actions are taken if the measurements are outside prespecified limits. A document specifying which actions to take in the case of unexpected measurements is called a mea-

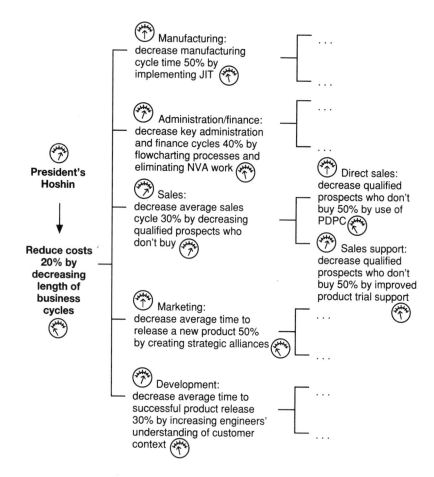

Figure 14-18. Deploying Metrics

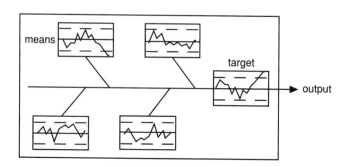

Figure 14-19. Using Metrics to Monitor Results and Means

surement implementation plan or control by measure plan. NEC Shizuoka's measurement implementation plan is a good example. See Table 14-3.

Table 14-3. NEC Shizuoka's Measurement Implementation Plan

Division manager	Section chief	Measure-ment (z item)	Goal (warning level)	When	Action at warning	Documents or graphs to be used
decrease defects of incoming parts	1. decrease major defects in incoming parts	number of major defects	0 (1)	1/month	details of actions	
	1.1 create a system for ZD					
	1.1.1 system to audit suppliers of major defects	suppliers audited		1/month		
	1.1.2 QC training for supplier	suppliers trained		1/month		
	1.2 direct control of worst two suppliers	number of defects caused by welding	0 (1)	1/month		

Unifying Daily Work with Hoshin Management

The purpose of hoshin management is to align every person and every activity so they address the key company goals. This makes it necessary to check whether people's daily work is currently in alignment with the top-level hoshins and, if not, to modify them appropriately. Managers have considerable discretion over which activities they emphasize, and the "natural" balance of activities may or may not support the current hoshins well. Thus a necessary and fundamental aspect of hoshin management is analysis of the daily work.

The components that support the objectives of each person's daily work need to be listed and organized. The result can be summarized in a tree (see Figure 14-20).

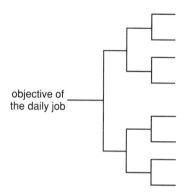

**Figure 14-20. Tree for Components Supporting
the Daily Job Objectives**

Next, the hoshins relevant to this person need to be correlated with the components which support his or her current daily job objectives, and new tasks must be added as necessary to accomplish the hoshins (see Figure 14-21).

From this correlation matrix it is possible

- to understand which daily job tasks have higher priority, because they address hoshins
- to understand that new daily job tasks have to be added so that the person addresses previously unaddressed hoshins
- for everyone to understand what each other is doing

You can then institute control by measurement methods (metrics and targets) that enable each person to monitor and control his or her own activities. Each must be sure to follow the process and accomplish the desired results. Thus, each person can run his or her own personal PDCA.

PHASE 4 — CHECK AND ACT (REACTIVE)

Once the annual Plan has been made (plan) and deployed over the year or half year (do), it is time to check for weaknesses

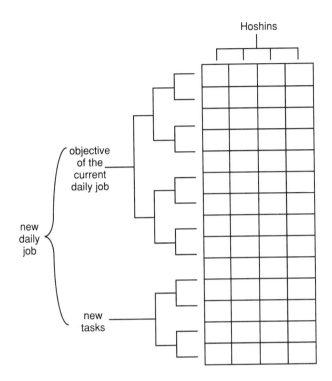

Figure 14-21. Correlating Hoshins with Components Supporting the Current Daily Job Objectives

in the plan or the way it was carried out (check) and to act appropriately to influence the next year's plan or possibly the long- or mid-term plans (act). (see Figure 14-22).

The check step entails discovering why the planned process didn't achieve the desired results. In other words, a process has been created that can now be analyzed using reactive improvement methods — you use the 7 QC steps to analyze the difference between the plan and reality, and determine the main causes of the difference. For instance, using the data taken as part of the measurement plan, you can discover whether parts of the plan weren't carried out or were carried out but didn't produce the planned result (see Figure 14-23). This provides feedback to the next planning cycle.

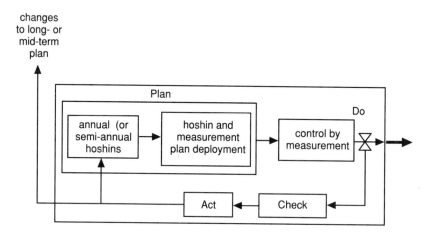

Figure 14-22. Checking and Acting to Modify the Plan

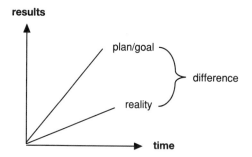

Figure 14-23. Analyzing the Difference Between Plan and Reality

It is important to enforce such fact-based analysis through use of the use of the 7 QC steps. For this purpose hoshin management dictates the use of analysis data sheets that the president or division head "diagnoses" to make sure they are done.

The act step then involves deciding on the key parts of the process to improve over the next cycle. This brings us back to *plan* and *do* as described previously.

get quantitative links between the president and management to balance.

- At the beginning the paperwork of hoshin management was time-consuming, but later it became easier.
- Shizuoka limited each manager's targets to three per year — these were their business targets.
- QA, profit, and manufacturing lead time were the president's three targets. These were derived from the previous year's results; more precisely, they were stated as less than x percent failure on final inspection, y percentage, and z days from order to ship.
- The president let his subordinates choose their means to achieve targets, but he reviewed the means with them.

Over the five years preceding our visit with the president of NEC Shizuoka, years during which the company implemented TQM and used hoshin management, NEC Shizuoka's sales rose at twice the rate of its staffing, and profits rose at five times the rate of staffing. The president attributes those excellent results to bringing costs down via factory automation and to embracing a process of systemization.

The president of NEC Kansai (another NEC subsidiary) said that the most important benefit of presidential diagnosis is that it enables him to detect latent problems and to adjust the hoshin management system to address them.

HOSHIN MANAGEMENT VERSUS MANAGEMENT BY OBJECTIVES

In the Japanese view, the United States may not have felt the need for hoshin management as strongly as Japan does. As shown in Figure 14-24, in Japan the CEO is felt to have less authority relative to vice presidents and division directors than do CEOs in the United States.[15]

Kogure quotes a 1980 survey of U.S. and Japanese companies in which it was revealed that U.S. companies were superior

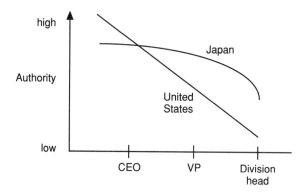

Figure 14-24. Comparison of Authority Levels

in formalization, concentration of authority in the upper levels, and systemization of management planning systems; U.S. companies were also strong in various aspects of cross-functional management (small business units) and in production management systems.[16] Therefore, Japanese companies felt it necessary to institute a formal system of deployment of policy from higher to lower levels in the company. They assumed that in the U.S. context, where top-down management prevails, top management directives may penetrate more easily to the bottom than theirs did.

Japanese companies don't have clear lines of authority — it is part of the Japanese culture to appreciate "softness" in such issues. Japanese companies prefer a bottom-up to a top-down system, and their hoshin management methods have developed accordingly. For instance, as mentioned earlier, the hoshin management system includes the explicit interlevel negotiation system of "catchball." Thus, hoshin management evolved to include a significant bottom-up component to modify the initial top-down policies.

In his book, Professor Kogure emphasizes the difference between hoshin management and management by objectives (MBO). Hoshin management puts stress on achieving results by controlling the process. MBO as typically practiced puts stress on achieving objectives by managing people.

MBO and hoshin management do the same job with regard to deploying company goals into individual goals and letting people try to achieve them. Even though Japanese hoshin management focuses on process, management does pay attention to results; emphasis on process is not permission to fail to achieve the results. Since hoshin management controls the process to produce results, you can analyze the process for the causes of failure and change the process until it does produce the desired results (see Figure 14-25).

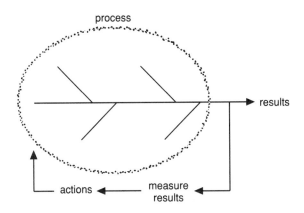

Figure 14-25. Analyzing and Changing the Process to Get Results

With its emphasis on making people responsible for results, MBO all too often abdicates responsibility for understanding the process used to meet the objectives. For example, it may not take into account whether the process is capable of achieving the objectives. Practiced this way, not only does MBO gamble on individuals and their own processes, which may or may not be capable processes, but MBO also has no way to learn how to improve if the individual or process is not capable — MBO typically does not even learn from an individual who is capable.

If only the targets and not the means are deployed, as frequently happens with management by objectives, the deployment shown in Figure 14-15 looks more like that shown in Figure 14-26.

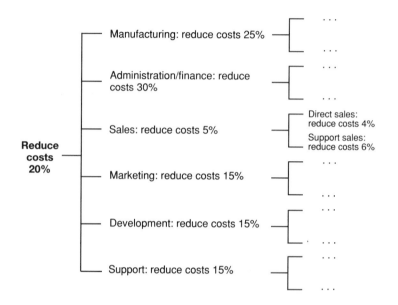

Figure 14-26. Management by Objectives

Note that the units of the metrics stay the same from level to level of the deployment. This is really a system of partitioning or dispersion of objectives rather than deployment.

Table 14-4 compares MBO and hoshin management based on our observations of actual use in U.S. companies.

Sales management often exemplifies the extremes of MBO. The cycle shown in the following figure will be familiar to many U.S. managers. In the MBO cycle illustrated above, the effort is to achieve sales performance by controlling the investment in salespeople and motivating their output, with little direct effort to understand, teach, and improve the sales skill of the organization. Managers and salespeople conspire to present sales as an individual skill that depends on the company's ability to attract

Table 14-4. Comparison of Management by Objectives and Hoshin Management

Management by Objectives	Hoshin Management
12-month planning cycle	6-month planning cycle
Deploy a portion of the top-level target to each segment at each level (no change of units of measure)	Deploy targets with different metrics to each segment at each level (change of units of measure)
Lower-level management is responsible for providing the means	Higher-level management suggests plausible means for key targets
Some negotiation of targets (considerable pressure for lower-level management to accept targets proposed by higher-level management	Catchball of targets and means based on facts and analysis
Little monitoring of the means (if it works, it's OK)	Some targets and metrics are aimed at controlling adherence to the means
	Analysis of causes and failure of the means of the last planning cycle is used to improve methods proposed in next planning cycle
Presidential recriminations for missing targets and sometimes replacement of the responsible manager	Presidential diagnosis of the PDCA cycle and suggestions on how to improve next time
New manager blames predecessor's system for past problems and begins to plan a new system	Old manager learns from past to do a better job next time
Dependence on undocumented skill in individual managers assumed to be capable	**Attempt to document needed skill and institutionalize it in the company**

successful salespeople. The company makes no effort to directly control its destiny by learning to sell its product and to develop salespeople who can do so.

While companies may perceive less need for a system to deploy and manage policy than Japanese companies, the purposes of hoshin management (listed at the beginning of this chapter) are equally important to both. The system is also useful to U.S. companies, as demonstrated by Texas Instruments and Hewlett-Packard.

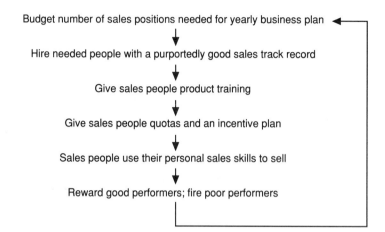

Figure 14-27. An MBO Model for Sales Management

Sarv Singh Soin of Hewlett-Packard gives the following view of hoshin management (which he calls Hoshin planning):

> You may ask the question, "Why adopt Hoshin planning? After all it is very similar to MBO and we have been successful with MBO." While MBO has many strengths, it has also many weaknesses. For example, there is a weak linkage between strategy and implementation; there is no detailed planning process; there is an insufficient consensus approach; a hierarchy of objectives, although apparent in theory, may not exist in reality; finally and most important there is no framework for a formalized review procedure to monitor and ensure success.
>
> Hoshin planning on the other hand has all the strengths of MBO and more to boot but none of its weaknesses. The strength of Hoshin planning is that it is a systematic and tightly coupled process. It does, however, require much more effort and consensus than MBO; but it helps provide a focus, a single-minded approach by the entire management team. The entire process is designed to en-

sure success. In the final analysis, Hoshin planning can be considered a more mature MBO process.[17]

Soin's view that hoshin management is a more mature form of MBO is consistent with our view of hoshin management as being complimentary to the conventional business planning process, as discussed in the next section.

HOSHIN MANAGEMENT AND CONVENTIONAL BUSINESS PLANNING

The conventional business planning process has many parallels to the hoshin management process we have described in this chapter (see the right side of Figure 14-28).

The conventional business process is substantially focused on results. In fact, MBO as it is often practiced can be viewed as a system to deploy desired results. However, process is necessary to achieve results, and providing the means to produce the results is the domain of hoshin management.

Hoshin management also takes a longer term view than the conventional annual business plan often takes. The actual goal of the company is not its annual results, but to achieve the company's vision and mid-term plan. The annual business plan is but a step towards the mid-term plan and vision. Hoshin management takes into account that some of the means necessary to achieve the mid-term plan and company vision may take more than one year. [It therefore builds into annual plans the means for achieving longer term objectives.] For instance, for a U.S. company to sell products in Japan takes more than a first year sales target. It takes a multi-year effort to understand the Japanese market and develop a capability to address that market. In this example, hoshin management will address the higher (longer-term) objective of selling products in Japan, while the annual business plan may specify only the Japanese sales expected for the next year.

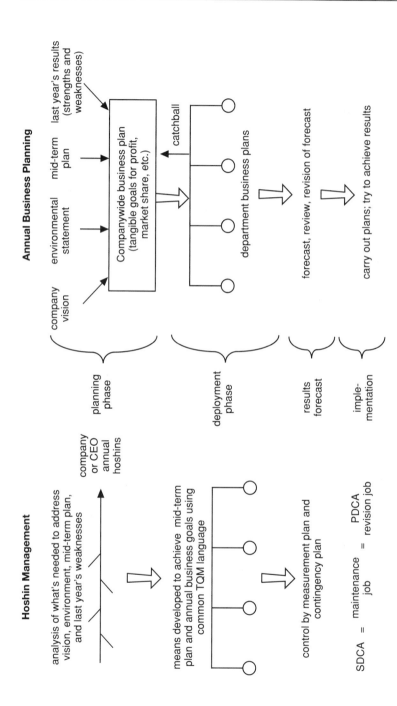

Figure 14-28. Hoshin Management Compared with Conventional Business Planning

As shown in Figure 14-28 (and discussed in detail earlier in this chapter), hoshin management begins by analysis of the environment, the vision, the mid-term plan, and last year's weaknesses to discover the top level (company or CEO) hoshins. These top level hoshins address the means necessary to achieve both the mid-term plan and the annual business goals. They are deployed downward through the organization using TQM's common language:

- Facts: using measurable data
- Process: using Ishikawa diagrams to understand what's really happening
- Focus: using Pareto diagrams to be sure to address the vital few

In the deployment of hoshins, the outcome at each higher level is the target of the means of the next lower level, as shown in the figure below:

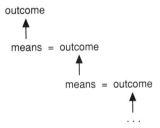

Let's put a 7 steps slant on this. In step 1, we state the theme, that is, the desired outcome.

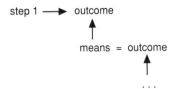

What is the means then? It is step 4, the solution.

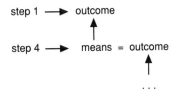

It is clear from this figure that we are missing something —
steps 2 and 3, data collection and causal analysis. This makes it
clear that creation of the means at the next lower level in hoshin
management should not be a speculative exercise. Rather, the
means is derived from data collection and causal analysis.

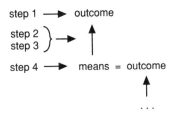

Then, control by measurement is used to develop the basis
of the interleaved SDCA (maintenance) and PDCA (incremental
improvement) cycles through which the deployed plan is implemented. As was stated earlier in this chapter, metrics are needed
to measure both the results and the means.

Hoshin management is a vehicle to integrate the entire organization to achieve the company goals. Kansai Electric
showed that to integrate the entire organization, two types of
PDCA were necessary — $PDCA_1$ and $PDCA_2$. $PDCA_2$ is hoshin
management (see Figure 14-29).[18] This is discussed in more detail in the next chapter.

AN ALTERNATIVE HOSHIN DEPLOYMENT SYSTEM

Earlier in the chapter we mentioned that the hoshin deployment system has a weakness in that it fails to make clear the connection between the means and its effect on the higher-level

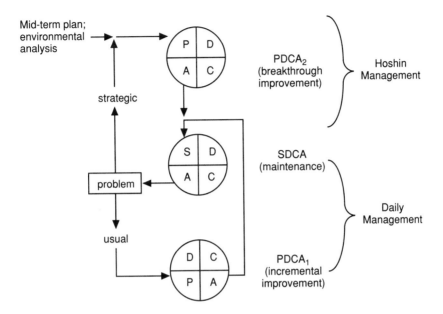

Figure 14-29. Two Types of PDCA for Organization Integration

outcome. MBO does not have this weakness, since it specifies to what degree each lower unit affects the result; however, MBO doesn't specify the means of accomplishing objectives. Akao describes a method of addressing this weakness.[19]

In this alternative deployment method, the top-level goal is stated and then guidelines are stated for the subdepartments. This first stage of deployment might look very much like the MBO deployment shown earlier (Figure 14-30).

Once the top-level outcome and guidelines for the next level are deployed, means are deployed (see Figure 14-31). The means are developed further on the basis of facts and 7 QC steps analysis of obstacles to the goal (see Figure 14-32).

Hybrid systems of deployment are also possible, where guidelines toward the top-level outcome are deployed and the alternating target and means system of deployment described earlier in the chapter is used to develop the means and process metrics and targets.

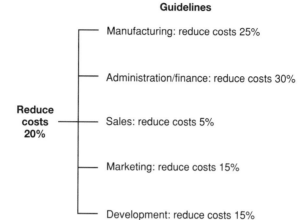

Figure 14-30. Guidelines from Top-Level Goal

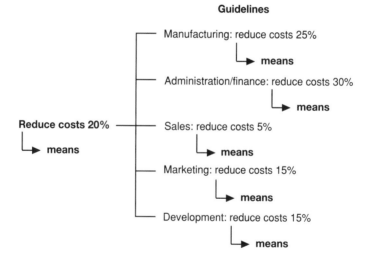

Figure 14-31. Means for Achieving Second-Level Guidelines

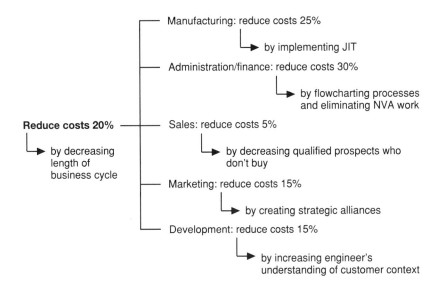

Figure 14-32. Top Management and Functional Means

HOSHIN MANAGEMENT AS "SYSTEMS ENGINEERING" FOR ALIGNMENT

Hoshin management is intended to systematize alignment (within the company and between the company and the environment) — to make it a form of engineering, like process engineering for manufacturing. Therefore, the same infrastructure elements are necessary for hoshin management as are needed for process engineering.

In the case of process engineering the elements of the system consist of physical elements such as the building or jigs; however, in the case of hoshin management, the elements of the system are invisible and influence the organization indirectly. "Soft" rather than "hard" elements must play key roles.

Table 14-5 shows the correspondence between the elements of process engineering and those of hoshin management.

Table 14-5. Process Engineering Compared with Hoshin Management

	System	Process	Tools	Operation
Production process engineering	building	machines	jigs	manuals
Hoshin management	hoshin management system	flow	data sheets	manuals

We have shown how hoshin management aligns the organization. In the next chapter we show how hoshin management enforces the use of PDCA by all managers.

NOTES

1. The discussion of hoshin management in this chapter introduces a number of concepts that are needed for the discussion of managerial development in Chapter 15.
2. For our discussion of hoshin management we are grateful to JSQC and its Research Committee on the Case Study of Hoshin Management for the document *Hoshin kanri unei-no tebiki (Guide for Hoshin Mananagment)*, 1989.
3. There is no one correct version of hoshin management. Each company adapts the basic concepts to its needs. The version we describe here is meant to be representative. It is based on a 1991 presentation by the president of NEC Shizuoka (Michio Ikawa), a 1991 presentation by Masao Kogure, a 1992 presentation by the president of NEC Kansai, and a 1992 presentation by Mitsuru Nitta of Tokyo Electric Power Company. Akao's book *Hoshin Kanri* provides an extensive description of hoshin management.
4. Some companies use a semiannual planning cycle because it allows more accurate prediction and thus more relevant planning and a more frequently improvement cycle.

5. The Japanese translation of what we are here calling hoshins is "policies." We are not using the latter term because hoshin management is describing something different from "policies" in the usual American sense of the word.

6. Many companies use variations from this ideal.

7. The material here draws on Hidemi Ueda, Yoshio Mitsufi, and Susumu Yamada, "Case Study of Hoshin Management, Daily Management, and Cross-functional Management (2)," *Total Quality Control* 38, no. 11, (1987): 79-89.

8. Russell Ackoff, *Creating the Corporate Future* (New York: John Wiley, 1981).

9. In Watts Humphrey's discussion of the software development process, his definition of insanity was "doing the same thing over and over and expecting things to change."

10. Michio Ikawa, "TQC Activities at NEC Shizuoka," *Reports of Statistical Application Research, Union of Japanese Scientists and Engineers* 37, no. 1-2 (1990-91): 67-68.

11. C.K. Prahalad and G. Hamel, "The Core Competence of the Corporation," *Harvard Business Review* 68, no. 3 (May-June 1990): 79-91.

12. Masao Kogure, "Some Fundamental Problems on Hoshin Kanri in Japanese TQC," *Transactions of the 44th Annual Quality Congress of the American Society for Quality Control*, May 14-16, 1990, San Francisco, CA, 5.

13. It usually stops short of the individual.

14. Nemoto, *Total Quality for Management.*

15. This figure is derived from Tadao Kagano, Yujiro Nonaka, Kiyonori Sakakibara, and Akihiro Okumura, *Nichi-Bei Kigyo no Keiei Hikaku (Comparison of Management Practices between U.S. and Japan)* (Tokyo: Nihon-Keizai-Shinbunsha, 1983).

16. Masao Kogure, *Japanese TQC: Its Review and New Evolution* (Tokyo: JUSE, 1988).

17. Sarv Singh Soin, *Total Quality Control Essentials* (New York: McGraw-Hill, Inc., 1992), 58. Soin's book came to our attention as this book was in publication, just in time to include the above quote, but not in time to point out other similarities or differences of viewpoint between him and us.

18. Figure 14-29 is adapted from a diagram in Kenji Kurogane, ed., *Effective Use of Control Items in TQC Activities* (Tokyo: Japanese Standards Association, 1990), 171.

19. Akao, *Hoshin Kanri*, 9.

15

Managerial Development

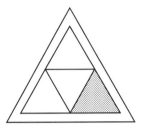

A difficult aspect of total participation is getting managers to practice TQM. Managers initially don't understand what their role is under TQM. Simply put, it is to teach and practice PDCA. Even when managers do understand their role under TQM, they find it difficult to practice. Developing managers so they can undertake their necessary role under TQM is the subject of this chapter.

The following case study illustrates both hoshin management (the subject of the previous chapter) and managerial development (the subject of this chapter).

CASE STUDY OF NIMS

Kiyoshi Uchimaru and his colleagues have written a book describing the efforts of NEC Integrated Circuit and Microcomputer Systems (NIMS) to implement TQM.[1] NIMS is a 1,000-person design subsidiary of NEC. It started as a contract engineering shop with little capability for managing development. Later, deciding that it needed to develop the highest level of self-sufficiency, it embarked on a path of TQM implementation, and in 1987 won the Deming Prize. This effort was led by the then president, Kiyoshi Uchimaru, who himself has decades of engineering management experience.

There are three ways to look at the NIMS story reported in this book. First, it can be seen as a story of TQM phase-in. As described in Chapter 12, TQM phase-in typically progresses through three phases: orientation (recognizing the need for TQM and learning its basic principles), empowerment (learning the methods of TQM and developing skill in practicing them), and alignment (harmonizing the business and TQM goals and practices of the company).

The management at NIMS began with orientation, but it became captivated by the concept of hoshin management as a method of aligning activities companywide. Therefore, from the orientation phase managers attempted to move directly to hoshin management and the alignment phase. Finding, however, that the NIMS staff did not have the necessary skill to work on companywide activities, they were forced to go back to the empowerment phase to teach the basics of TQM. With a little empowerment, they tried alignment again and were again forced to go back for more empowering skills. This cycle repeated several times until they had reached truly extraordinary levels of individual empowerment, after which they finally succeeded in alignment. In effect, hoshin management became the tool NIMS used to deploy each year's improvement ideas and to systematize successful ideas.

Second, the NIMS story is a story of the application of TQM in a creative engineering environment. We have all heard statements such as "TQM might be applicable to manufacturing, but it cannot be applied to a creative task such as engineering." The feeling at NIMS was no different. The NIMS technical staff cited all the usual reasons why TQM could not apply to them. However, Uchimaru makes the point that the history of science is itself a quality improvement story: develop a theory and plan how to test it, do an empirical experiment, check the result to see if the experiment confirmed the theory, and act to publish (standardize) the result. This PDCA cycle continues with each new theory being built on — or correcting — a previously held theory.

As Uchimaru sees things, an engineer who doesn't think TQM applies to technical activities must not understand either engineering or TQM or both. TQM is the application of the scientific method to business (pick an important problem, get the facts, analyze the facts, find the underlying truth, plan a method of improvement based on the underlying truth, systematically test it to verify that it works, standardize the new method, and then cycle around again). Uchimaru also explains why the complexity of modern business and technology requires a teamwork approach rather than each engineer "doing his own thing." In the case of NIMS, Uchimaru applied TQM both to the business of the company and to engineering methods.

Third, the NIMS story is a story of managerial development arrived at through hoshin management. When TQM is taught or explained, the first question from most managers is, "How will I have to change what I am doing?" The NIMS case illustrates the evolution and development of the role of technical managers under TQM.

Uchimaru and his colleagues didn't see a clear path to successful TQM implementation in a technical group when they started. They applied continuous improvement over a period of many years, incrementally discovering methods that worked to improve NIMS design quality dramatically. During these repeated cycles, Uchimaru and his colleagues focused on two fundamental issues: (1) making the development process ever more visible, and (2) inserting quality ever further upstream (that is, earlier in the design and development process). These two fundamental issues are represented by the horizontal and vertical axes of Figure 15-1.

Hoshin management cycles are often referred to as CAPD rather than PDCA cycles to emphasize the control and feedback aspects of hoshin and to focus on the manager's primary role of planning the next phase of the improvement process. A later

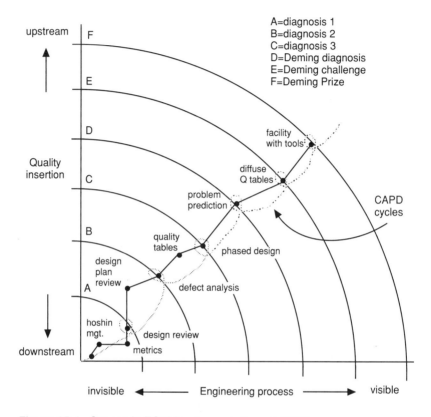

Figure 15-1. **Stages in TQM Implementation at NIMS**

section in this chapter describes the distinction between CAPD and PDCA more fully.

Like most companies, NIMS started in the lower left corner of the figure — with nearly invisible development process and with quality insertion relatively far downstream (e.g., catching defects after they have been shipped to customers). By the time NIMS won the Deming Prize, it had evolved a highly visible development process with quality inserted as far upstream as possible, as the upper right of the figure shows. This didn't happen overnight. It took many years of what Uchimaru calls "trial and error," by which he means repeated CAPD. The shaded curving loops indicate the CAPD cycle repeated over many years; the tight loops represent CAP and the long arches represent D. The labeled dots along the straight line segments show successive areas of improvement activity. The following paragraphs briefly describe these successive improvement activities.

Because hoshin management is regarded as a pillar of TQM in Japan, NIMS immediately tried to implement such a system (see slanting line segment nearest to the origin of the figure).[2] However, hoshin management did not immediately produce results as good as NIMS had sought. In fact, NIMS discovered that it was trying to implement hoshin management (a tool normally used during the alignment phase) before its staff had gone through the empowerment phase (in which basic quality capabilities are developed). In other words, it attempted to skip from the orientation phase of TQM phase-in to the alignment phase, but was forced to go back to the empowerment phase to build basic capabilities relating to quality.

The next step in NIMS's implementation was to install some quality metrics. By doing this it was attempting to make the development process more visible. It discovered first that getting technical people to agree on a set of metrics, or even agree that there should be metrics, took many months. Once the technical people had agreed on a small set of metrics, NIMS discovered that metrics alone didn't provide much improvement. In other words, it began to realize the need for focusing on process instead of results.

Next NIMS tried to improve its development processes by initiating design reviews. We all know about design reviews — meetings in which experienced and skilled designers from around the company review a proposed design. This was an attempt to insert the quality further upstream, that is, to find the bugs while still in the design stage rather than implementing poor designs. This activity helped some, but not as much as NIMS hoped it would.

NIMS then figured out that if finding problems in the design further upstream was good, then finding problems in the design plan would be even better. Thus, the company initiated design plan reviews in which experienced managers and technologists from various areas reviewed development plans, looking for potential problems that could be corrected before the project got under way. Design plan reviews proved to be quite beneficial.

While the design and design plan reviews were proactive efforts to eliminate defects and other forms of waste, NIMS soon realized that it was not making good use of all of the data on defects — it was not using this data to eliminate root causes of defects, that is, to do reactive improvement. Thus, it changed its operating methods so that if defects were found, investigations would be undertaken to figure out at what earlier time the problem should have been detected and when the problem was actually created.

This process was called defect analysis (see Figure 15-2). By doing this analysis and trying to shorten the two time intervals shown in the figure, NIMS made the development process clearer and also learned how to insert quality (or at least detect lack of quality) further upstream.

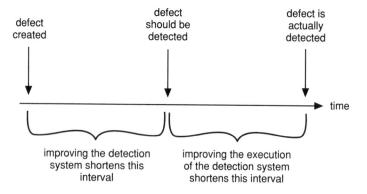

Figure 15-2. Defect Analysis

Having concentrated early improvement activities on detecting various types of defects, NIMS attempted to use quality tables (QFD) to better capture customer-defined quality. For a chosen project, it determined product requirements and built a big quality table to show how to achieve the requirements, but it took so long and was so big that it was not useful. So it reconsidered the customer requirements in light of which ones needed innovation (a small fraction) and which could be handled routinely (a large fraction). In other words, it learned to separate a development activity into parts requiring breakthrough improvement (e.g., invention of a new technology) and incremental improvement (e.g., a small change to an existing module). The activities requiring breakthrough it called the bottleneck, and the necessary innovative activity became known as bottleneck engineering (BNE). Then it used quality tables to plan how to do the bottleneck engineering. This proved to be very effective.

The chronology of NIMS improvement activities described to this point illustrates an important aspect of CAPD. NIMS didn't limit itself to reacting only to measured weaknesses of the previous cycle. The plan part of CAPD also includes an often qualitative assessment of the next important direction. Thus we see NIMS's improvement targets moving through several cycles of defect detection and elimination and then changing direction to focus on effective deployment of customer requirements. The successful parts of each improvement effort were added to NIMS's overall product development system.

Once the defect detection and customer requirements deployment systems were made explicit, it became clear that NIMS's design process was not very explicit. Thus, NIMS embarked on what it called phased hierarchical design. Of course, we all know about phase review systems for product development in which the development process is divided into five or six phases, each of which is several to many months long. NIMS divided these phases into subphases that were much shorter. This subdivision served two purposes. First, it provided many more points in time at which the process was visible (e.g., clear interfaces, clear test procedures); second, it permitted earlier feedback about problems. Making the process more visible allowed NIMS to understand which methods worked and which didn't, helped teams of engineers to work together efficiently, provided standard models for successive steps in the process for which standard tools could be built, and enabled greater reuse of modules.

By this point NIMS had progressed significantly both in making the process visible and in moving the quality insertion upstream. However, it still was not making the progress it wanted. In particular, the ultimate source of defects is mistakes by engineers, and it was not clear how engineering managers should help engineers to improve their skill — in Uchimaru's words, "to become more professional." By "professional," Uchimaru does not mean someone who gets paid for doing something each day; rather, he means the equivalent of a golf pro — someone who shoots par.

Uchimaru says that any professional (at golf, the game of go, or VLSI design) has three characteristics: a strong grounding in theory and the ability to apply the theory practically, a strong capability for analyzing failure (the professional understands why he or she made a mistake and learns from it), and a large set of tools he or she knows how to use in different situations, acquired through experience (many turns of the PDCA cycle).

The traditional way professionals are developed is by having a student study with a master. However, in the engineering field all too often the method used to teach engineers is the school of hard knocks. Companies hire engineering graduates from good schools and assign them to projects without much guidance on how to do good engineering. In fact, many engineering managers think their only jobs are to allocate staff and tasks and monitor results, and they don't have any explicit system to develop better engineers. Uchimaru makes the point that the engineering managers frequently use the notion that engineering is an individual art, learned through personal experience, as an excuse for why they can't do much to improve the ability of their engineers. However, Uchimaru says that if companies are to develop their engineers so that they create fewer defects, engineering managers must become coaches who teach the young engineers professional skills.

This recognition led to a system called problem prediction. The subphases of phased hierarchical design are divided into still shorter phases, each a few days long. The engineering manager's job is to sit down regularly with each engineer and ask what he is going to do in the next few days. Having heard the engineer's design plans, the manager asks the engineer to predict what might go wrong. Then the manager tells the engineer to go about his work for the next few days. A few days later, the manager again sits down with the engineer and asks him to describe his recent design work — what went wrong that the engineer thought would go wrong, and what went wrong that he didn't think would go wrong. The manager then helps the engineer evaluate the quality of the design, because a nonprofessional engineer is incapable of judging whether he has a good design. Through this problem prediction and coaching process, the engineering manager teaches other engineers to be professionals. Uchimaru says that a good manager must know the capabilities of his or her engineers well enough to accurately predict the areas in which they will have problems; then the manager can subtly guide the engineer to provide maximum learning from the engineer's process of prediction and reflection.

In the last two phases of the NIMS story, managers spread the techniques (such as quality tables) and facility of tool use throughout the company. Each of the concentric circles (labeled A, B, etc., in Figure 15-1) represents roughly a year's time. By trying iteratively to improve and control its development process, NIMS used TQM as a learning system that eventually taught it how to bring its development processes to the point where it won the Deming Prize, and it has results far better than industry averages. With each CAPD cycle it made another quality improvement — from the relatively superficial to recognizing and efficiently correcting defects and eventually to the profound level of improving the professionalism of their engineers. Uchimaru describes this as the "spiral up of craftsmanship."

COMPANY STRATEGIES

Having obtained an overview of hoshin management and seen how NIMS used it incrementally to improve its development process, we can now return to the question of management development in TQM. Improvement of managers' skills and managers' job processes is more complex than improvement for lower-level employees[3]; company improvement strategies and systems must typically be augmented for managers. There are three ways in which the necessary skills and processes for managers are more complex, and thus require extended improvement strategies.

First, managers are responsible for more complex processes. Managers are responsible not only for low-cost incremental improvements, but also for making larger-scale breakthroughs and deciding issues of resource allocation. If a company's improvement system focuses only on quality improvement teams (QITs) of lower-level employees, managers are likely to equate QITs with improvement, and therefore exclude major breakthrough and resource-using processes from systematic improvement. In addition, if improvement strategy and systems focus improvement on teams — be they high- or low-level — managers can lose sight of available improvements they themselves can make to their own daily jobs. Also, long cycle time processes tend to require a variation from PDCA as applied to short cycle time processes. We saw this in the CAPD step of the year-long hoshin management cycle. These issues are discussed in the following.

Second, more than anyone else, managers must take responsibility for achieving results, whatever the difficulties. If they don't, who will? However, many company strategies focus only on the desirability of accomplishing objectives and not the means of accomplishing actual results. To systematically improve the company's capability to achieve results, managers must learn to improve processes in which both the improvement and the consequences take more than a short time to ascertain; they must also learn how to discover what part of a process prevents the desired results and how to fix it. These issues are discussed later in the chapter.

Third, there must be a system to mobilize managerial participation in improvement activity in the company hierarchy. If the company uses a system of voluntary participation in improvement activities, a manager might choose not to participate — a decision that can leave those below with no leadership or support in quality improvement. However, the activities of managers differ significantly according to their level in the organization. Therefore, different mobilization strategies are needed for each level of the organization. These strategies are also discussed later in the chapter.

Ubiquity of the Dual Function of Work

When they first learn about TQM, managers often think that all improvement work is to be done by quality improvement teams, and that the teams will use the 7 QC steps, 7 QC tools, QFD, and so on. The managers think that their own daily job, on the other hand, has no relation to the 7 QC steps or PDCA. By extension of the dual function of work, we mean extension of explicit improvement activity to managers' daily work in addition to the activities of improvement teams.

Many managers recognize that the systematic improvement methods of TQM can make incremental continuous improvement to specific processes. They often don't recognize, however, that TQM also includes systematic methods of seeking breakthrough improvements.

Incremental and Breakthrough Improvement

The following figures illustrate the three improvement levels to which all systematic methods are applied.[4] To a considerable extent, these parallel the three types of problem solving from the WV model — process control, reactive improvement, and proactive improvement.

The first level of improvement comes from greater adherence to standards. This is SDCA, as shown in Figure 15-3.

The second level of improvement comes from incremental improvement by QC circles and QITs. This is one type of PDCA, which we call $PDCA_1$, as shown in Figure 15-4.

The third level of improvement comes from focusing on the most important issues across the company and on cross-company breakthroughs. Current information about the environment and company goals is needed for this. This is another type of PDCA, which we call $PDCA_2$, as shown in Figure 15-5.

These figures suggest different PDCA systems for continuous and breakthrough improvements. These are made explicit in Figure 15-6, which shows how Japanese companies apply appropriate TQM methods to both incremental and breakthrough improvement.[5] Coming out of the SDCA cycle near the bottom left of the figure are two types of problems that require improvement: (1) routine problems and accidents or acts of God, and (2) critical problems or profound problems (such as changing the company's quality culture). The first type of problem can be addressed by continuous improvement activities, while the second type of problem requires breakthrough activity and can be addressed by the company's system of hoshin management.

Daily Work and Improvement Work

Once managers understand the two types of PDCA, they must then discover how these are relevant to their own daily work.

Typical managers in non-TQM companies spend perhaps 75 to 95 percent of their time on daily work and routine fixes. Unfortunately, the improvement methods for these problems are intuition at best and guesswork at worst — not very efficient. This leaves the managers only 25 percent of their time or less for critical problems and breakthrough improvements.

If managers are to have time to work on breakthrough improvements they must reduce the time they spend on daily

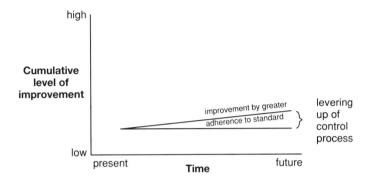

Figure 15-3. The SDCA Improvement Cycle

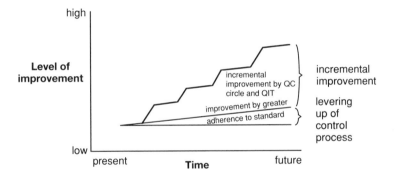

Figure 15-4. The PDCA₁ Improvement Cycle

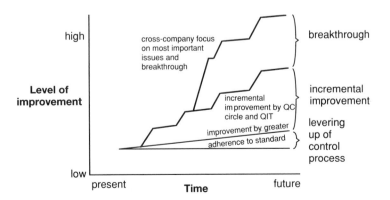

Figure 15-5. The PDCA₂ Improvement Cycle

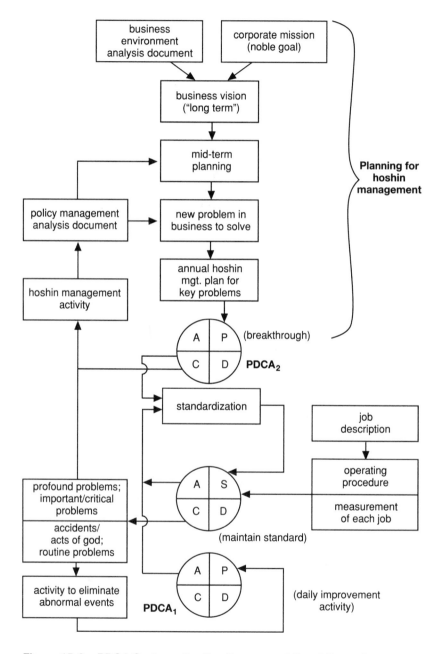

Figure 15-6. PDCA Systems for Continuous and Breakthrough Improvement

work and routine improvements. This means they have to obtain the benefits of standardization and use an efficient improvement process (i.e., the 7 QC steps) on routine issues. Increasing use of explicit SDCA and $PDCA_1$ actually makes more time available for working on breakthrough improvements. Furthermore, the explicit improvement methods of SDCA and $PDCA_1$ produce more valid data and experience and improvement skill. Not only do SDCA and $PDCA_1$ provide more time; they also develop intuition and innovation skill. In effect, they convert intuition from guesswork to mastery.

In TQM companies, managers do $PDCA_1$ themselves, as part of their daily job. There are three systems for getting managers to this level. In the first, QITs use the 7 steps, $PDCA_1$, and a little $PDCA_2$. They do this both to solve problems and to get on-the-job training in applying the 7 steps and PDCA. However, this first approach has two weaknesses: (1) diffusion of QITs is limited — that is, all managers can't participate in QITs; and (2) QITs move away from the idea that PDCA is a part of daily work.

Therefore, a second system is needed. This is hoshin management. Hoshin management forces all managers to use PDCA (in the form of CAPD) as part of their annual or semiannual plan for accomplishing key company objectives. In other words, hoshin management requires managers to practice $PDCA_2$.

Third, when managers have experience with $PDCA_2$, they are ready to tackle the hardest task of all, running $PDCA_1$ on their own daily work. Once a manager has experienced the PDCA as a member of a QIT or through hoshin management, the manager can begin to use systematic improvement in his or her own daily job, as described in the next section.

Using the Concept of Hoshin Management in a Department

We mentioned that hoshin management provides an opportunity for managers to practice PDCA themselves. However, hoshin management as normally practiced includes participation of managers from throughout the company, interlevel catchball, and a month or two to make the yearly plan. To many U.S. managers, hoshin management appears complex and documentation-intensive, making them reluctant to try it.

We have two observations on this. First, the empirical result — companywide improvement — is commensurate with the effort. Second, like so many TQM models, the hoshin management model is applicable at many levels. A company's first experience with hoshin management doesn't have to be at a companywide level; a divisional or departmental team can apply the model to a planning task. Consider the hoshin management figure again (see Figure 15-7).

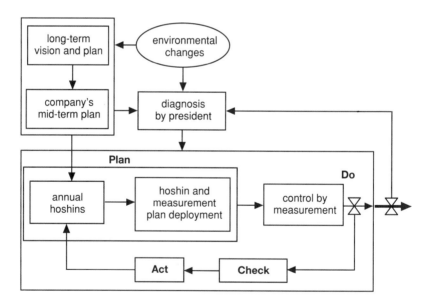

Figure 15-7. Hoshin Management

A department, for instance, has some longer-term (e.g., yearly) goals. As a result, they have decided that some specific significant task has to be accomplished ("significant" means a task that has several independent subtasks to be performed by individuals or groups). Such a task might be a marketing communications plan (e.g., advertising or brochures) for the year. Rather than doing interdivisional and interlevel catchball, the entire department planning team might get together to deploy this task (i.e., plan the subtasks and perhaps subsubtasks) and to develop an appropriate plan to control the subtasks (monitor adherence to the plan for accomplishing the subtasks and monitoring results).

The departmental deployment of tasks and measurement parallels hoshin management as described in the previous section, except it is done on a more contained scale and with all of the managers participating. Thus, it should be a shorter and more straightforward process, requiring, for example, a day or a few days of planning. Approaching the planning of the task in this way has the benefits of the hoshin management system — a plan that closely targets accomplishment of the task (rather than one that is based on guesswork), and a system for taking data to discover what actually happened both with adherence to the plan and its results. This provides the necessary information to run the CAPD cycle, so that each annual plan for this task benefits from the previous year's experience.

CAPD versus PDCA

As stated earlier in this chapter, we write PDCA in the CAPD form to emphasize the control and feedback aspects of PDCA. The distinction between PDCA and CAPD is subtle, as their difference is to a considerable extent a point of view.[6]

PDCA applies well to manufacturing, administrative, or other processes where the past is repeated over and over and the ultimate target remains more or less constant. For instance, consider the process of preparing a monthly financial schedule. The ultimate goals are to make the schedule ever more accurate, clear, and cheaply and quickly done.[7]

As shown on the left of Figure 15-8, initially the process has considerable variation.

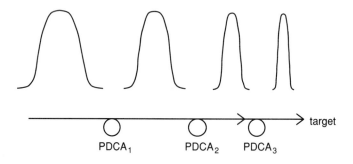

Figure 15-8. Repeating PDCA

The PDCA$_1$ cycle is used to improve the process and its results, as follows:

P: Pick the problem that is most responsible for the variation in results, analyze the root causes of the problem, and plan countermeasures to fix the root causes.
D: Do the improvement.
C: Check that the improvement was effective.
A: Standardize it as appropriate, and go to the next improvement.

Under continuous improvement, the PDCA$_2$ cycle is then run again to eliminate the next most important problem and thus further reduce the variance of the process and its results. Then PDCA$_3$ is run again, and so on. Every month the process is repeated, and the target remains the same — reduced variance to achieve an ever improved and economically produced financial schedule.

CAPD applies well to planning situations, which take up the bulk of managers' time. In these situations the past is unlikely to repeat — emphasis must be on planning the future. Consider, for instance, the yearly sales plan. As with PDCA, initially the process has considerable variation, as shown at the left of Figure 15-9.

However, the target for the next planning cycle (target$_1$) is likely to differ from the target for the previous planning cycle,

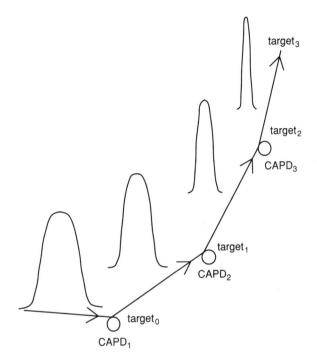

Figure 15-9. Repeating CAPD

because times will have changed. Even so, you want less variance in the way you carry out the plan for the next year and the amount by which you miss objectives. So you run the $CAPD_1$ cycle. The letters of CAPD have the following meanings.

CA: Discover what was wrong with the previous process that prevented achievement of the desired results; what are the key things to improve for the next cycle.

P: Determine what is desired for the future (e.g., what is the next target).

D: Carry out the plan for the year

CA: Check whether target was achieved, and if not, why not (repeat CAPD).

The purpose of CAPD is to improve the process in the face of changing goals. Thus, standardization in CAPD differs from standardization in PDCA — you must standardize on improvements to the process but at the same time change the process to be able to achieve changing goals.

PDCA is often compared to the scientific method: plan an experiment to test a theory, do the experiment, check the results of the experiment, and take appropriate action to publish or revise the theory. In fact, PDCA is a very good description of the scientific approach as applied, for instance, in an industrial, quality assurance situation where the target is known and relatively constant. CAPD is more representative of the scientific method as applied by research scientists. Such scientists have to decide what theory to test next on the basis of previous results and events in the technical environment. Then they must plan an experiment, trying to control as many variables as possible so they can accurately interpret the results but recognizing that some variables will be uncontrollable. Finally, they analyze the results, extracting all possible information that will enhance their understanding — what seemed to work, what didn't seem to work, what parts of the experiment they were unable to carry out and why, and so on. Then, they act to adopt and apply parts of the theory that were validated and to decide which key insights they should investigate in the next cycle.

CAPD is fundamentally the same as PDCA but differs in degree and emphasis in three ways:

1. In CAPD greater effort is required to conduct a controlled experiment, or at least an experiment where it's clear what couldn't be controlled. In a typical manufacturing or administrative process to which PDCA would be applied it is relatively easy to carry out a controlled experiment.
2. Processes to which CAPD is applied are often so complex and interleaved with other processes or external events that the goals of the process change over the course of an improvement cycle.
3. In repetitive manufacturing and administrative processes enough data can often be collected during the plan stage

so that root causes can be identified. In the complex, evolving processes to which CAPD is applied, one often has to run the cycle several times to gain an understanding of the potential root causes — the NIMS case study at the beginning of this chapter is an example.

Using the CAPD Cycle in the Daily Job

It has become a cliché that Japanese managers take a long-term view of process while U.S. managers take a short-term view of results. The short-term versus long-term distinction is in many cases an illusion — the true distinction is between correcting the superficial and correcting that which endures. Results focus on the superficial. Process focuses on that which creates enduring improvement.

Control of Process

Most people in a company don't understand that results are a function of process, that the results in fact come directly from the process. Figure 15-10 illustrates the process for baking a cake; the result comes from the process, which deals with methods, operators, materials, equipment, and so on. The results of the baking process include taste, texture, color, and so forth — the cake's quality characteristics.

Many companies largely ignore the relationship between process and results and focus instead on objectives, with the hope that by delegating aggressive objectives to capable people, they will somehow obtain the desired results.

You can control the process by monitoring it appropriately and taking appropriate actions to produce the results desired — for instance, moist cake, as shown in Figure 15-11.

The figure shows two types of monitoring. At point *a* in the figure, an aspect of the process for making moist cake (in this case, the temperature of the oven) is monitored. When the temperature deviates from the target temperature (350 degrees), action

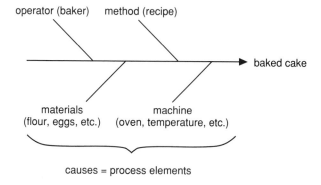

Figure 15-10. Process Elements of Cake Baking

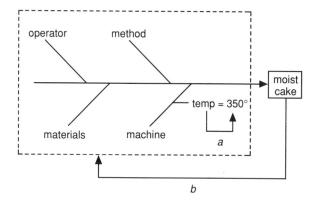

**Figure 15-11. Process Control of Cake Baking —
Monitoring Process and Results**

is taken to bring the temperature back to its proper level. This is control by measurement, as described in hoshin management. You can control the process by monitoring the deviation of the process from standard and bringing it back to standard as necessary.

At point *b* in the figure, you monitor the result of the process (in this case against some standard of moistness), and if the result is not as desired, you analyze the process to discover and fix the problem. Perhaps the process was not followed accurately, or perhaps the process should be modified to produce cake with improved qualities of moistness. In any case, the focus is on the actual results, what aspect of the process produced those results, and how to improve the process so that better results are obtained. In this case, you control the process by monitoring the deviation of results from the standard and improving the process as necessary.

The above example shows that there are two kinds of metrics: results metrics and process metrics. Few managers understand the distinction. Most focus on results while ignoring process ("I want to motivate the staff," or "I can't improve what I can't measure"), but a focus on results metrics alone is highly unlikely to succeed. As TQM has spread it has become more common for managers to focus on process metrics, but this alone is also unlikely to succeed. The point of paying attention to either process or process metrics is to find out what is causing or preventing success. If you don't look at results metrics, you won't know whether the process is working or not. If you don't look at process metrics, you won't be able to figure out what worked or didn't work. Managers must understand that process causes results, and that process metrics tell you why results metrics happened. The purpose of studying both kinds of metrics is to pinpoint what must be done to improve the process and thus improve the results.

There actually are three levels of control of process in the concept of CAPD. Two of them, control of process by monitoring deviation of process and control of process by monitoring deviation of results, have already been described.

Consider again the example of cake baking, where the desired result is moist cake.

The process of making moist cake requires an oven temperature of 350 degrees. The temperature can be monitored, and deviations from 350 degrees used to adjust the oven temperature until it is 350 degrees. This is control of process by deviation of process from standard — *a* in Figure 15-12.

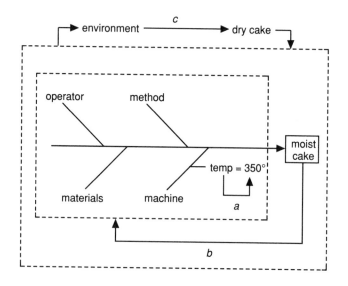

**Figure 15-12.   Process Control of Cake Baking —
Monitoring the Environment**

The moistness of the cake can be monitored, and deviations from the desired results used to adjust the process appropriately. This is control of process by deviation of result from
standard — *b* in Figure 15-12.

However, a third type of control is needed so that changes
in the environment can be addressed. By monitoring the cultural
environment, you can use deviations between current process
goals and new cultural desires to adjust the total process and its
goals to the new cultural norm. This is control of process by
monitoring deviation of goals — *c* in Figure 15-12.

For instance, suppose that the environment changes such
that dry cake is more desirable than moist cake — *c* in the figure. A company cannot simply say, "We make moist cake, and
people who want dry cake can go elsewhere." Such a product-
out orientation has lost out time and again to market-in competitors. The auto industry provides many such examples,
starting with its original victory over the horse and buggy
companies and continuing with General Motors' besting of

(any-color-so-long-as-it's-black) Ford, and the European and Asian car companies' trouncing of (Americans-want-large-fuel-guzzling-cars) U.S. companies.

Assumption of Responsibility

The highly developed manager must become capable of controlling a company's destiny in an uncertain world. This requires taking responsibility for developing processes that address the real situation. It means applying CAPD at successively more difficult levels, as follows:

Level 0: **Watch results but give little feedback beyond assigning blame to individuals.**

You know the results you want to achieve. Assign the job of achieving the results to someone and leave it to that person to run the process for achieving the results. When the results are not what you hoped, you suspect that the person to whom you assigned the job was not as capable as you had thought.

Level 1: **Take responsibility for the process — control by monitoring deviation of process from standard.**

Presumably there is a process for achieving the desired results. You take responsibility for adherence to that process, monitoring the process for any deviations from standard procedure and, when necessary, bringing the process back to standard. If you don't take responsibility for the process, you won't be able to maintain good results if they happen; and, if they don't happen, you won't know why — that is, whether the process didn't work or whether it wasn't followed.

Level 2: **Take responsibility for results — control by monitoring deviation of results from standard.**

Having followed the process you intended, monitor the results to see if they deviate from the goals of the process (presumably something to do with satisfying customers). The results tell you if the process is capable of producing the results desired. If the results are not what the process is supposed to produce, you trace those results back to the process and figure out what must be changed to produce the desired results. You rely not on opinion or intuition but on data leading to the real root causes of the results. Take responsibility for studying the process and then make the change necessary to achieve the desired results. Don't blame failure on individuals, the process, or circumstances.

Level 3: **Take responsibility for learning to survive in a changing environment — control by monitoring deviation of goals.**

The world keeps changing. What you thought were good results (i.e., what you thought would satisfy customers) may after a while no longer be good (satisfy them). Take responsibility for monitoring deviations between goals and changing customer demands, and change the process and its goals so that customer demands are met. Take responsibility for helping the company survive in a changing world.

Institutionalizing the CAPD Cycle

Recall the domino theory described in Chapter 10, which is that the CEO or president must mobilize the TQM officer and senior managers before the middle managers can be mobilized (see Figure 15-13). Typically, there may be a few unconvinced senior managers who also need further mobilization.

Mobilize all levels of the organization to use the CAPD cycle. Work from the top down, from the bottom up, and in the middle, making special effort to get the middle managers to do CAPD (see Figure 15-14). Since the nature of the job is different at each level, requiring different applications of CAPD, it is appropriate for companies to use a different mobilization strategy at each level.

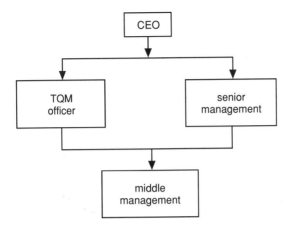

Figure 15-13. Domino Theory of Mobilization

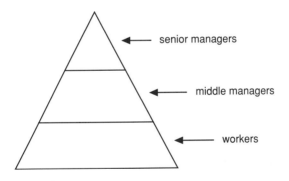

Figure 15-14. Mobilizing All Levels

Top-down Mobilization — President's Diagnosis

Diagnosis by the CEO or president and by the division head is an important tool to mobilize the company to CAPD.[8] These diagnoses have three purposes:

- To enforce the CAPD cycle in the organization and to communicate to all employees the TQM concept and use of the 7 QC tools

- To bring about the company goals, and to examine adherence to the planned means
- To give the president an understanding of the support subordinates need and insight into the work environment of the lower third of the organization, particularly into employee attitudes

Achievement of these purposes yields clear benefits to the organization. The president's diagnosis has other benefits as well:

- Once the company is doing periodic analysis, it will have a vast amount of data about its TQM and business activities; once this data is available, there is great opportunity for improvement.
- Diagnosis contributes to the TQM education of a president. Whereas teaching is a first step to understanding TQM, diagnosis is the next step, requiring study of what questions to ask and enough skill at TQM to give prescriptions for improvement.

Table 15-1 shows a typical plan for such a presidential diagnosis.[9]

Mobilizing the Middle — Ochibo-hiroi *("gleaning")*

The previous section described the presidential diagnosis as a top-down strategy for institutionalizing use of CAPD. This section deals with a strategy for the middle of the organization.

Since 1952, the Hitachi Corporation has used a system it calls *ochibo-hiroi. Ochibo-hiroi* is Japanese for the name of the painting by Jean-François Millet entitled *The Gleaners,* in which three women farmers are shown picking up wheat that was missed in the harvest. To Hitachi, *ochibo-hiroi,* or gleaning, means to pick up and use old experience.

In the Hitachi system, once a year middle managers reflect on mistakes and complaints related to customers. Each section picks out its most serious or critical mistake of the past year and analyzes it in detail to see what it can learn from it.

Table 15-1. Plan for Presidential Diagnosis

1.	Decision about which division and who will be diagnosed	1 month ahead of diagnosis day
2.	Planning of diagnosis — main issues	1 month ahead
3.	Distribution of detailed schedule for diagnosis day	10 days ahead
4.	Submission of presentation transparencies and diagnosis document to the president	1 week ahead
5.	Logistics preparations	1 day ahead
6.	Diagnosis day	1 day ahead
7.	Reflection on weaknesses, and comments by the diagnosis team	Within 1 week of diagnosis day
8.	President and executives make a formal document of their diagnosis	Within 15 days
9.	Division submits analysis of problems found by diagnosis and solutions	Within 1 month

Symptoms that there is something to be gleaned from the year's experience are:

- interacted poorly with a customer or another company
- received a complaint that it didn't believe or didn't accept
- gave a customer excuses or an explanation for a problem rather than taking action on it

To understand and gain enduring benefit from the year's experience, middle managers must follow two guidelines:

- Take the viewpoint of the customer and assume responsibility for the problem.
- Focus on processes and root causes to find out why such a problem happened.

Figure 15-15 illustrates how the Hitachi group uses *ochibo-hiroi* to institutionalize CAPD in middle management. The people in the section do the *ochibo-hiroi* analysis under the leadership of the section head. Thus, the section head must learn about CAPD to lead the analysis and present its results. The section head has to give an explanation in front of these managers. The division head then diagnoses the section head's presentation. Thus, managers learn all the facts of what is going on in the division, as well as CAPD focused on the customer.

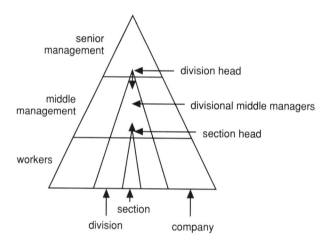

Figure 15-15. Institutionalizing CAPD in Middle Management

Bottom-up Mobilization — 5S Activities

5S activities are very popular in many factories in Japan, where the 5S symbol is frequently seen. The 5S's, as one Japanese company taught one U.S. supplier, are as follows:

- *Seiri*: Keep only needed material at the job site; remove unnecessary items immediately.
- *Seiton*: Store materials in an orderly fashion.
- *Seiketsu*: Observe overall cleanliness; in neat and clean surroundings it is more obvious when something is wrong.
- *Seiso*: Clean tools, equipment, and job site whenever necessary; clean equipment works better.

- *Shitsuke*: Practice self-discipline.[10]

Use of 5S has two purposes:

- To set CAPD in motion from the workers to the supervisors and their managers.
- To bring CAPD to the bottom of the organization — that is, to mobilize the workers to adhere to standards and see the benefits of standardization for long-term (not just immediate) improvement (see Figure 15-16). 5S activities find the implicit standard and highlight deviation from it.

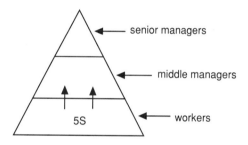

Figure 15-16. 5S from the Bottom Up

INDIVIDUAL PRACTICE OF CAPD BY MANAGERS

We have given a number of examples of company strategies for developing management practice of CAPD: hoshin management, presidential diagnosis, *ochibo-hiroi*, and 5S. All of these are intended directly or indirectly to force managers to practice CAPD. However, to practice CAPD most effectively, managers also have to take personal responsibility for understanding the full scope of application of CAPD and for developing their CAPD skills.

Suppose a manager sees a problem (N) in a certain process over the course of several months; problem N is the most serious problem in July, the second most serious in August, and again the most serious in September. [11]

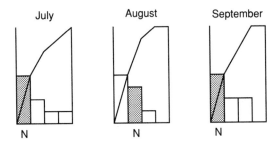

Stages of Managerial Action

The manager's job is to take some action about this problem. The manager can take a variety of actions, each indicative of a further stage of development of individual practice of CAPD.

Stage 0

At this stage of managerial development, the manager does not understand the concept of dual function of work and thinks that quality improvement is "not my job" and that the job of the manager is to give instructions. Therefore, the manager passes all jobs on to subordinates and asks a subordinate to fix the problem. In this case, the manager's action may be summarized as giving instructions. TQM does not recognize this approach as adequately rising to managerial responsibility.

Stage 1

At this stage, the manager shows understanding of the dual function of work. The manager thinks improvement is everyone's job and an important personal responsibility, but does not truly understand PDCA. Thus, the manager may think intuitively about the cause of the problem and devise a solution, and then delegate implementation of the solution to a subordinate — jumping from problem to solution without data collection and causal analysis. In this case, the manager's action may be summarized as intuitive analysis, for the purpose of managerial implementation of the dual function of work.

Stage 2

At this stage, the manager understands PDCA and the value of prevention versus a one-time fix. The manager undertakes formal causal analysis of the problem and formal planning of a solution, and only then delegates implementation to a subordinate (or perhaps even participates in the implementation). However, the manager at this stage does not have enough skill to create an SDCA system for the solution. In this case, the manager's action may be summarized as causal analysis, for the purpose of prevention of recurrence of the problem.

Stage 3

At this stage, the manager understands that a process or system must be created if an improvement is to be maintained. The manager undertakes formal causal analyses and solution planning, estimates the effect of the solution or evaluates the solution in an experimental way, and revises the standard if appropriate; the manager also creates a set of measurements to control the process — for example, a control chart. However, the manager does not understand the concept of cross-functional or cross-product improvement. In this case, the manager's action may be summarized as revision of standard, for the purpose of adherence to process.

Stage 4

At this stage, the manager understands the great benefit of finding cross-functional or cross-product instances where analogous problems may be prevented through a transfer of the improvement. The manager examines other products and processes to see if they have the same problem and uses the analysis of the first product to improve the others. In this case, the manager's action may be summarized as applying learning to other situations, for the purpose of eliminating latent problems. This is the expert level of TQM managerial practice.

Stage 5

At this stage, the manager is skilled in the dual function of work, prevention of recurrence, adherence to process and eliminating latent problems — the activities of stages 1 through 4. Moreover, the manager understands that further improvement requires that these activities be used in concert. In this case, the manager's action may be summarized as integration of efforts, for the purpose of achieving business success.

Table 15-2 summarizes these stages.

Means Associated with Each Stage

The means of achieving each managerial purpose is listed in the right column of Table 15-2.

Stage 1 Means

To implement the dual function of work, the manager must not delegate all problems to a subordinate. Rather, the manager

Table 15-2. Stages of Managerial Action

Stage	Managerial Action	Managerial Purpose	Means
0	Giving instructions		
1	Intuitive analysis	Dual function of work	Do own improvement work
2	Causal analysis	Prevention of recurrence	Use real information
3	Revision of standard	Adherence to process	Install system
4	Applying learning to other situations	Eliminating latent problems	Self-innovation
5	Integration of efforts	Leveraging for business success	Focus

must personally do two things — provide a clear mission and goals, and carry out the improvement work.

Regarding the first task, the manager must make clear two types of goals — noble goals and practical goals. The noble goal usually benefits the customer; the manager must constantly speak of personal belief in the primacy of the customer. Practical goals are what must be accomplished immediately by the manager and subordinates.[12]

However, it is not sufficient for the manager just to make the mission and goal clear. The manager must demonstrate personal belief in improvement methods by using them in practice, for example, by running PDCA. Practicing improvement behaviors is hard for managers and subordinates. Nevertheless, it is essential; if managers do not personally practice improvement activities in their own daily work, the staff will not believe in the methods and the manager will not gain skill in them. Managers should err on the side of not delegating improvement work. Hence the TQM slogan "No delegation."

Stage 2 Means

Just fixing a problem is not sufficient. Future occurrences of the problem must be prevented. The key to prevention is to find out what is really happening, that is, to get and use real information. The people with the true information are the people doing the job day in and day out. To get the true information from the people doing the job, the manager must adhere to two important practices: no criticism and active listening.

No criticism means that the manager must not ask who was at fault, why the problem wasn't found sooner, or how people could let this happen. Even when receiving a presentation of a plan, managers should encourage employees to speak openly, for example, by encouraging them to be candid about what they think should be done and why. Critiquing the plan seldom elicits as much real information as does encouraging employees to speak openly.

Critical questions, explicit laying of blame, or critical analysis will at the minimum stop employees from speaking, and such tactics may make them falsify the information they present. Employees quickly learn what managers want to hear and don't want to hear, and then they give them what they want to hear. All managers have experienced this.

In fact, offering no criticism is not enough; praise is required. Divide the problem into small steps in which good points can be found and praised immediately. Praise is more effective if directed at specifics ("it is good that you constructed a Pareto diagram") rather than generalities ("you are doing an excellent job").

A famous anecdote about Yokio Horie, CEO of Pentel, illustrates this point. One of Pentel's engineers had worked on 100 potential products and had only one success. The engineer hesitated to report his results. However, Mr. Horie told the engineer, "It is great that you could create one good product; you must repeat the process you used for that product and you will create more good products."

Active listening is also necessary for eliciting the real information. If managers just talk and state their own opinions, employees will clam up. If managers want all of the real data, they must listen and encourage employees to talk until they have said all that is to be said.

In a famous Japanese novel a creative but undisciplined young girl named To To Chan has to change schools several times. On a visit to yet another school, the girl and her mother are informed by the schoolmaster that the mother's presence is not necessary. The schoolmaster brings his chair close to the young girl and tells her to speak whatever is on her mind. No one has given her this freedom to speak before, and she speaks for several hours. The schoolmaster encourages her, actively listening. When the girl is exhausted, the schoolmaster asks if there is anything else she wants to say. She remembers that her mother doesn't like the color of the clothes she is wearing, and says that. Then, when she can think of nothing more to say, the schoolmaster says, "you are now a member of this school." The girl goes on to success at the school.

Stage 3 Means

TQM is a mass movement. A system or process is needed that everyone can follow; however, this system or process shouldn't be rigid. Disneyland provides an example of such a system. At Disneyland there is just one entrance/exit. Everyone enters at the same place. Entering visitors pass a cheerful guard and then meet Mickey Mouse, who greets them. Next, they come to a mall, which is carefully laid out (with high ceilings, etc.) to suggest openness (despite a second-floor streetscape that is 80 percent of real size and a third-floor streetscape that is 60 percent of real size). As they come out of the mall, everyone gets a view of the magic castle in the distance. All of these attractive design features keep people moving and prevent unpleasant congestion. Although the visitors follow a process designed to ensure an enjoyable visit, the process happens automatically and without explicit discipline.

Another example of such a process is the theme selection matrix used as step 1 of the 7 QC steps. This matrix guides improvement teams through the process of selecting appropriate tasks without imposing a rigid structure on the discussion.

Managers must learn to create business systems and processes that enforce work standards without rigid discipline. They must make the systems easy and enjoyable to use.

Stage 4 Means

The half-life of knowledge is getting shorter and shorter. Skills required for the job and society change rapidly. Managers must constantly renew their knowledge and themselves. We call this self-innovation.

There are three keys to self-innovation:

1. *Curiosity*: Curiosity is critical because it provides natural motivation to find out what needs to be changed and how to change it.
2. *Openness to learning from others*: Curiosity is not enough. One doesn't learn fast enough from personal investigation. One needs openness to learning from others. Thus, managers must listen empathetically, not critically. They must get rid of the I-already-know-it (IAKI) attitude.
3. *Fishbowl approach (going on site):* Observing people in their own environment is often the most effective way to learn from others. The fishbowl principle is described in Chapter 7: one discovers more from observing things in their actual environment than from getting prestructured information — such as surveys or reports from subordinates. With regard to self-innovation, the fishbowl approach has three benefits:
   - It offers an alternative to the question/response model of learning, which leaves important questions unasked.
   - It enables triangulation — that is, it lets one look at things from several angles to discover what is actually happening.
   - The person with the most knowledge will learn the most from a visit — therefore, the manager should personally go on site.

Stage 5 Means

Companies have many problems and many capabilities, skills, and practices. We can apply the capabilities, skills, and practices to many problems simultaneously, as shown in Figure 15-17.

This approach might be how the world would look to managers at Stage 4, when they have developed many skills but have not yet learned to integrate their efforts.

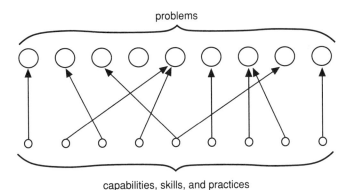

Figure 15-17. **Attacking Many Problems at Once**

But such an approach is both time-consuming and self-defeating, diluting the effort that may be necessary to conquer any of the problem. Practically speaking, you must integrate your efforts somehow. Focusing on a specific target puts sufficient capability on a problem to solve it; it provides the only feasible means of using many capabilities simultaneously and thus improving the way the capabilities are used together (see Figure 15-18).

Actually succeeding in solving a problem is the most important component for future success. Integrating and focusing your capabilities so that you can solve a problem is the first major step to this success.

The Kumon system, developed in Japan but now taught worldwide, is an example of an integrated system of pedagogic practices that uses a tight focus on individual problems to assure overall success, specifically teaching college calculus to precollege-age children.[13]

The Kumon math process builds good study habits, responds to individual students' needs, and teaches only the mathematics needed to learn calculus. The lessons in the Kumon process are small independent segments that the students focus their capabilities on. The Kumon tutoring sessions are organized as PDCA cycles.

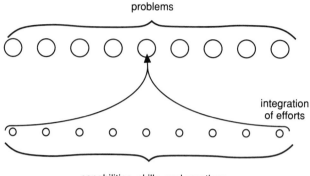

Figure 15-18. Focusing on a Specific Target

The Kumon system of teaching mathematics illustrates the benefit of success. Children have natural curiosity, enthusiasm, and confidence in their ability to solve problems. Initial success in the process gives them a sense of achievement, thus reinforcing their desire to know, and so the cycle repeats itself. The enjoyment that comes from repeated success leads to more success. With success and enjoyment come ability and creativity (see Figure 15-19).

Ability in the preceding figure means an integrated set of learning habits, attitudes, and skills that can be applied not only to college calculus, but also to many other topics. The ability to deal skillfully with many new things is virtually a definition of creativity.

To summarize the details of the means for the five stages of managerial development, we add another column to the table (see Table 15-3).

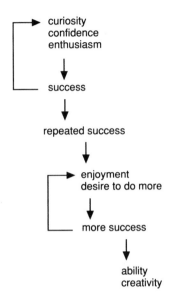

Figure 15-19. Reinforcing Ability and Creativity Through Success

Table 15-3. Managerial Action, Purpose, Means, and Components

Level	Managerial Action	Managerial Purpose	Means	Components of the Means
0	Giving instructions			
1	Intuitive analysis	Dual function of work	Do own improvement work	Clear mission and goals Personal practice of improvement
2	Causal analysis	Prevention of recurrence	Use real information	No criticism Recognition of staff Active listening
3	Revision of standard	Adherence to process	Install system	Enjoyable, not rigid
4	Applying learning to other situations	Eliminating latent problems	Self-innovation	Openness to learning Curiosity Swim in the fishbowl
5	Integration of efforts	Leveraging for business success	Focus	Narrow focus Repeated use

NOTES

1. Kiyoshi Uchimaru, et al., *TQM for Technical Groups: Total Quality Principles for Product Development* (Cambridge, MA: Productivity Press, 1993).
2. This figure is our interpretation of the NIMS documentation, and the directions of the line segments are qualitative estimates.
3. These remarks include engineering managers — "senior managers" — as much as any other kind.
4. Based on a figure in Kozo Koura in Yoji Akao, editor, *Hoshin Kanri: Policy Deployment for Successful TQM* (Cambridge, MA: Productivity Press, 1991), 105; and on a figure in Ishikawa, *Introduction to Quality Control*, 170.
5. Kozo Koura, *Total Quality Control* 42 (March 1991): 273.
6. Each company implementing TQM needs to decide whether to use both PDCA and CAPD in its TQM vocabulary, or to only describe variations of PDCA. Having both PDCA and CAPD could cause confusion and debate — "are we doing PDCA or CAPD now?" "what exactly is the difference between PDCA and CAPD?" — which doesn't necessarily add value. On the other hand, in some companies managers or other professionals are loath to use the same tools that work in manufacturing and administration, that is, PDCA. In this case it may be useful to emphasize the differences between PDCA and CAPD.
7. This statement can apply equally to the manufacturing of a steel cylinder, in which the ultimate goals are to make the cylinder ever more precisely, quickly, and cheaply.
8. We use the terms *CEO* or *president* to mean the top manager in the organization. In companies with both a CEO and a president who reports to the CEO, the two officers should consider doing the diagnosis together.

9. This table is adapted slightly from Kunabura and Matsuzowa, "QC Audits by Top Management," *Quality, JSQC,* 17 (April 1987), 163; see also Ishikawa, *What Is Total Quality Control?* 161-69.

10. James P. Walker, "A Disciplined Approach to Continuous Improvement," Packard Electric monograph, 1988.

11. This case was developed from a case briefly mentioned in *Hoshin Kanri unei-no tebiki (Guide for Hoshin Management)* (1989), 172 (published by the JSQC Committee on the Case Study of Hoshin Management.

12. The benefit of hoshin management is that it breaks down these immediate targets and aligns them with the company goals, and provides a fact-based process for deciding which goals the managers should personally undertake, and which should be delegated and to whom.

13. Shoji Shiba, "The Excellent Eduction System for One and a Half Million Children," *Journal of Programmed Learning and Educational Technology* 23-24 (1987).

The Fourth Revolution:
SOCIETAL NETWORKING

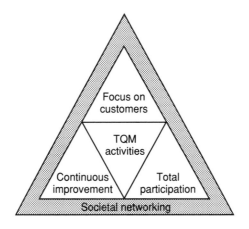

16

Networking and Societal Diffusion: Regional and Nationwide Networking

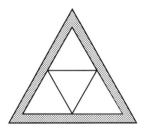

An important characteristic of TQM is societal learning. Societal learning can be thought of as network learning or learning from the network of companies, customers, suppliers, and others who are trying to improve their quality practices. Such learning is necessary because TQM is not a theory that a company can simply learn and follow. Rather, TQM is a continuing societal and organizational experiment in our companies. TQM practices have developed through trial and error. People learn how to do it by trying to do it, and learning what they must do. This changes as they learn more and as the world changes. However, it is too limiting for each company to discover the organizational means of developing TQM by itself. Reinventing the wheel consumes time and resources that even the largest and smartest company can't afford. Reinventing the wheel also risks developing an inferior version.

reinvented wheel

If one company develops a method that works, that method should be diffused so that other companies can use it as well. For this reason, Japan has the tradition of "no secrets" about the methodology of quality improvements.

There are many examples in Japanese TQM of such diffusion, such as guidelines for how QC circles meet and exchange factory visits. These were not theory. They evolved in QC circles and were a great success, and were then diffused throughout Japan. Milliken's "sharing rallies," mentioned in Chapter 11 as an example of the diffusion of quality improvement success stories, are a U.S. invention that has become popular and has been diffused to other companies.

One problem in implementing TQM is that for some types of information and skill a catch-22 exists that makes internal development of methods difficult, so that societal diffusion becomes all the more important. For example, it is difficult for CEOs to be taught new methods of leadership by those below them in the company hierarchy; therefore, CEOs must get most of their information about TQM from outside their company hierarchy.

At all levels in a corporation, the existence of success stories and managers experienced in TQM makes TQM easier to practice. But how does a company that is just beginning its TQM implementation find success stories on which to model its own activities or experienced managers on whom to model its behavior? Executives should be looking outside their own companies or organizations for knowledge, training, and examples of TQM practice. This chapter is about the structure of

TQM beyond the individual corporation and about the methods by which TQM understanding and skills are diffused from the broader quality culture into individual companies.

Companies need to participate in societal networking of TQM for reasons beyond the simple desire to gain efficiency in their TQM implementations. A company is unlikely to be able to do high-quality work in a low-quality culture. If a company resides in a national or regional environment of poorly trained workers, customers tolerant of low-quality products, and weak competitors, it is unlikely that the company can find the will and the means for producing high-quality products. In particular, a company cannot stand on quality alone, without quality suppliers. The quality of the suppliers must be developed, and this is more possible within an industry or geographical quality culture. Participation in a widespread process of diffusion can be considered an investment in the creation of a regional or national quality culture, which in turn is an investment in a company's future ability to do business.

In brief, companies participate in regional and national efforts and organizations that diffuse TQM for three reasons: to avoid having to reinvent 40 years of quality practices internally; to create mutual learning and sharing of current discoveries among corporations; and to create a quality culture in which to do business. This chapter describes the elements of regional and national infrastructure, explaining how companies participate at each level.

The primary focus of discussion about regional and national infrastructure is the Japanese case, because the Japanese infrastructure is more developed and more organized than that in the United States. However, some U.S. examples are also included.

Japan has found three elements necessary for successful societal diffusion of TQM:

- an infrastructure to support networking
- openness with real cases
- change agents (or catalysts)

INFRASTRUCTURE FOR NETWORKING

The Japanese have identified six elements of the infrastructure for networking.[1] As shown in Figure 16-1, these elements are:

1. National promotional organization
2. Training
3. Knowledge dissemination
4. Societal promotion activities
5. National standard certification
6. Development of new methods

A seventh element, the change agent (shown in the figure), is considered to be in parallel with this six-element infrastructure. It is described in a later section.

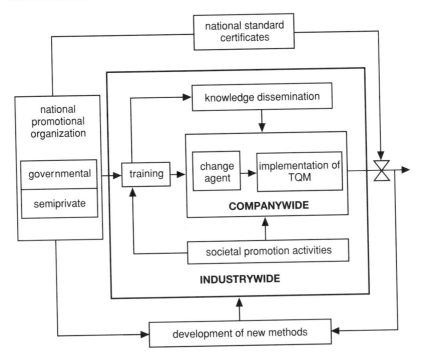

Figure 16-1. Infrastructure for Networking

National Promotional Organization

To support quality improvement, two types of national organizations — government and semiprivate — developed in Japan. Each has a role to play.

One key in the development of TQM is to start from a standard. The national government organization is involved in standardization and sometimes in certification of quality. For instance, the government organization MITI (Ministry of International Trade and Industry) played an important role in providing an initial standard and establishing a certification process (JIS). Certification, which deals with quality standards for products and company practices, is another of the six elements of the infrastructure for networking.

Building on the activities of the government organization, which provide some of the basics, the semiprivate national promotional organizations do the follow-on work. Two nonprofit national organizations for TQM exist in Japan — the Union of Japanese Scientists and Engineers (JUSE) and the Japanese Standards Association (JSA). The two organizations are complementary, and together serve the needs of large, medium, and small Japanese companies. JSA has a closer relationship with MITI, which has tried to diffuse standardization throughout Japanese industry. The primary roles of JUSE and JSA are training, knowledge dissemination, societal promotion activities, and development of new methods — the other four elements of the infrastructure for networking.

JUSE and JSA are highly effective organizations. They have a suitably long-range perspective, and they are neither as rigid as government organizations tend to be nor as shortsighted as commercial private consulting organizations tend to be.

JUSE and JSA also have an informal atmosphere, bringing together a variety of people interested in quality. In keeping with its name, JUSE brings together scientists and engineers from all disciplines, as well as managers. This is in contrast to the American Society for Quality Control (ASQC), which tends to be oriented toward a single discipline, that of quality specialists. JUSE also brings together people from different industries, the universities, and the national research institutions (e.g., agriculture, commerce). JUSE and JSA provide a place and opportunity for all these people to interact so they can draw on one another's knowledge and resources.

The participation of the national research institutions and universities is particularly valuable to industry, for several reasons: They are a source of intellectual capital, especially regarding statistics; workers there have more discretionary time than in industry; they tend to have a longer-term perspective; and university people in particular have another specialty and need not get their support from TQM activities.

Historically, JUSE and JSA have not done any consulting work (although that is now changing), which meant they weren't trying to sell their collective wisdom. Therefore they have permitted great openness about information and know-how related to quality control.

JUSE is a particularly influential quality organization in Japan.[2] When W. Edwards Deming visited Japan in 1950 and began teaching statistical quality control, it was JUSE that embraced his teachings and spread them. It was JUSE that invited Joseph Juran to Japan to teach in 1954. JUSE promoted the quality circle movement.[3] In 1951 JUSE instituted the Deming Prize, the prestigious award given to quality innovators in Japan and abroad, and JUSE organizes many of the conventions and events that lead up to the awarding of this prize each year. The Deming Prize has played a central role in the promotion of TQM.

Quality control (QC) education has also played a central role in the promotion of TQM. In 1949, JUSE started a 30-day basic QC course for engineers. Over the next 10 years it programmed courses for middle and upper management and, in 1967, for foremen, so that every enterprise level was covered. A good deal of money was invested in training young engineers and managers, but in consequence it is earning large returns for Japan. Ten or twenty years after beginning their quality education, people with solid QC backgrounds are sitting on the boards of Japan's top corporations. Dr. Koji Kobayashi, the former president of NEC, is an example of this trend.

The JUSE organization proper is chiefly involved in arranging logistics for its activities rather than itself being the source of quality knowledge. For example, in 1989, the full-time staff of JUSE was 84, with an additional 31 people employed by JUSE Press. By contrast, about 2,000 people from universities, corporations, and government collaborate to teach JUSE courses and serve on the committees that create and improve JUSE courses. The "lean staff with extensive networking" structure is an interesting innovation, for it virtually guarantees that TQM knowledge is integrated and preserved within corporations, not hoarded in JUSE or other external organizations such as consulting companies or universities. Also, members of JUSE are corporations rather than individuals, numbering about 1,850 in 1989. JUSE's aim is clearly to increase knowledge within corporations, and its membership and staffing policies support this aim.

JUSE approaches corporate implementation from the top down as well as using middle-up, middle-down, and bottom-up approaches. JUSE's board of directors is made up of high-ranking industrialists; by tradition, the president of JUSE is the chairman or an ex-chairman of the Keidanren, the most prominent organization of Japanese CEOs.[4] When Deming taught statistical quality control in the 1950s, he taught classes with presidents of corporations, not just engineers. Joseph Juran's focus in 1954 was top and middle management. As of 1991, nearly 5,000 top executives had gone through JUSE's five- day top executive's course, and another 9,000 had been participants in the JUSE five-day course for executives. Both courses have long waiting lists.[5]

Independent consulting organizations do not play a major role in implementing quality improvement in Japan, even though other areas of business are richly supplied with consulting companies, both Japanese and foreign-owned.

The Center for Quality Management was designed to be like JUSE in several respects. The membership comprises corporations rather than individuals, and the dual focus of the CQM is education and top management. Like JUSE, CQM uses instructors from member corporations rather than in-house staff. CQM was modeled on JUSE because many of JUSE's features appeared to be what the member companies most needed. CQM is described in more detail in the next sections.

In comparison with their Japanese counterparts, American quality organizations are fragmented and numerous. A thorough survey of quality organizations would therefore be quite beside the point, at least for now, in understanding how a regional or national infrastructure works. However, a few brief descriptions should give the flavor of the membership, functioning, and curricula of quality organizations in the US.

The American Society for Quality Control (ASQC) is a professional organization for quality specialists, and is probably the largest quality organization in the United States.

The American Supplier Institute (ASI) was spun off from Ford Motor's efforts to improve the quality of its supplier base.

GOAL/QPC originated with a group of followers of W. Edwards Deming, and has evolved into an independent training organization with both individual and corporate members. Its tools and practices have been adapted from the Japanese versions, observed on study trips. Instructors are both employees and free-lancers.

There are many independent consulting companies, most of which have entered the arena of quality consulting from other, more traditional consulting arenas. Consulting companies vary enormously in focus, ranging from specialty providers of everything from statistical software to mission- and vision-setting training, to "full-spectrum" companies whose services cover more or less the full range of TQM.

Finally, a unique type of consulting company should be mentioned — the TQM company spinoff. In the case of Corning Glass and Florida Power & Light, the consulting company remains a company unit that provides services both to the parent company and to commercial clients. In other cases, a number of key individuals leave the parent company to form their own consulting company.

Training

National training infrastructure includes instruction in a variety of skills for a variety of target students, from CEOs to line workers, from engineers to administrators. Training is a means of mutual learning among companies, in which knowledgeable instructors from one company teach people from many others.

One of the most important roles of the semiprivate national promotional organizations is education and training. JUSE's courses, for instance, are the source of quality instruction for many different organizations. This particularly helps the diffusion of TQM. Many companies find it less expensive to get training from JUSE, with its 2,000 collaborators (committees of people from industry and universities who develop course curricula and teach the courses), than to create their own training activities.

JUSE offers 270 courses to 33,560 people per year, but only in Tokyo and Osaka, whereas JSA offers 250 courses to 15,000 people per year in 58 smaller cities. Table 16-1 lists examples of JUSE courses for 1991. Notice when each course was established. Also noteworthy is the fact that some of the courses in each subject area are as long as 2 to 4 weeks.

Knowledge Dissemination

Knowledge dissemination includes publishing cases, instructional material, and research in books and periodicals for a variety of audiences. It also includes holding conventions and other events on quality. Within a quality culture where companies share information about their TQM successes and failures, such dissemination activities are an important means of mutual learning among companies.

Table 16-1. Examples of 1991 JUSE Courses

Subject	Number of Offerings	First Course Established
Quality control	27	1949
Reliability	9	1960
Design of experiments	3	1955
Multivariate analysis	3	1970
Software production control	2	1980
Operations research	4	1962
Industrial engineering	2	1963
Marketing	1	1951
Sensory test	1	1957
Product liability	1	1973
Other management techniques	6	1972

Especially in the early years of the Japanese push for quality improvement (before quality became a popular subject), JUSE and JSA were a primary source of journals, magazines, and books related to quality. For example, JUSE publishes three monthly journals, including *QC Circle*, which has a monthly circulation of 170,000. Furthermore, between 1960 and 1985, about half of all quality control books published were publications of JUSE or JSA, as shown by the graph in Figure 16-2.

Since TQM in Japan began teaching that quality is everyone's job, the demand for books has increased. JUSE and JSA helped create a quality culture that provides an ongoing economic base for continuing dissemination of quality knowledge.

The role of knowledge dissemination should not be underestimated. It includes more than just publishing activities. There are nine national districts for QC circles, each of which contains a chapter that holds local conventions, mutual visits, study meetings, and discussions. Once every two days, there is a convention somewhere in Japan.[6]

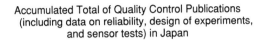

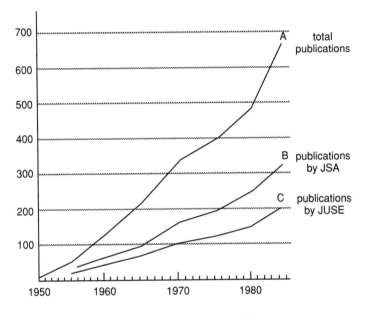

Figure 16-2. Publications of JUSE and JSA

Again, TQM is not a theory: it is a system for managing improvement based on fact, and is itself evolving, according to the facts of success in practice. Quality control was introduced into Japan from the United States. There it evolved into a set of practices that fit the Japanese culture and needs extraordinarily well. Out of statistical quality control, the Japanese created quality circles, kaizen, companywide quality control, and other concepts to develop what we know as TQM today. America needs a more explicit system for experimenting with quality methods in companies and diffusing the results of the experiments to evolve a version of TQM suitable for American culture and needs, and for the culture and needs of each company attempting to practice TQM. Knowledge dissemination is an important element in getting TQM to work.

Societal Promotion Activities

There are many types of societal promotion activities. These activities increase social awareness of quality, and they transfer quality techniques to different levels of company hierarchy and to different types and styles of industries (e.g., mass production, one-piece manufacturing, chemical industry). Examples of these activities are quality days, quality month (November), and quality awards. For instance, one of the major societal promotions in Japan is the Deming Prize for "Nationwide Promotion and Dissemination of TQC."

The U.S. version of this prize is the Malcolm Baldrige National Quality Award (MBNQA).[7] The main benefit of the Baldrige Award is its promotion of quality in the United States. Companies are advertising that they have won the award, a practice that focuses on both the prize winning company's attention and that of its competitors on quality. Companies are demanding that their suppliers prepare themselves to apply for the Baldrige Award. Companies are undertaking full or superficial self-evaluations of their quality practices using the Baldrige criteria. Hundreds of thousands of copies of the Baldrige criteria have been distributed to companies and individuals requesting them. The press, trade, and academic journals include many articles discussing the award. States and regions are establishing their own versions of the Baldrige Award, in some cases viewing them as an intermediate step on a company's path to the Baldrige Award.

There is much discussion in the United States about whether the Baldrige Award helps or hurts company quality practices.[8] Its real or purported problems seem secondary compared with the benefit of national promotion of quality.[9]

National Standard Certification

National Standard Certificates are issued by the government certifying that a given product meets certain quality specifications. JIS (Japanese Industrial Standards) are the province of the JIS Committee. To earn the right to display the JIS mark on its products, a company must standardize its manufacturing processes and allow its QC levels to be examined and certified.[10] At present, about 11,000 plants in Japan have passed JIS inspection. The International Standards Organization (ISO), of which the United States is a member, seems to be filling a similar role with the ISO 9000 series of quality standards and certification processes.

Development of New Methods

As quality concepts change, different methods are needed. The national infrastructure of societal networking provides a mechanism for the development of new methods, and JUSE and JSA have invested heavily in the development of new quality methods. For instance, in the 1950s JUSE invited Deming to Japan to learn about statistical quality control from him, and JUSE invested in the development of statistical methods. More generally, JUSE set up the QC Research Group, and JSA set up the QC Research Committee. Meetings of these groups and less formal occasions provided the opportunities for debate among those who were taking the lead in developing new methods for total quality control. A participant recalls that it was normal for meetings to last for one to two hours, and then to continue informally well into the wee hours of the morning. These activities gradually built a consensus on how to adapt U.S. quality control methods to Japan.

The tradition of consensus building lives on. JUSE holds two three-day QC residential symposia every year. Invited attendance is limited to about 100. The participants stay in the same hotel and are together from early in the morning until late at night. This proximity enables them to discuss the day's topics in both formal and informal settings. A consensus emerges not from the forceful leadership of a few people but from face-to-face communication among the entire group.

JUSE follows a sequence of steps in the development of new methods. First, the JUSE Research Group regularly researches a new method. Next there is a symposium to introduce the new method to a larger population. When the method has come into practical use and there are real cases to study, a seminar is held. These steps were followed, for example, when the 7 management and planning tools were developed in the 1970s.

The 7 management tools consist of six methods and tools for processing qualitative or linguistic information, and one tool for processing numerical data (in particular, for doing multivariate analysis). Methods and tools for processing linguistic information were necessary because of the continuing evolution of the quality concept. The quality concept moved beyond just statistical process control, and it became increasingly important to create a formulation process for problem solving. Also, quality activities had spread to a variety of industries, functions, and company positions — quality was no longer relevant only on the factory floor.

The history of the development of the 7 management tools proceeded as follows:[11]

- A JUSE research committee for developing QC tools worked from 1972 to 1977.
- Professor Yoshinobu Nayatani and others proposed the 7 management and planning tools in 1977.
- A workshop on the 7 management and planning tools was started in 1978.
- A symposium on the 7 management and planning tools was started in 1978.
- The first book on the 7 management and planning tools was published in 1979.
- The 7 management and planning tools enjoyed great popularity in quality-related fields in Japan after 1979.

OPENNESS WITH REAL CASES

The second of the three elements necessary for successful societal diffusion and networking is sharing actual cases. As stated at the beginning of this chapter, TQM is a societal experiment. After one organization has success with a method, the method must be diffused. Therefore, companies must be open with real cases. Real cases means detailed processes of quality practices, such as improvement, or of quality assurance systems. This policy of openness applies not only to documents and presentations but also to demonstrations of their use in practice. For example, several of the companies in CQM are trying to implement a system of diffusion of quality improvement success stories such as the system described in Chapter 11. Even with the Japanese and Milliken models to study, it is difficult for a company to develop an efficient and effective presentation system. Therefore, within CQM, companies have allowed representatives of other companies to attend their presentation days (QI story days), and the methods presented on such occasions have served as models for other companies.

In Japan, companies demonstrate that there are no secrets in the know-how of quality improvement by distributing a wide range of information and success stories. For example, 33 books on quality were published by JUSE in 1988. Two-thirds of them dealt with concrete examples and case studies rather than with theoretical work.

Another mechanism for diffusion of real cases and success stories in Japan is Quality Month. For example, the schedule and activities for Quality Month in November 1988 were as follows:

Week 1
- Quality Conference for Foremen — 92 case studies, and 15 plant visits and on-site debates

Week 2
* Quality Conference for Managers — 92 case studies, and
  9 plant visits, debates, and panel discussions
* Top Management Conference
* Deming Prize Ceremony

Week 3
* Conference on TQC in the Service Industry

In all, 250 actual cases of implementation were presented during this period.

CHANGE AGENTS

The third key factor for successful societal diffusion and networking is the use of change agents. Revolution from insiders is very difficult because the revolution represents a paradigm change for the organization. Strong change agents from outside often play a necessary role in thought revolutions.[12] If they have sufficient knowledge and personality or prestige, and the necessary sense of mission, change agents serve as catalysts for change. From the Japanese point of view, it is difficult for some consultants to serve as change agents because they lack the necessary sense of mission.

Deming and Juran had the necessary qualifications, so in 1950 and 1954 they served as national change agents for quality in Japan. Professor Kano and others served as change agents to Florida Power & Light, and Professor Shiba has served as a change agent for TQM in Hungary and for several of the CQM companies in the United States.

CQM CASE STUDY

In early 1990, seven Boston-area companies formed the Center for Quality Management to learn from and aid each other in their TQM implementations. The companies that formed the CQM had characteristics (described in Chapter 13) typical of companies that decide to implement TQM. With few exceptions, the seven companies that formed the CQM were all suffering from the economic slowdown that began in the late 1980s. Also, the CEOs of several of the companies had personally visited Japan and observed its business practices. At least one of the CEOs had lived in Japan, most had divisions in Japan and traveled to Japan frequently, and some had studied Japan's business practices through trade association committees on international competitiveness. Furthermore, several of these CEOs were regularly in contact with each other through existing business associations, such as the Massachusetts High Tech Council. Thus, business crisis and awareness of TQM as practiced in Japan motivated these CEOs to practice TQM.

In November 1989, Professor Shiba gave a seminar at MIT that several of the CEOs attended. Professor Tom Lee of MIT, who had been Shiba's colleague at the International Institute for the Application of Systems Analysis in Vienna in the 1980s, arranged for Professor Shiba to give the seminar.

As a result of whatever problems they were having at their companies, their knowledge of Japan and TQM, and Professor Shiba's introduction to TQM, the following seven Boston-area companies decided to form the Center for Quality Management:

- Analog Devices
- Bolt Beranek and Newman, Inc.
- Bose
- Digital Equipment Corporation
- General Electric
- Polaroid Corporation
- Teradyne, Inc.

Chairman of the board was Ray Stata of Analog Devices, president was Professor Lee of MIT (on a part-time, pro bono basis), and the board of directors consisted of the CEOs or other senior managers of the founding companies.

The CQM was formed on the basis of the three-element model for societal diffusion, as expressed in its mission statement:

> The mission of the Center for Quality Management is to accelerate understanding and implementation of quality management concepts and methods by creating a network of like-minded organizations to share knowledge and experience. This will require a common language and a shared understanding of the basic methodologies to define problems and design solutions. In the broadest sense, the long-term objective of the Center is to promote organizational and societal learning about how to improve the performance of human systems.

Having decided to form the CQM, the founding CEOs needed a plan for what the CQM would do specifically and how it would function, and they needed a joint understanding of what TQM is. To this end, they undertook a five-week design study in March and April of 1990. This design study, described in Chapter 9, was led by Shoji Shiba. All of the participants were senior line managers or senior quality staff members from the CQM companies, except three participants from MIT.

The plan resulting from the CQM design study led to a committee structure, as shown in Figure 16-3. The intention was to have a lean staff and active committee structure (like JUSE) — to put the know-how in the companies and not in the CQM staff.

After the design study ended, it took a few more weeks for the board to read the plan and approve it. Although a number of committees were proposed, not all of them became active in 1990. Activities that did take place in 1990 included the following:

- The seminar committee was active, sponsoring seminars by Florida Power & Light, Xerox, Motorola, and Corning.
- The research committee commissioned translation of the book *TQM for Technical Groups*.[13]
- Shoji Shiba offered several one-day courses called CEO Introduction to TQM.

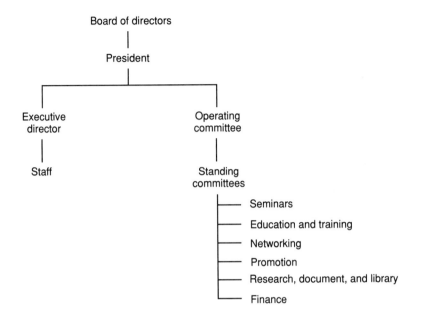

Figure 16-3. CQM Committee Structure

- The first CQM tool manual was developed.
- The six-day course, TQM for Senior Managers: Planning and Implementation, was offered in two parallel sessions in October, November, and December to 48 executives of CQM companies.
- The 1991 plan was prepared, its starting point being PDCA on 1990 activities.

The six-day course on TQM for senior managers was a particularly noteworthy achievement of 1991. The course was developed by Shoji Shiba with help from the CQM design team. It was attended by several CEOs and their direct reports and was taught by Professor Shiba. It included much group work with TQM tools and a number of case studies presented by CEOs, senior managers, and members of the design team. The design team took notes on the entire six days and converted them into transparencies and draft text that could be used again by other presenters and as the basis for this book. A key concept of the course was "no delegation of improvement," which was demonstrated in many ways; for example, the CEOs themselves presented case studies.

1991 Activities

Activities of the CQM in 1991 included the following:

- Membership in the CQM expanded from 7 to 24 companies and from 1 to 5 university affiliates.
- The six-day course on TQM for senior managers was offered three more times to 72 more CEOs and senior managers. The courses were taught by CEOs and senior managers who had taken the course with Professor Shiba, to show executive leadership in TQM and to learn the material better. Companies also took the material into their own companies and based internal activities on it.
- This book was drafted.
- Staff members of the member companies cooperatively developed five additional TQM manuals.
- Member companies offered skills courses to attendees from all of the companies, and member companies took the teachings back for use inside their companies.
- There were opportunities for considerable networking, including a trip by CEOs and development VPs to Japan, a CEO roundtable, and a Quality VP day.
- There were seminars by Federal Express, Texas Instruments, and Digital Equipment Corporation.
- A research effort was undertaken on process metrics for R&D.
- There was a reunion of participants in the six-day course, at which the participating CEOs presented company activities based on what they learned in the course.

- There were many interchanges among companies, such as the sharing of experience or methods, and courses that were open to enrollees from other companies.
- The 1992 plan was drafted, its starting point being PDCA on 1991 activities.

Key aspects of the CQM are top management involvement (companies, not individuals), emphasis on open sharing and mutual learning (common language, materials, cases), and continued connection to practitioners in Japan.

Key accomplishments of the CQM to date have been transfer of some of the Japanese technology of TQM to the CQM companies, and having industry people (including senior managers and CEOs) teach TQM.

The first year, 1990, was a year of organization. The second year, 1991, was a year of orientation — deciding what was really important to do and getting it started. The challenge for the third year, 1992, was to figure out how to address demands for growth: how to select new member companies who will actively participate; how to provide services to the expanded membership while still depending on the committee structure; and how to expand the staff without diminishing the intellectual leadership of the companies.

The CQM has several long-term aspirations:

- To handle CQM company facilities outside of New England (California, Europe, Japan, and so forth)
- To participate in development of a national quality culture in the United States
- To expand the CQM model or help others copy the CQM methods (assuming that this model works well)
- To develop improved, advanced methods of TQM, moving beyond what was copied from Japan

The last point is particularly important. The CQM companies copied Japan because it was efficient to do so. Of course, they had to adapt what they learned from Japan to the U.S.

business culture. Also, Japan is continuing to evolve TQM, for instance, to address the fact that long-range planning has not been a strong part of TQM. The CQM companies have the opportunity and necessity to develop improved methods of TQM and to integrate them with their existing practice of TQM.

DYNAMICS OF A SOCIETAL LEARNING SYSTEM

Strong market pressure for innovation provides pull for societal learning. A nationwide quality promotion infrastructure provides push for societal learning. Change agents (particularly external change agents) with sufficient knowledge and prestige and the necessary sense of mission provide the catalyst for societal learning. Openness with real cases provides data for societal learning.

In Japan, people from three types of institutions participate in the societal learning system. Semiprivate agencies, with some help from the government, provide the infrastructure. Business or industry provides openness with real cases. Change agents primarily come from academia. Change agents in Japan have come from universities and national research institutions because they traditionally have had social prestige, especially popular universities such as Tokyo University, Tokyo Institute of Technology, and Kyoto University and others (see Table 16-2).

In the United States, the government and semiprivate agencies provide the infrastructure of quality diffusion; however, the situation is much more fragmented than in Japan. For instance, although the Department of Commerce gives its imprimatur to the Baldrige Award, the bulk of the effort to administer the Baldrige Award comes from individuals from industry and consultancies. Basically, the Baldrige Award organization is a semiprivate organization. Furthermore, as in Japan, the major effort of addressing the need for a quality promotion infrastructure comes from industrial consortia. However, while there are only two major consortia in Japan (JUSE and JSA), there are many quality organizations in the United States.

Table 16-2. Elements and Institutions of Societal Learning in Japan and the United States

Learning Element	Institution in Japan	Institution in the United States
Quality promotion infrastructure	Government and semi-private agencies (focused)	Government and semi-private agencies (fragmented)
Openness with real cases	Industry ("no secrets in quality")	Industry (often wary of sharing quality methods)
Change agents	Universities, national research institutions (knowledge, prestige, sense of mission)	? (Retired CEOs?)

U.S. industry is becoming increasingly open with real cases; but many companies remain wary of sharing quality methods.

Finding outside change agents is an unsolved problem in the United States. Although university professors have intellectual prestige, many in U.S. industry consider academics to be out of touch with real-world practices. American consultants have the same problem as Japanese consultants in acting as change agents; their short-term self-interest sometimes conflicts with their long-term sense of mission. Retired CEOs may be good candidates for change agents, since they have both prestige with industry and the necessary knowledge, but to fill the bill they must retain a vigorous sense of mission in their post-industry years.

TQM requires change throughout the company organization. The traditional method of effecting change is from the top down, by order and enforcement of top-level managers. Most top managers can testify to the difficulty of such an approach. Managers just below the top argue against the changes, middle managers delay implementation, and much of the rest of the staff swears that the changes can't work in their company. They tend to continue doing whatever they have been doing. The alternative is outside influence and outside power for change. A societal learning system provides an effective alternative to top-down change. The modern quality promotion program uses a regional or national organization or quality culture to exert outside influence for change.

This outside influence is beginning to emerge in the United States. The Baldrige Award has generated interest in quality in thousands of U.S. companies. Some companies are putting pressure on their suppliers to focus on quality. For instance, Motorola has asked its suppliers when they will be ready to apply for the Baldrige Award. More specifically, Globe Metallurgical, which won the Baldrige Award in 1988, was motivated in part by its desire to get Ford's Q-1 quality rating. Similarly, Wallace Company, which won the Baldrige Award in 1990, was seeking to satisfy the quality requirements of Hoechst Celanese, which in turn was seeking to satisfy the quality requirements of Ford.

Diffusion of QI stories is another example of outside influence. When workers in one company see workers in another effectively using improvement methodologies, they think in terms of application to their company. A manager is going to be more receptive to TQM if all the other companies the manager might work for are also implementing TQM. Young engineers would not be so negative about the use of basic quality methods if their universities required mastery of the methods for graduation.

There are many ways such outside forces for quality infusion are manifested, as shown in Figure 16-4. If TQM is to be spread throughout a society, it is not enough for parent corporations to require and teach TQM to subsidiaries, or for large customers to require and teach TQM to suppliers. Moreover, TQM is a complex set of knowledge and practices, so that no single channel of diffusion is sufficient. A regional and national infrastructure requires several channels in several dimensions.

Indeed, Figure 16-4 implies 135 kinds of diffusion channels (this book of standards for top management is one example). All of the elements on each of the dimensions are opportunities for societal diffusion in an industry, region, or nation.

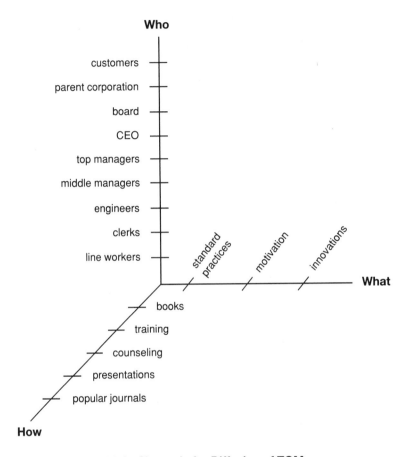

Figure 16-4. Multiple Channels for Diffusion of TQM

NOTES

1. Parts of this section were previously published in Shiba, "Quality Knows No Bounds," *Look Japan*, May 1989, 30-31.
2. The information describing JUSE is primarily taken from JUSE's descriptive brochure, "JUSE: Organization and Activities."

3. Robert E. Cole, "The Macropolitics of Organizational Change: A Comparative Analysis of the Spread of Small-Group Activities," *Administrative Science Quarterly* 30 (December 1985), 560-87; Cole, *Strategies for Learning* (Berkeley: University of California Press, 1989).

4. Cole, *Strategies for Learning*, 272-296 (chap. 13, "The Building of a National Infrastructure in Japan").

5. Remarks by Mr. J. Noguchi in an informal lecture at JUSE headquarters, March 12, 1990.

6. Lecture by MIT professor Tom Lee on his visit to JUSE, November 7, 1989.

7. John Petrolini of Teradyne provided us with a briefing on the Baldrige Award. See also Mark G. Brown, *Baldrige Award Winning Quality: How to Intrepret the Malcolm Baldrige Award Criteria* (White Plains, N.Y.: Quality Resources/Milwaukee: ASQC Quality Press, 1992).

8. David A. Garvin, "Does the Baldrige Award Really Work?" *Harvard Business Review* (Jan-Feb 1992), 126-47.

9. Besides, over time and with continuous improvement, it should be possible to eliminate many of the problems people find with the Baldrige Award.

10. For a more detailed description see David A. Garvin, *Managing Quality*, 185-186.

11. From Kaoru Ishikawa, ed., "Special Issue; Seven Management Tools," *Reports of Statistical Application Research* 33, no. 2 (June 1986).

12. Everett M. Rogers, *Diffusion of Innovations* (New York: Free Press, 1962).

13. Uchimaru, et al., *TQM for Technical Groups* (Cambridge, MA: Productivity Press, 1993).

17

TQM as a

Learning System

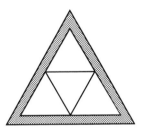

In the previous chapters TQM is described as a hierarchical model for improving the skill of individuals, teams, organizations or companies, and regions or nations. According to this model, activities at each level are supported by the next larger unit:

- Individual problem-solving is supported by teams. A person trying alone to improve his or her skill may not have the necessary motivation and may find complete understanding difficult to attain. Working in a team will usually accelerate learning (see Chapter 9).
- Team activities are supported by the organization or company infrastructure. Teams without organizational support will find it difficult to become empowered (have authority and capability) and may in fact find it difficult to survive. The organization's mobilization infrastructure will accelerate team learning (see Chapter 11).
- The organization or company, especially its senior management, is supported by the regional or national quality culture and infrastructure. It is difficult for a company to make the changes necessary to improve its skill if no

other company is doing the same thing, customers don't expect improvement, and competitors are not improving. Networking at the regional or national level accelerates the learning of an organization or company (as discussed in the previous chapter).

Common to these four levels of total quality management is the existence of a system of learning at each level. The real quality being totally managed is the quality of human capabilities. The real improvement activity taking place is improving skills and the ability to learn. Through TQM every size of unit, from individual to team to company to region or nation, can learn how to learn. TQM can be thought of as a system for learning new skill for the benefit of society.

This is the focus of this chapter: TQM as a learning system; TQM as a system for developing individual, team, company, and national skill.

KEEPING PACE WITH THE NEED FOR SKILL

As Lester Thurow, dean of MIT's Sloan School of Management, points out:

> In the century ahead natural resources, capital, and new product technologies are going to rapidly move around the world. People will move — but more slowly than anything else. People become the only sustainable competitive advantage."[1]

Learning can be divided into three categories: job-specific capabilities (knowledge needed to do one job versus another); skills (abilities in one field of endeavor or another, such as engineering or advertising); and basic education (reading, history, working with people, and so on). As illustrated in Figure 17-1, skills are built on top of basic education, and job-specific capabilities are built on top of skills.

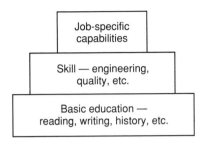

Figure 17-1. Three Categories of Learning

In most countries, basic education is provided in the public school systems, while job-specific capabilities are learned on the job and taught by the employing company. Skills, however, are taught differently. Thurow points out that in American and British firms skill acquisition is an individual responsibility. People invest their own time and money to get college degrees. Someone without a college degree in engineering, for example, will find it virtually impossible to advance into an engineering career. One must go to night school, or take time off to complete a degree program.

In Japan, by contrast, skill training is done primarily by employers. At NEC's IC/Microsystems subsidiary, for example, new engineers receive a full year of training initially, learning skills that the company deems necessary for engineers to master. However, in the rapidly changing world that TQM addresses, companies must change their systems and equipment to deal with changing realities. These changes are coming faster and must be accomplished more rapidly. With these changes, jobs change rapidly and job-specific capabilities rapidly become obsolete. New job-specific capabilities and experience must be obtained.

Skill level is paramount in determining how quickly people can develop new job-specific capabilities (the level of basic education also matters, but not as directly). These changes are shown in Figure 17-2.

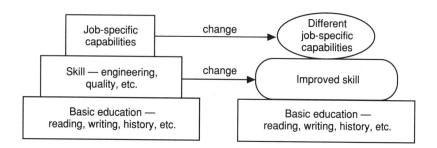

Figure 17-2. Changes in Needed Skills

During times of rapid change, needed skills change, so people can no longer depend on college training from many years ago. To keep skills current, employees must acquire new skills as a normal part of employment. To rely on exceptional people acquiring new skills by making exceptional sacrifices is to doom most employees to becoming further and further out of date with every passing year, and less and less productive in terms of their potential.

As Thurow pointed out, human capability is the key resource that companies must develop. Although skill is not directly related to the job, it is an important aspect of human capabilities; thus, companies must invest in its development. Shoji Shiba believes that Japan's greater willingness to invest in the development of skill is an important competitive advantage.

David Kearns was chairman of Xerox during the period of its transition from near-victim of Japanese competition to world-class competitor and American exemplar of TQM. Kearns has made similar statements about the need to continually develop skill. In the concluding sections of his book describing those years, he writes:

> [A critical success factor for corporate success is] organizational learning. Even those [companies] with great strategies, total quality, and innovative organizational architectures don't always get it right the first time. They make mistakes. The best competitors do have a unique ca-

pacity to reflect upon and understand the meaning in those mistakes very quickly, and turn insight into action; they are learning-efficient organizations. They learn from customers, competitors, and suppliers. They learn from success and they learn from failure. They encourage the notion of "productive failure" as a key ingredient in the learning process. They recognize that the sources of success in the past are often the seeds of failure in the future.

Competitive effectiveness will therefore require companies to invest in the development of their capacity to learn. It will require significant improvements in the capacities of individuals, groups, and whole organizations to reflect and gain insight. The key ingredients are the structures, processes, and environments that enable and encourage learning, but also empower people to translate learning into action.[2]

Deming has expressed similar thoughts, along the lines that doing your best is a dead end and that permanent improvement comes from learning how to change what you do.

A TQM MODEL FOR SKILL DEVELOPMENT

In the following four sections we describe a TQM model that any entity can use to develop itself.

Parallels in the Stages of Learning

At any level of practice — individual, team, organization, or region — TQM engenders the ability for self-development, or the ability to change for the better. The three phases of the TQM process — orientation, empowerment and self-invention — are nearly the same at each level, as summarized in the top row of Table 17-1. Generally speaking, by orientation we mean being introduced to a new skill. By empowerment we mean learning the craft of the new skill, typically from someone who is already expert in the conventional body of skill. By self-invention we mean having enough craft to adapt the skill effectively to one's specific needs or to extend the craft beyond what one has learned from others.[3]

Table 17-1. Levels of TQM Practice and Phases of Learning

Phase ⟹ Level ⟱	Orientation	Empowerment	Self-invention
Individual	Knowledge	Understanding	Skill
Team	Belonging	Achievement/ recognition	Self-actualization
Organization	Orientation	Empowerment/ synchronization	Alignment/ localization
Region/nation	Crisis	Imitation/ Benchmarking	Systematic development

Consider the parallels within each of the four levels to these three phases of learning.

As we described in the preface and have summarized in the second row of Table 17-1, individuals start their learning in a particular subject with knowledge — facts about the way things work, like the 7 steps of reactive problem solving, or about their own job. With use of facts in conversations on the job or in the classroom, individuals acquire understanding. Use of knowledge and understanding in actual situations or applications produces skill.[4] Skill provides the ability for effective self-development.

The third row of the table highlights teams. In Chapter 9 we described the developmental progression of teams (Figure 9-3). This progression is summarized in Figure 17-3.

Teams formed from work groups begin with social cohesion — in the sense of belonging to a group. Groups often form social bonds, ranging from management teams to assembly-line bowling teams. This is the orientation phase for teams. However, when a team begins to function as a team and achieve as a team, it will begin to be recognized as a team, and members will

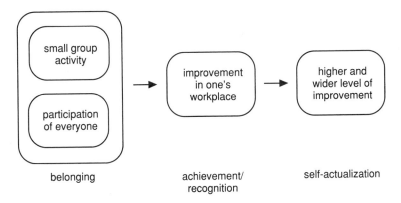

Figure 17-3. Developmental Progression of Teams

begin to work explicitly for the team because it brings recognized achievement. This is the empowerment phase. When a team becomes proficient at its task, it begins to experiment and change continually. Being on the team becomes a creative exercise, a form of self-actualization. This is the self-invention phase. The self-development sequence for teams is analogous to certain levels in Abraham Maslow's hierarchy of needs, ranging from satisfying affiliative needs to recognition needs to the need for self-actualization.

Organizations also go through transitions in learning. TQM implementations in Deming Prize and Baldrige Award winners were described in Chapter 12 as having three phases. An orientation phase occurs when the organization recognizes the need for change (either crisis or powerful vision) and involves exploration and experimentation with the means of change. The empowerment phase includes the setting of a new course and provision of the persuasion, education, and reorganization necessary to achieve it. (Sometimes this phase is broken into fluctuation, unfreezing of existing practices, and synchronization, or getting the organization to follow a new set of common practices.) When an organization becomes proficient at its new set of practices, it adapts them to the organization's particular needs.

For example, the transition from companywide 7-steps reactive problem solving to formal hoshin management is often a transition from the empowerment phase to an alignment phase, as described in Chapter 12. The term denotes aligning TQM practices and systems with all other practices and systems of the business, in addition to alignment of individuals to common purposes. However, Shoji Shiba often has called this phase "localization," meaning that the company has reinvented TQM practices to suit its local situation. This is self-invention at the company level.

Learning by regions and nations may seem less clear-cut than the other levels we have discussed, perhaps because of the relative scarcity of examples. However, TQM learning in Japan and the United States seems to follow the orientation/empowerment/self-invention model. In Japan, the orientation phase encompassed the export crisis in the late 1940s and early to mid-1950s, and the search for foreign experts such as Deming and Juran. Next followed an empowerment phase in which the lessons of the 1950s were deployed through a national infrastructure that included the Deming Prize process and the intercompany educational processes organized by JUSE and JSA. The subsequent history of Japanese TQM is the story of a systematic search for new approaches (self-invention) in response to global economic and social pressures. The history of the 1960s through the present seems analogous to the localization phase for organizational TQM learning, and the self-actualization phase for team development.[5]

The United States went through an orientation phase in the late 1970s and 1980s, during which people recognized that the quality practices in many industries, notably automobiles and consumer electronics, were substantially below world-class levels. Beginning in the 1980s, many companies empowered themselves by adopting and practicing the TQM concepts of Deming and Juran as practiced in Japan. At the same time, some U.S. companies had the necessary skill to search systematically for improved approaches. Motorola's six sigma and Xerox's benchmarking approaches are examples. Although there are many such success stories for individual companies, a clear standard set of quality practices and reliable means of diffusing them throughout the country has yet to emerge.

Forces for Accelerated Learning — Infrastructures and Triggers

The left box in Figure 17-4 illustrates the three phases of learning or self-development described in the previous section.

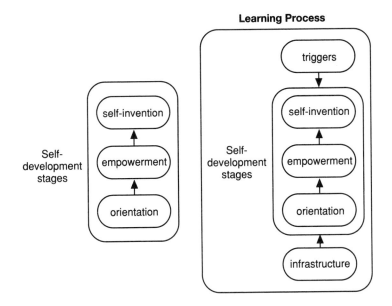

Figure 17-4. Triggers and Infrastructures for Self-Development

These phases of self-development don't just happen by themselves. The entity trying to learn needs outside forces to catalyze self-development. Two key types of external forces are triggers and infrastructures, shown in the figure's right box.

Individual learning is encouraged and facilitated by the infrastructure of standardized problem-solving methods (7 steps, 7 QC tools, 7 management and planning tools), teams (in which people help each other), managers (who guide and advise subordinates), and the 7 elements of organizational infrastructure (goals, organization, education, promotion, diffusion of success stories, incentives, and management diagnosis).

Teams, like individuals, find learning support in management and organizational infrastructure.

Organizational learning is facilitated by internal monitoring and diagnosis infrastructure, and external regional and national quality infrastructure, through organizations such as JUSE in Japan, and the ASQC and CQM in the United States. Such "transcorporate" organizations provide publication of real cases, classes, national and regional quality awards, quality promotion and conferences, and so on.

Regional and national learning is enhanced by internal monitoring, diagnosis, and systematic exploration and development, as well as by other regions or nations.

In other words, the infrastructure for each level tends to come from one level above. This is illustrated in the following table.

Level	Infrastructure from Level Above
Individual	Team or group learning
Team	Seven organizational infrastructure elements
Organization	Societal networking

Triggers complement infrastructures in initiating rapid learning. As was explained in Chapter 9, the learning process does not steadily increase over time. Rather, it remains at a level for a while and then jumps. Triggers are normally needed to instigate these jumps (see Figure 17-5).

Teams provide triggers (i.e., facilitate rapid learning) for individuals. Enthusiastic managers provide triggers for teams, as was noted in Chapter 9. Business crisis, the voice of the customer, and excellent practices in other companies are triggers for the CEO and senior management. In turn, the CEOs and senior managers articulate strategy to trigger the orientation phase of TQM mobilization in an organization. Meanwhile, inability to compete in world markets is a potent trigger for nations.

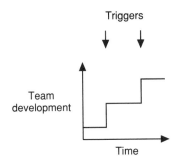

Figure 17-5. Triggers for Rapid Learning

Indirect Activities to Push and Pull the Learning Process

Despite their necessity and effectiveness, triggers and infrastructures do not mobilize the learning process and stages of self-development enough so that companies can keep pace with rapid change in society. To compensate, TQM offers a number of indirect activities that further mobilize learning. These indirect activities are not typically used in our hierarchical and functionally partitioned companies; using them to speed learning is an important innovation of TQM, another revolution in management thinking.

Some of these indirect activities "push" the learning process, while others "pull" it. There are two types of indirect pushing activities, or pressures — *nonhierarchical* elements and *outside* elements — and two types of indirect pulls — *noble goals* and *noble practices* — as shown in Figure 17-6.

Indirect Pressures — Nonhierarchical Elements

TQM activities cause people to work outside the normal relationships based on work group, function, or level in company hierarchy. Nonhierarchical structures are therefore used to push forward or drive learning. Such nonhierarchical structures are available at each of the four levels, as shown at the bottom left of Figure 17-7.

The dual function of work was discussed in Chapters 3 and 9. It provides a nonhierarchical push for self-development. The

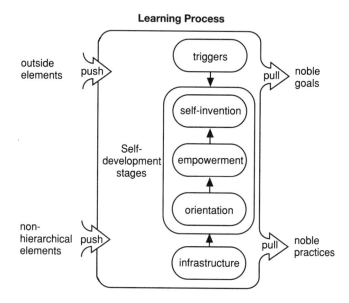

Figure 17-6. Push and Pull in the Learning Process

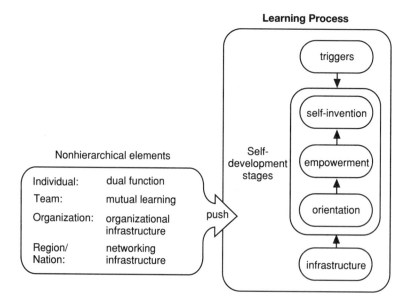

Figure 17-7. Indirect Pressure from Nonhierarchical Elements

dual function of work principle asserts that it is the job of every-one to do both improvement work and daily work. It abandons Taylor's hierarchical approach, which calls for managers and quality specialists to do the improvement work and workers to do the daily work. Thus, individuals are given freedom, not direct command, to improve themselves.

Mutual learning adds a nonhierarchical aspect at the team level of learning, as opposed to the traditional (hierarchical) teacher-to-student method of learning. Anyone who has had difficulty studying alone is aware of the benefits of group study. Learning by oneself is more difficult than learning in a group, which provides a sense of momentum, responsibility, and motivation. (Methods of mutual learning for teams were described in Chapter 9.)

At the organizational level, companies use the seven elements of infrastructure for TQM mobilization (introduced in Chapter 11) as a nonhierarchical push for development of organizational improvement skills. Table 17-2 contrasts the traditional direct approach to organizational development (left column) with the indirect approach (middle column) resulting from the TQM mobilization infrastructure (right column).

A given organization will usually fall between these two extremes, both in the style of daily work and in the style of improvement activities. As we explained in Chapter 16, even at the regional or national level, learning is indirectly spread from organization to organization through the quality culture and infrastructure. Such diffusion occurs in regional and industry associations and in initiatives and consortia formed for the purpose of creating networks between industries and countries.

All of the above provide learning driven through distinctly nonhierarchical channels.

Indirect Pressures — Outside Elements

The natural complement to the nonhierarchical push to acquire learning skills is a push from the outside — another form

Table 17-2. The TQM Indirect Approach to Organizational Development Compared with the Traditional Direct Approach

Traditional Hierarchical Daily Work Methods	Nonhierarchical Improvement Infrastructure	Related Infrastructure Elements
Goals and regulations	Vision	1. Goal setting
Hierarchical chain of command	Networking organization	2. Organizational setting
Direct enforcement	Mutual learning	3. Education and training
Top-down sloganeering	Permeating the organization	4. Promotion
Penalty and correction	Praise and encouragement	5. Diffusion of success stories
Order	Support	6. Awards and incentives
Results	Process	7. Monitoring and diagnosis

of indirect pressure. As with non-hierarchical methods, outside pressure applies at all four levels of TQM practice (top left of Figure 17-8).

Individuals change more readily when clearly apprised of customer desires and needs. This is the market-in concept, which emphasizes that the purpose of work is to satisfy customers, not just do the job (see Figure 3-3).

Teams change more rapidly when a systematic program of customer visitation, analysis, and action is in place. Also effective are the QI story presentations, which make it clear that peers can accomplish significant improvements. Meanwhile, the internal QI story presentation system disseminates information across department and division barriers, while the QC circle conventions disseminate information across company and industry barriers. Both mechanisms create ties between otherwise unrelated parties and raise their overall level of improvement.

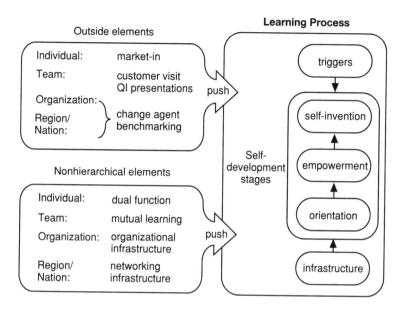

Figure 17-8. Indirect Pressure from Outside Elements

Organizations change more readily when needed changes are identified by "existence proof" of the feasibility of dramatically improved operations (benchmarking — see Chapter 13) or by an experienced but objective observer (a change agent — see Chapter 16). Benchmarking makes clear both the level of performance others are capable of and their process for achieving that level of performance. Change agents, outsiders with sufficient knowledge, prestige, and sense of mission, can serve as catalysts to bring about paradigm changes in an organization — revolutions in thinking that would be difficult to cause from within.

National change can be speeded up similarly by outside pressures such as benchmarking and change agents. Benchmarking at the national level occurs when U.S. delegations from government and industry go to Japan to study the results and methods there. The creation of the Baldrige Award is an example of moving a successful Japanese practice (the Deming Prize) to the United States. Similarly, change agents can come from outside a company. Deming went to Japan as a change agent. A number of Japanese experts have come to the United States as change agents for successful quality initiatives.

Individuals, teams, organizations, and countries are motivated by outside forces. TQM systematically takes advantage of these outside forces, building on their ability to create change.

Indirect Pulls — Noble Goals

At every level there are also pulls, or forces that create a desire for learning. "Noble goals" are one such force. Traditionally, noble goals reflect *loyalty to the (well-being of the) larger unit.* That is, individuals are motivated by the desire to serve the team, company, or country. Similarly, teams are motivated by the need for the company to do well. Ishikawa often said that quality must serve the nation, not the company. Such loyalty to the higher unit reveals an understanding of interrelatedness, as shown in Figure 17-9.

**Figure 17-9. Serving the Well-Being
of the Larger Unit**

The pull of the noble goal of loyalty to the larger unit is shown in the pulling force at the bottom right of Figure 17-10.

Although some people are willing to sacrifice their own well being for that of the larger unit (such as those who sacrifice

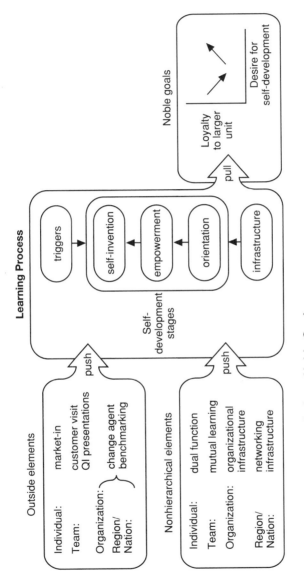

Figure 17-10. Indirect Pulls from Noble Goals

career advancement in order to enhance company performance, and those fighting forces who sacrifice their lives for their countries), loyalty to the larger unit is generally tempered by loyalty to oneself (the downward slope of the left arrow).

Therefore, TQM adds another goal — self-development — to the noble goals. In other words, TQM elicits the learning it needs by appealing both to the higher loyalty and to the individual's own desire for self-development (the upward slope of the right arrow).

For example, a major part of the QC circle movement in Japan is use of teamwork to enhance the development (skills, happiness, capabilities, quality of working life) of the individual members. As shown in Figure 17-11, one of the three purposes of QC circles is to accomplish the company goals; the other two are related to the development of the individual.

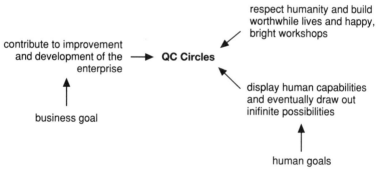

Source: *How to Operate QC Circle Activities* (Tokyo: Union of Japanese Scientists and Engineers, 1985), 4.

Figure 17-11. Purposes of the QC Circle

A major reason for the success in diffusion of QC circles in Japan was likely this emphasis on developing human potential in addition to meeting the business goals, and that more emphasis on business goals would have inhibited diffusion.

Thus the pull from traditional goals such as loyalty to the larger unit increases when human goals are being fulfilled. Companies that develop employees win loyalty and heightened motivation. Similarly, countries like the United States, which bring impoverished immigrants to new levels of education and prosperity, win the patriotism of those groups.

Indirect Pulls — Noble Practices

A final pull toward learning comes from what might be called noble practices: exercise of universally recognized and valued skills and processes. Traditionally, the successful and revered practices in business have been decision making and action based on intuition, judgment, and experience — management as an *art*. (The Japanese have reduced this to an acronym, KKD, which translated stands for knowledge, experience, and guts.) To the traditional artistic practice of management, TQM adds the higher goal of fact-based management (*science*). As was noted in Chapter 4, management by facts (PDCA, WV model) is really the practical application of the scientific method. The arrows at top left of Figure 17-12 show an increase in "scientific" noble practices, and a slight decrease in "artistic" noble practices. Experience, intuition, and judgment are not abandoned; rather, total dependence on them is decreased.

For example, in the NEC/IC case of implementation, PDCA (a "scientific" method) was used to enhance engineers' sensitivity and ability to anticipate problems.[6] This approach served to elevate intuition — the "art" of engineering — to a higher plane. The same thing happens at many levels. The empirical knowledge on teamwork in this book is intended to give managers more perceptiveness — intuition, as it were — about what goes on in their teams. The empirical generalities about CEO campaigning and TQM education are intended to enhance what is ultimately an intuitive ability, namely the ability to design and diagnose a TQM program. So the top right arrow in Figure 17-12

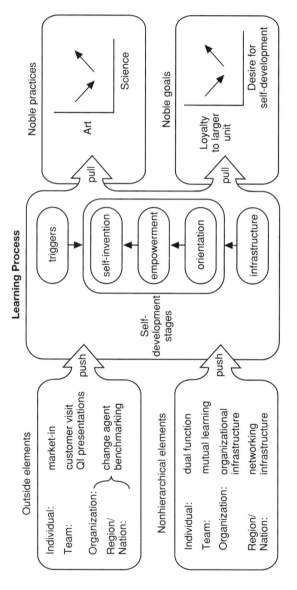

Figure 17-12. Indirect Pulls from Nobel Practices

slopes upward, indicating improvement in the traditional realm of intuition and judgment when science is applied.

The addition of fact-based noble practices motivates learning by offering a clear process and appealing to many types of people with many types of abilities.

Indirect Forces for Learning Complement Direct Forces for Learning

While TQM has added the indirect forces described above (which experience has shown are enormously effective), it has not abandoned the traditional direct forces. Just as organizational charts of improvement have dual functions, one part networked and one part hierarchical, so does learning. For example, learning takes place directly through the hierarchy and through inside pressures, as well as through indirect channels. The learning system of TQM embraces both the direct and indirect modes of learning; anything less cannot prove effective in the long run.

For each of the elements of indirect learning outlined above, there is a complementary direct element that also plays a role in learning systems. These are shown in Figure 17-13.

In addition to self-development capabilities, there are also trained-in capabilities. The same is true with triggers and infrastructure. The triggers for these capabilities may be more mundane (being hired, coming up next on a training schedule), and the infrastructure more familiar (a corporate training department). The complements to nonhierarchical elements and outside elements are hierarchical elements and inside elements. People undergo training (or learn by repetition of experience) because their manager tells them to do it, and the training is typically designed to help them to perform the job better. But the dual function of work requires that many types of training (both problem-solving methods and standardized ways of doing a job better) be part of hierarchical learning.

Total Quality Management

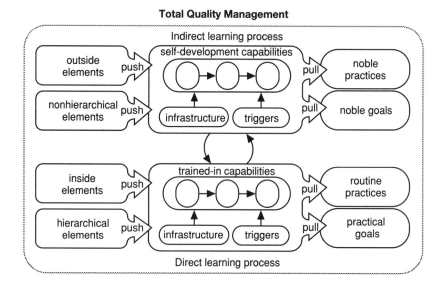

Figure 17-13. Complementary Elements of Indirect and Direct Learning

The complements to noble goals are practical goals. A business plan that calls for new skills is certainly a pull for training. Similarly, the complements to the noble practices (of art and science) are routine practices. An example would be the routine practice of doing a project retrospective at the end of every development task — making this bit of PDCA a standard part of daily work.

SUMMARY OF SKILL DEVELOPMENT

This chapter opened with a discussion of the need for skill development. TQM was described as a learning system that focuses skill development at every level. It improves products and services. It improves human resources. We conclude the chapter by returning to the issue of skill development.

Arguably the most important aspect of TQM is its development of the individual — its encouragement of human learning.

In particular, it requires senior managers to develop their knowledge of the theory and practice of quality.

In TQM, the learning style of geniuses is fitted to a model that everyone can use. This learning style often follows the skill development phases described earlier in this chapter — orientation, empowerment, and self-invention. Geniuses first study a new topic (read books, observe current practice, etc.) — this is orientation. Next, they imitate current masters (practice traditional techniques) — this is empowerment. Finally, with theory and skill at their disposal, geniuses invent their own methods — this is self-invention.

The example of the brilliant Dutch painter, Vincent van Gogh, illustrates an application of this three-phase method. Around 1886 van Gogh began seriously studying Japanese prints. He collected some 400 Japanese prints, and in 1887 he presented exhibitions of Japanese prints in the Café du Tambourin and the Restaurant du Chalét in Paris. This was van Gogh's orientation phase with regard to Japanese prints. He invested time and money in learning something new.

Next, van Gogh painted copies of Japanese prints. For example, the Vincent van Gogh Rijksmuseum in Amsterdam shows his *Japonaiserie: The Tree* (1887), a close copy of *The Plumtree Teahouse at Kameido* (1857) by Hiroshige (1797-1858). This was his empowerment phase. During this phase he perfected his ability to paint in the conventional manner. Copying the masters, imitation, is a very powerful tool for empowerment. If we refuse to or can't imitate those who already have skill, it is very difficult to empower ourselves.

Finally, van Gogh created his own methods. He moved beyond imitation. But traces remain, for example, in the shape of the tree trunks and the flowers in *The Sower*[7] or *Pear Tree in Blossom* (both 1888). Once he had studied and become empowered, van Gogh moved on to self-invention like *Still-Life with Irises* (1889).

As individuals, teams, companies, and nations we can use TQM to follow this learning style of geniuses. First, the crisis provides orientation. Next, we gain empowerment by imitating those who are succeeding, that is, by imitating best practice. Finally, we will be in a position to evolve our own system, to reinvent ourselves.

Since we are in a crisis, we must move through these steps quickly. We cannot remain long in the orientation phase, debating whether best practice applies to us or not. We must quickly see the implications of the crisis and then move on quickly to gain skill. We must adopt the best practices of others, even if we are unsure that those practices apply to us. Until we master those practices, we will not be in a position to make a well-founded judgment about their worth and applicability, or to tailor them to our situation.

We have now come full circle:

- from the preface, where we discussed the three-part model of learning and skill acquisition, whereby knowledge becomes understanding and understanding becomes skill
- to this chapter, where we discussed TQM as a learning system, moving individuals, teams, companies, and nations from orientation to empowerment to self-invention

Thank you for taking this journey with us.

NOTES

1. Lester Thurow, *Head to Head* (New York: William Morrow, 1992), 51-52.
2. David T. Kearns and David A. Nadler, *Prophets in the Dark: How Xerox Reinvented Itself and Beat Back the Japanese* (New York: Harper Collins, 1992). The discussion of TQM as a success factor separate from organizational learning gives the flavor of TQM as equivalent to customer focus. The discussions of organization-wide diagnoses suggest that Kearns and Nadler may not con-

sider this "organizational learning practice" as an integral part of TQM.

3. In an ideal world, the terminology at the four levels would be identical. In practice, the terms developed independently, and we have used the now-standard terms in the respective chapters. Table 17-1 therefore includes five sets of terms.

4. Educators will recognize this sequence as akin to the Kirkpatrick model of skill acquisition.

5. It might be instructive to examine other historical instances of need for rapid learning. For example, at the beginning of the Industrial Revolution, the French government made a concerted effort to acquire British technology in a variety of industries. Likewise, in the nineteenth century, Europeans were cognizant of the need to learn "the American system of manufactures."

6. See the case study in Chapter 15, based on Kiyoshi Uchimaru, et al., *TQM for Technical Groups: Total Quality Principles for Product Development* (Cambridge, MA: Productivity Press, 1993).

7. All of the paintings referred to here (even the Hiroshige) are in the collection of the Rijksmuseum Vincent van Gogh in Amsterdam, with the exception of *The Sower*. There are several works of that name from 1888; the one with the tree hangs in Zürich, Stiftung Sammlung E.G. Bührle.

Afterword

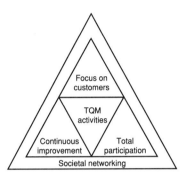

We began this book by describing the evolving nature of quality (in Chapters 1 and 2); we described TQM as an evolving system of concepts and practices for creating higher-quality products and services for increased customer satisfaction in a rapidly changing world. The key words in this description are "evolving" and "rapidly changing." We have described TQM as we see it effectively practiced today, but what works today will probably be insufficient for tomorrow.

The main body of this book (Chapters 3 to 16) is organized according to four concepts — we called them four revolutions in management thinking — that have proved fundamental to successful implementation of TQM today. These are focus on customers, continuous improvement, total participation, and societal networking. Focus on customers keeps a company's attention on those whose changing needs define the criteria for company success. Continuous improvement provides the idea of a learning cycle. Total participation recognizes the modern reality that everyone in the company has a stake in the company, and that everyone's participation and skill are needed to remain competitive. Societal networking provides a supportive culture and the means of acquiring rapid experience and refinement in the implementation of quality methods.

Chapter 17 describes the four revolutions of TQM as a learning system with emphasis on developing capabilities. These four revolutions don't apply just to the way a company implements its quality methods, improves its business processes, and develops the human capabilities of its employees. They also apply to the evolution of TQM itself. TQM must evolve in directions that satisfy the changing needs of its customers — companies, company stakeholders (employees, investors, suppliers, communities where the company resides), company customers, and society at large. TQM must continually improve and evolve. Broad participation in the evolution of TQM is needed. All of the elements of society must work together for the quick and efficient evolution of TQM.

Whether it is applied to the evolution of a company's TQM implementation or to the evolution of TQM in general, continuous improvement is perhaps the most basic of the four revolutions. Continuous improvement is PDCA. Continuous improvement means that you identify the weakness in a current system and discover what must be changed to remove the weakness (plan). Continuous improvement means that you then try the change and discover if it really works (do and check). Continuous improvement also reminds you that, being human, you won't follow through and use the improvement methods on a continuing basis unless you install systems that force you to do so (act). We have described several systems and models designed to assure action, such as the WV model, the four levels of practice (individual, team, organization, region/nation), and systems of teams.

Finally, continuous improvement means that you repeat the cycle forever to bring your company up to the current level of best practice and to react to a changing environment. In this sense, TQM may be thought of as a system for changing demands of the environment — TQM is a system for learning. Customer support, total participation, and societal networking are concepts that support and focus the learning system.

By applying the principles of TQM to itself, TQM will invent or acquire those quality concepts and practices necessary to meet the changing demands of the modern world. We look forward to the refinement of the current practice of TQM , to the evolution of the concepts of quality beyond the four fitnesses, and to additional revolutions in management thinking.

About the Authors

Shoji Shiba is a professor of business administration at Tsukuba University in Japan and currently an adjunct professor at MIT, where he teaches graduate courses in Total Quality Management at the Sloan School of Management and in the Leaders for Manufacturing program. Dr. Shiba helped found the Center for Quality Management.

As an international expert in Total Quality Management, Dr. Shiba is responsible for disseminating the practices and methodologies of TQM to nationwide or regionwide industries and governments in several countries, including France, Ireland, Italy, the former USSR (1990 and 1991), and Sweden. In honor of his work in Hungary, the ministry established the Annual IIASA Shiba Award, presented to groups and individuals who make significant TQM contributions.

Alan K. Graham works with the Center for Quality Management, developing TQM practices for new product development and corporate strategy formation. He is also a principal of Product Development Consulting (Cambridge, Massachusetts). Dr. Graham holds a Ph.D. from MIT in electrical engineering, and served on the faculty and staff of MIT's Sloan School of Management, teaching and researching system simulation models for corporate and economic strategy. He is the author of numerous articles and one book in the system dynamics field.

David C. Walden got his undergraduate degree in mathematics at San Francisco State College and did graduate study in computer science at MIT. Since college, he has worked at MIT Lincoln Laboratories, Norsk Data (Oslo, Norway), and Bolt Beranek and Newman, Inc. (Cambridge, Massachusetts). In his nearly 30-year business career he has held a succession of technical, technical management, and general management positions. Mr. Walden is a frequent author, speaker, and editor on various technical and management topics.

Index

ASI. *See* American Supplier Institute

ASQC. *See* American Society for Quality Control

AT&T mission statement, 341

Abe, Masanobu, 377

Abstraction, levels of, 166-68

Ackoff, Russell, 419-23

Affinity diagram, 158. *See also* KJ method

Akao, Yoji, 384, 455

Alcoa Aluminum, 391

American Society for Quality Control, 511, 514, 542

American Supplier Institute, 323, 514

Analog Devices, xii, 264, 321, 401, 523

Broken Pellicle QI Team case study, 87-101

Errorbusters case study, 127-40, 289

Arrow diagram, 158

Artzt, Edwin, 321

Asahi Brewery, 182

Awards and incentives. *See* TQM implementation

Baldrige Award, 30, 266, 317, 371-72, 380, 518, 528, 530, 539, 547

Bannister, Roger, 38

Benchmarking, 332, 343, 344, 380, 392-95

Bodek, Norman, xiii

Bolt Beranek and Newman, Inc. (BBN), xi, 181, 187, 264, 335, 523

customer visitation case study, 170-79, 193, 196, 217, 237

internal TQM education, 358-60

TQM introduction strategy, 327-30

Bose Corporation, xii, 264, 523

Bridgestone Tire Company, 411

565

Burchill, Gary, 201-05, 231, 242, 244-45
By chance principle, 148

CAPD cycle, 463-64, 467, 475
and daily work, 481-86
individual practice of, 491-501
institutionalizing, 486-91
and PDCA cycle, 477-81
stages of practice, 492-94
Camp, Robert C., 393
Catchball, 433, 466, 447, 449
Cause-and-effect diagram, 85, 103, 119, 120
Cause and result chain, 78
Center for Quality Management, xx, 522-28
CEO involvement, 307-13
CEO crusades, 317-21
Teradyne case study, 313-17
in training, 351-52, 353
Change agents, 522
Check sheet, 85, 102
Commitment
to mutual learning, xxv
to openness to learning, xxvi
to serious application, xxiii
Contextual inquiry, 197-200
Continuous improvement. See Improvement, continuous
Control chart, 85, 104
Corning Glass, 37-38, 40-41, 344, 366, 514, 524
CEO crusade, 317-21
internal TQM education, 357-58
TQM implementation, 377, 380
Corporate culture, fitness to. See Fitnesses, future

Cost, fitness to. See Fitnesses, four
Cost down 10 percent (CD10), 13
Creativity. See Innovation
Customer interview, 202
Customer requirements, 207, 211, 214-41
definition of product based on, 240-43
determination of, 207-16
operationally defining, 237-39
qualitative definition of, 217-31
quantitative definition of, 231-40
selection of, 216-17
Customer visitation, 170
diminishing returns, 184
fishbowl approach, 184-85
seven key points, 178
Customer, voice of the, 196-98
contextual inquiry and, 198-201
See also Transforming the voice of the customer

Daily work, 249-51
d'Arbeloff, Alex, 313-17, 321, 324-25, 334, 339
Data, kinds of, 55-56, 145
Data analysis
language, 156-57, 164-66
numeric, 156-57
Data collection, 53, 56
for proactive improvement, 145-150
qualitative, 55, 149-50, 194

quantitative, 55, 91-93, 116-21, 129-31, 138, 145-46
Defect analysis, 466
Deming, W. Edwards, 4, 17, 56, 59, 62-63, 320, 512-14, 522, 537, 540
Deming Prize, 266, 317, 371, 518-19, 539, 540, 547
  FPL, 368
Diagnosis, management. *See* Management diagnosis of QI story
Digital Equipment Corporation (DEC), xi, 108, 264, 523, 526
  benchmarking, 395-96
  contextual inquiry at, 197-200
  cycle time reduction, 404
  employee circles, 282-85, 288
  TQM introduction strategy, 331-33
  six sigma at, 402-03
Disneyland, 497
Domino theory. *See* Total quality management

Edison, Thomas, 74

FPL. *See* Florida Power & Light
Federal Express, 317, 526
Federal Reserve Bank, 38
Feedback, 9
Fishbowl principle, 183-85, 197, 498
Fisher, George, 170, 172, 187, 403
Fitnesses, four
  evolution of, 16, 19, 25
  cost, 8

latent requirement, 11
  standard, 4
  use, 5
  See also Fitnesses, future
Fitnesses, future
  corporate culture, 26
  global environment, 26-27
5 evils, 79, 84, 90, 98, 112, 144, 405
5S activities, 490-91
5 whys, 120
5 Ws and 1 H, 167-68
Florida Power & Light (FPL), 10, 108, 282, 340, 514, 524
  CEO crusade, 312, 317, 319
  mission statement, 341
  QITs (Quality Improvement Teams), 367-68
  TQM introduction, 352, 380, 384, 386
Ford Motor Company, 64, 485, 530
  mission statement, 341
Fortune 500, 332
4 Ms, 119
4 Ps, 119
Fuji Xerox, 312-13. *See also* Xerox

GOAL/QPC, 514
Gantt chart, 115
General Electric, xii, 523
  Jet Engine Division, 264
General Motors, 484
Global environment, fitness to. *See* Fitnesses, future
Globe Metallurgical, 317-18, 320, 530
Goal setting
  annual goals, 340

Goal setting (*continued*)
  intermediate goals, 339
  noble goals, 339-40, 495,
    548-50
  U.S. and Japanese approach-
    es, 342-43
  value/mission statements,
    341-42
Graphs, 85, 103, 116-17

Hall, Edward T., 297
Hallmark Cards, 394
Hayakawa, S.I., 166, 186-87
Henry Ford Health Care, 344,
  367
Hewlett-Packard Company,
  42, 244, 366-67, 449
  mission statement, 342
Histogram, 85, 104, 117
Hitachi Ltd., 282, 359, 488-89
Hoechst Celanese, 530
Hong Kong, 10, 17
Horie, Yukio, 496
Hoshin management, 384
  alternative deployement
    system, 454-57
  and business planning,
    451-54
  CAPD cycle, 463, 475. *See also*
    CAPD cycle
  catchball, 433-34
  components and phases,
    413-15
  and daily work, 439-41
  definition, 411-13
  hoshin deployment, 426-36
  and management by object-
    ives, 445-51, 455
  metrics and targets, 437-39
  NEC Shizuoka case study,
    423-27

president's diagnosis,
    443-45
  strategic planning, 417-23
  and three types of problem
    solving, 415-17
Hoshins, aligning, 433-34
  alignment matrix, 434-36
Houghton, James, 317-20

IBM, 353, 372, 380, 387
ISO 9000, 519
Ikawa, Michio, 340, 424
Improvement
  iterative, 56. *See also*
    Improvement, continuous
  proactive, 53-54, 141-185
  reactive, 51-53, 73-105
  three types of, 49-54
  WV model (integrated), 151.
    See also WV model
Improvement, continuous, 28
  WV model of, 47-49
Improvement, systematic, 48
Inference, 165
Infrastructure for TQM,
  337-72
  organization structure,
    344-47
  seven elements of, 337-39
  See also TQM implementation
Innovation, 65, 67-68
Integration, evolution of
  company, 20, 25
International Standards Org-
  anization (ISO), 519
Interview script. *See* Customer
  interview
Intuition, 149

JIS (Japanese Industrial Standards) Committee, 519

JUSE. *See* Union of Japanese Scientists and Engineers
Japanese government support of TQM, 511
Japanese Standards Association (JSA), 30, 511-12, 515-16, 519, 528
Judgment, 165
Junguzza, Joe, 344, 365, 372
Juran, Joseph, 377, 513, 522, 540
Just-in-time (JIT), 134-35, 137

KJ diagram, 175
  in BBN customer visitation, 174-77
  customer image KJ, 202, 205-206
  customer requirements KJ, 217-220
  See also Kawakita, Jiro
KJ method, 153, 156. *See also* Kawakita, Jiro
Kaizen (continuous improvement), 37, 303, 517
Kanban system, 134, 138
Kano, Noriaki, 221, 223-29, 239, 334, 377
Kano diagram, 221-22, 226, 229
Kano evaluation table, 224, 226-27
Kano questionnaire, 223-25, 228
Kansai Electric Co., 312, 380, 454
Kawakita, Jiro, 160, 195
  five principles, 146-150
  and KJ method, 153
  W model, 48
  See also KJ diagram

Kearns, David T., 313, 318-20, 393, 536
Keidanren, 513
Key person, 126
Kobayashi, Koji, 513
Kobayashi Kosei Ladybug Circle, 272-77, 280, 291
Kogure, Masao, 428, 445-46
Komatsu Co., 411, Korea, 10, 17
Kumon education system, 499, 500

L.L. Bean, 38, 394
LUTI (learn, use, teach, inspect), xxiii
Ladder of abstraction. *See* Abstraction, levels of
Ladybug Circle. *See* Kobayashi Kosei Ladybug Circle
Language, affective, 162
Language of reports, 162
Latent requirement, fitness to. *See* Fitnesses, four
Leach, Ken, 318, 320
Lead users, 193-04, 204
Learning
  infrastructures for, 541-43
  model for, xxii
  organizational levels of, 537, 538-41
  push and pull elements, 543-44
  societal. *See* Societal networking

  triggers for, 541-43
  types of, 534-35
  See also Skill
Lee, Thomas H., xi, xvii, 523

Level of experience, 54
Level of thought, 54
Levy, Stephen, 171, 327
Lillrank, Paul, 377
Luther, David, 318

MPM (multi-pickup method),
  160, 161, 175-77, 216-17, 245,
  266
MacDonald, Marshall, 312
McGregor's Theory Y, 160
Malone, Tom, 318-19, 361
Management by objectives
(MBO), 446-51, 455
Management by process, 45-47
Management diagnosis of QI
  story, 107-40
  diagnostic matrix, 109
  external assessments, 371-72
  at FPL, 368-71
  general guidelines, 108-12
  reasons for, 107
Managerial development,
  461-501
  NIMS case study, 461-70
Market-in, 35-42
  and WV model, 142-44
Maslow, Abraham, 290, 539
Massachusetts High Tech
  Council, 523
Matrix data analysis, 158
Matrix diagram, 158
Milliken, Roger, 318
Milliken Co., 508, 521
  CEO crusade, 317-19
  sharing rallies, 360-61
Mission statements, 341-42
Motorola, 38, 187, 340, 366,
  372, 524, 530
  benchmarking, 395-96
  CEO involvement, 317-20

Communications Products
  Division, 380
customer orientation, 10,
  41-42
customer visitation, 170
introduction of TQM, 331,
  353, 357, 359
6 steps to 60, 153
six sigma, 332, 367, 401-07,
  540
Multi-pickup method. See
  MPM
Multi-valued thinking, 168-69

N.A. Phillips, 367
  mission statement, 341
NEC Corporation, 26, 339
NEC Integrated Circuit and
  Microcomputer Systems
  (NIMS), 535, 551
  case study, 461-70
NEC Kansai, 445
NEC Shizuoka, 340, 423-27,
  444
NIMS. See NEC Integrated
  Circuit and Microcomputer
  Systems (NIMS)
Nayatani, Yoshinobu, 157, 520
Nemoto, Masao, 434
New product development,
  189-243
  role of proactive improve-
    ment in, 190, 241-43
  stages of, 190-92
  WV model in, 241-43
Noble goals. See Goal setting
Noble practices, 551-53

Ochibo-hiroi (gleaning), 488-91
Oil crises, 17
Olsen, Ken, 332

PDCA cycle
  in breakthrough improve--
    ment, 472-73
  in customer visitation, 182-83
  definition, 56-57
  to improve TQM education,
    357-59
  in reactive improvement, 65
  and SDCA cycle, 66, 67,
    251-54, 385-86, 472-75
  and 7 tools and 7 steps,
    139-140
PDPC diagram, 158
Parallel organization, 384-87
Pareto diagram, 85, 102, 119,
  124
Participation, total, 29
Pasteur, Louis, 149
Pentel, 496
Polaroid Corporation, xi, 264,
  344, 365, 523
Polaroid Land camera, 11, 15
Proactive improvement.
  See Improvement, proactive
Problem exploration, 78
Problem identification, 75
  four-part process, 76
Problem solving
  determining priorities, 81
  steps and tools, 85
  theme. *See* Theme, problem-
    solving
  three types of, 49-54
  See also Improvement
Process, management by,
  45-47
Process control, 59-64
  basic principles, 60
  definition, 49-51
  model for, 60

and process improvement, 64
Procter & Gamble, 321, 327
Product-out, 35-36, 142

QI story presentation, 107-40
  case study, 127-39
  diagnostic matrix, 109
  general guidelines for diag-
    nosing, 108-12
  in Japan, 360-65
Quality concept
  changes in dominant, 16
  evolution of methodology,
    18-20, 25
  See also Fitnesses, four
Quality function deployment
  (QFD), 20, 197, 199, 201, 240,
    244, 384
  in proactive improvement,
    141
Quality metrics, 231-39
Quality month, 521
Quality of design, 23-24
Quality of conformance, 23-24
Quality satisfaction decay,
  229-30

Reactive improvement.
  See Improvement, reactive
Reflection on process, 126
Relations diagram, 158
Revolutions in management,
  xix, 27-29
Rogers, Carl, 293, 305
Root cause, 121

SDCA cycle
  and PDCA cycle, 65, 66, 67,
    251-54, 385-86, 472-75
  in process control, 51, 64-65

SDCA cycle (*continued*)
  in reactive improvement, 53
  in expanded WV model,
    151-52
SQC. *See* Statistical quality
    control
Scatter diagram, 85, 105
Sears Craftsman tools, 6
Self-innovation, 498
Semantics, 161
7 improvement steps.
    See 7 steps
7 management and planning
    tools, 157-60, 520-21
7 QC steps. *See* 7 steps
7 QC tools, 85-87
  described, 101-05
7 steps, 52-53, 85-87
  case study, 87-101
7 translation guidelines.
    See Transforming the voice
    of the customer
Shell Oil mission statement,
    342
Shewhart, W.A., 56, 59, 62, 69
Shingo, Shigeo, 404
Shizuoka. *See* NEC Shizuoka
Simms, Arden, 318
Singapore, 17
Sisphysus model.
    See TQM phase-in
Six sigma, 392, 401-05.
    See also Digital Equipment
    Corporation; Motorola
Skill
  changing needs, 534-37
  development model, 537-38
Small group improvement
    activities (SGIA), 201
Smith, Bill, xvii, 321, 523

Snowball model. *See* TQM
    phase-in
Societal networking, 29
  CQM case study, 522-28
  definition, 507
  infrastructure for, 510-21
  in Japan, 508, 509-22, 528-29
  sharing actual cases, 521-22
  in U.S., 528-30
Soin, Sarv Singh, 450-51
Sony Walkman, 11, 229-30
Standard, fitness to.
    See Fitnesses, four
Standard steps
  for proactive improvement,
    150
  for reactive improvement.
    See 7 steps
Standardization, 125-126
Stata, Ray, xvii, 321, 523
Statistical quality control
    (SQC), 4, 9
Statistical variation, 7
Stepping stone approach, 147
Stratification, 85-86, 102, 104,
    117
Stripping basket case study,
    193, 196, 201-06, 208-16,
    218-38
Swatch, 12
Systematic improvement. *See*
    Improvement, systematic

TOP (Technical and Organiza-
    tional Mapping), 197
TQM. *See* Total quality
    management
TQM implementation
  awards and incentives,
    365-68

large companies, 331
midsize companies, 351, 384
promotional activities, 359-65
small companies, 331
training and education, 347-59
See also Infrastructure for TQM; TQM phase-in; Total quality management
TQM phase-in, 377, 379
alignment phase, 378, 379, 383-84
empowerment phase, 378, 379, 381
orientation phase, 378, 379, 380-81
Sisyphus model, 381-82
snowball model, 381-82
three phases, 377-79
U.S. strategies for, 391-407
Taiwan, 10, 17
Tampering by management, 64
Teams, 255-56
cross-functional, 259-263
development, 276-81
meetings, 294-99
QC circles, 269-72, 281-82
types of, 257-58
voluntarism, 285-89
Teamwork, 255-56
case study, 264-69, 272-75, 282-85
creativity in, 301-03
principles for activating, 289-300
Teradyne, Inc., xi, 13, 264, 339, 523
CEO involvement, 313-17
TQM introduction at, 321-27, 358-59

Texas Instruments, 316, 323, 344, 449, 526
Theme, problem-solving
selection of, 79
statement of, 81
360-degree view, 146
3M, 10, 366
mission statement, 341
Thurow, Lester, 534-36
Tokyo Electric Power, 361, 363
Tokyo University, 528
Total quality management (TQM)
domino theory of implementation, 309-10, 311
four levels of practice, 29-30
four revolutions in concepts and practices, 28-29
initiation strategies, 307-33
See also Infrastructure for TQM; TQM implementation
Toto Ltd., 9
Toyota, 386, 411
Transforming the voice of the customer, 207
iceberg model, 214-215
refining the key item, 214
stripping basket case study, 211
translation guidelines, 208-211
Translating the voice of the customer. *See* Transforming the voice of the customer
Tree diagram, 158
Triangulation, 202
Two-valued thinking, 169

Uchimaru, Kiyoshi, 461-65, 468-69

Union of Japanese Scientists and Engineers (JUSE), xxi, 30, 511-16, 519-21, 524, 528, 542
 Research Committee on the 7 Management and Planning Tools, 157
U.S. Department of Commerce, 528
United Steelworkers of America, 320
Use, fitness to. *See* Fitnesses, four

van Gogh, Vincent, 555
Varian, Ion Implant Division, 387
Vital few principle, 56, 150
von Hippel, Eric, 148, 193-94, 244

WV model, 47-49, 142-144
 expanded model for proactive improvement, 151-52
 and 3 kinds of data, 145-146
Wallace, John and C.S., 318
Wallace Company, 317, 530
Weakness orientation, 76-78, 84, 112

Xerox Corporation, xxiii, 41, 407, 524, 534,
 benchmarking at, 331-32, 393-94, 396, 401, 540
 CEO involvement, 312-13, 317-20
 introduction of TQM, 344, 347, 352, 366-68
 mission statement, 341
 quality improvement process, 153
 setting goals, 340, 380
 USMG, 10
 See also Fuji Xerox

Yo-one, xxiv, 299

BOOKS FROM PRODUCTIVITY PRESS

Productivity Press publishes and distributes materials on continuous improvement in productivity, quality, and the creative involvement of all employees. Many of our products are direct source materials from Japan that have been translated into English for the first time and are available exclusively from Productivity. Supplemental products and services include membership groups, conferences,seminars, in-house training and consulting, audio-visual training programs, and industrial study missions. Call toll-free 1-800-394-6868 for our free catalog.

The Management Master Series
William F. Christopher, ed.

The Management Master Series offers business managers leading-edge information on the best contemporary management practices. Written by respected authorities, each set deals with a major theme; each of the six books within the set is a short "briefcase book" addressing a specific topic in a concise, to-the-point presentation. These are ideal books for busy managers who want to get the whole message quickly. (For information on other sets in the series, call toll-free.)

Set 1—Great Management Ideas
Management Alert: Don't Reform, Transform! — Michael J. Kami
Vision, Mission, Total Quality: Leadership Tools for Turbulent Times — William F. Christopher
The Power of Strategic Partnering — Eberhard E. Scheuing
New Performance Measures — Brian H. Maskell
Motivating Superior Performance — Saul W. Gellerman
Doing and Rewarding: Inside a High-Performance Organization — Carl G. Thor
ISBN 1-56327-091-9 / 6 volumes, each 50 pages / $85.00 the set / Order MMS1-B218

Fast Focus on TQM
A Concise Guide to Companywide Learning
Derm Barrett

Definitions and detailed explanations of over 160 key terms used in TQM have been compiled in this concise, easy-to-read handbook. Organized in glossary form, but presented in much greater depth, it is a perfect primer for introducing anyone to TQM. This book will help to align teams, departments,or entire organizations in a common understanding and use of TQM terminology. For anyone entering or currently involved in TQM, this is one resource you must have.
ISBN 1-56327-049-8 / 186 pages / $20.00 / Order FAST-B218

PRODUCTIVITY PRESS, INC., DEPT. BK, P.O. BOX 13390, PORTLAND, OR 97213-0390
Telephone: 1-800-394-6868   Fax: 1-800-394-6286

Handbook for Productivity Measurement and Improvement
William F. Christopher and Carl G. Thor, eds.

An unparalleled resource! In over 100 chapters, nearly 80 front-runners in the quality movement reveal the evolving theory and specific practices of world-class organizations. Spanning a wide variety of industries and business sectors, they discuss quality and productivity in manufacturing,service industries, profit centers, administration, nonprofit and government institutions, health care and education. Contributors include Robert C. Camp, Peter F. Drucker, Jay W. Forrester, Joseph M.Juran, Robert S. Kaplan, John W. Kendrick, Yasuhiro Monden, and Lester C. Thurow. Comprehensive in scope and organized for easy reference, this compendium belongs in every company and academic institution concerned with business and industrial viability.
ISBN 1-56327-007-2 / 1344 pages / $90.00 / Order HPM-B218

The Unshackled Organization
Facing the Challenge of Unpredictability Through Spontaneous Reorganization
Jeffrey Goldstein

Managers should not necessarily try to solve all the internal problems within their organizations; intervention may help in the short term, but in the long run may inhibit true problem-solving change from taking place. And change is the real goal. Through change comes real hope for improvement. Using leading-edge scientific and social theories about change, Goldstein explores how change happens within an organization and reveals that only through "self organization" can natural, lasting change occur. This book is a pragmatic guide for managers, executives, consultants, and other change agents.
ISBN 1-56327-048-X / 208 pages / $25.00 / Order UO-B218

TO ORDER: Write, phone, or fax Productivity Press, Dept. BK, P.O. Box 13390, Portland, OR 97213-0390, phone 1-800-394-6868, fax 1-800-394-6286. Send check or charge to your credit card (American Express, Visa, MasterCard accepted).

U.S. ORDERS: Add $5 shipping for first book, $2 each additional for UPS surface delivery. We offer attractive quantity discounts for bulk purchases of indi-vidual titles; call for more information.

INTERNATIONAL ORDERS: Write, phone, or fax for quote and indicate ship-ping method desired. For international callers, telephone number is 503-235-0600 and fax number is 503-235-0909. Prepayment in U.S. dollars must accompany your order (checks must be drawn on U.S. banks). When quote is returned with payment, your order will be shipped promptly by the method requested.

NOTE: Prices are in U.S. dollars and are subject to change without notice.

PRODUCTIVITY PRESS, INC., DEPT. BK, P.O. BOX 13390, PORTLAND, OR 97213-0390
Telephone: 1-800-394-6868   Fax: 1-800-394-6286